SNOWSTORM

Volume 1

The Art and Life of Carmelo "Snow" Sigona

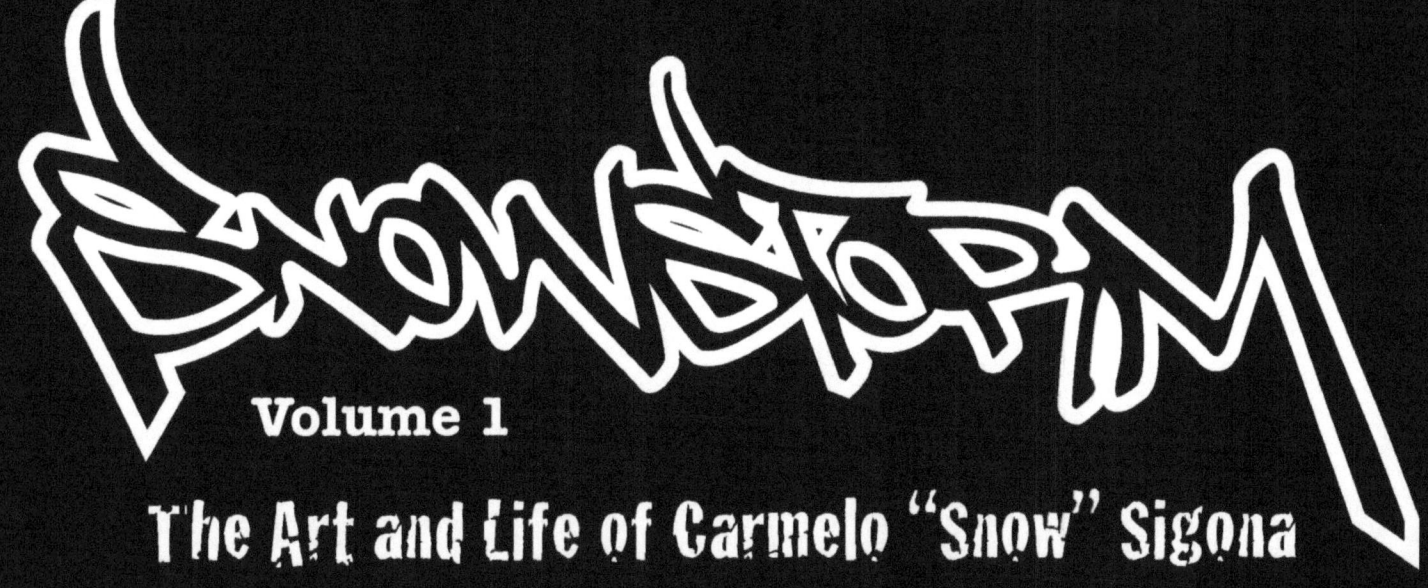

SNOWSTORM

Volume 1

The Art and Life of Carmelo "Snow" Sigona

By
Carmelo "Snow" Sigona
Michael J. Murch

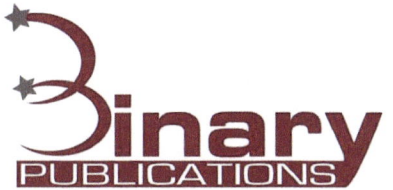

Published by Binary Publications

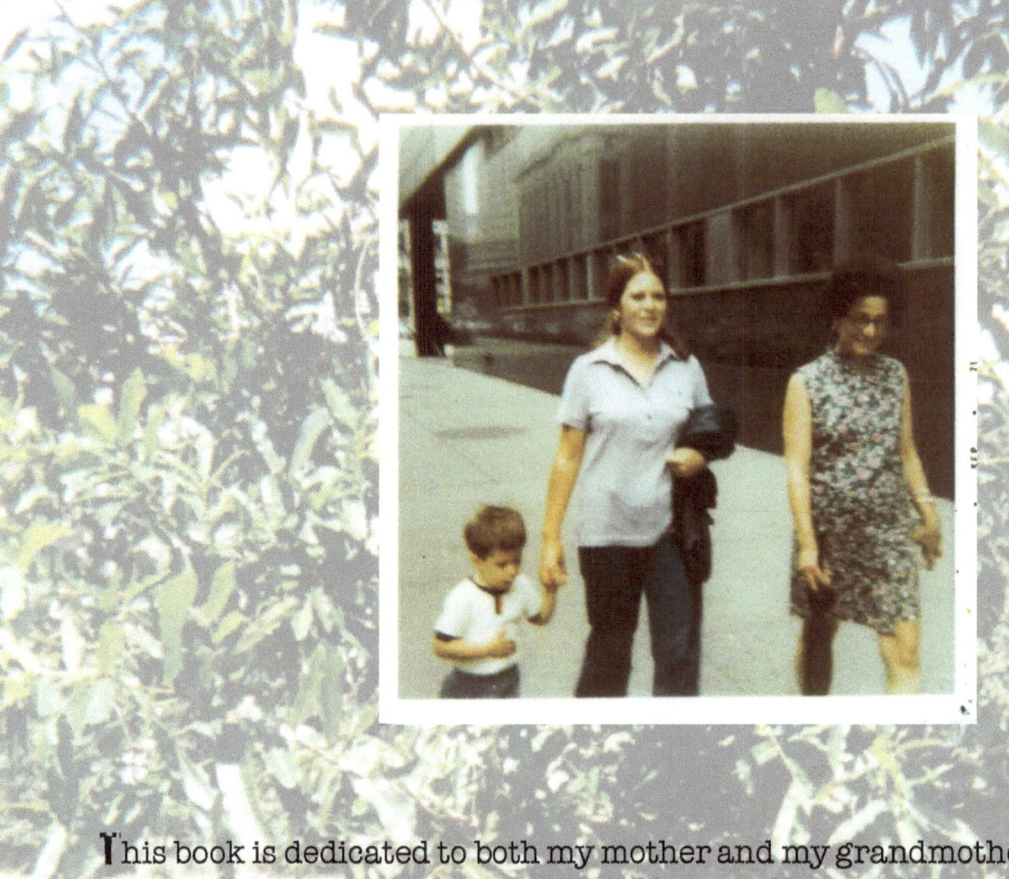

This book is dedicated to both my mother and my grandmother, who raised me to be a gentleman and to never give up on myself or my dreams. They will always walk hand in hand with me and for that I am eternally grateful. May they both rest in peace!

ACKNOWLEDGEMENTS

Written by Carmelo "Snow" Sigona and Michael J. Murch

Layout and Design by Carmelo "Snow" Sigona and Stephanie Jones

Edited by Stephanie Jones

Photo Contributions: SELF QM8, Joe Labisi, Jack Ferrante, Steve "The Victim" Hamady, Gentrifried QM8

I would like to acknowledge and thank:

My family, most especially my father and sister; my art teachers, especially Mrs. Austin for believing in me; Sister Letizia and my St. Anthony's family; all of my QM8 brothers: special thanks to SWITCH QM8, SELF QM8, and the HITMAN LEEN; my Funkadelphia family: DJ SAT-ONE and KING KARE AFU; all of the guys from McFarlane Toys, past and present; Steve "The Victim" Hamady; the Summer Madness Crew of 1988; Jerry Gant; my Brick City homeboys from NRG and BNS; my Silk City home boys from Park Avenue and SPB, especially my main man Nestor; all my Chilltown family; DJ SYKOPATH; my FX family: special shout to my brother Jamie HEF, POSE 2, POEM, MEK, REK, and LOOMIT; Joe Bachstadt; Joel Hecht; Bobby Harper; James CHILD Byrne (RIP); ROM MAD, for keeping me crazy; The G-Force and Soul City Warriors; the Bronx Team; the Reddin family, most especially "Dirty" Don and Ray; the folks at Binary; my dear friend and mentor Tony "Capitan" Billotto; Ken Zen (RIP); Kaiz; DTM; Michael and Mamma Murch.

Last but not least. my one and only soulmate and boo Stephanie "Mizz" Jones for keeping it ALL together, ALL the time. Love you!

Peace and respect to my fellow seekers.

Carmelo "Snow" Sigona

ArtofSnowOne.com

Table of Contents

Foreword

This foreword serves as a preview; the tip of the iceberg regarding a complex and sensitive human being, a gifted and imaginative artist, a former student, and a great friend, Carmelo "Snow" Sigona.

I've always admired the quality and complexity of Snow's abstract compositions. They require his complete focus and concentration; there can be no loose ends. I see Pollack, Kandinsky, and Picasso in his wall pieces, and I feel J.R.R Tolkien and Lewis Carroll in his storytelling.

The first time I met Carmen was in early February, 1995. McFarlane Toys, for whom I worked, was preparing for its second International Toy Fair, and we needed to make a dynamic impression in our New York City showroom for both the retail buyers and the media.

An acquaintance, from the town in which I lived, suggested that I give a local graffiti artist a chance to help out in our showroom by having him create some mural treatments. He said that "the kid" was a huge Spawn fan. I've always been willing to give emerging artists and designers a shot. After all, there were folks who did that for me, and I felt a responsibility to continue the chain, so I said, "Yes."

Snow showed up at our Manhattan showroom with a duffle bag full of spray cans, some Spawn comics, and a respirator. He was quiet, humble, and confident. I showed him a room that displayed all of our awards, packaged action figures, play sets, T-shirts, and other ancillary merchandise. Snow suggested painting a larger-than-life Spawn image, with his living cape billowing and twisting around the entire room and embracing a large Spawn logo. I said, "Great idea! How long will it take? We're on a tight schedule." He answered, "An hour, maybe two."

What happened next was magic. With only a spray can, Carmen transported us from a bare dark room to the very pages of a Spawn comic book! The room was now exciting, vibrant, and alive. In fact, he was so fast and bold that we let him "have fun" with our sales office as well, where he painted other dynamic Spawn characters and logos. Everyone, including Todd McFarlane, was very impressed. From that day on, Carmen was not only included in all of our showroom and display projects, he became a key member of our special, small team of "creative commandoes" that designed and built the cutting edge McFarlane showrooms each and every year.

Carmen also has a vast capacity for learning. He pays attention to what others say and do, and he grasps the significance of any situation. Since the "old McFarlane days", Carmen and I have teamed up for many projects, including toy showrooms, displays, product development, murals, and video sets. More often than not, he now includes me in his projects. For that I am thankful.

It is said that interesting people attract other interesting people. Through his great talent of networking, Carmen has introduced me to a host of unforgettably interesting people. He has enriched the lives of many, from all walks of life. I am fortunate to say that mine is one of those enriched lives. Carmen often says that I mentored him, but what he may not realize is how much he has mentored me.

Anthony Billotto

Introduction

After decades of friendship, I was asked by Carmelo to lend my skills to the telling of his storied career. The following is my account of the life and art of graffiti artist and legend, Carmelo "Snow" Sigona. Like many great artists, Snow's story is a lifelong journey of pursuing graffiti fame and greatness; A story of a young man who finds guidance and salvation through art.

More recently, Snow's art has taken him around the world and he has enjoyed international acclaim. But it wasn't always a peaceful, fun, and fulfilling experience. In this book, volume one of two, Snow's early life, struggles, and rise to fame (or infamy) will be explored. Through much adversity, he persevered and has gone on to reap the rewards of the seeds sown by his early struggles.

Snow has always been blessed to enjoy a life filled with many influential people. From his parents, friends, and mentors to a rough street wise detective, they all played a major role in the shaping and influencing of Snow's character and life.

We will see Snow's visual transformation from young street amateur to masterful stylist and professional designer who ultimately goes on to form a successful studio of his own. All of this springing from his amazing art and creative contributions.

This volume will give you a peek into Snow's mind and his creative passions. So, turn the page and enjoy this legendary artist's story...

Michael J, Murch
aka "Dise Man"

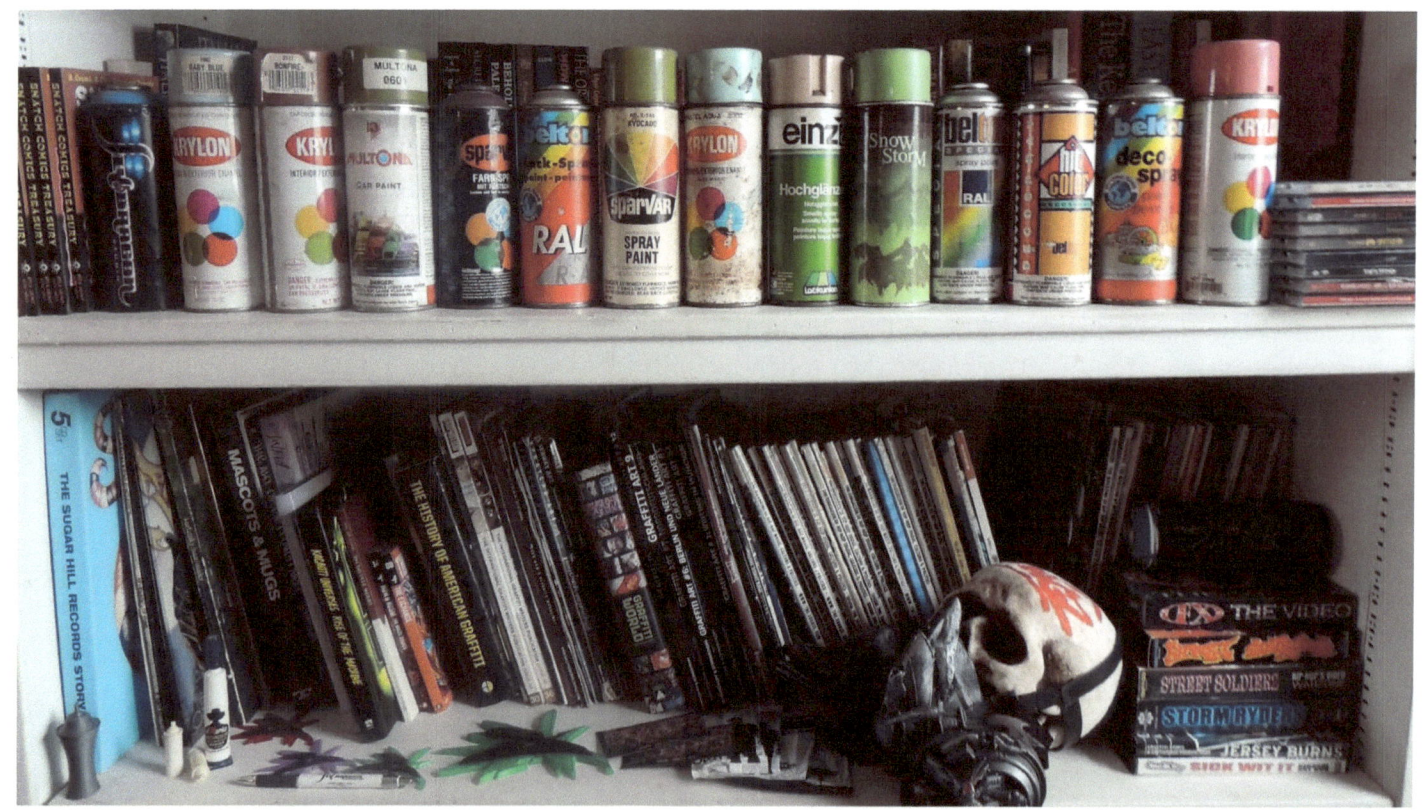

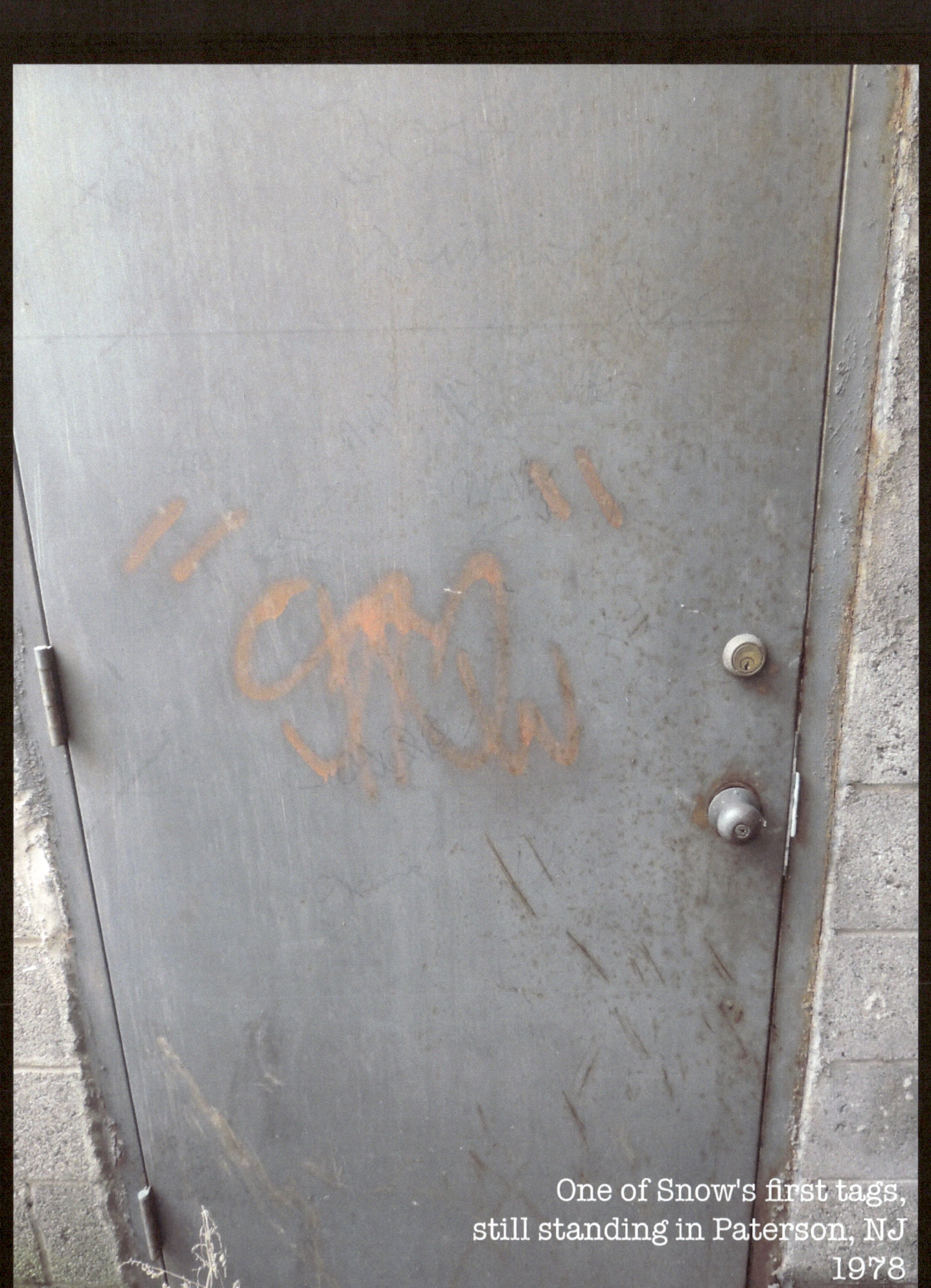

One of Snow's first tags,
still standing in Paterson, NJ
1978

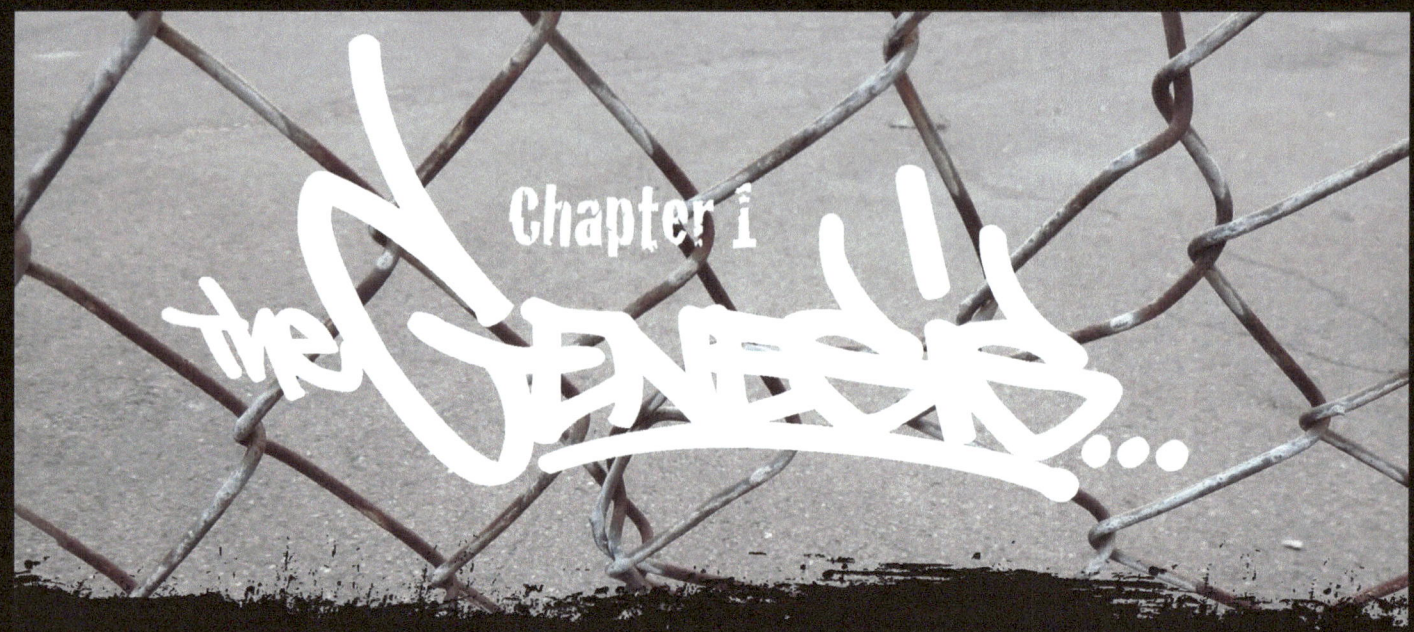

Chapter 1
the GENESIS...

In 1968, ten years before Dr. Daniel Conte appeared in Martin Scorsese's Raging Bull, he was delivering Carmelo "Snow" Sigona to his proud parents Carmelo and Noreen Sigona at Saddle Book General Hospital in Saddle Brook, NJ. Awaiting Little Carmen's arrival to his first home in Paterson, NJ were some of his earliest and most influential inspirations.

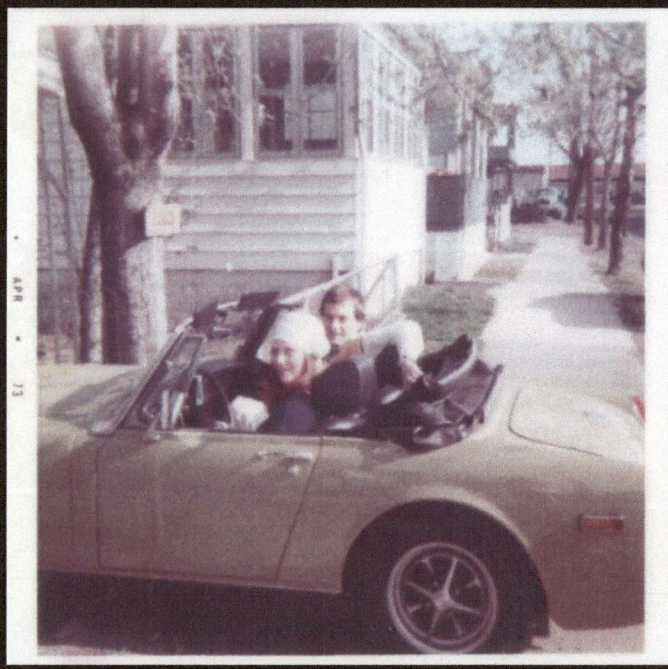

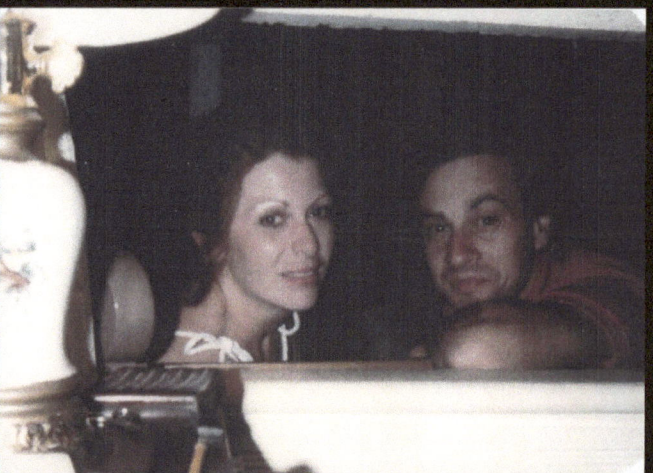

During these formative years, young Carmelo's parents both held two jobs while attending school. Even with their demanding schedules and their struggles to make ends' meet, his parents still made time to help shape Carmelo's character and impact his young mind.

Young Carmelo was exposed to the arts even before he started school. His mother had him listening to a variety of different music at a very early age and his father, a sci-fi/fantasy fan, in his own right, turned him on to serials such as Flash Gordon, one he himself had grown up watching. Carmelo and his dad would watch Planet of the Apes, Sinbad, Gunga Din, and King Kong. These were films and themes that sparked Carmelo's undeveloped mind and imagination, many of which still bring joy and entertainment to he and his father today.

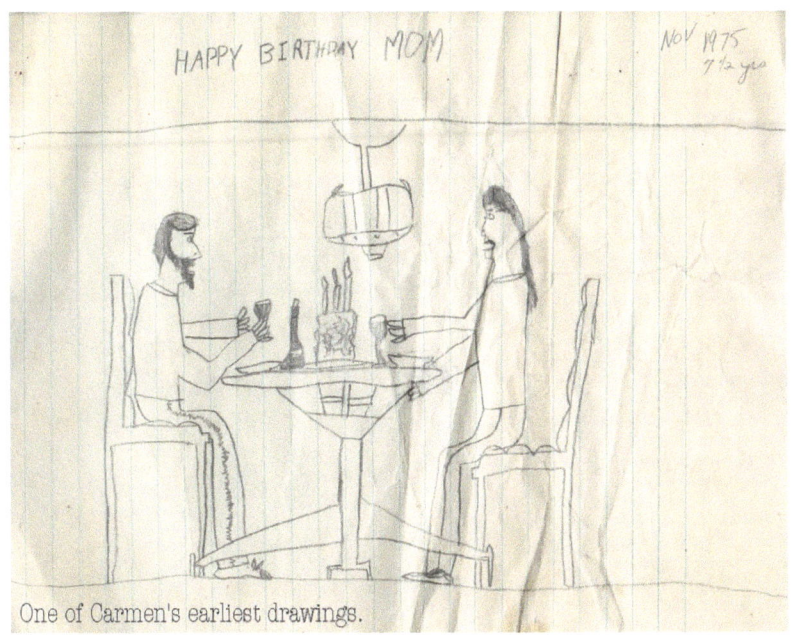

One of Carmen's earliest drawings.

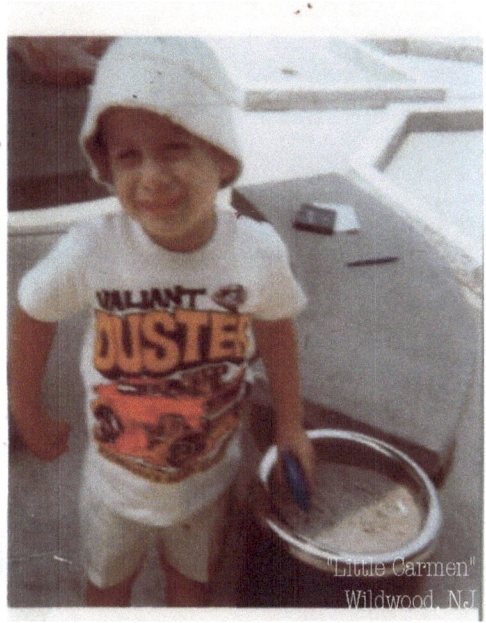

"Little Carmen"
Wildwood, N.J.

After the films were over, he and his dad would reenact them and their favorite scenes in the living room of their small apartment. Like most young boys, Carmelo loved to play with action figures, toy soldiers, dinosaur models, cars, cowboys and Indians, to name a few. Many a Sunday afternoon was spent indulging his imagination, while the aromatic scent of his mother's homemade Italian cooking permeated the apartment. His father would use blankets and couch pillows to layout the fictional movie set. Dad's awesome awareness to detail using couch pillows and blankets to replicate Skull Island is something that makes Carmelo smile even today.

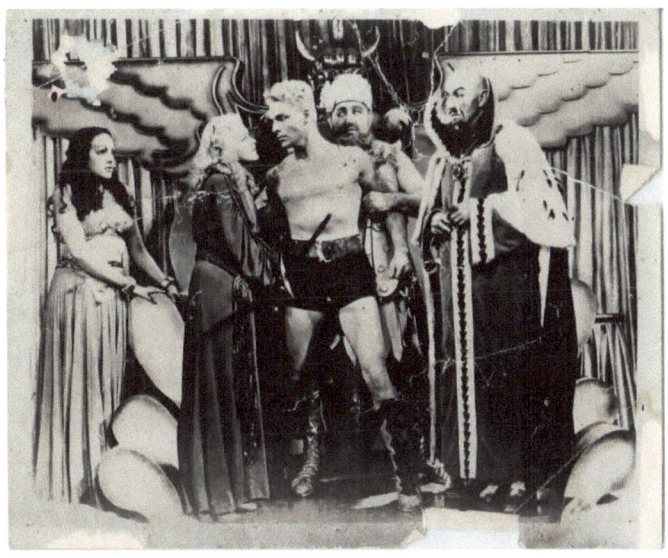

Original Flash Gordon Series (1936), starring Buster Crabbe was a household favorite

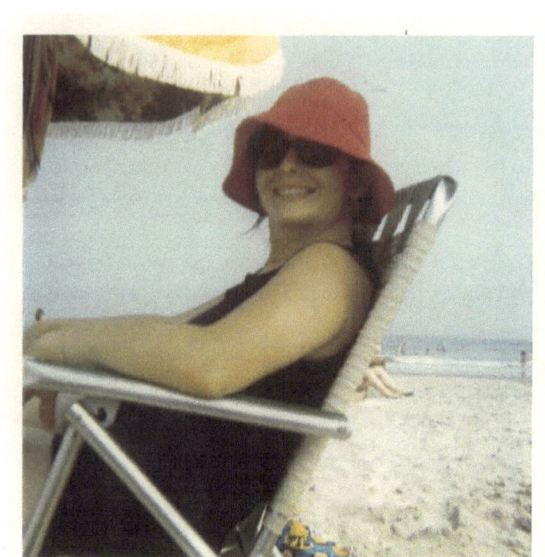

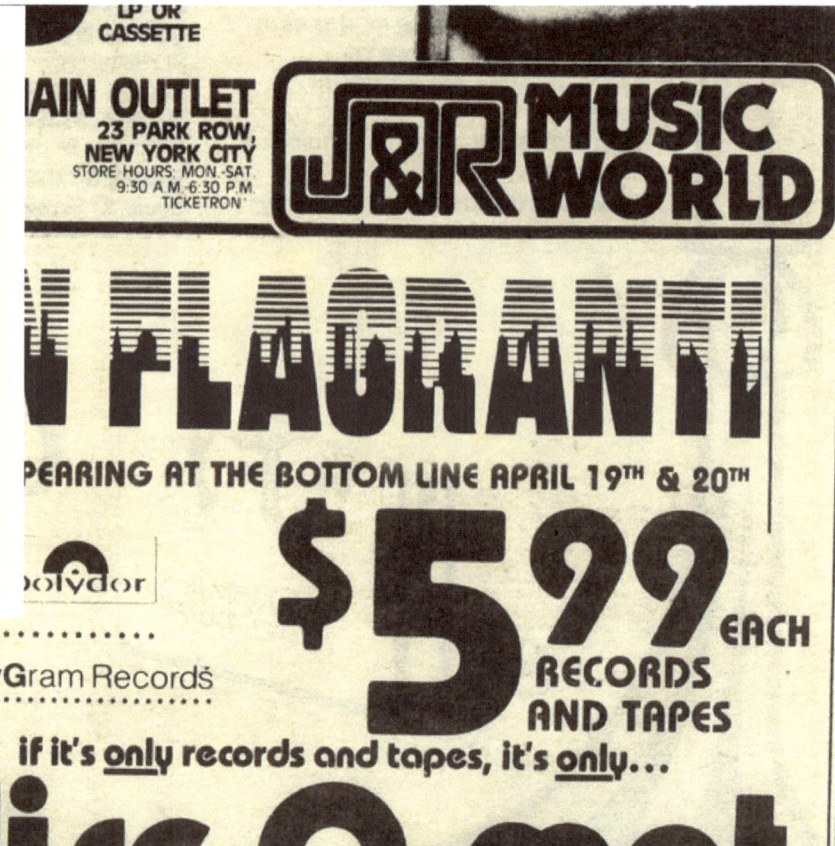

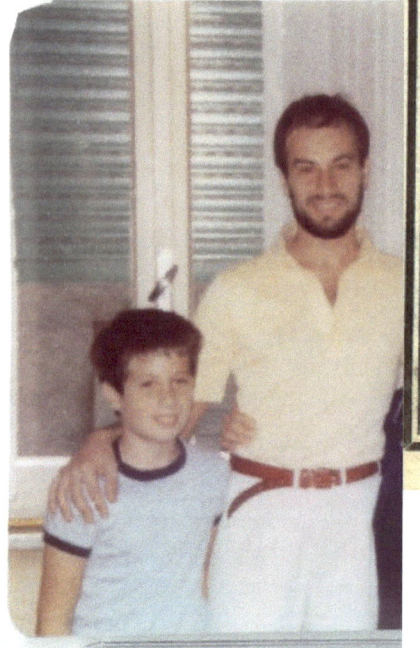

"I remember my mom always getting me into new and different types of music. She used to take me to disc-O-mat, a record store in Wayne, NJ, to buy my first vinyl records."

Carmelo

Back in the day, with mom and dad

Some of the first vinyl records that his mother took him to buy

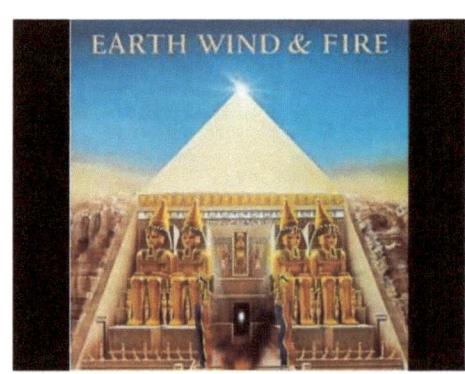

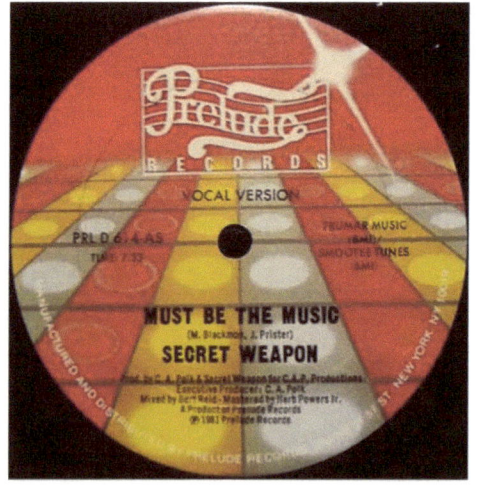

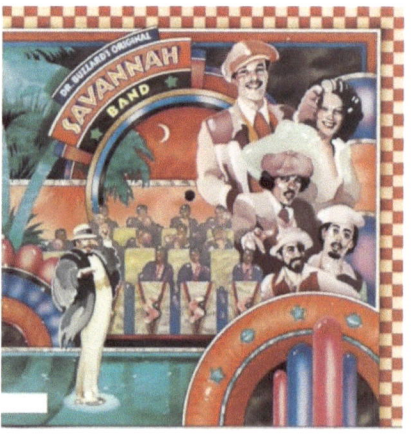

During the 1970's, Carmelo began to explore his artistic side. He spent a lot of time at his Aunt Joan's house. His aunt often babysat him for his parents. She was a very talented oil painter who often shared her work with Carmelo. There, he spent his time both studying her paintings and drawing comic book characters with his cousin Greg. Star Wars had just hit theaters and became their subject of choice. As he recalls, he and his cousin would draw epic space battles across page after page of sketch pads and sketch books. The George Lucas classic and the Marvel universe offered a wide range of characters for these two young boys to draw inspiration from. Carmelo's drawings quickly caught the attention of his family.

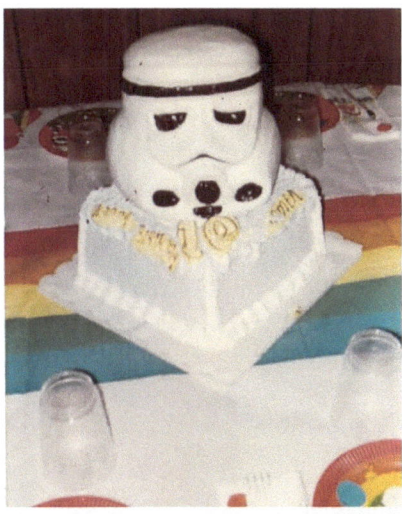

10th birthday cake
1978

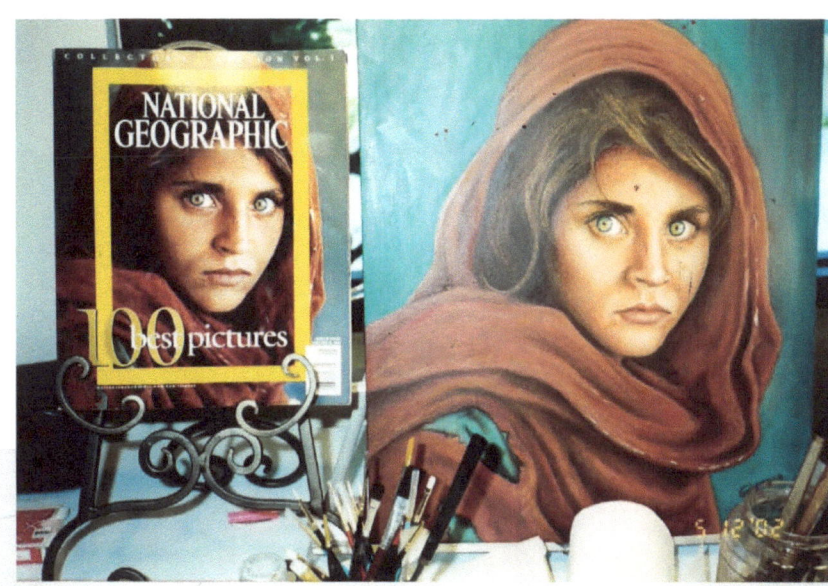

Joan Sigona

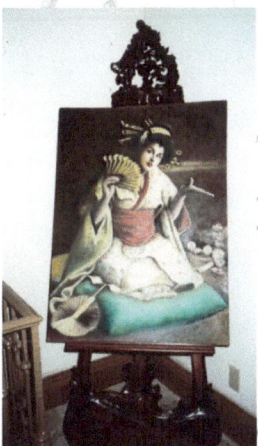

"...My nephew Carmen's talent and achievements never cease to amaze me. Carmen sets his sights high, supported with hard work and dedication that will always make an impact on his career path. Well done."

Joan Sigona

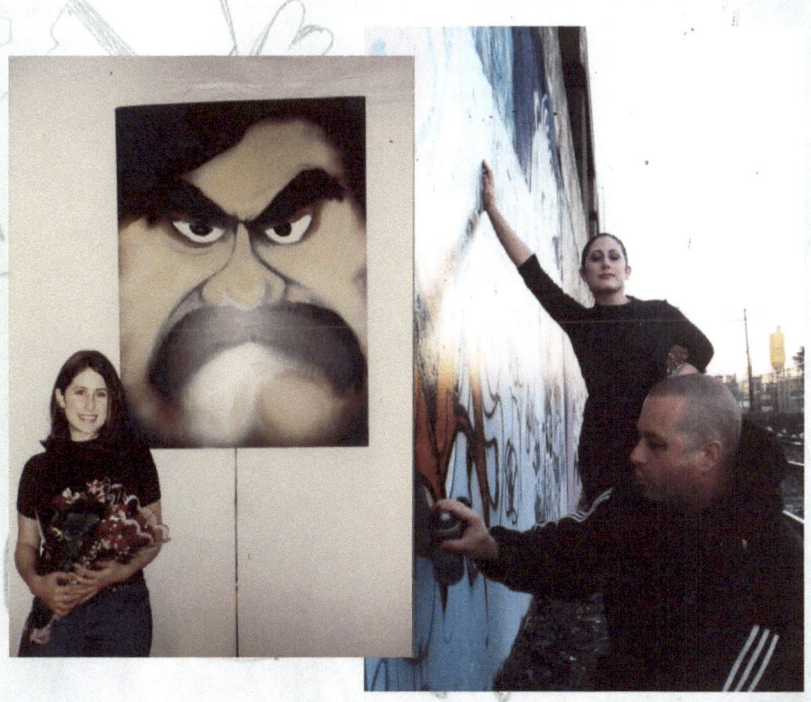

Little sister and Big brother

Carmelo attended St. Anthony's Elementary School on Beech Street in Paterson, NJ. By the late 1970's, he had regularly spent time drawing all sorts of comic book and cartoon characters, continuing to do so even during school hours. Through his 5th grade classroom window, Carmelo would catch his first glimpse of graffiti art in Paterson. Through this portal, his graffiti journey would truly start. Through that window, across the street from his school, he read the tags Evil, Bug, Mad, Red, and Dice. He immediately became intrigued and started to develop a tag, name, and style of his own.

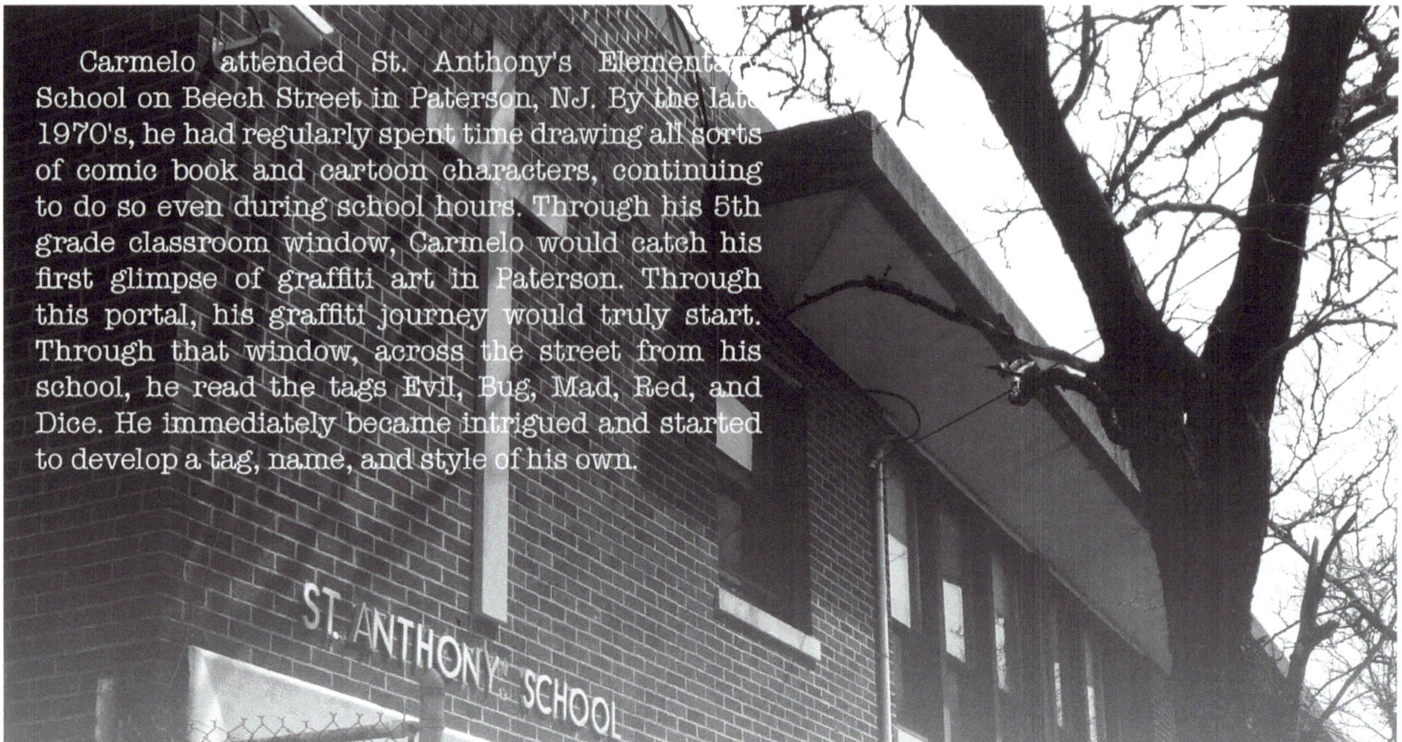

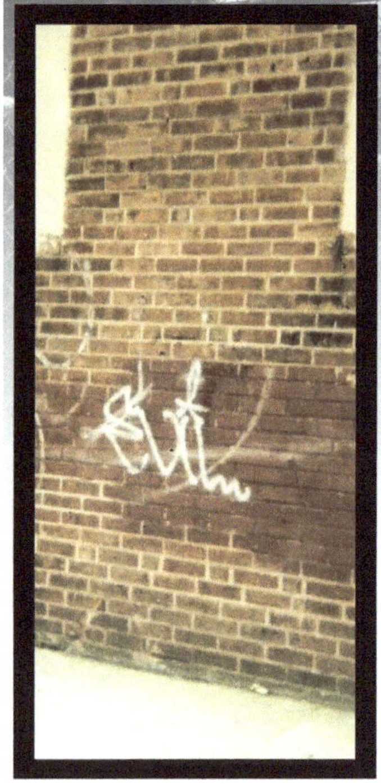

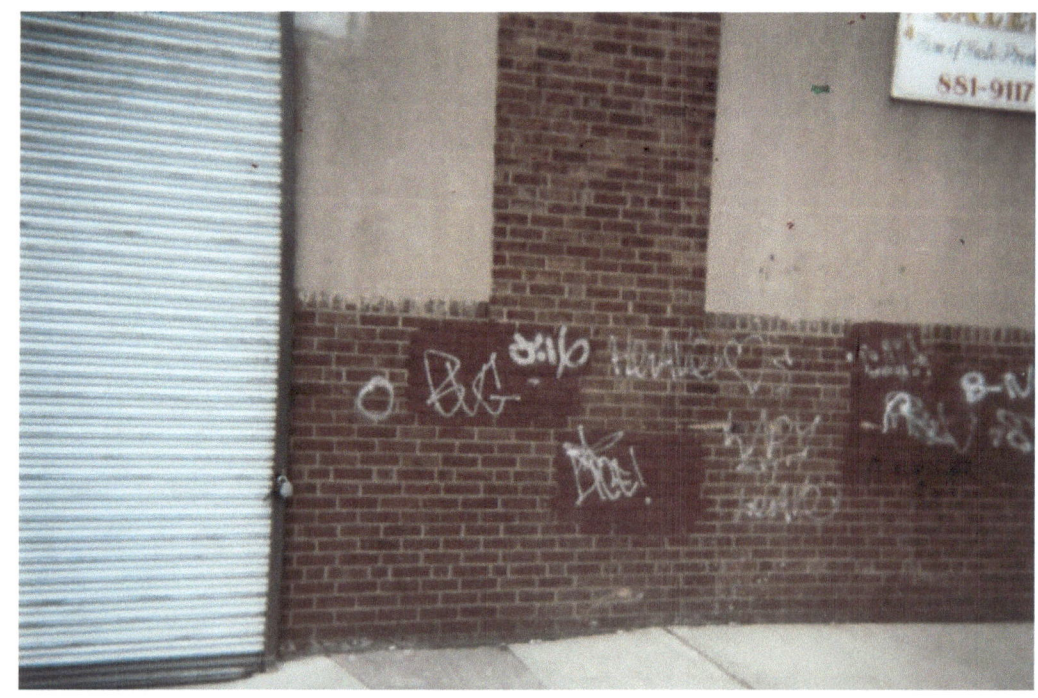

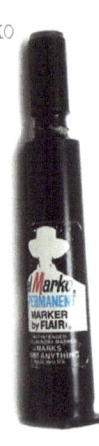

El Marko

Raised as a New York Yankee fan (Carmelo is a huge Yankee fan to this day), he and his dad would often go to the Bronx to the legendary Yankee Stadium to see the Bombers play. They would watch guys like Thurman Munson and Mr. October, Reggie Jackson, Carmelo often listening to his father explain the finer points of the game of baseball. However, more often than not, his father would find himself exclaiming, "Carmen, turn around! The game is over here!"

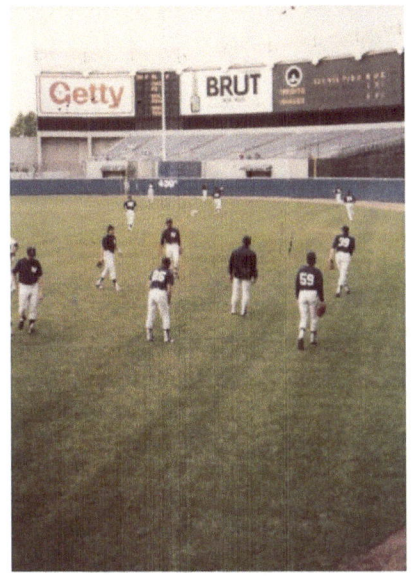 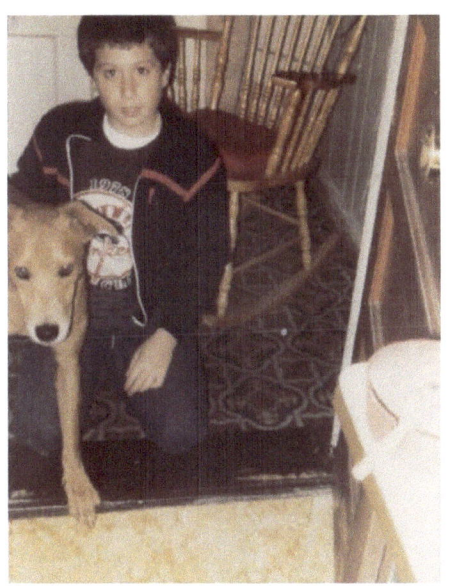

You see, back then at the Old Yankee Stadium, deep in the right field stands, there was a gap in the wall that allowed a clear view of the NYC subway trains. These trains took millions of New Yorkers from one borough to the other. However, for Carmelo, these trains were more than a mode of transportation; they were rolling steel canvases that displayed graffiti art, giving Carmelo his first glimpse into a world that would captivate and consume his imagination. Of course, at this time, Carmelo was a young impressionable artist, trying to decipher where those trains would take him.

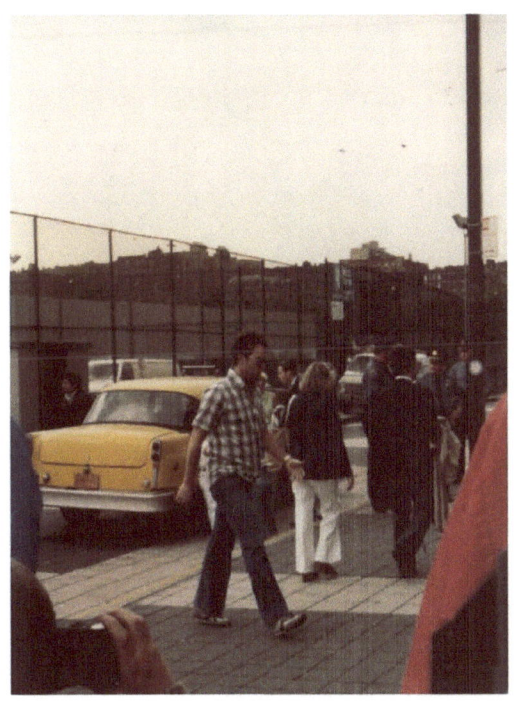 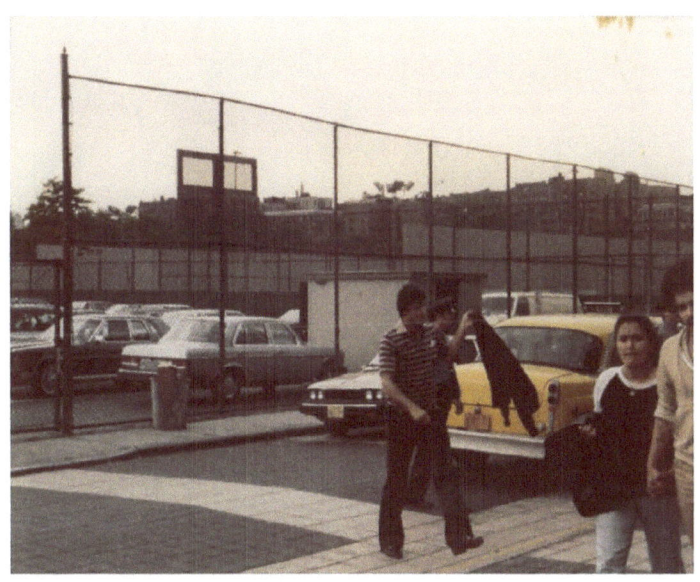

"In the late 70's, my Dad used to take me to the game real early so we could see the players walking in. We saw players like Nettles and Pinella and for me, they were larger than life."

Carmelo

By 1979, graffiti was thriving on trains all over NYC and slowly becoming an "epidemic" in Paterson, a.k.a Silk City. The art was growing and so was Carmelo's obsession with it. He was seeing it all over the city and once he tried it, it was clear to him that this was what he was going to do. Carmelo has been quoted as saying, "Graffiti artists think outside the box." Clearly that window at St. Anthony's School would be the first "box" that Carmelo would think beyond. Carmelo remembers being scolded by Sister Letizia for looking out that window and drawing on his notebooks and desks. Sister Letizia was a no-nonsense nun who demanded attention and structure. Carmelo credits Sister Letizia with helping him to form his character. He often referred to her as his third parent. In an interview with Carmelo's father, he described his son as very intelligent, with grades and comprehension never being a problem, but he had early concerns with his son being able to maintain his academic structure effectively. The consensus was that Sister Letizia helped Carmelo to adjust and later channel his rebellious energy in time to complete his elementary education.

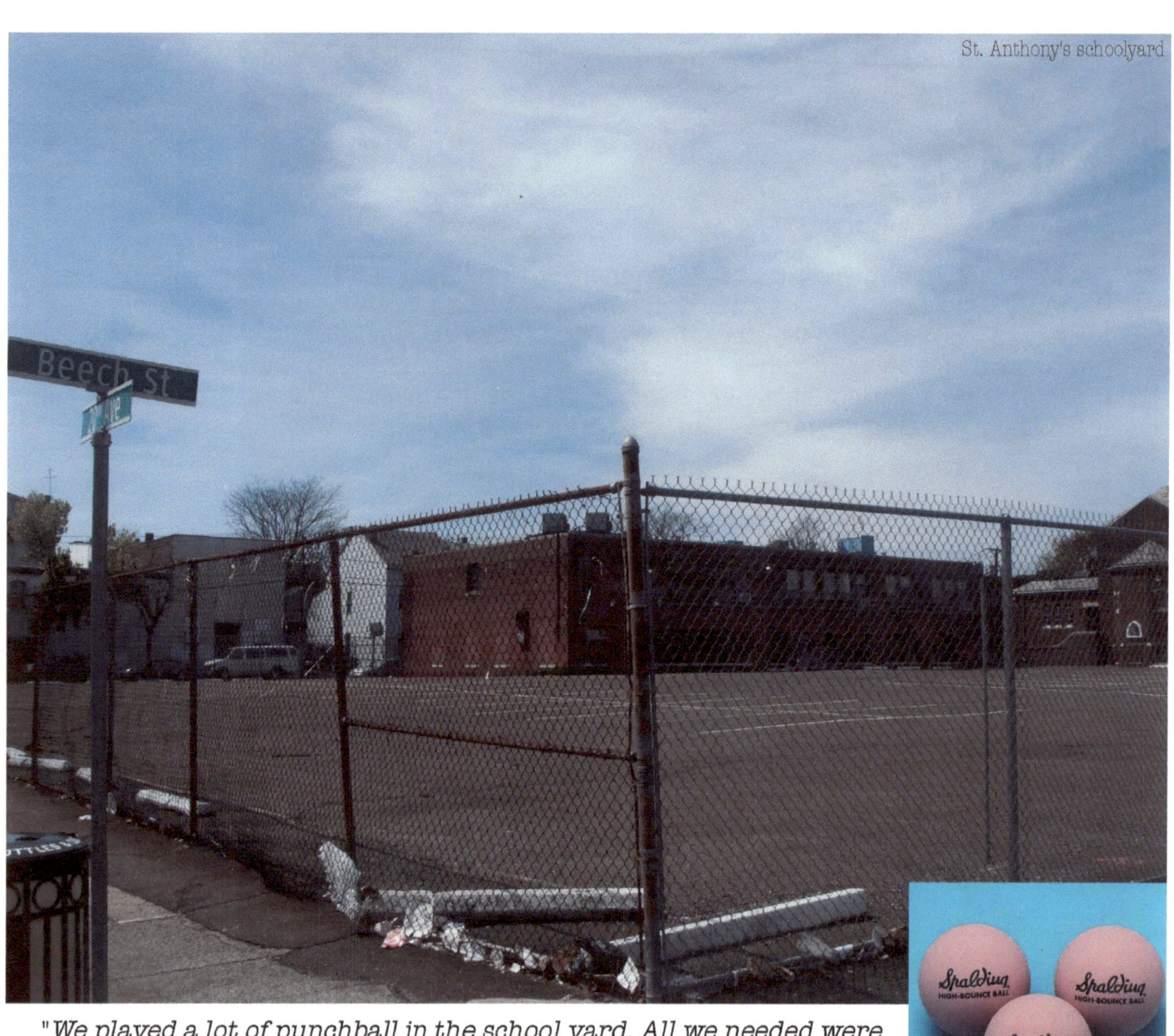

St. Anthony's schoolyard

"We played a lot of punchball in the school yard. All we needed were 'Super Pinkies' to keep us occupied for hours."

Carmelo

While at St. Anthony's, Carmelo discovered he had classmates that were also graffiti writers in his school. His classmates SCAT CPW, AERO TGF, and SM (SAME, ROM's cousin) were influences and "accomplices" in some of his earlier graffiti mischief.

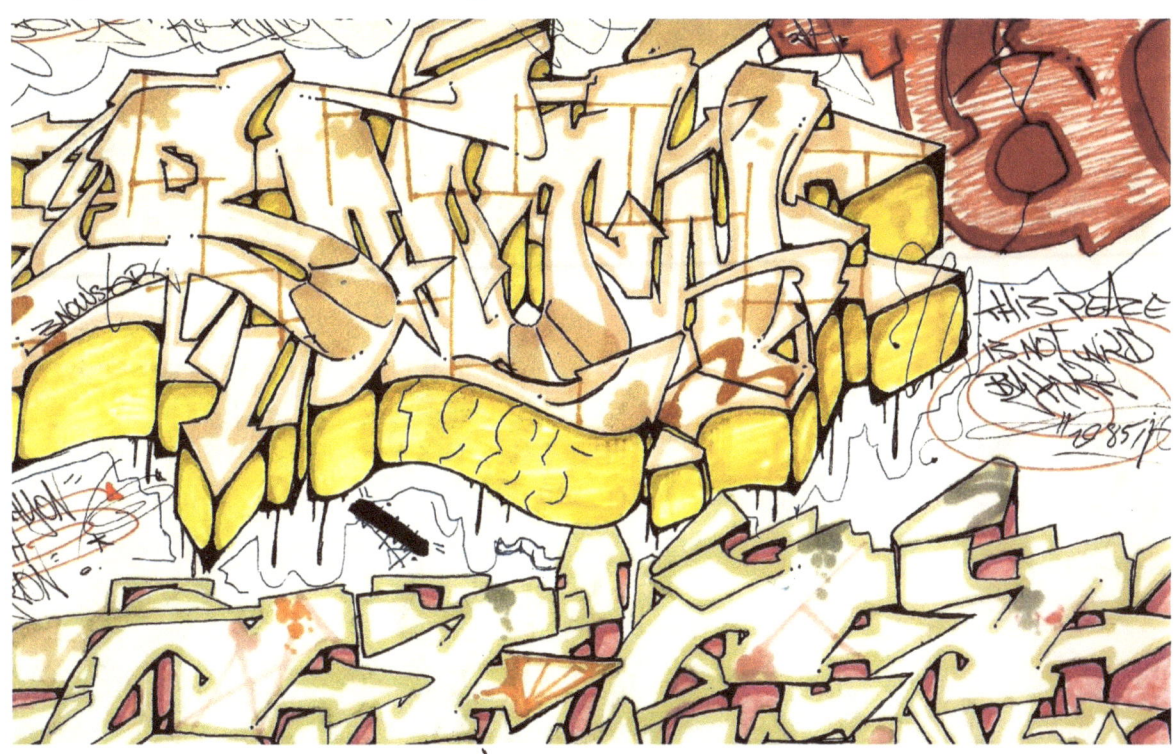

SNOW by KULL

"*There were so many guys with crazy styles back then in Paterson: KULL, DUE, SOAP, ROM, SACE, SES, MIN, KOF Crew, and the list goes on and on...*"

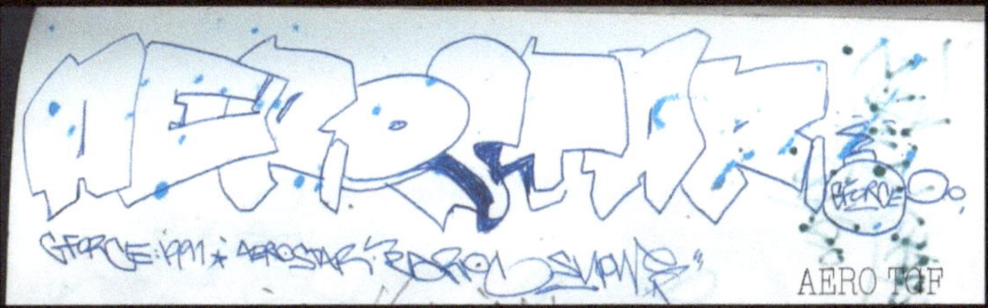

Kul by Due

SCAT CPW

AERO TGF

SE by SAME

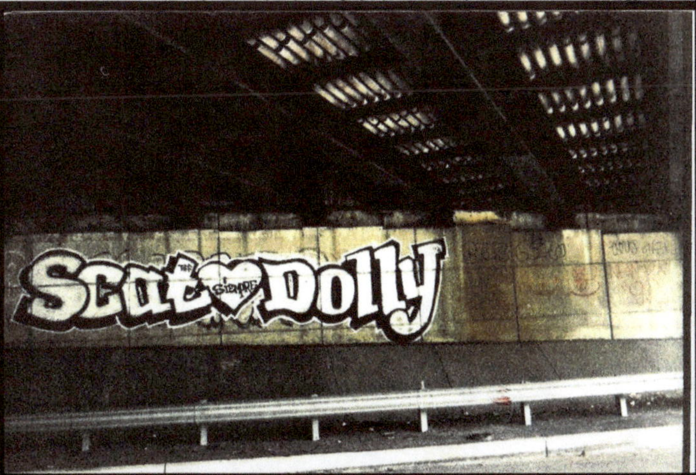

SCAT on Route 21
Passaic, NJ

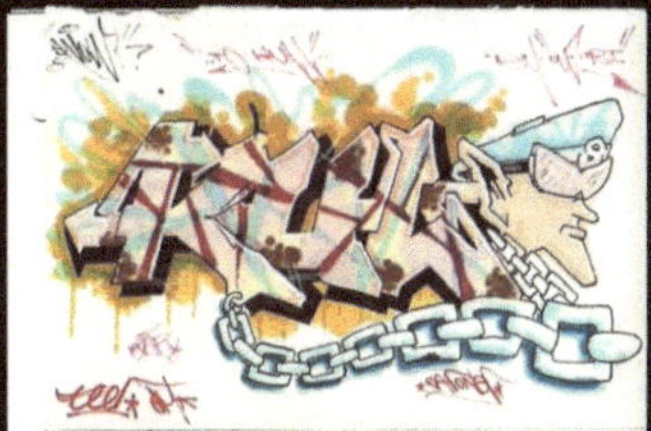

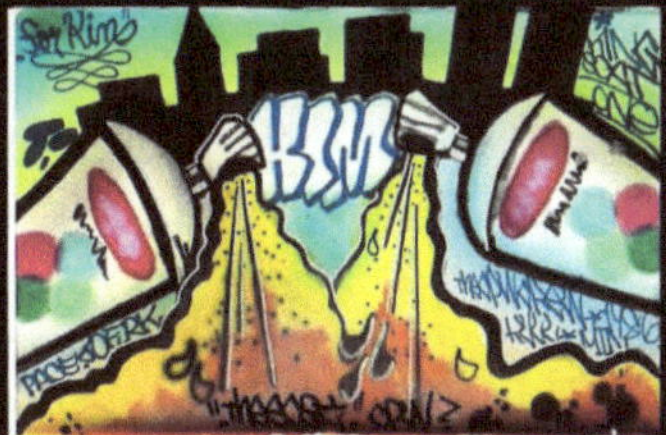

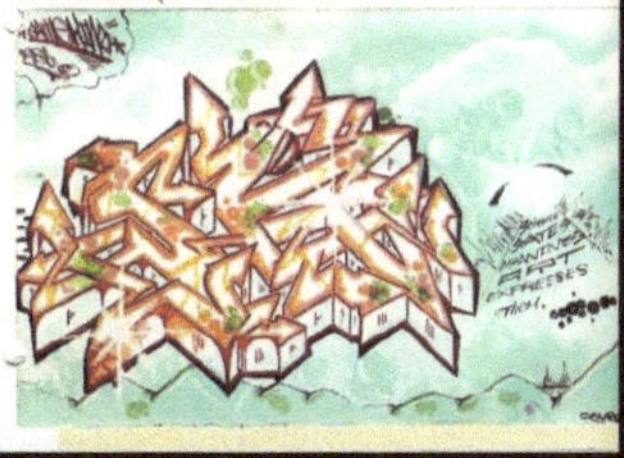

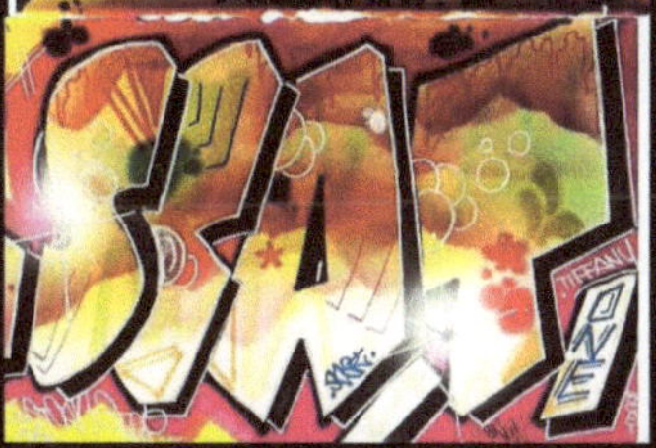

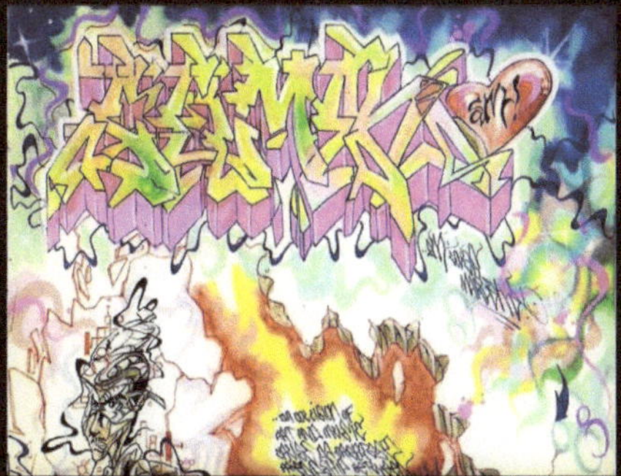

SAME by ROM

Like most graffiti artists, Carmelo spent his free time looking for places to "display" his name. As a kid, he would find himself in places like abandoned factories, train tracks and school yards. School numbers 15, 16, 24, 25, and 30 would become his favorite stomping grounds. In 1980, at the age of 12, Carmelo was painting in the now demolished Alabama Avenue Projects, and this is where he was given his name "Snow White". Carmelo was one of the few white kids tagging in his neighborhood, and his friends joked that this would be a good name for him. Being thick-skinned in a rough neighborhood, he ran with the name, dropped the "white", and was thereafter known as Snow. Snow said he loved the way the letters flowed and thats why he kept the name.

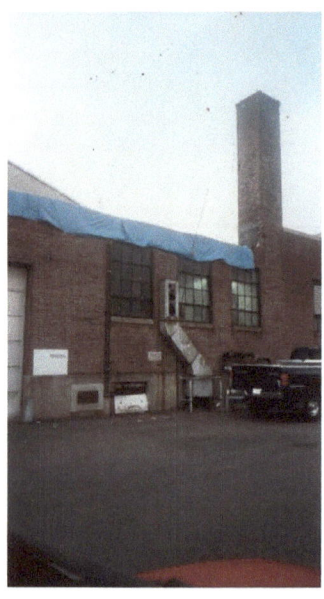
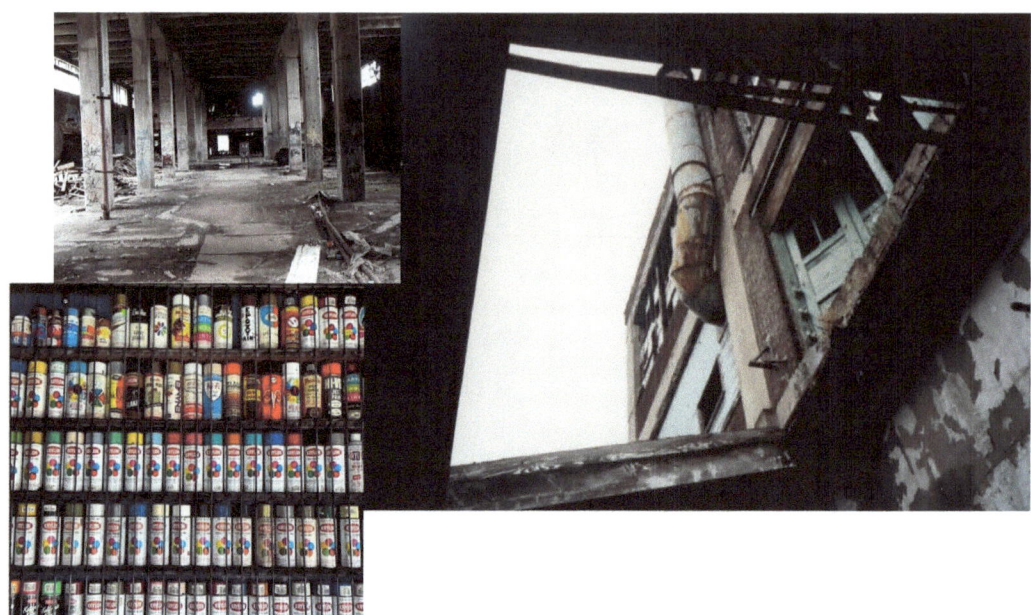

Spray paint was not the easiest thing to conceal and hide, stains and cans alike. Snow's parents could see it a mile away. His dad called him "walking evidence". At 12 years old, in 1980, Snow's graffiti was not only consuming all of his energy, but rapidly improving as well. He painted his first "piece" (piece is short for masterpiece in the graffiti world), and his style was taking on a life of its own.

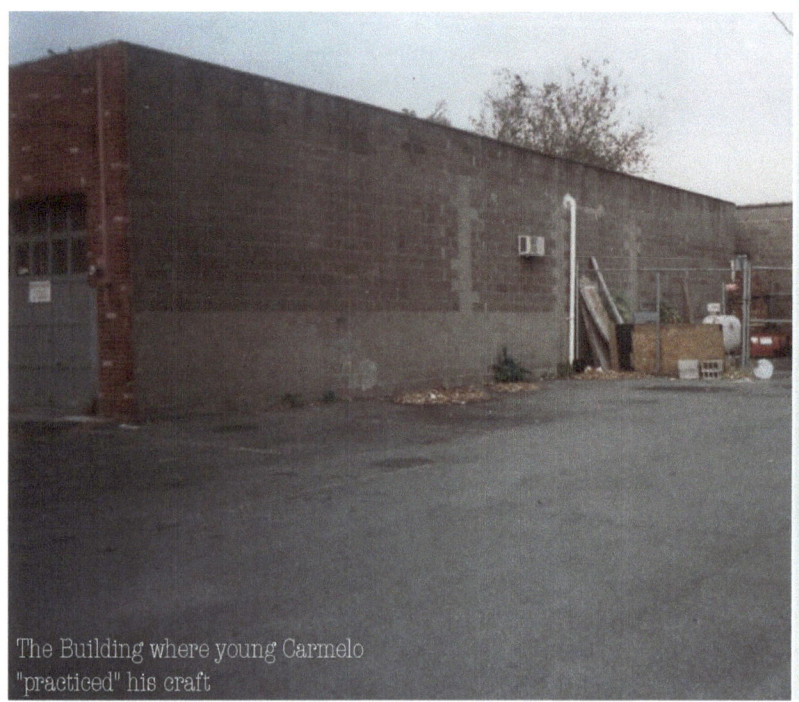
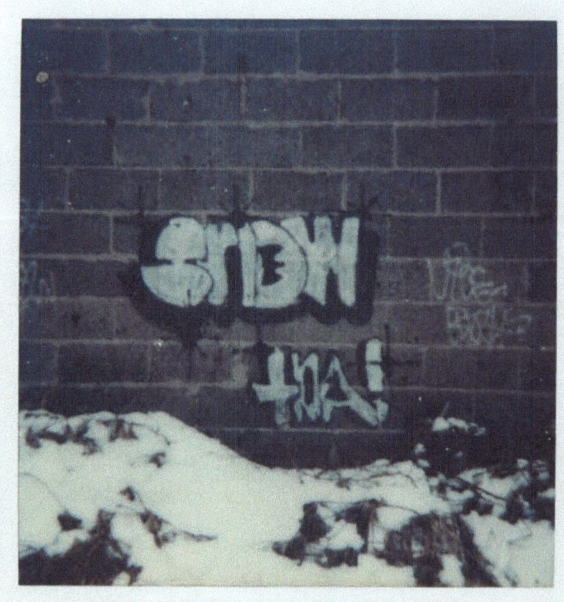

The Building where young Carmelo "practiced" his craft

Snow's very first piece, still standing! 1980

By 1983, Snow and his family moved to the suburbs of Newark. Graduating from St. Anthony's, he would receive an academic scholarship to attend Monclair Kimberly Academy, a private high school in Montclair, NJ. However, his stay at MKA would be short lived. Being raised in a more urban environment, Snow had difficulty adjusting and would go on to leave the school and his scholarship behind in 1984. He completed his remaining two years at Verona High School, where he graduated in 1986.

1986 also marked the year Snow was painting on everything from utility boxes and street signs to "abandoned" vehicles. Highway bridges would come later and essentially bring Snow local infamy. However, these canvases were usually privately owned or taken care of by city workers, which would not only get the attention of Snow's parents, but by now, local law enforcement officials were well aware of Snow's tag. At 15 years old, Snow appeared representing his custom wild style painted Lee brand jacket in the 1983 PBS special on Newark, NJ graffiti artist TooSweet Hakeem. The event was held in downtown Newark at the City Without Walls Gallery on Halsey Street. Snow, by himself, took the bus to Newark to attend. Snow's self painted jacket grabbed just

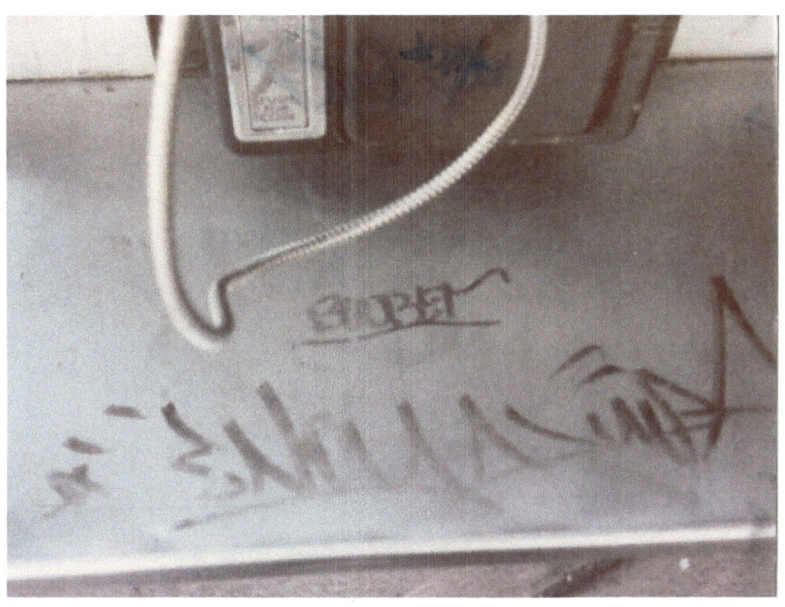

Payphone? What's a payphone? Believe it or not, there are some of these still floating around!

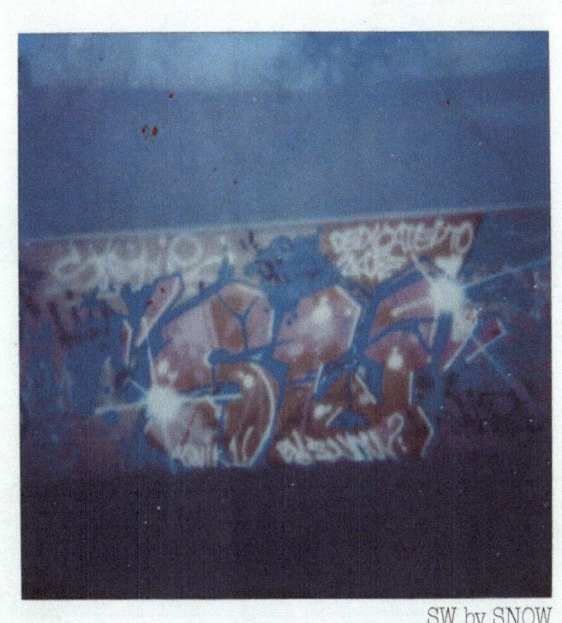

SW by SNOW
The Great Falls in Paterson
1985

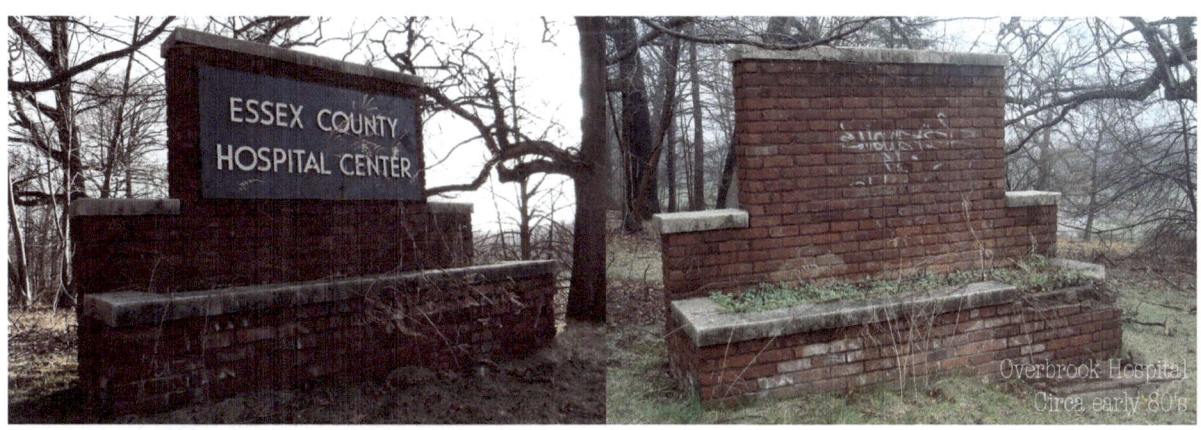

ESSEX COUNTY HOSPITAL CENTER

Overbrook Hospital
Circa early 80's

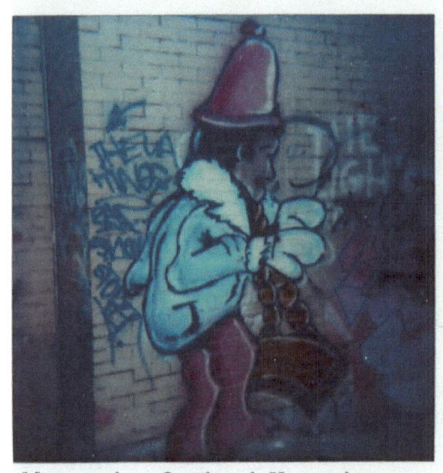
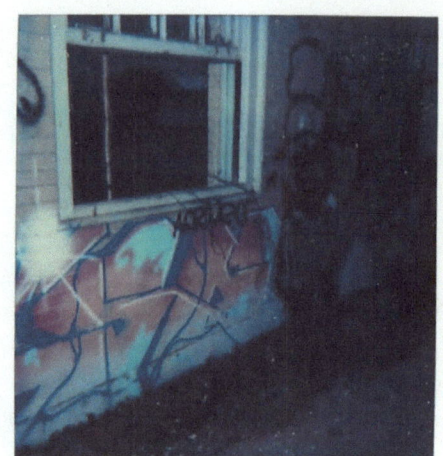
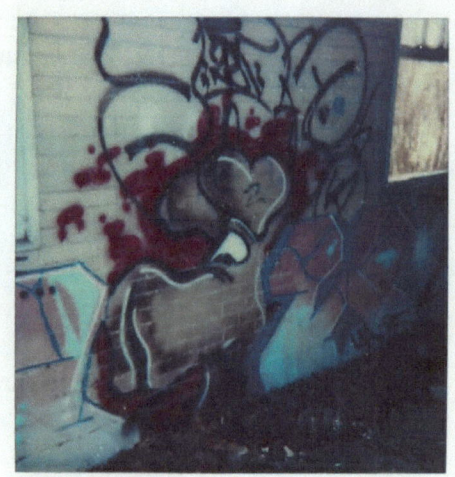

More work at Overbrook Hospital
Early 80's

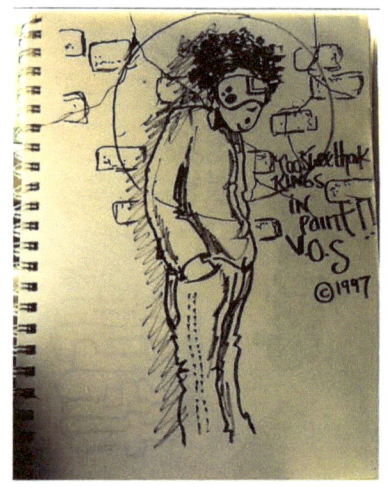

TOOSWEET HAKIM
1997

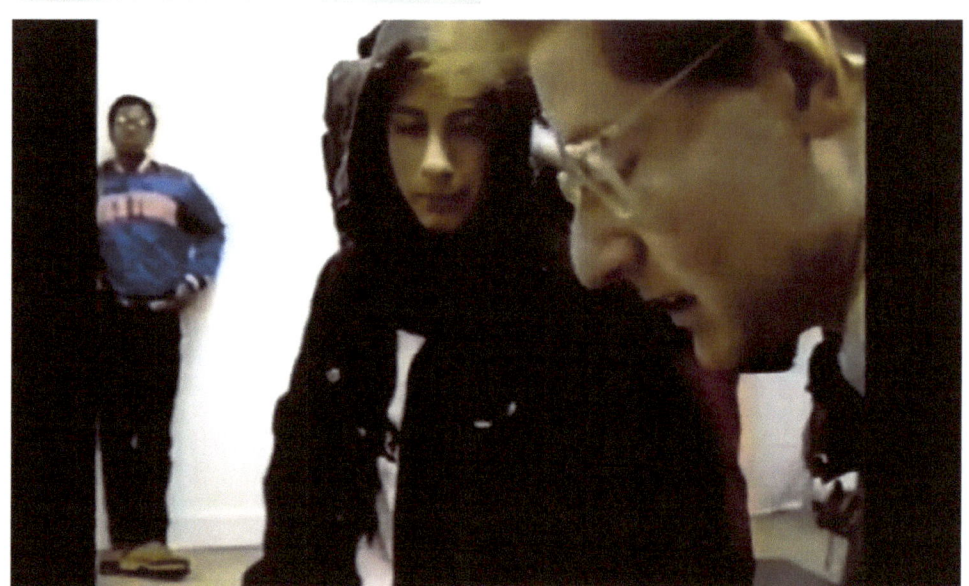

Young Snow appears on PBS graffiti art special.
Newark, NJ
Early 80's

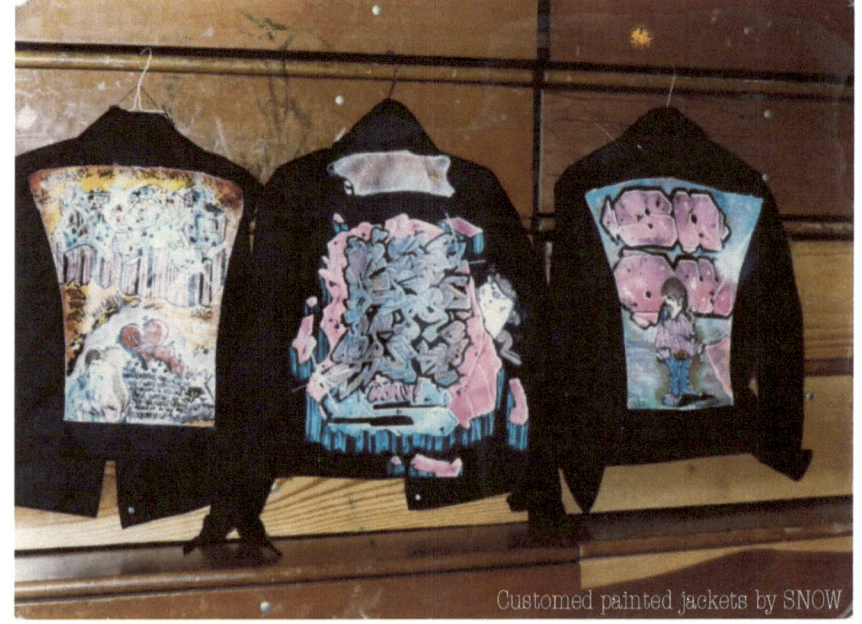

Customed painted jackets by SNOW

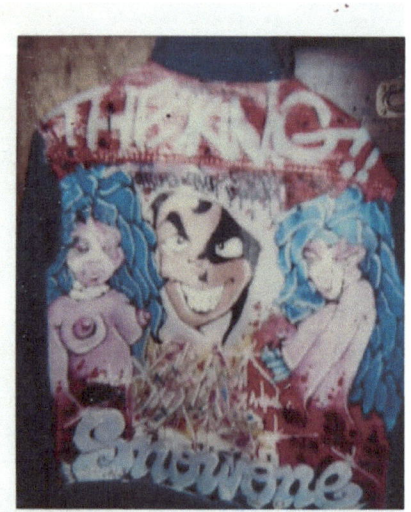

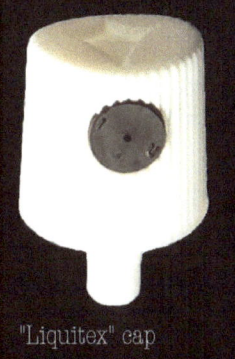

"Liquitex" cap

Graffiti wasn't the only art Snow was practicing; break dancing, DJing, and MCing had taken the country by storm, and he tried his hand at them as well. It wasn't uncommon to see these street performers do their thing on an old refrigerator box or a piece of linoleum, taped to the ground. The slick surface would easily allow dancers to spin on their backs, heads, and hands. When dancing on the street, graffiti decorated the walls, motivating these incredible entertainers. Also, dance clubs were getting an influx of these dancers and Snow would be right there in the mix. Through 1983-1985, Snow frequented a teen club in West Orange, NJ called Creations. Recognized as the crew's top graffiti talent (Snow also danced), Snow aligned himself with the crew: The Dead End Breakers. The Hip Hop crew soon became the All City Rockers (SONIC-D, DJ DANNY, GWHIZ, JUICE, and PAT BONEZ). Having Snow as their graffiti "ambassador" gave them plenty of status. Now becoming well traveled himself, Snow, through members of the All City Rockers, was introduced to Blaster, a graffiti artist from the Vailsburg section of Newark, NJ. (Snow's mother had grown up in nearby Irvington.)

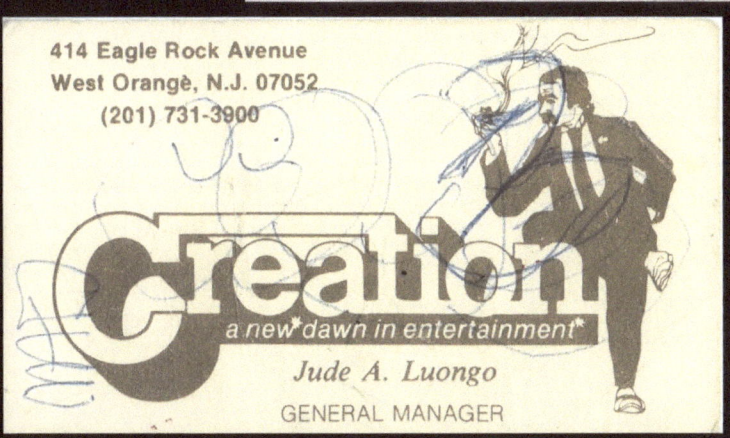

414 Eagle Rock Avenue
West Orangè, N.J. 07052
(201) 731-3900

Creation
a new dawn in entertainment

Jude A. Luongo
GENERAL MANAGER

"Clubs like The Meadowbrook and Creations served as a gathering place for writters (graf) and bboys."

SNOW

OLD
ACD
ACR
DEB
TNC

DISCO   DISCO

THE   ALL   CITY
DJs

DISCO

DJ   DANNY   DJ   BENNY

239-5086

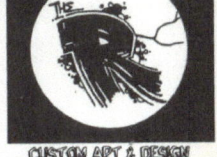

THE R
CUSTOM ART & DESIGN
You Name It We'll Design It

Gary R. Conway
ARTIST/OWNER

15 WILLIAM STREET
NEWARK, NJ 07103
TEL (201) 242-4973
PAGER (201) 613-9209

In 1985, Blaster, impressed with Snow's ability, brought Snow to meet NRG/NAM Crew member PRINS. PRINS was a talented graffiti artist in Newark. This would be far more than just two great artists chopping it up about bombing trains and highway bridges. At this point, Snow was using oven cleaner caps, aka Fat Caps, for bombing, and Stock Nozzles, aka Bone Caps, for artwork and piecing.

Snow was about to receive a new tool in his arsenal, as PRINS introduced him to "Liquitex", aka New York thin caps.

"This cap created a much cleaner look. It allowed us to get a sharp, tight look, as if we used stencils or tape. But using stencils, tape and cardboard cutouts was a definite no-no in the street arts back then. These new caps would allow for our graffiti art game to be elevated and transformed to the next level exclusively through our (spray)can control."

SNOW

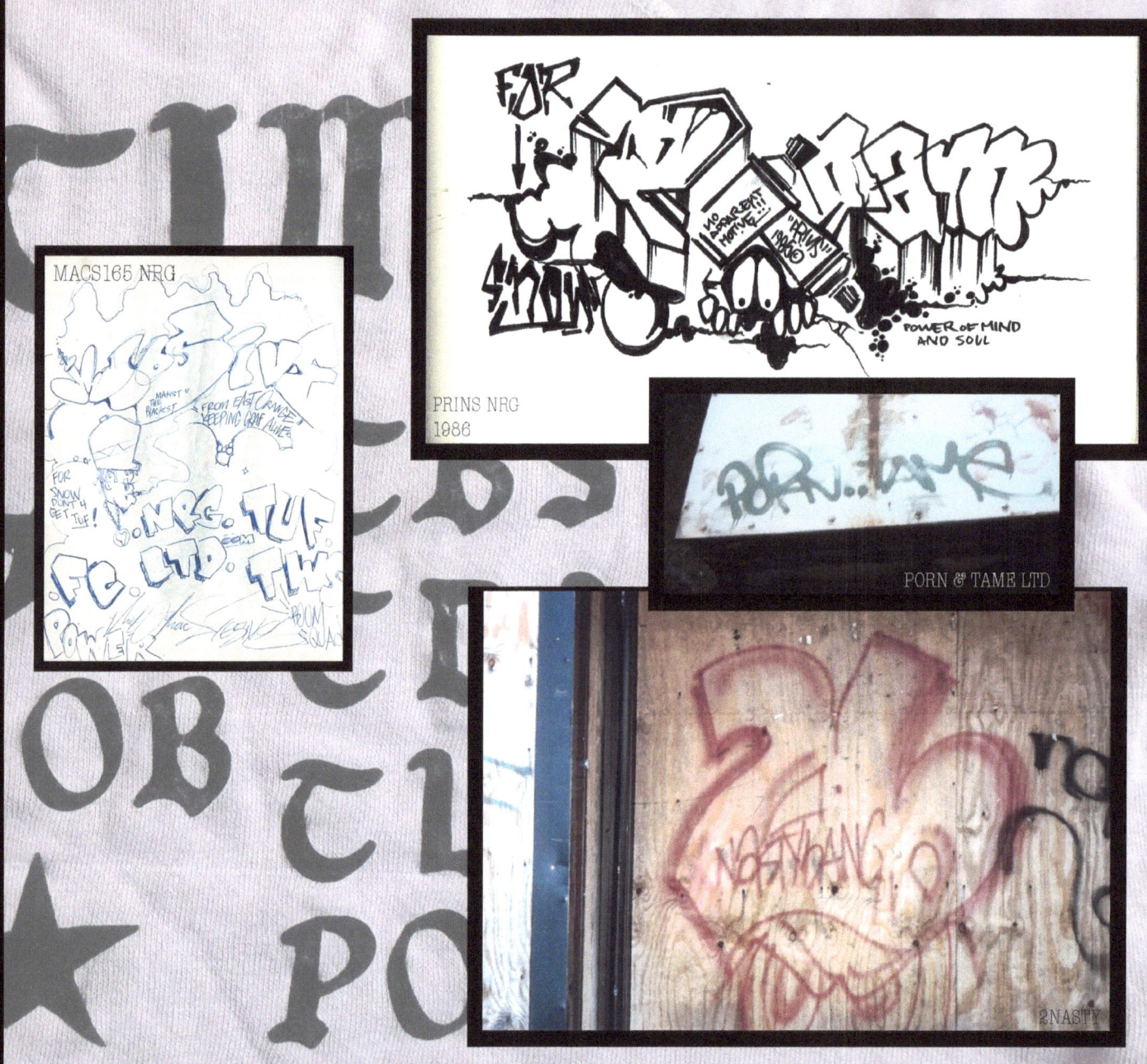

MACS165 NRG

PRINS NRG
1986

PORN & TAME LTD

2NASTY

"Besides PRINS there were so many writers in The Bricks that influenced me to get up, and so many unique styles: REVENGE VOS, PEZ, 2NASTY, PROE, TAME, PORN, MAX165, TENS, KECE, JEROO NRG, SOUL and CIRE BNS, MANE TWS, DUNE, EPIC, RUDE, TITO T... too many to list!"

SNOW

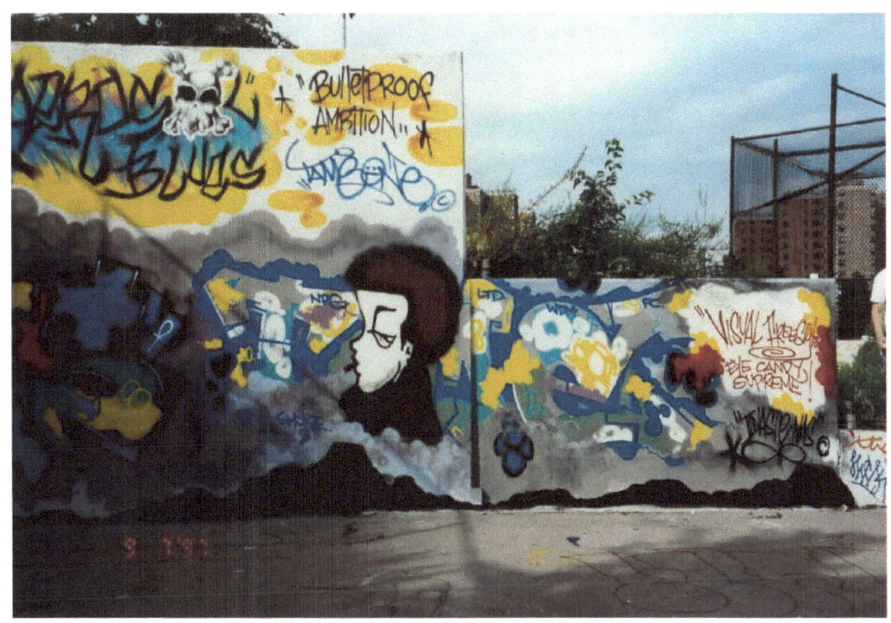

TAME LTD and 2NASTY NRG

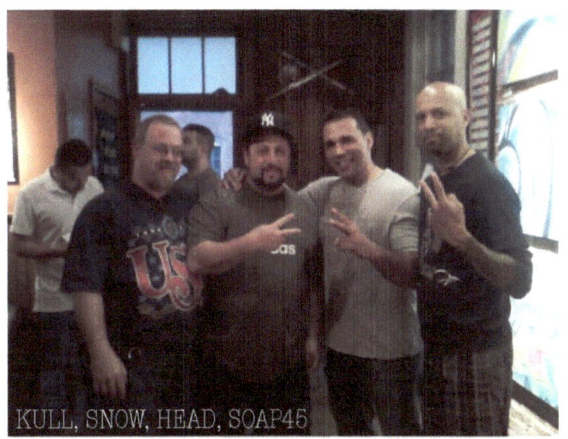

KULL, SNOW, HEAD, SOAP45

Old school reunion
The Ivanhoe, Paterson, NJ

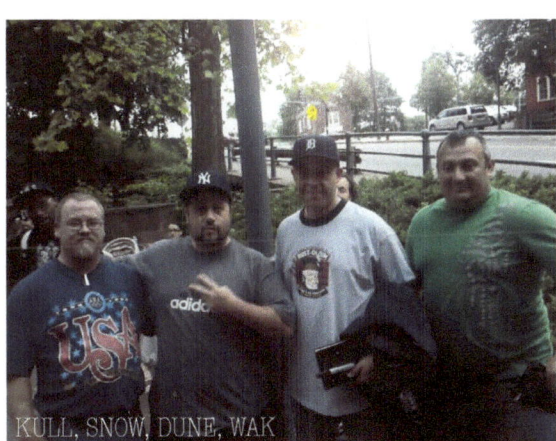

KULL, SNOW, DUNE, WAK

"KULL and MIN really showed me how
to come correct in blackbooks. They
were very inspirational in my early style
development."

SNOW

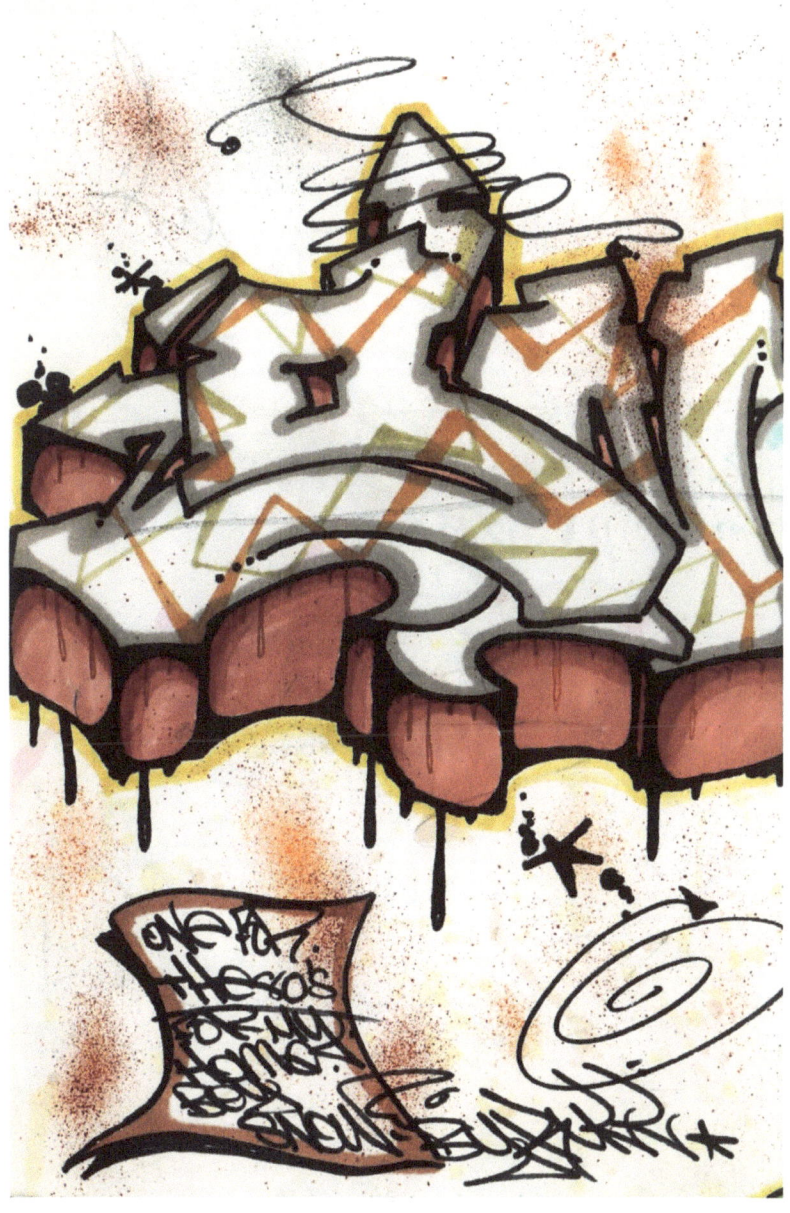

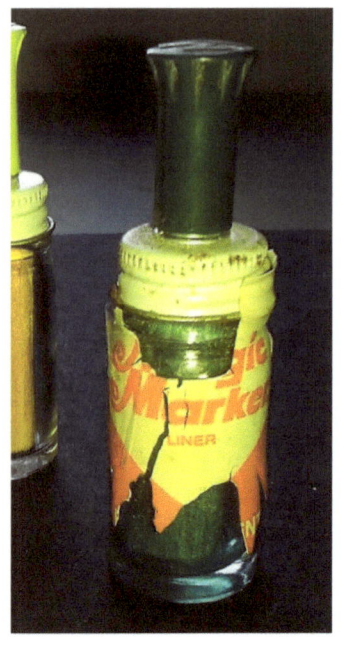

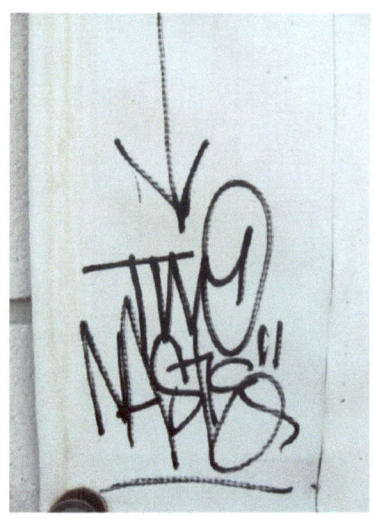

2NASTY NRG

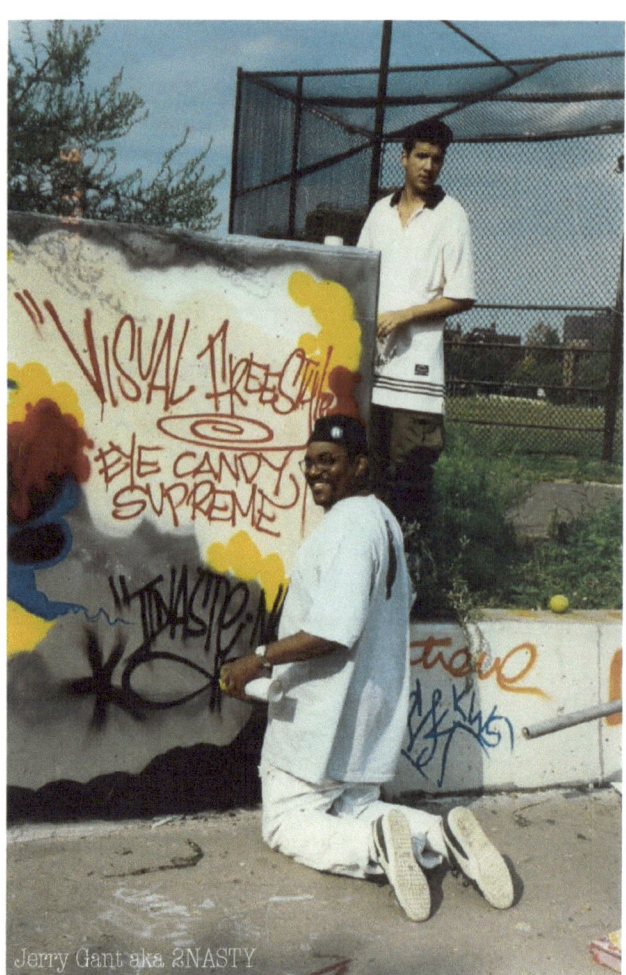

Jerry Gant aka 2NASTY

Some old blackbook action
SNOW by KULL
1985

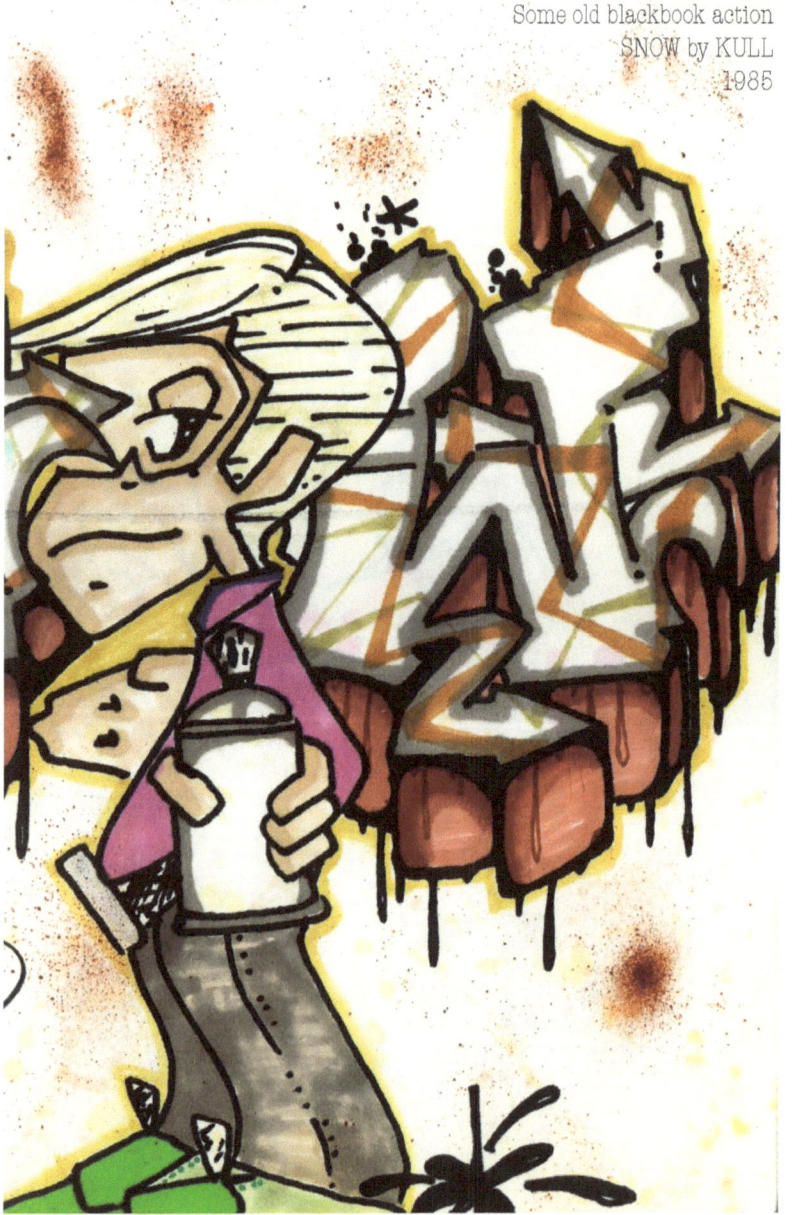

"I used to ride the Parkway when I was really young. I looked out the window and I would see 2NASTY tags when we got into the Newark area. He had the freshest handstyles."

SNOW

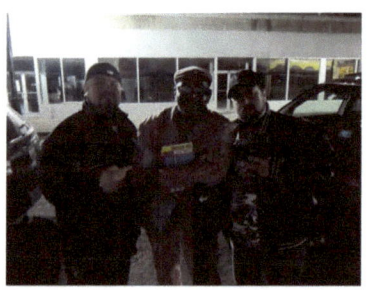

CENT, 2NASTY, and SNOW

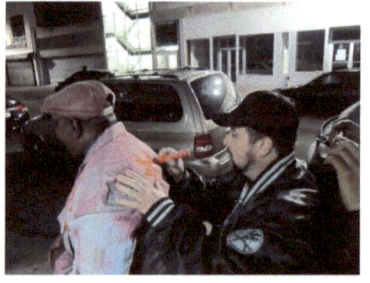

As Snow's reputation grew throughout the mid 80's, law enforcement was cracking down hard on graffiti writers; Snow was at the top of their list. Graffiti can be a truly beautiful and unique art but to some, the tags can be a misplaced eyesore, to say the least. During 1984-1985, graffiti in North Jersey was at epidemic proportions.

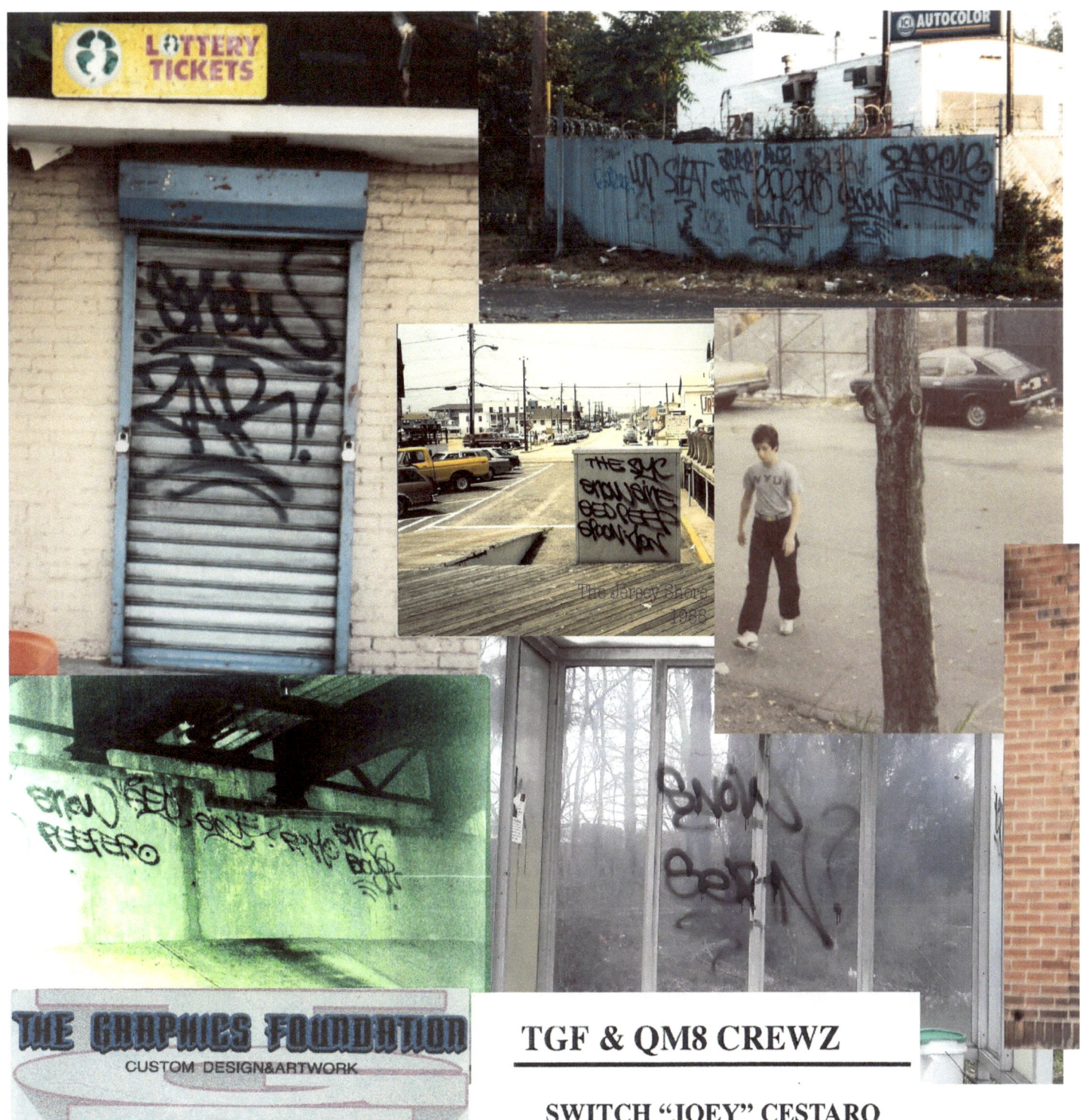

TGF & QM8 CREWZ

SWITCH "JOEY" CESTARO

PATERSON NJ 2000 TIL ?????

973 956 7588   E MAIL
SWITCHONEQM8@HOTMAIL.COM

Snow was invited by ZAR to be part of The Graffiti Force (TGF), a crew out of Paterson. Its members were: ZAR, AERO, SIC, CAP, and STOPER. Snow himself tagged highway bridges all over North Jersey, including routes 3, 46, 10, 287, 17, 1 & 9, 495, 287, and 80, and is credited as being one of the, if not the first, writers to bomb the highly exposed route 280. Snow, at 17 years old, even made his way southward to hit the Toms River Bridge, Seaside Heights, and Wildwood, NJ. (Graffiti had not really hit central or southern Jersey at this point. Although there was a heavier Philly influence slowly growing in the southern part of the Garden State, Snow was one of the first North Jersey writers to have a presence there.)

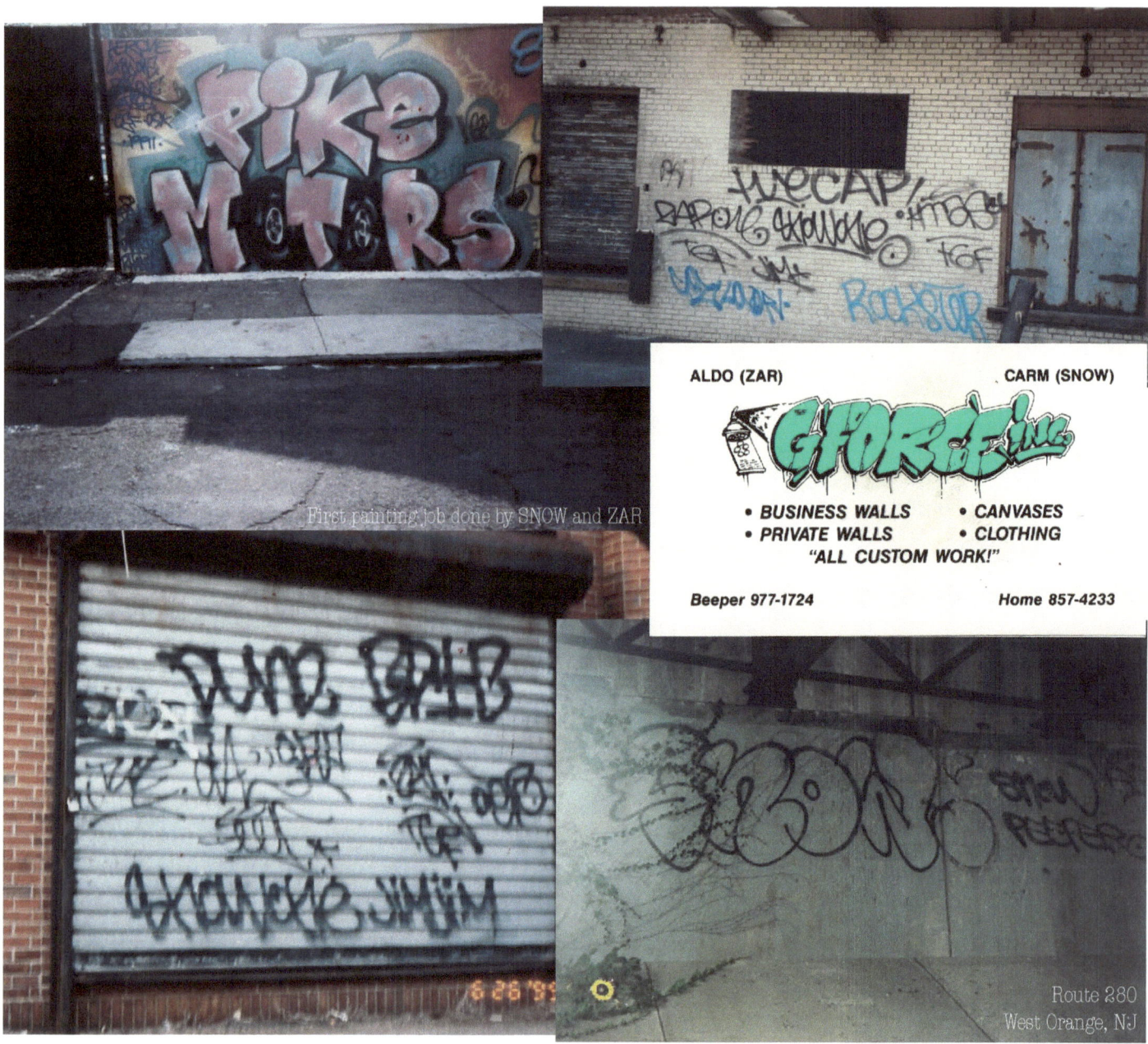

First painting job done by SNOW and ZAR

ALDO (ZAR)   CARM (SNOW)

GFORCE inc.

• BUSINESS WALLS   • CANVASES
• PRIVATE WALLS   • CLOTHING
"ALL CUSTOM WORK!"

Beeper 977-1724   Home 857-4233

Route 280
West Orange, NJ

Needless to say, Snow was covering ground, and law enforcement officials were at a point where they were offering rewards and going public with their fight against vandalism. Snow's mother, while preparing one of her tasty dishes in the kitchen, heard a public service announcement on Guardian Angel Curtis Sliwa's 77WABC radio show that her own son was wanted for countless acts of vandalism. His parents concerns grew deeper as Snow took more and more to graffiti and the adrenaline rush that it gave him.

"I started taking bus trips into NYC with ZAR and later with The SMC guys. I used to marvel at what I saw: guys like DONDI, SEEN UA, TKID, DUSTER, TACK FBA, SKEME, POEM, FLITE, SHAME 125, DOC TC5, WEST FC, TATS CRU, JON 156, DC3, SHOROZ AND DOME TDC, VULCAN, PART TDS, KOZE, RIZE, SERVE...just too many to name!!"

SNOW

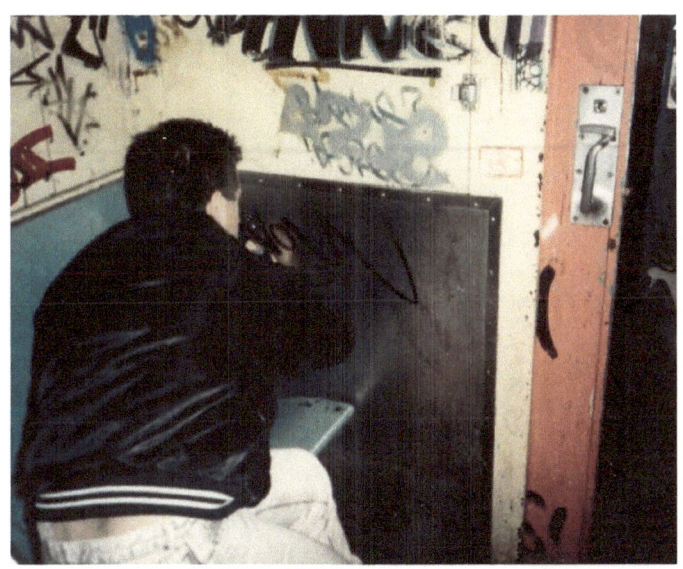
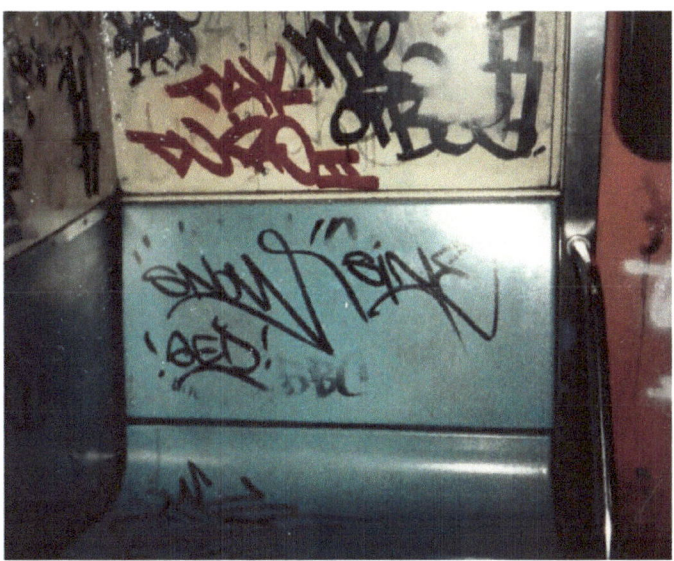

Circa 1987

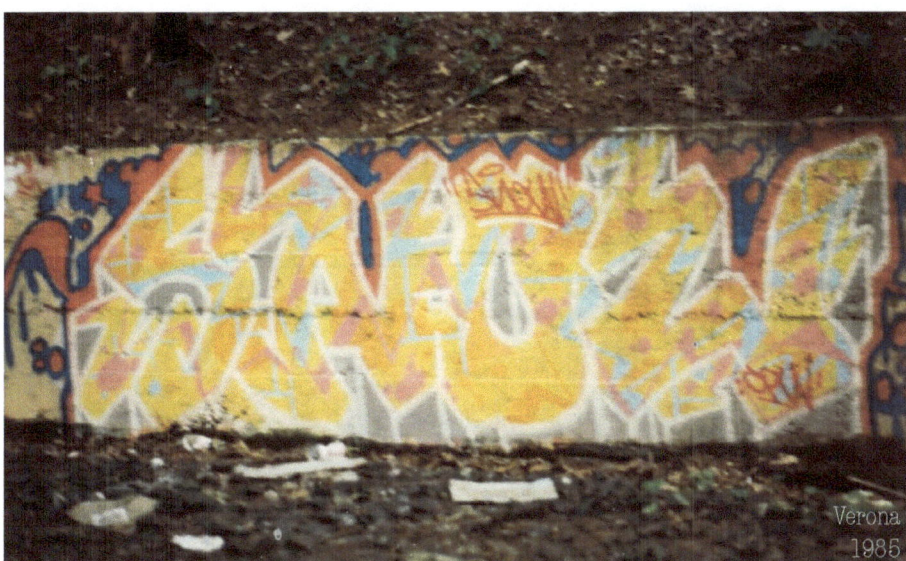

Verona
1985

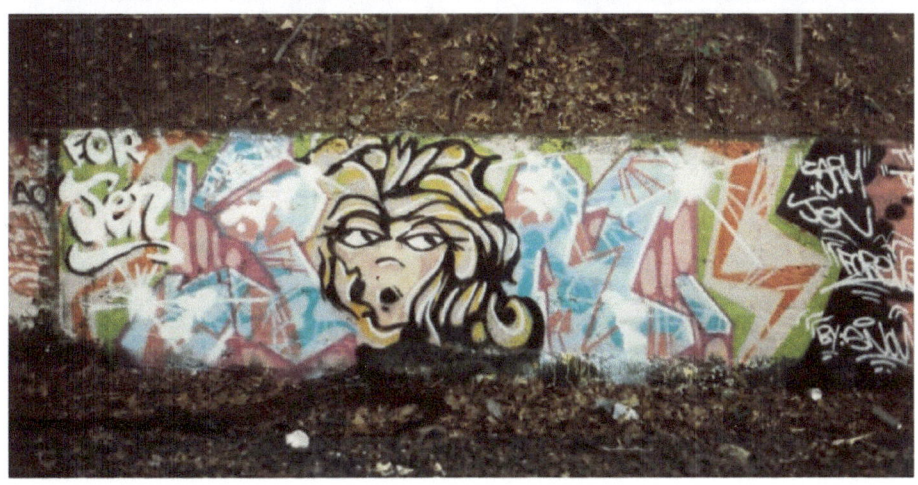

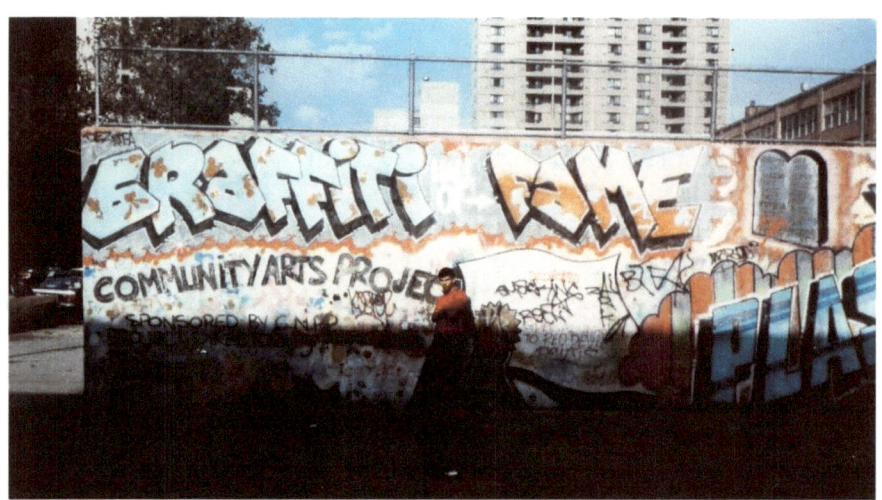

KANE TGF chilling at the Graffiti Hall of Fame
Harlem, NYC
mid 1980's

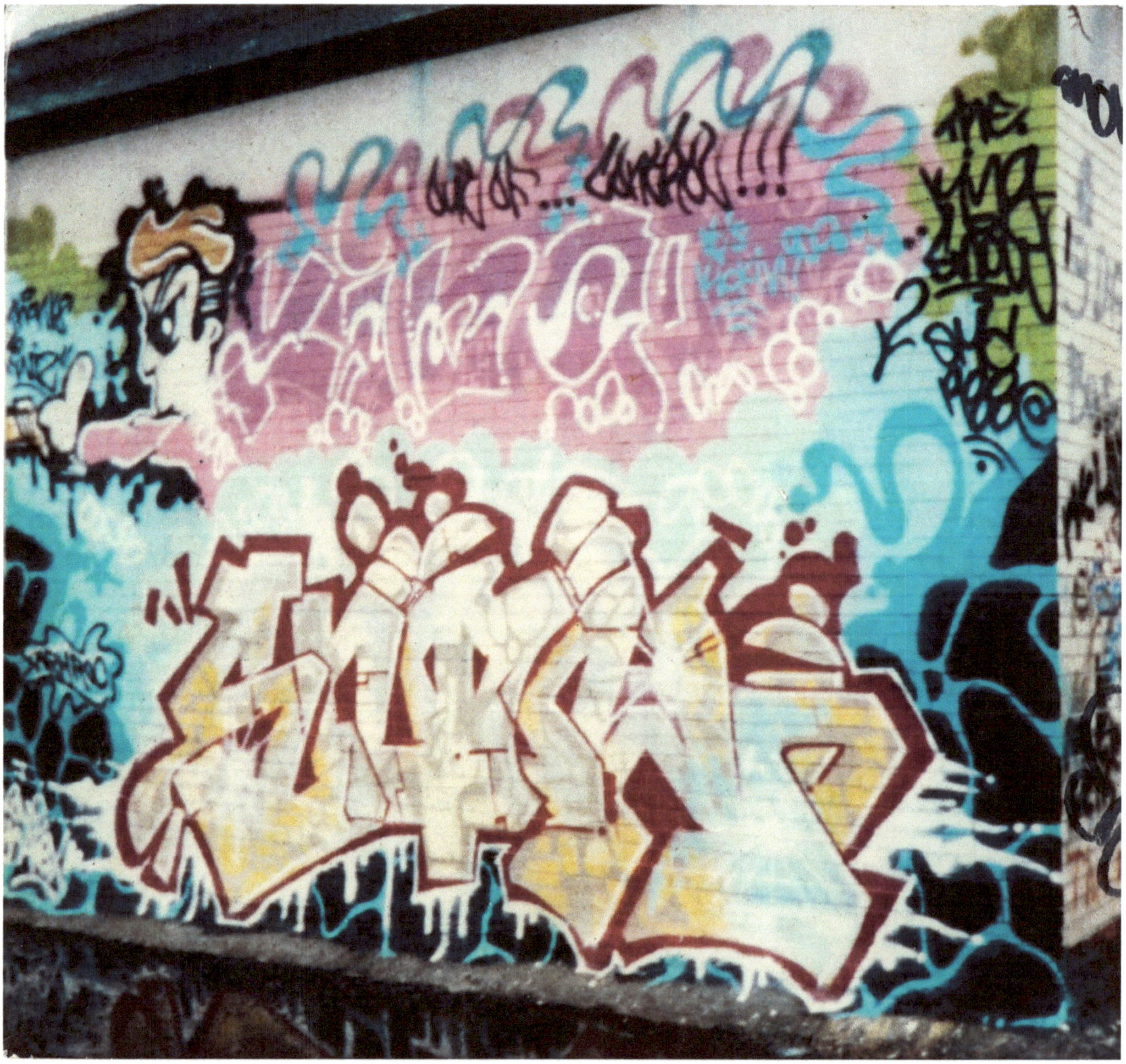

SNOW - Overbrook Hospital
1988

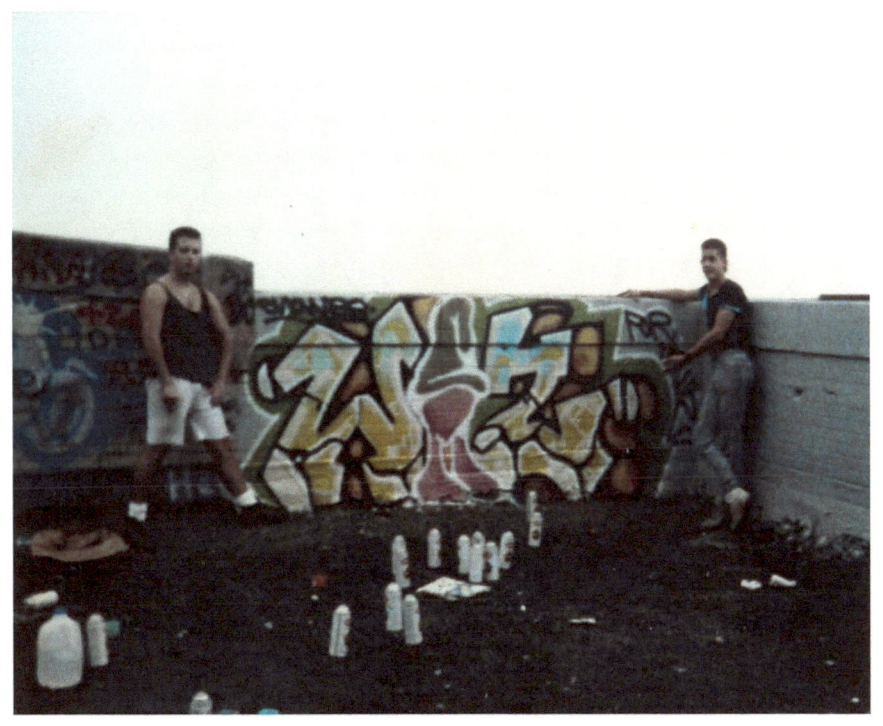

"Painting at the abandoned Overbook Hospital was one of my favorite past times. It was virtually like our playground. Sometimes we had 20-30 people up here, partying and playing manhunt into the wee hours of the night. I was the first one to bring some of my graffiti writer friends to this spot."

SNOW

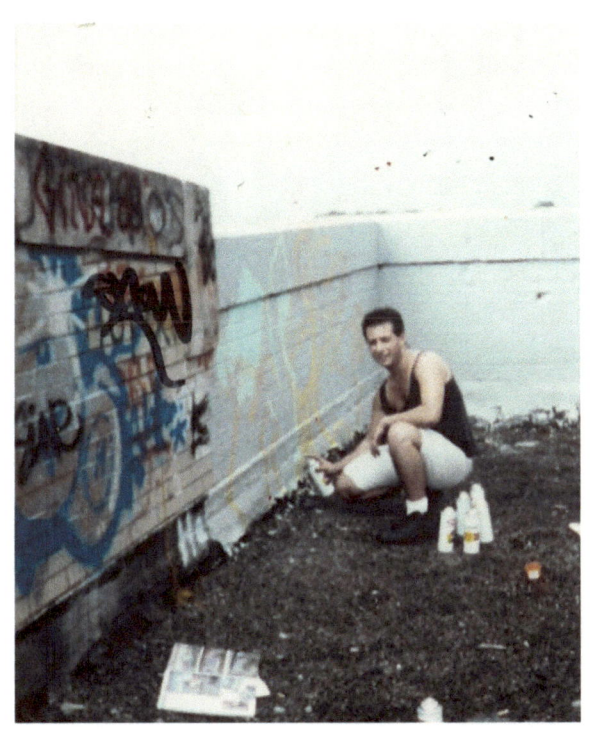

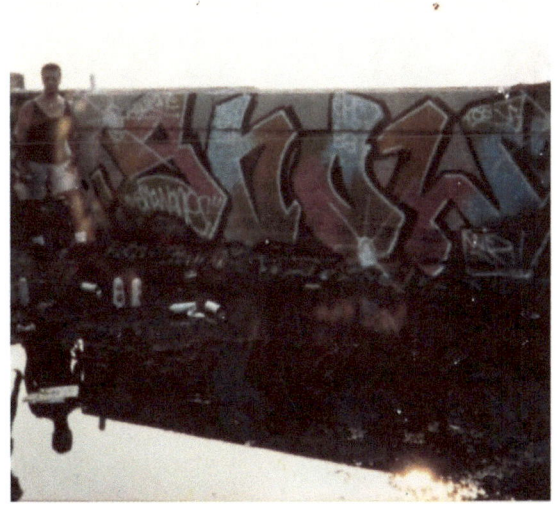

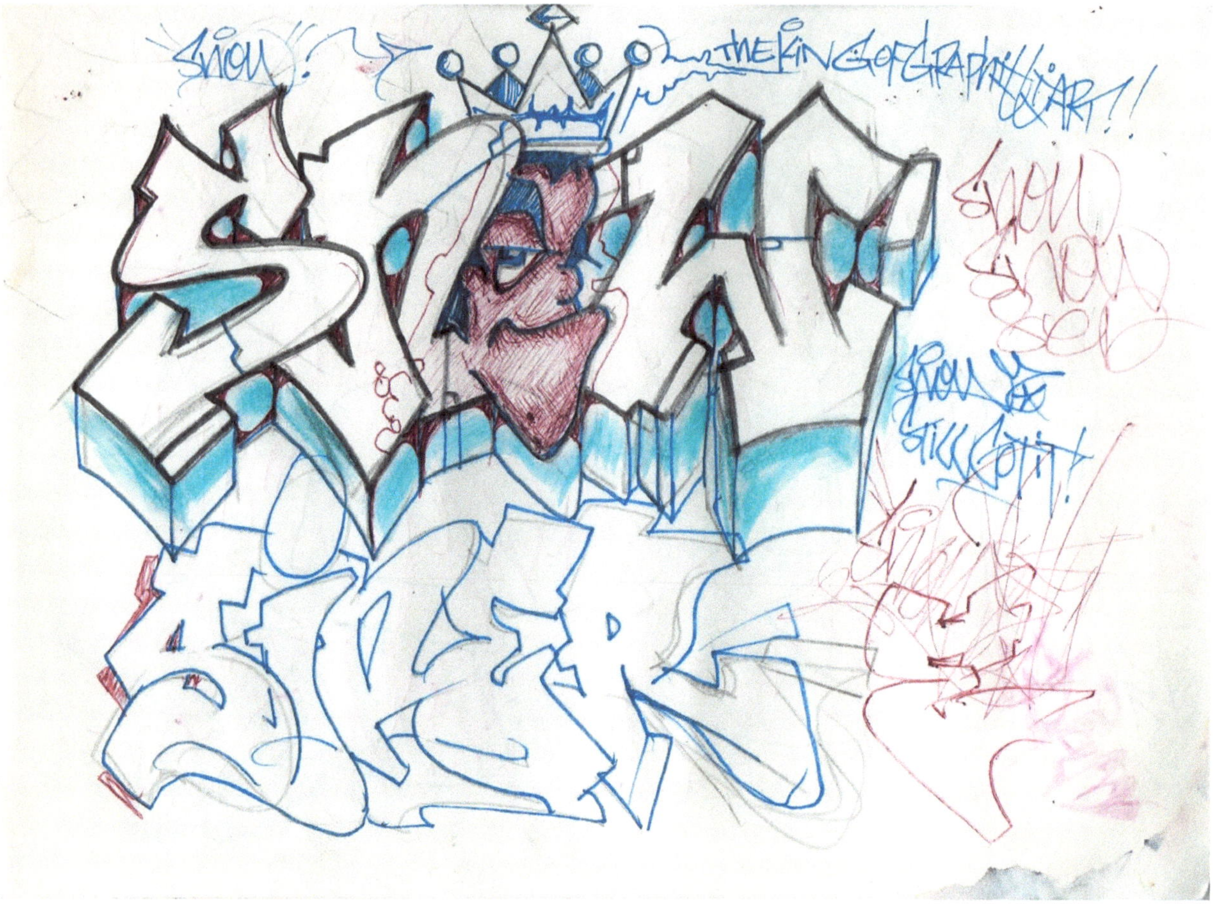

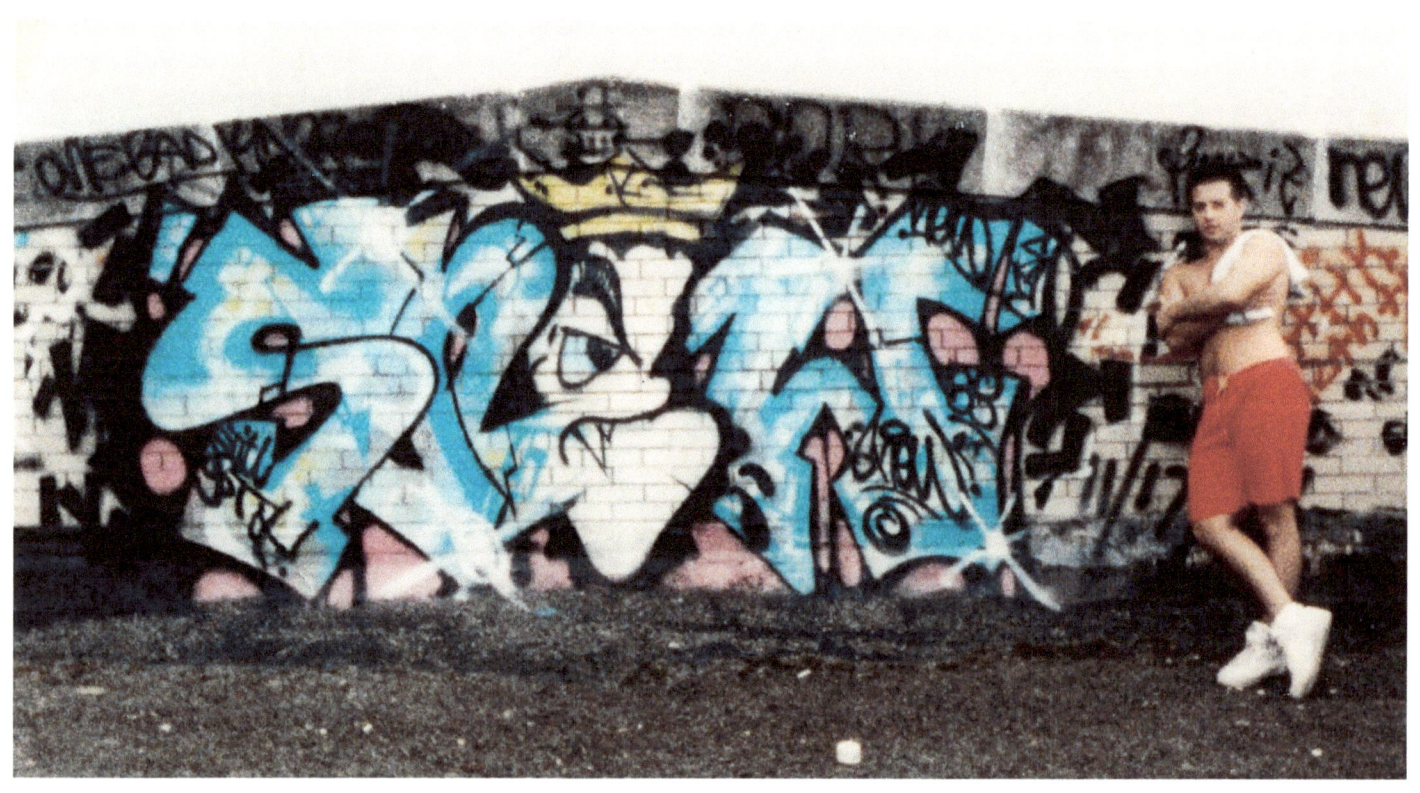

Sketches by SNOW and SINE SMC

SNOW - Overbrook Hospital
1988

In 1986, Snow was now attending Verona High School in Verona, NJ. As a senior, art classes were actually created in the curriculum to challenge his advanced abilities. This was made possible by Mrs. Austin, Snow's art teacher, who recognized his unique talents. His grades never suffered, but he did have to hand paint and scrub lockers and desks that he bombed relentlessly throughout the halls and classrooms. Although residing in Verona, NJ, Snow was spending all of his spare time in Paterson and Newark and bombing all points in between. This only created more legal problems for Snow, who by 1986 was being harassed regularly for petty and sometimes even non-graffiti related offenses. Snow's face started to become recognizable in 1985 to local police when he was caught exiting Overlook Park during a raid at the historic Great Falls in Paterson, NJ after painting a wall that was overlooking the Falls. While doing this, he and another writer were stopped by the cops. Everyone else ran. Unfortunately for Snow, he and his friend were covered in paint, making their guilt painfully obvious. After a slap on the wrist and a fine, law enforcement was anxiously circling, waiting and watching for Snow to screw up again.

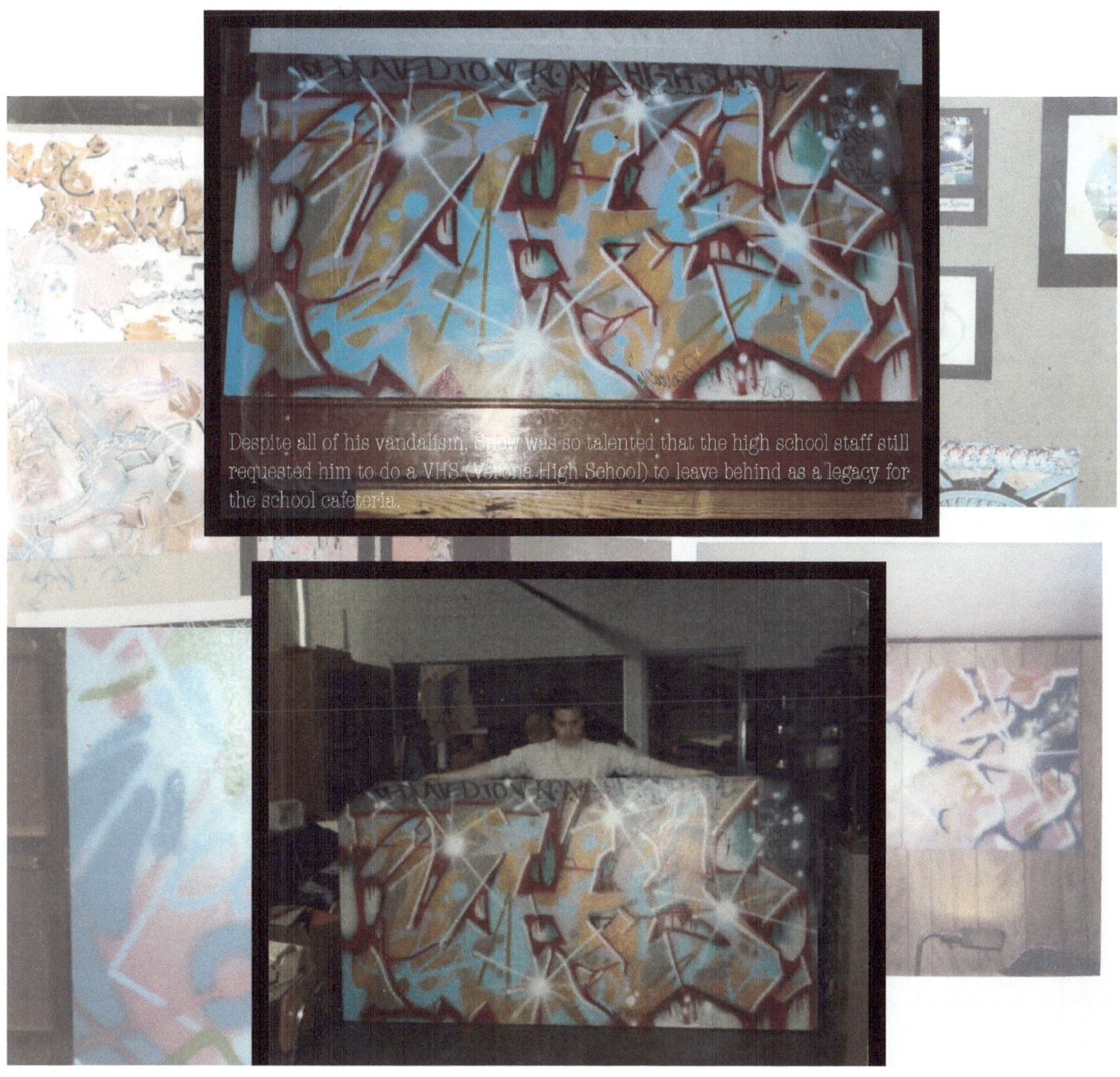

Despite all of his vandalism, Snow was so talented that the high school staff still requested him to do a VHS (Verona High School) to leave behind as a legacy for the school cafeteria.

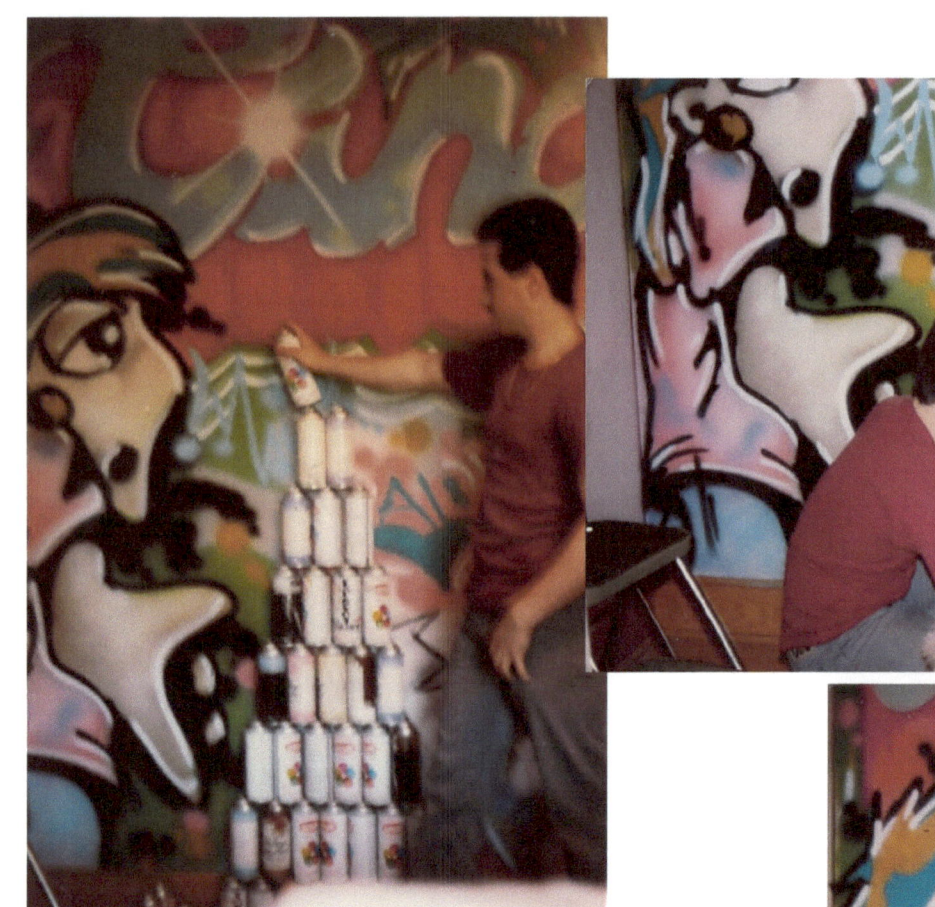

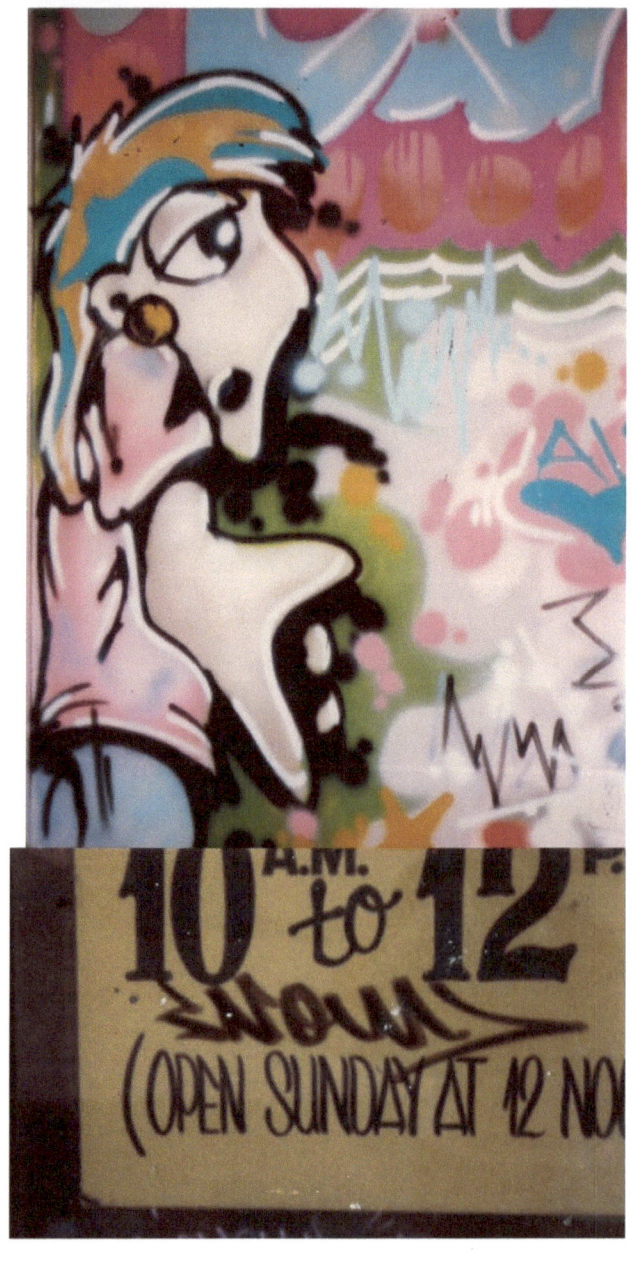

"I remember all of my friends and classmates asking me to do stuff for them, like paint their names in their bedrooms and such. This was the first room I remember doing for a friend of mine, Cindy, in West Caldwell, NJ. I remember her mom paid me in a delicious meal of macaroni and meatballs. Not a bad trade!"

SNOW

"I met Snow back in the early 80's. I was a young writer back in 'P-Town', and I remember seeing some of Snow's work when passing through Verona, NJ. I thought to myself, 'This guy has talent, and I have to meet him!' Just by luck, my partner in crime KULL happened to know who Snow was. We hooked up not too long after that, started gettin' up and started a crew together. We had some of the best writers from Paterson and Essex County. We made a lasting impact on the graffiti scene during the 1980's."

Michael "MIN" Mc Ilwrath

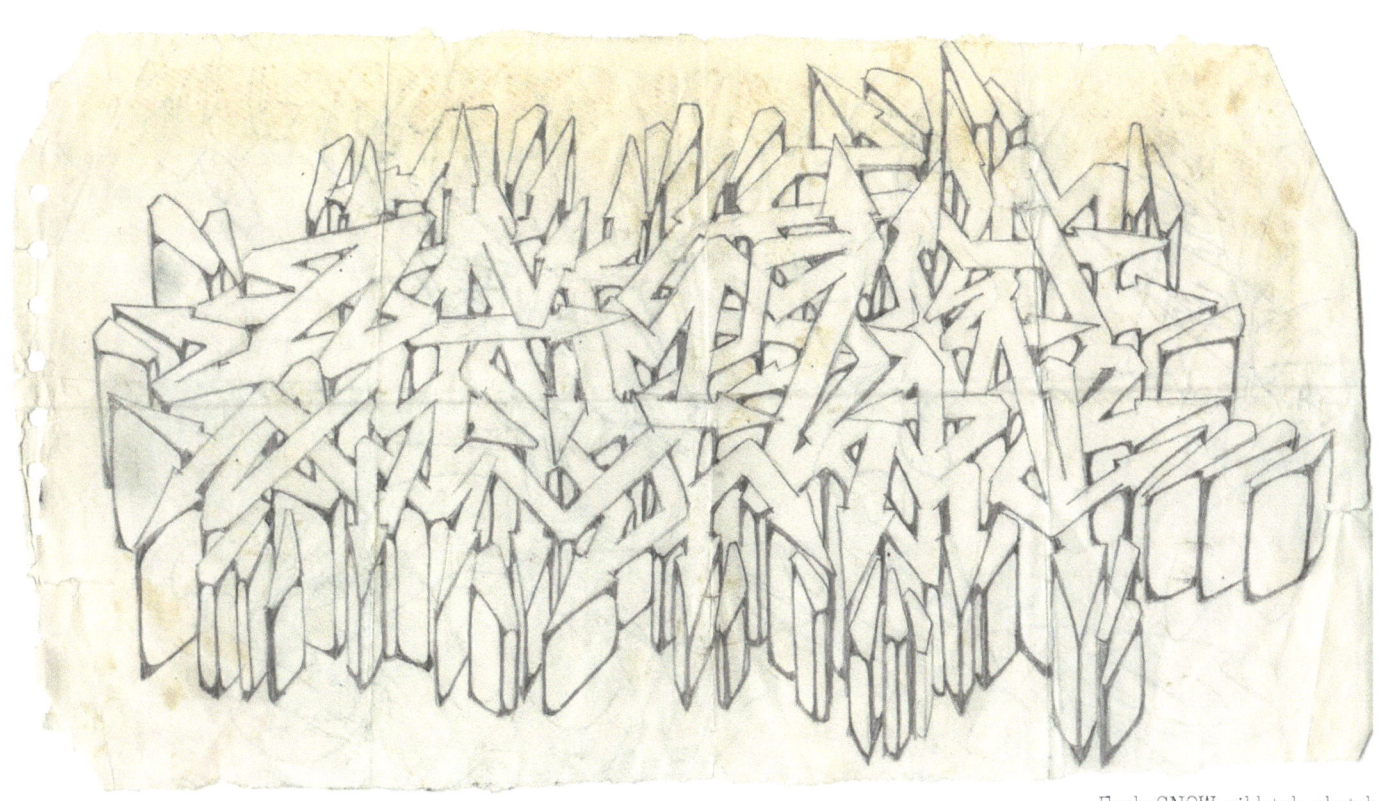

Early SNOW wildstyle sketch

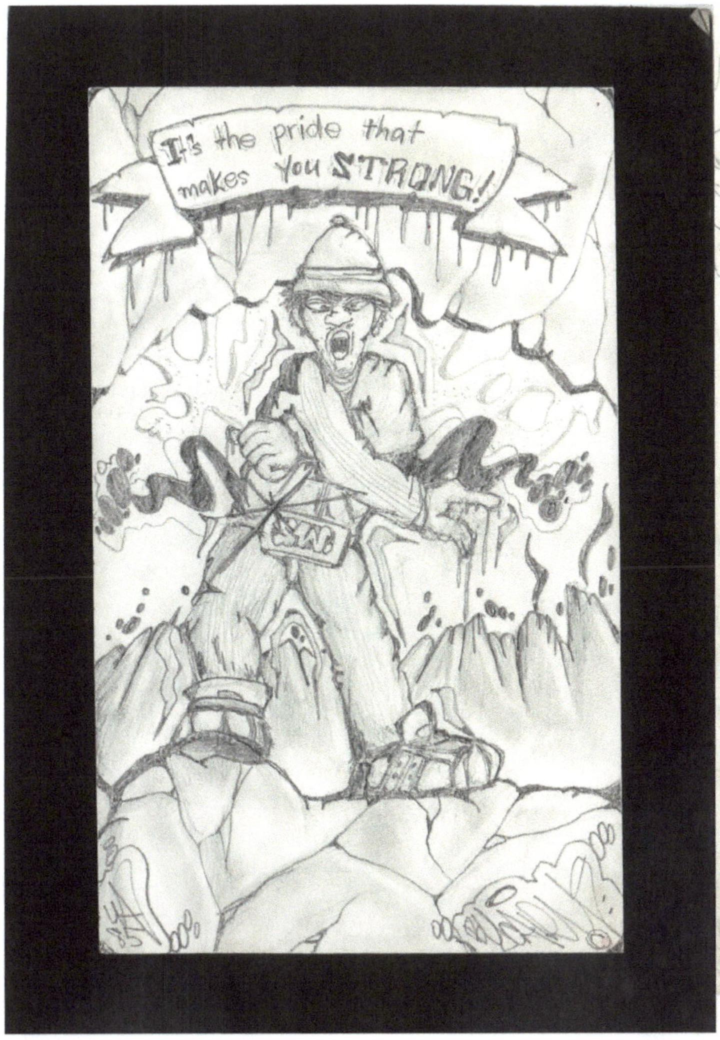

It's the pride that makes YOU STRONG!

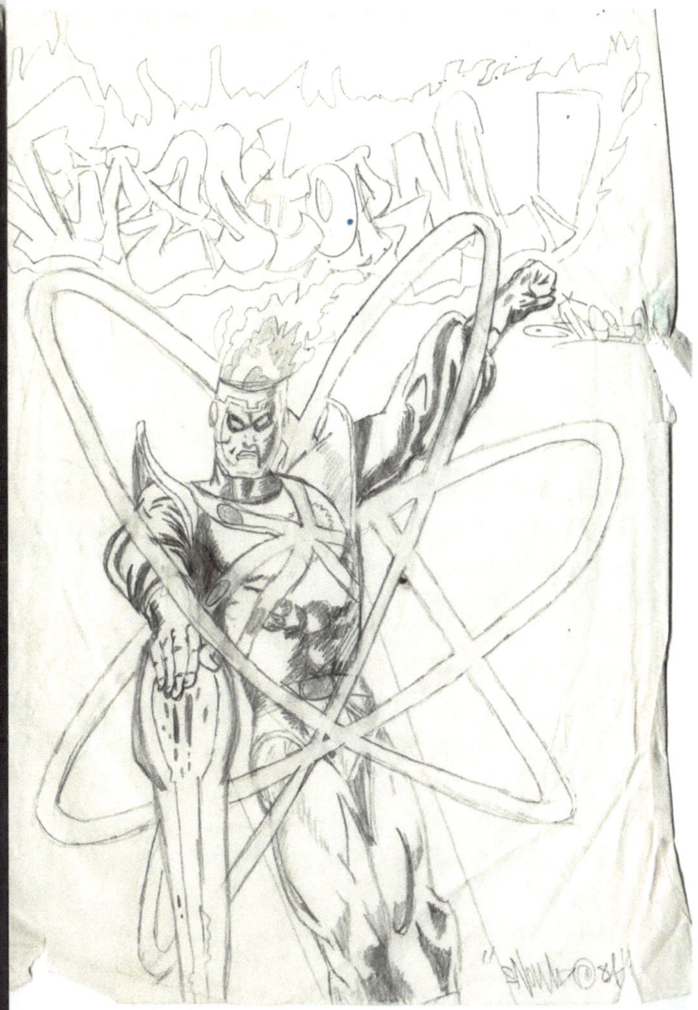

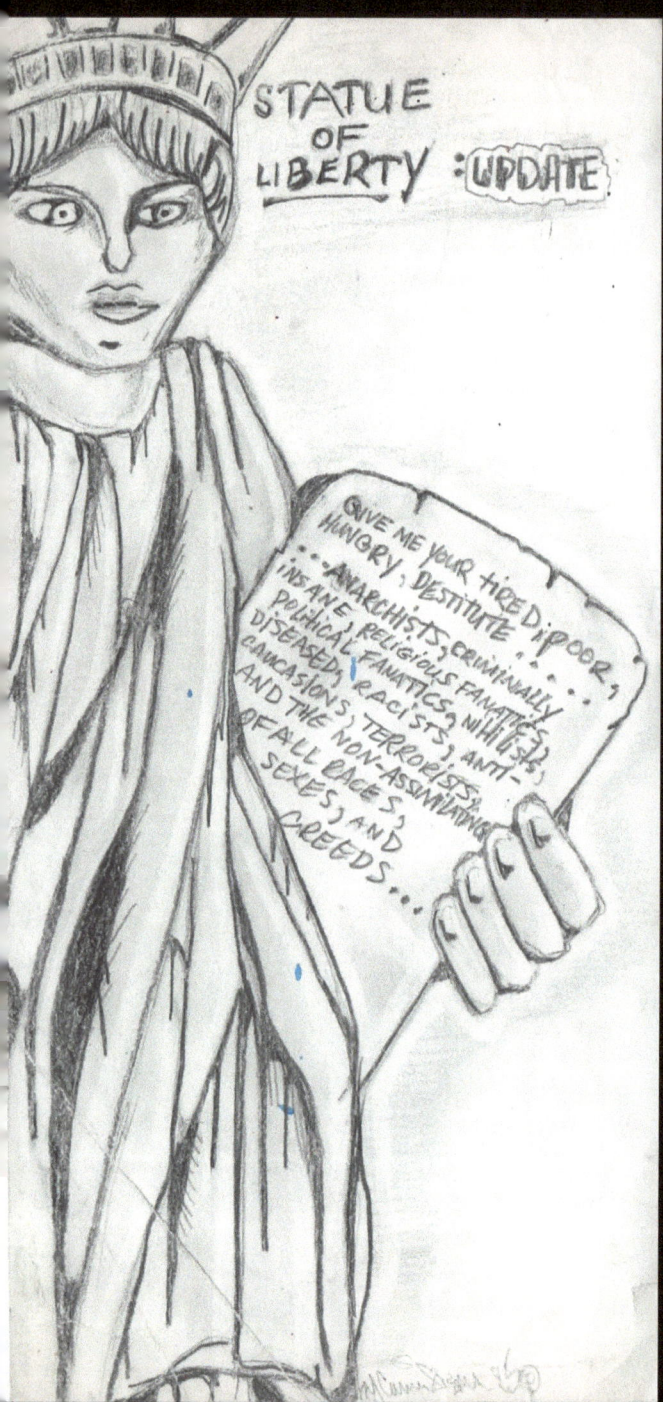

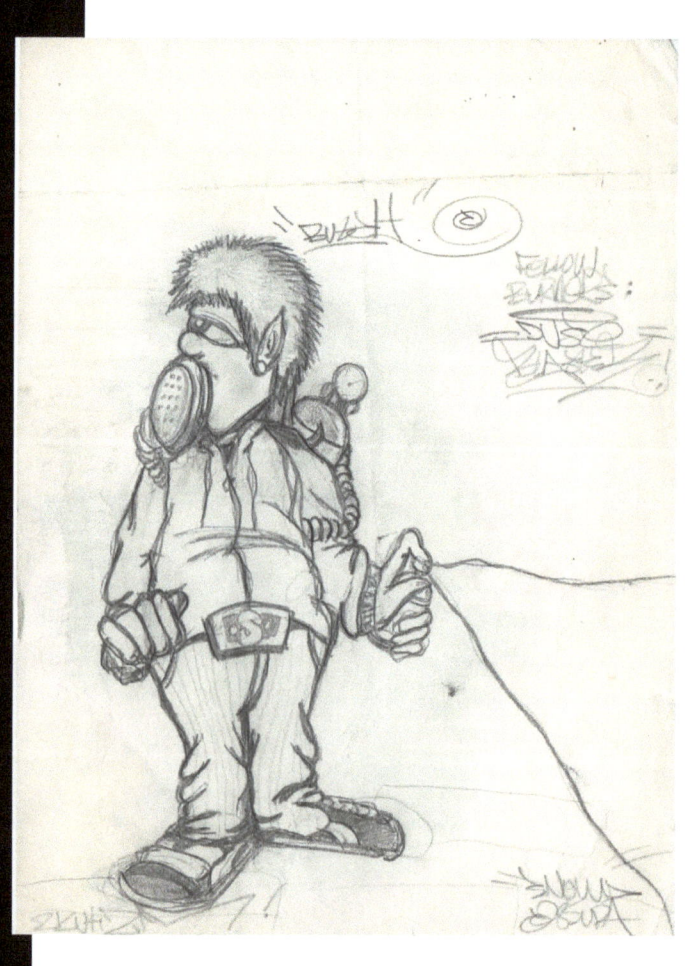

"I've always sketched. Everyday. Sometimes all day. Any chance I could get. For close to 40 years, that's all i've done, is sketch. It's the foundation of every artist and without sketching, the artist's work will suffer. Their work will reflect how much discipline and dedication the artist really has."

SNOW

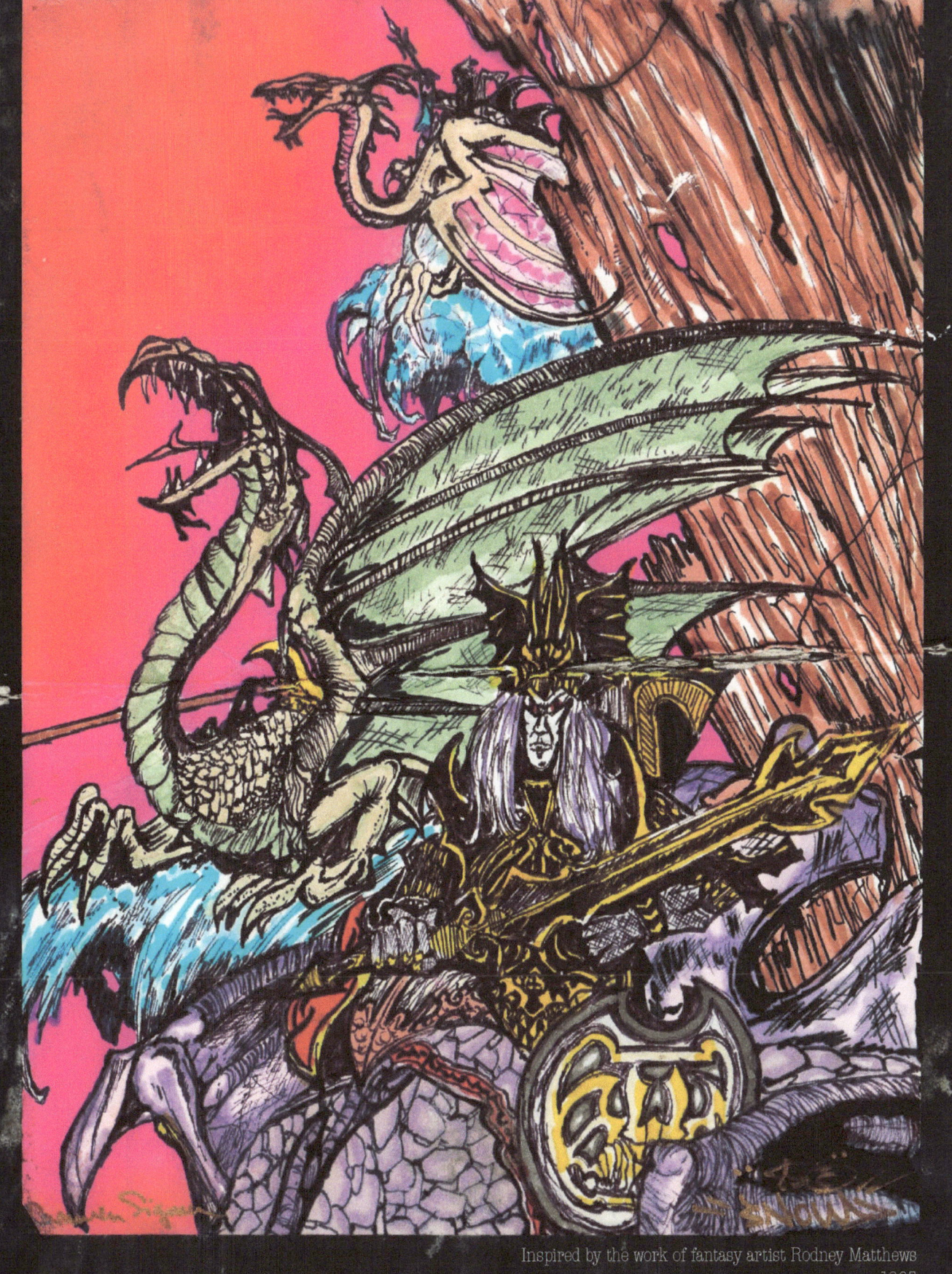

Inspired by the work of fantasy artist Rodney Matthews
1985

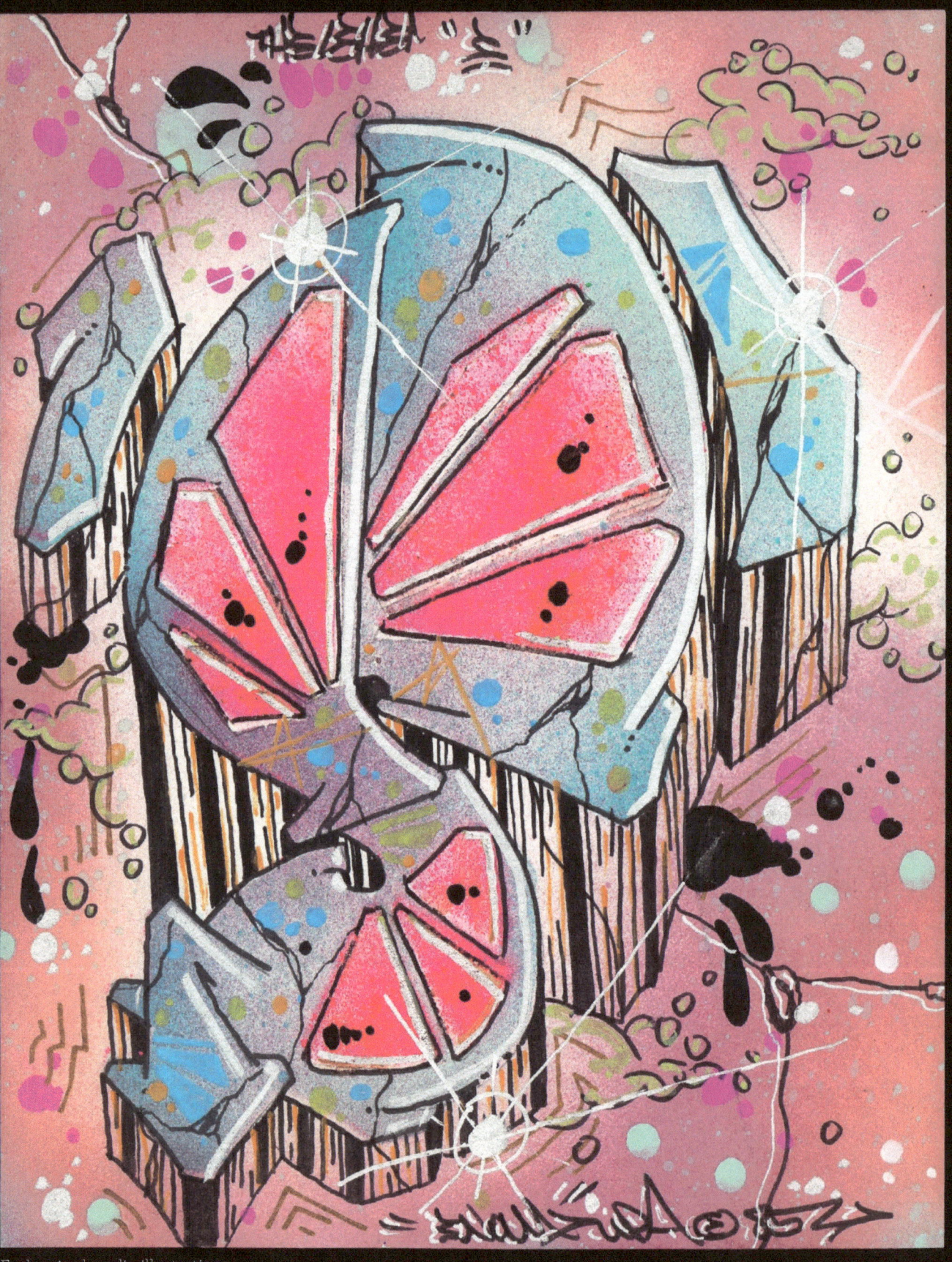

Early mixed media illustrations.
1985

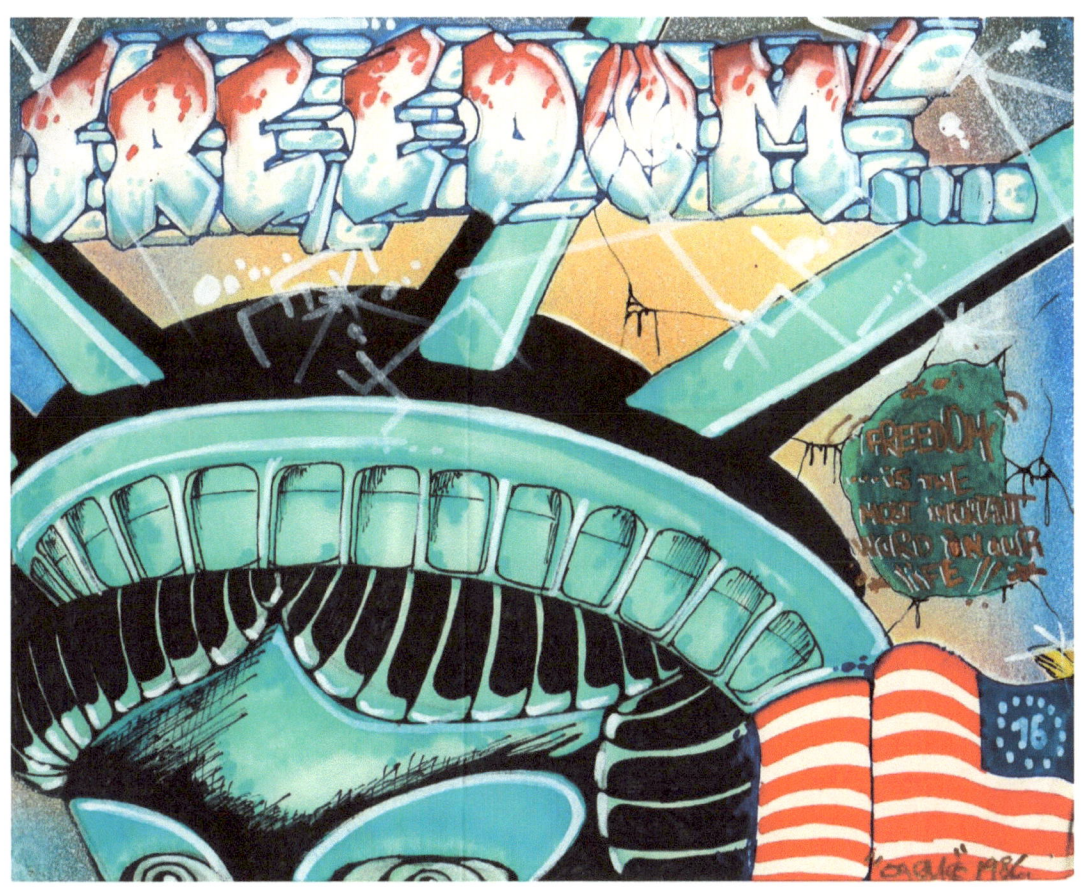

Early Illustrations - 1986

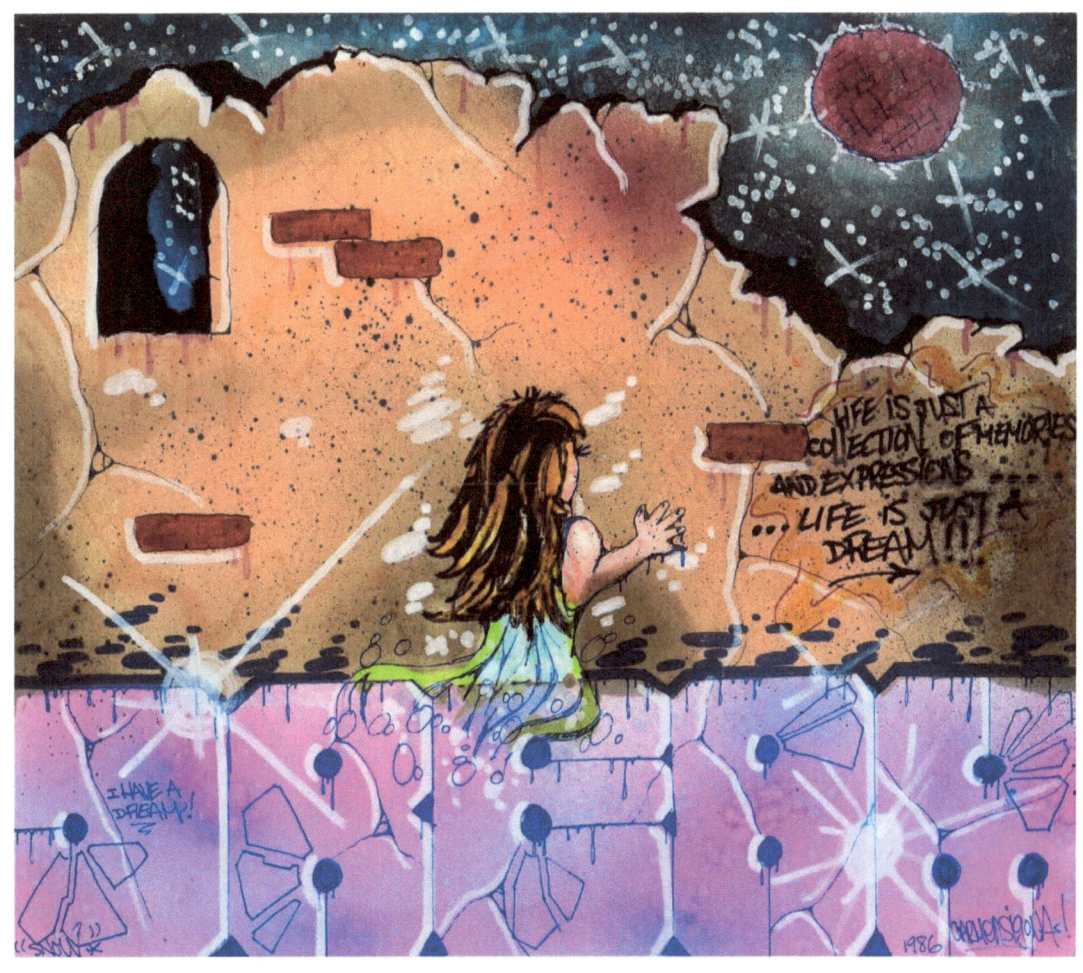

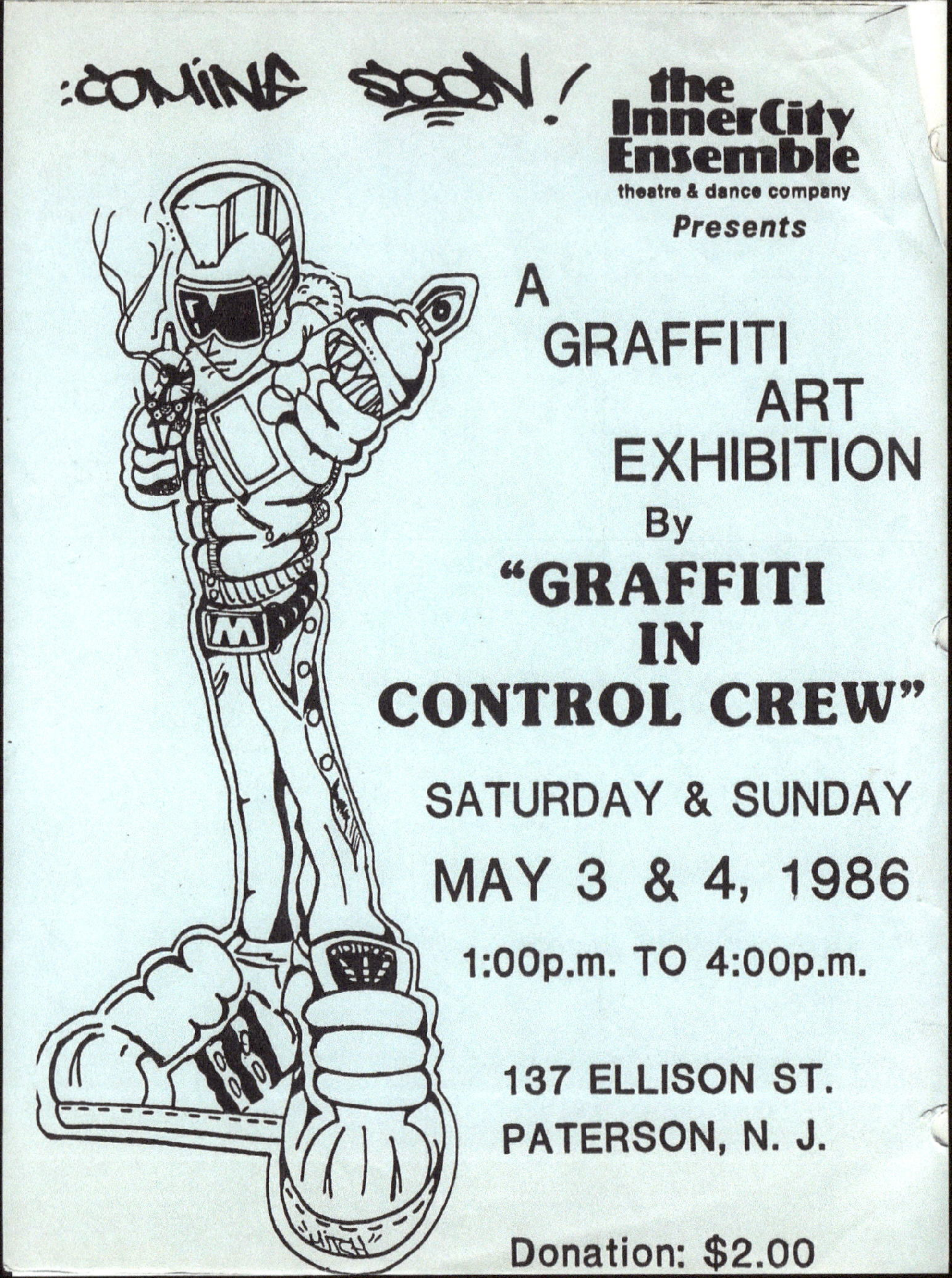

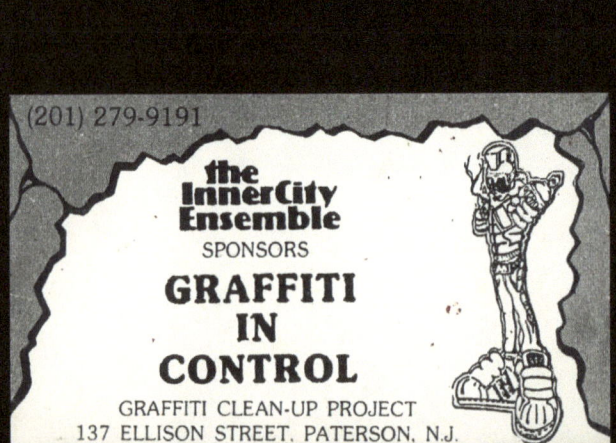

:COMING SOON!

the InnerCity Ensemble
theatre & dance company
Presents

A
GRAFFITI
ART
EXHIBITION

By

**"GRAFFITI
IN
CONTROL CREW"**

SATURDAY & SUNDAY

MAY 3 & 4, 1986

1:00p.m. TO 4:00p.m.

137 ELLISON ST.
PATERSON, N. J.

Donation: $2.00

"*Graffiti in Control (GIC) was a group and program started by the late Ralph Gomez of the Paterson inner city ensemble. It was the first attempt in Silk City to provide amnesty to taggers to enroll in the program and persue their art career. I myself refused the invitation when I found out I had to sign a document stating I promised to stop 'bombing' the city of Paterson. SCAT, ZAR, and a few others joined for the art supplies and to participate in the art shows that the program sponsored.*"

SNOW

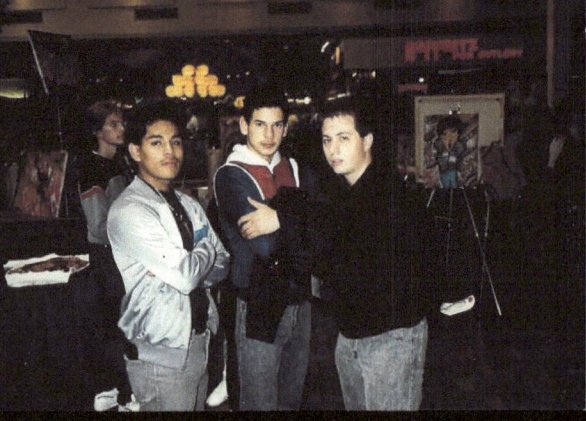

SCAT, SPY007, and SNOW attending GIC art show
Willowbrook Mall, 1986

(201) 279-9191

the InnerCity Ensemble
SPONSORS
GRAFFITI IN CONTROL
GRAFFITI CLEAN-UP PROJECT
137 ELLISON STREET, PATERSON, N.J.

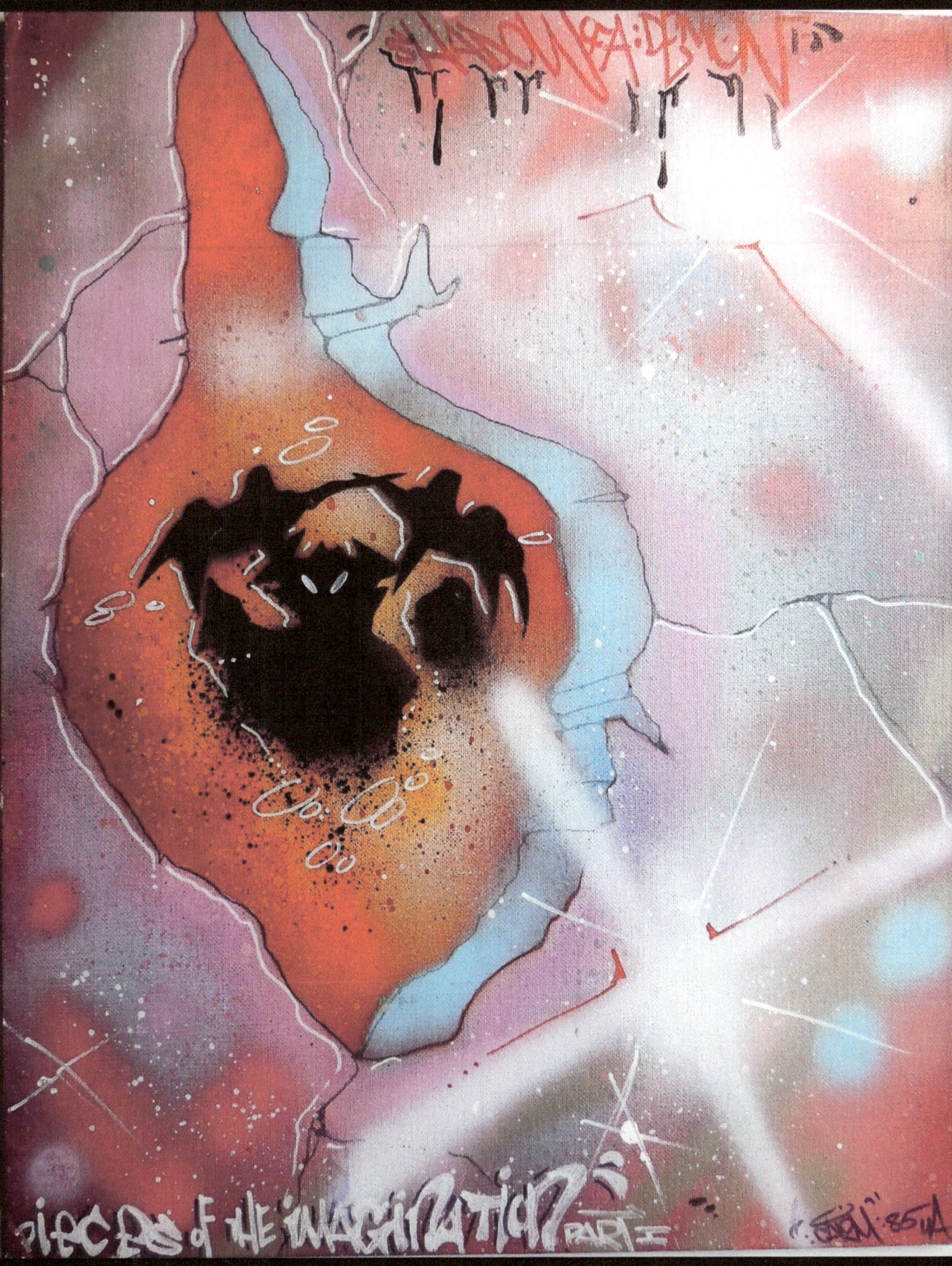

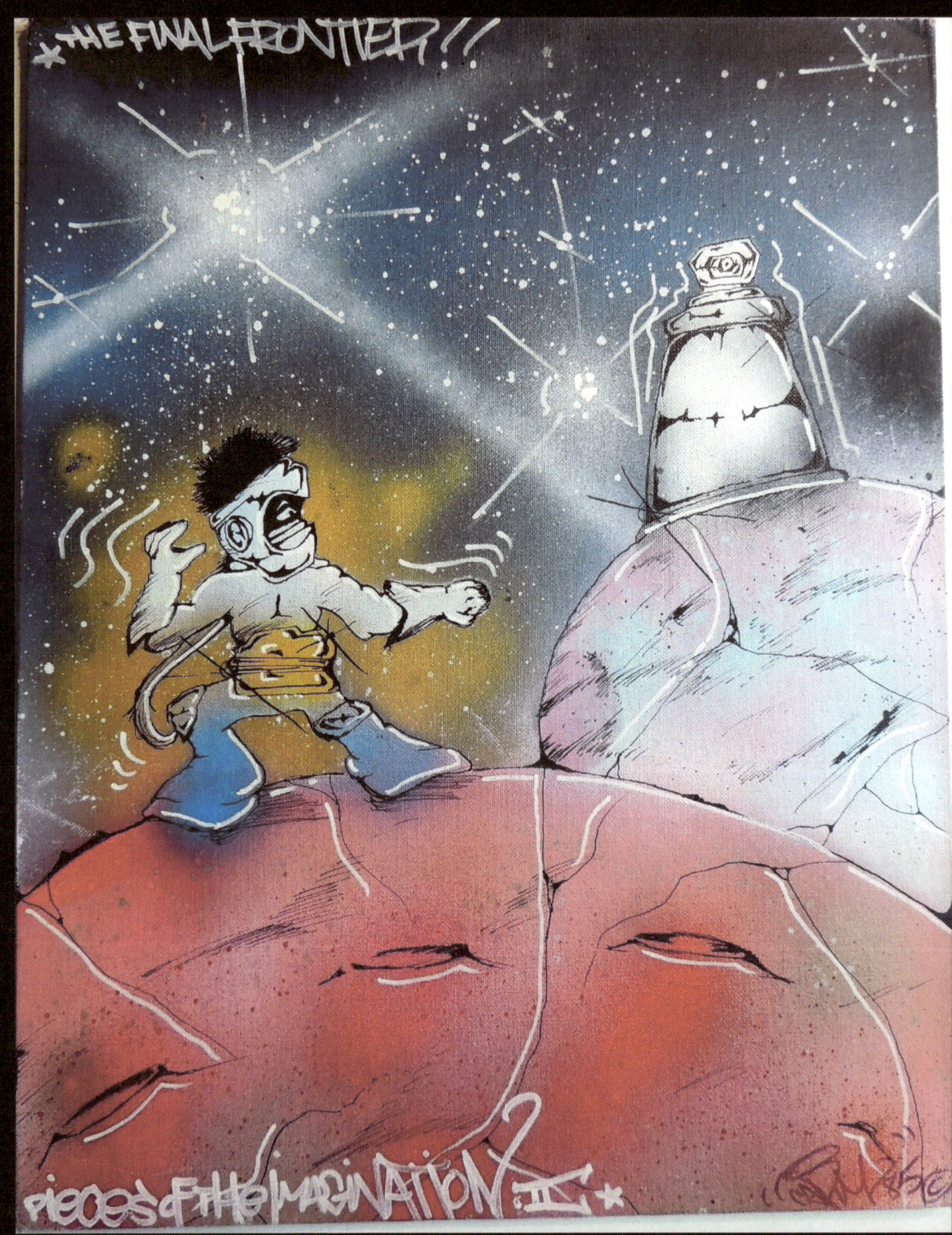

Some of Snow's earliest canvases done mostly in aerosol with a touch of marker
1985

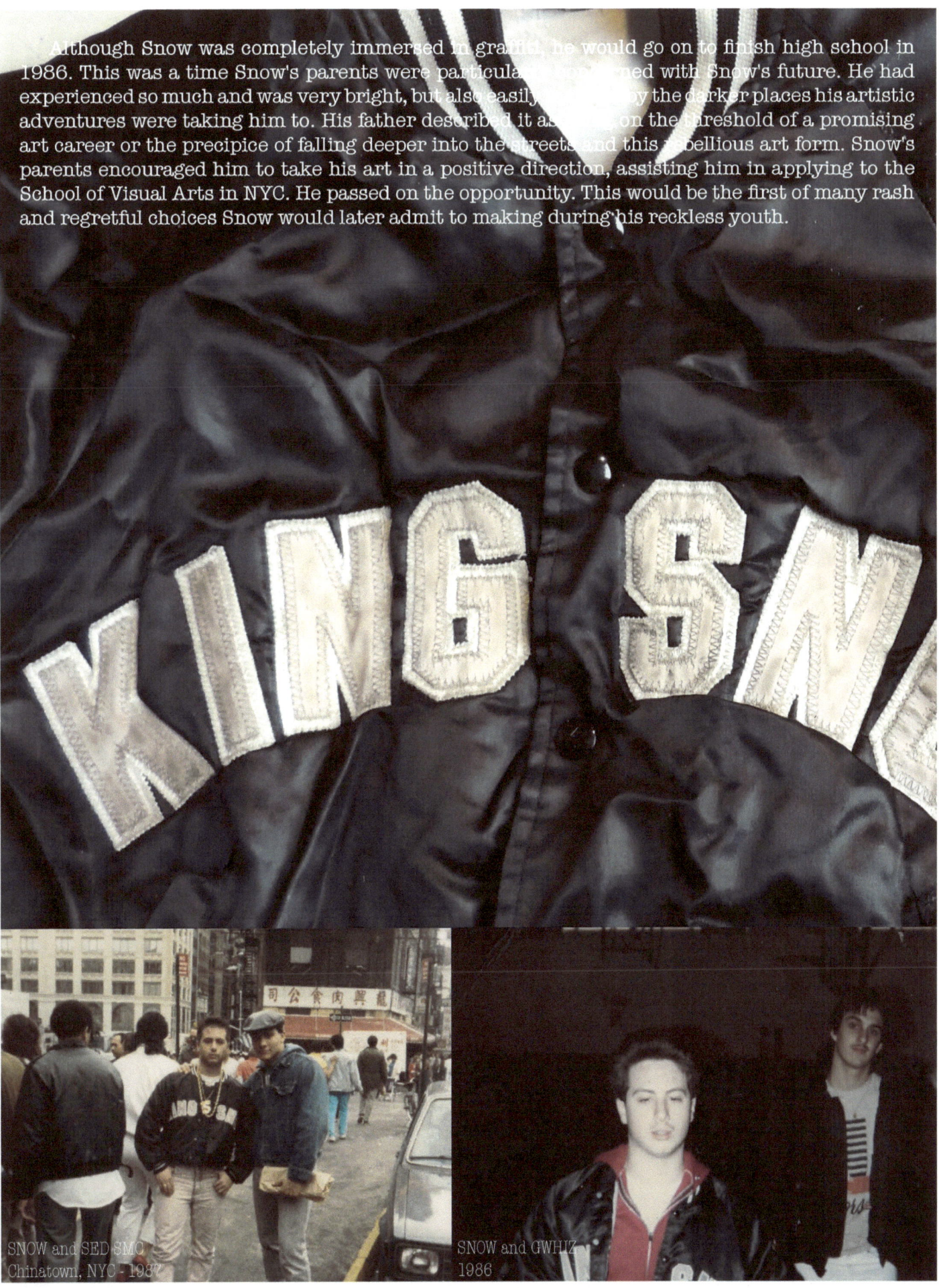

Although Snow was completely immersed in graffiti, he would go on to finish high school in 1986. This was a time Snow's parents were particularly concerned with Snow's future. He had experienced so much and was very bright, but also easily influenced by the darker places his artistic adventures were taking him to. His father described it as being on the threshold of a promising art career or the precipice of falling deeper into the streets and this rebellious art form. Snow's parents encouraged him to take his art in a positive direction, assisting him in applying to the School of Visual Arts in NYC. He passed on the opportunity. This would be the first of many rash and regretful choices Snow would later admit to making during his reckless youth.

SNOW and SED SMC
Chinatown, NYC - 1987

SNOW and GWHIZ
1986

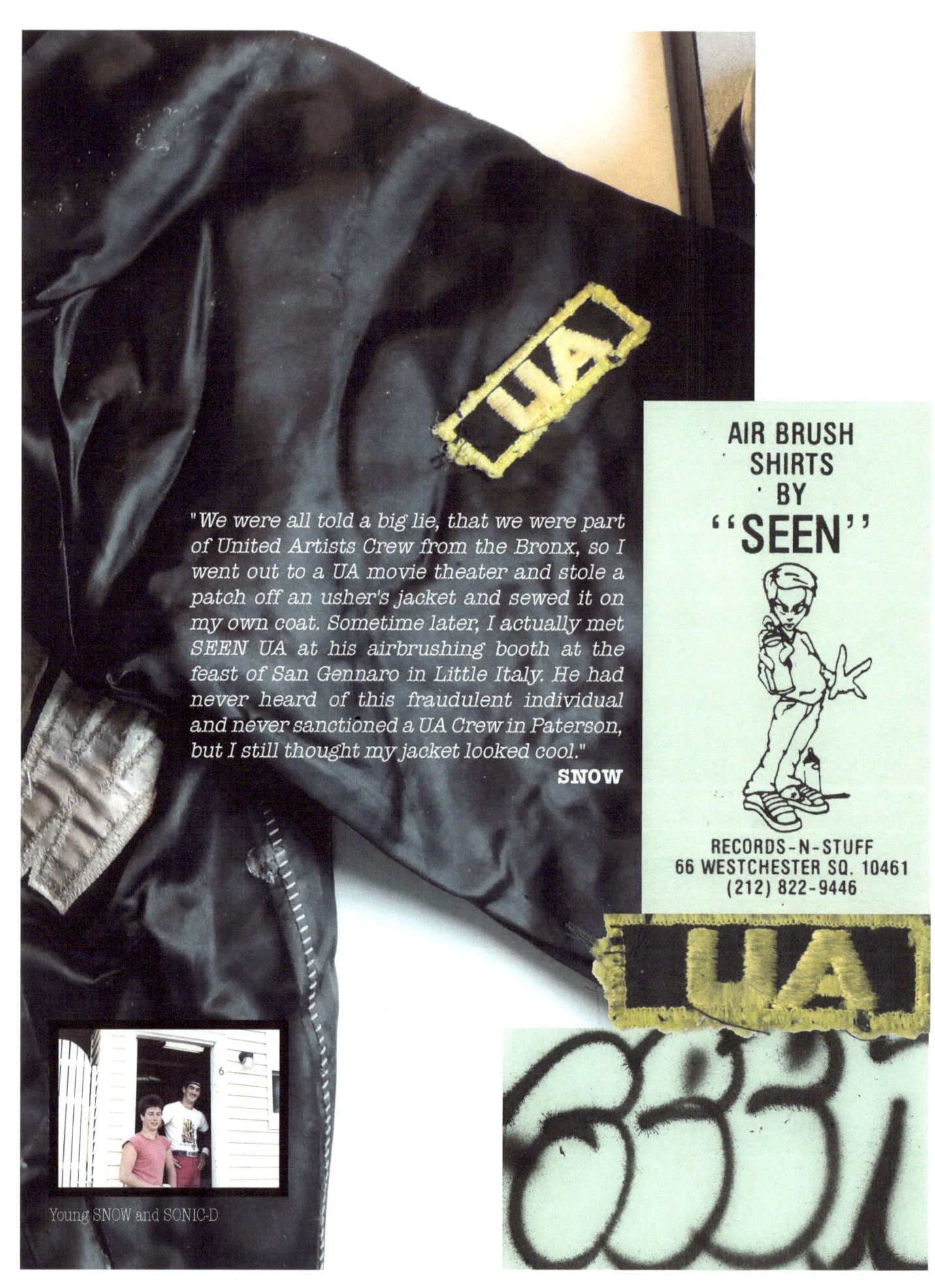

"We were all told a big lie, that we were part of United Artists Crew from the Bronx, so I went out to a UA movie theater and stole a patch off an usher's jacket and sewed it on my own coat. Sometime later, I actually met SEEN UA at his airbrushing booth at the feast of San Gennaro in Little Italy. He had never heard of this fraudulent individual and never sanctioned a UA Crew in Paterson, but I still thought my jacket looked cool."

SNOW

Young SNOW and SONIC-D

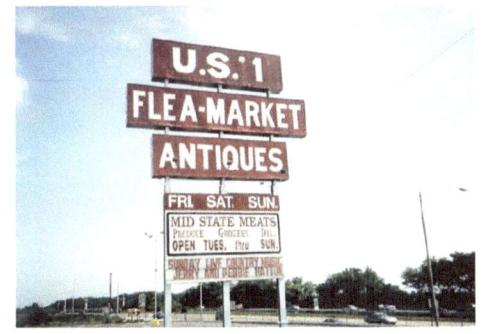

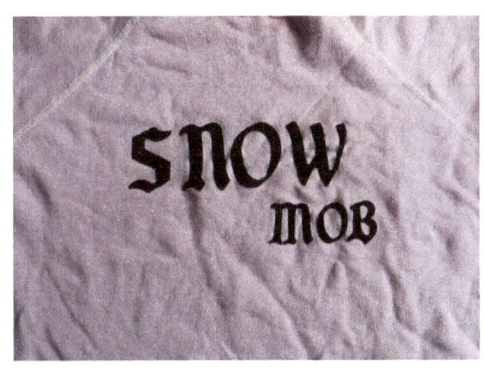

"I remember going to Union Flea Farket to buy records and get sweatshirts lettered up. There was also a dude named Topper who had an air brush stand where I would see a lot of graffiti tags from people who stopped by."

SNOW

Cross-out wars and beefs with rivals were beginning to brew for Snow, and the local and state law enforcement were keeping an eye out for him. All this time, Detective Don Reddin was transferring from Narcotics to the Gang/Juvenile unit. The veteran and gritty street detective would play a serious role in Snow's life.

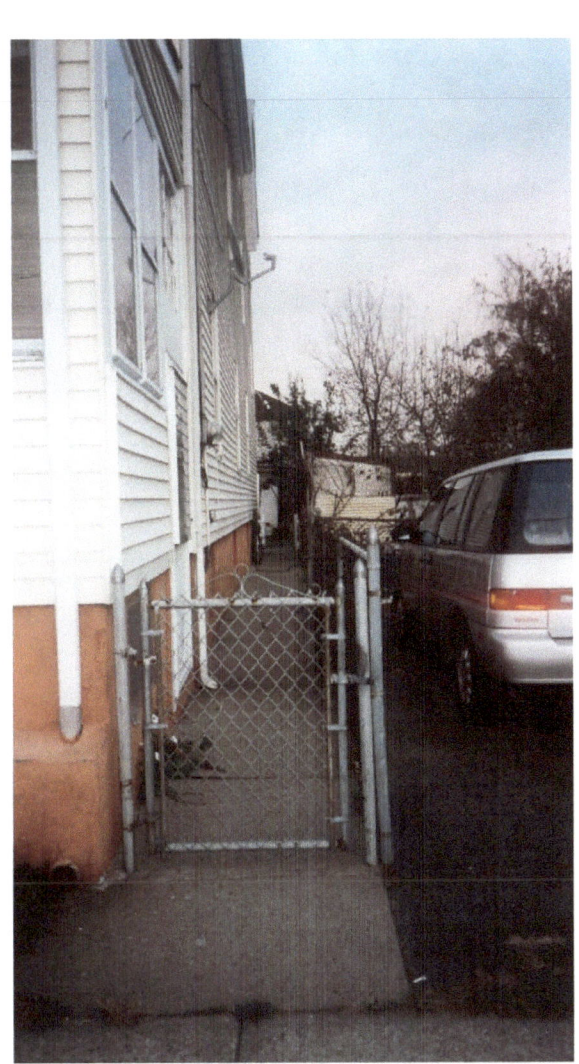

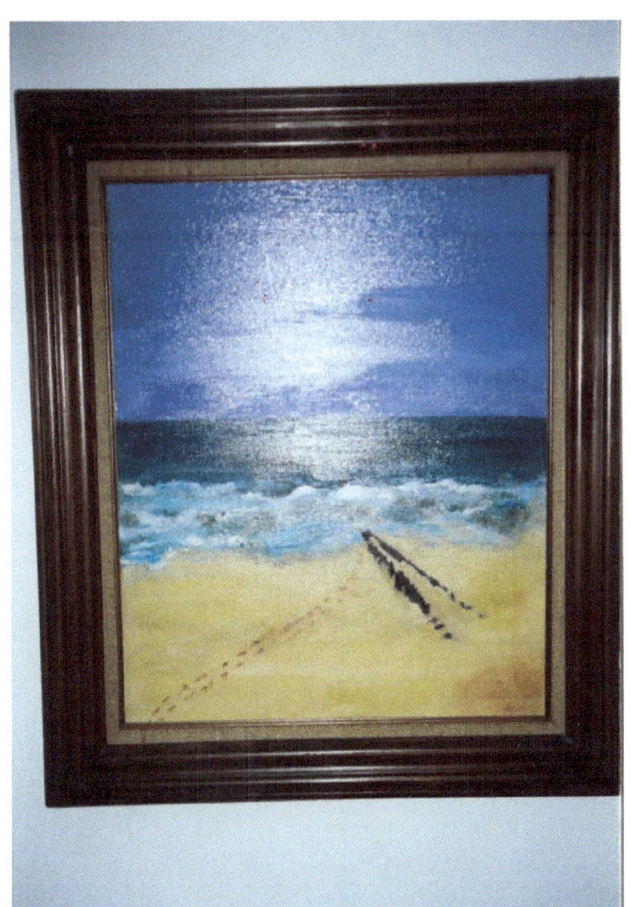

"This was the first piece of non-graffiti fine art that I did for my parents while I was at MKA. My mother had it framed and always displayed it wherever they lived."

SNOW

By 1987, Snow was enthralled with the Hip Hop and street culture. He felt there was increasing heat on himself, and he did not want to burden his parents with his own troubles. So, he elected to leave home and move out, renting a room in Bloomfield, NJ. He found himself a job working at a print shop and continued his quest for graffiti greatness under the cover of the night sky.

Blackbook Illustrations
1983-1988

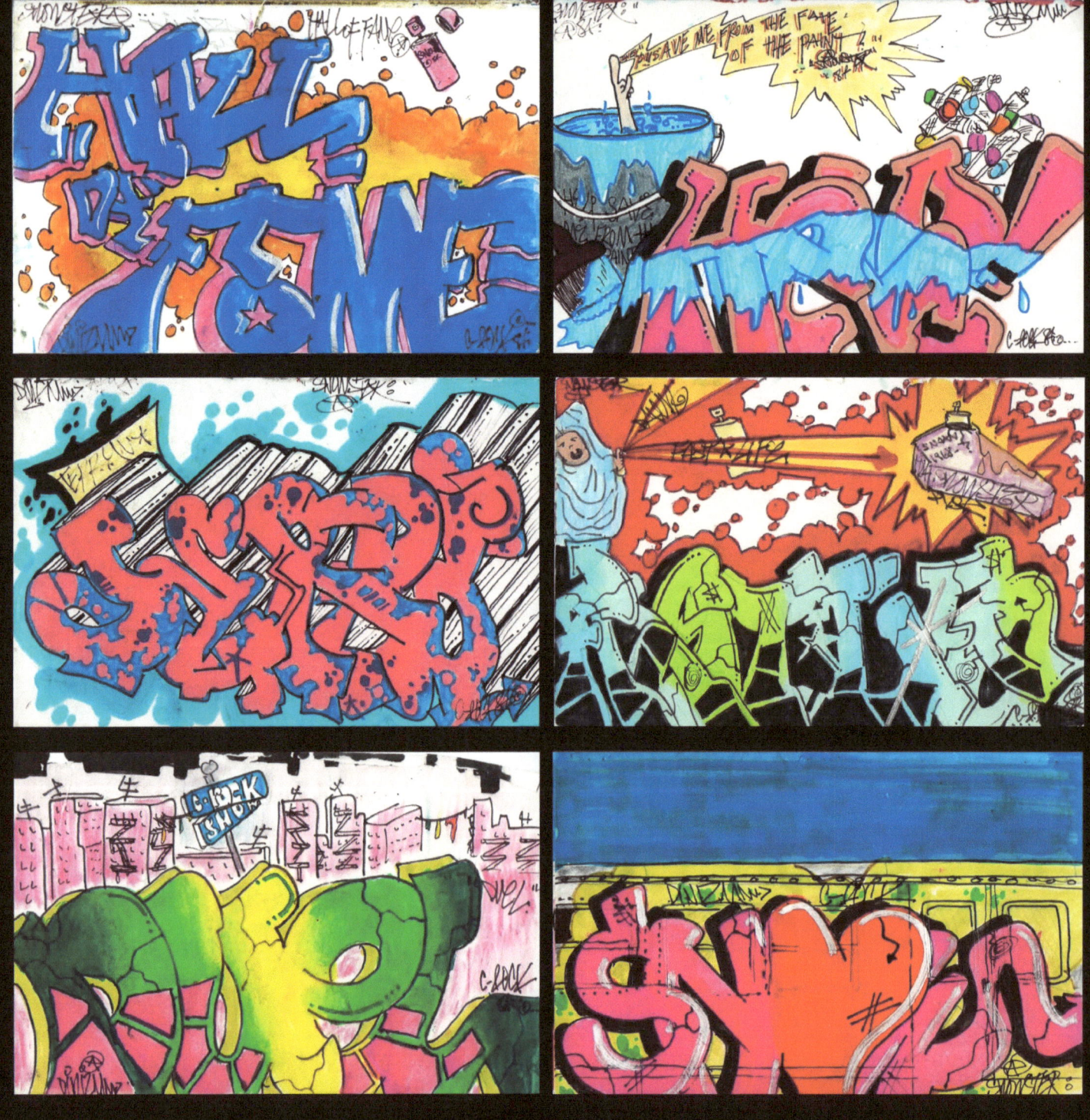

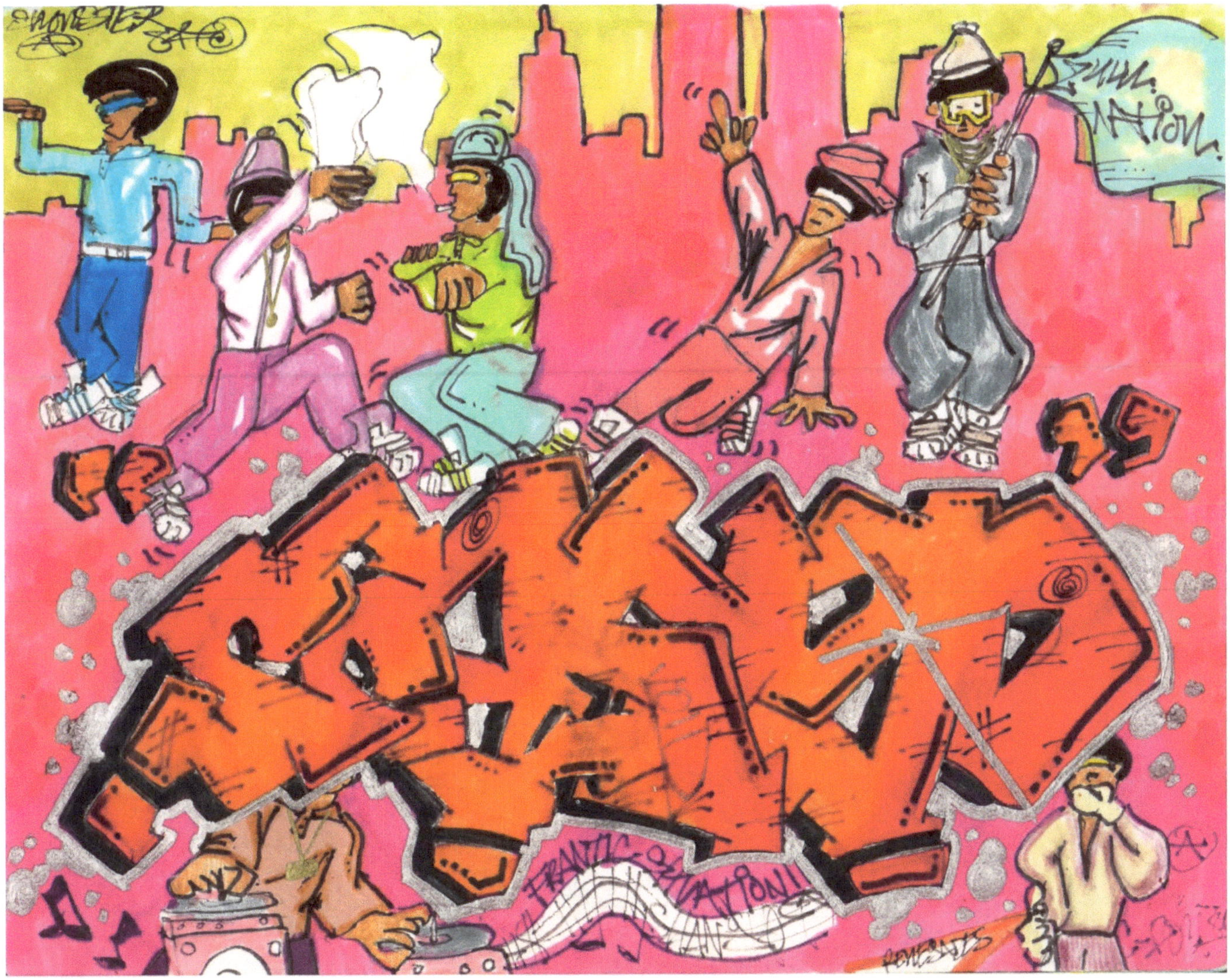

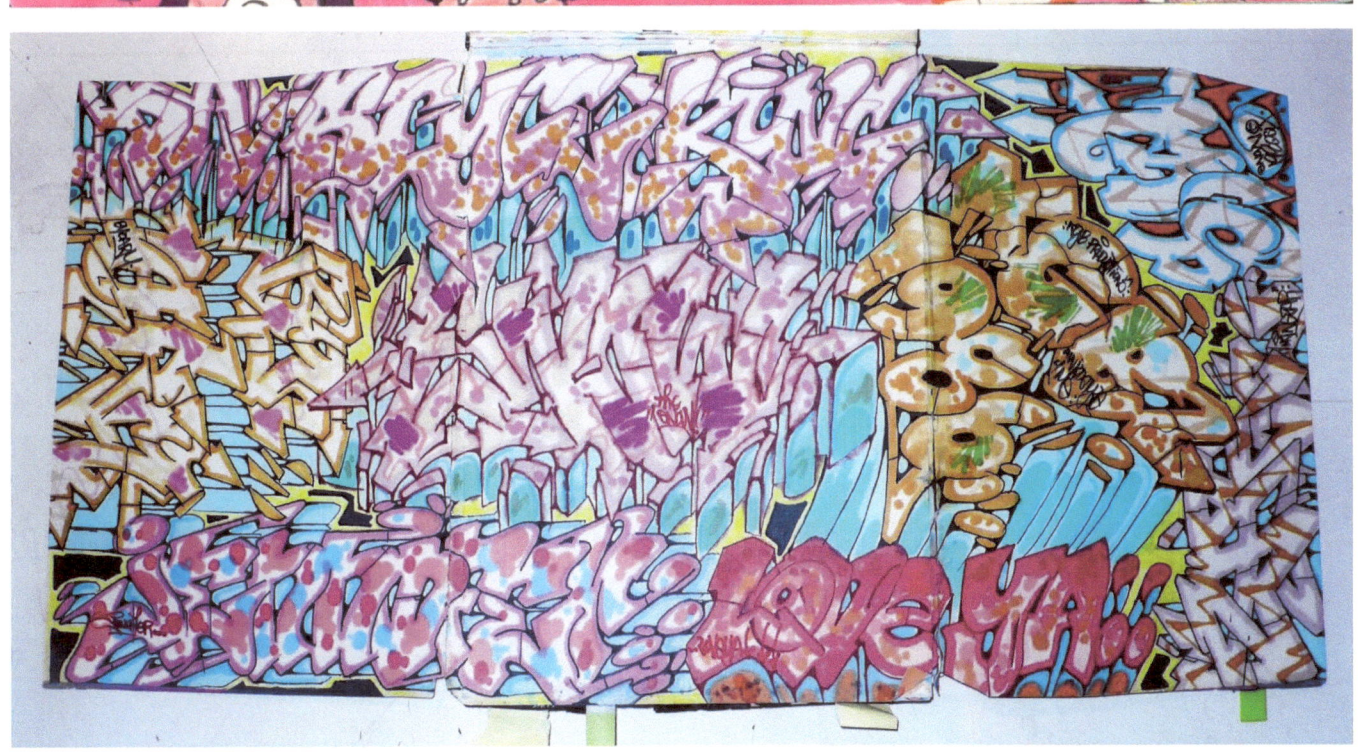

SNOW's first trifold blackbook page
1986

In the beginning there was a tag;
but not good or of something to brag.
And then there was a throw-up;
which would undoubtedly
    blow-up;
into something new from crew
    2 crew;
then someone burned;
from which everyone teamed.
And then it was prophecized;
that graphitti would grow...
    ... but never surpass the
    murals of ...

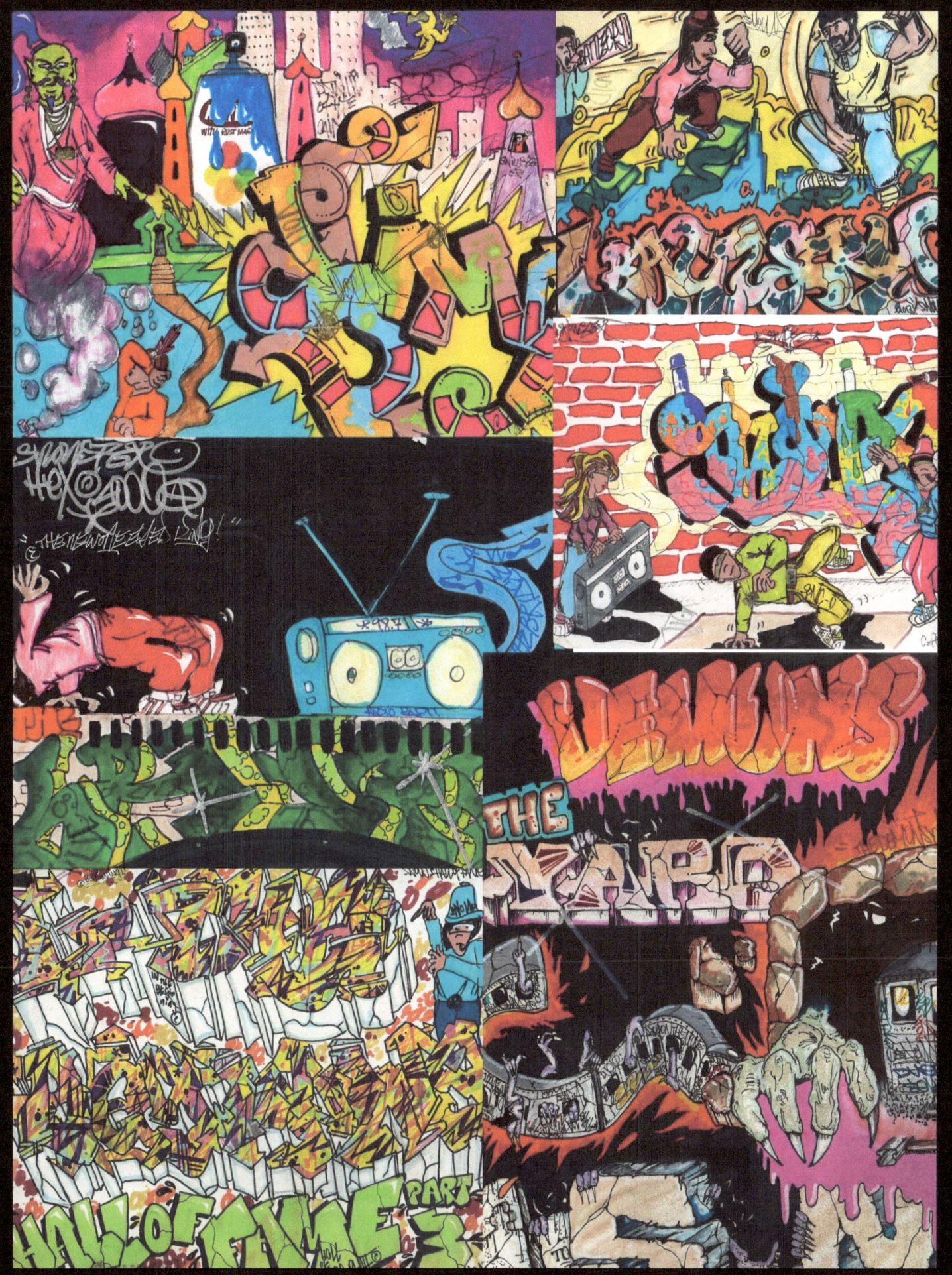

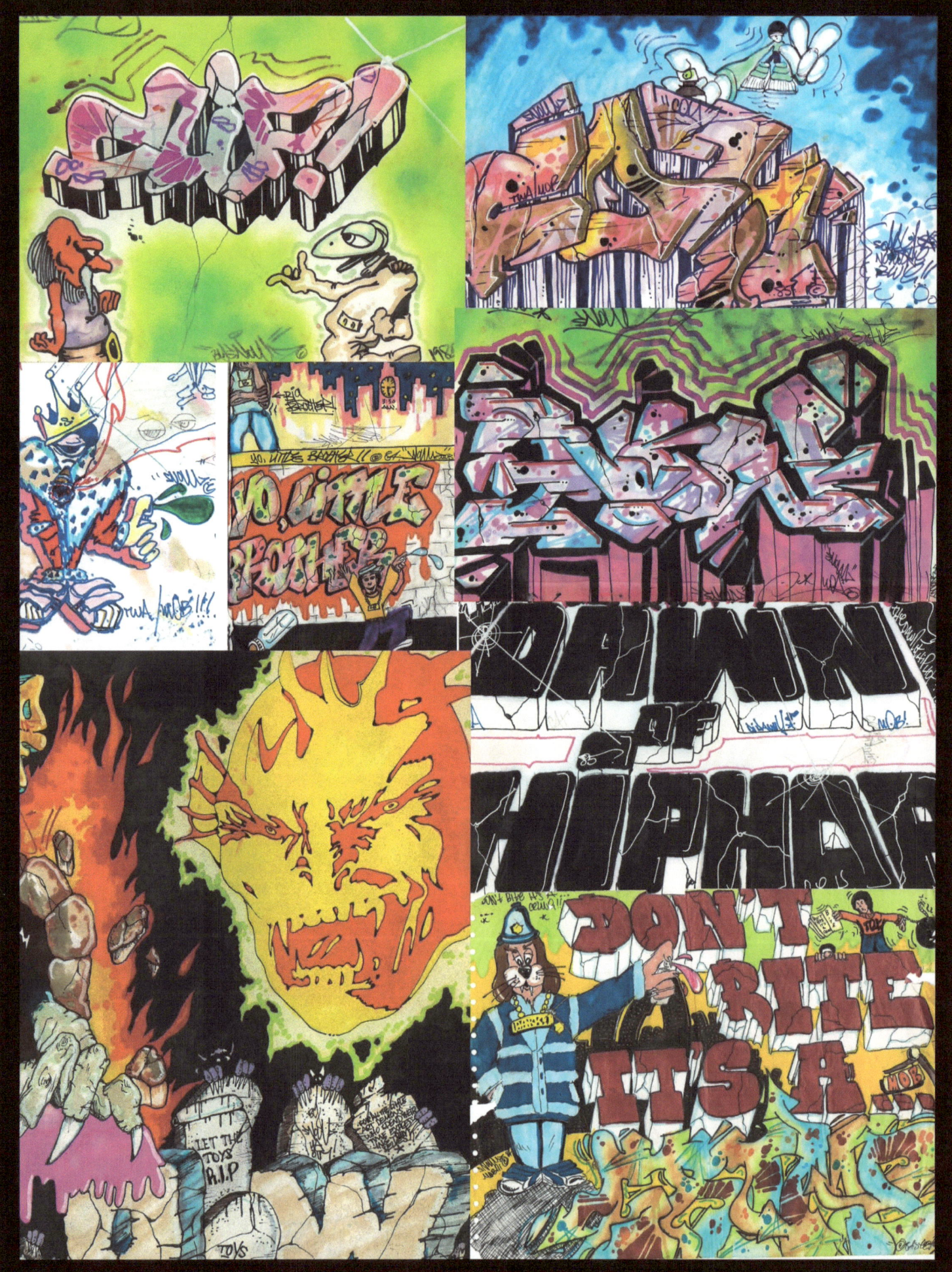

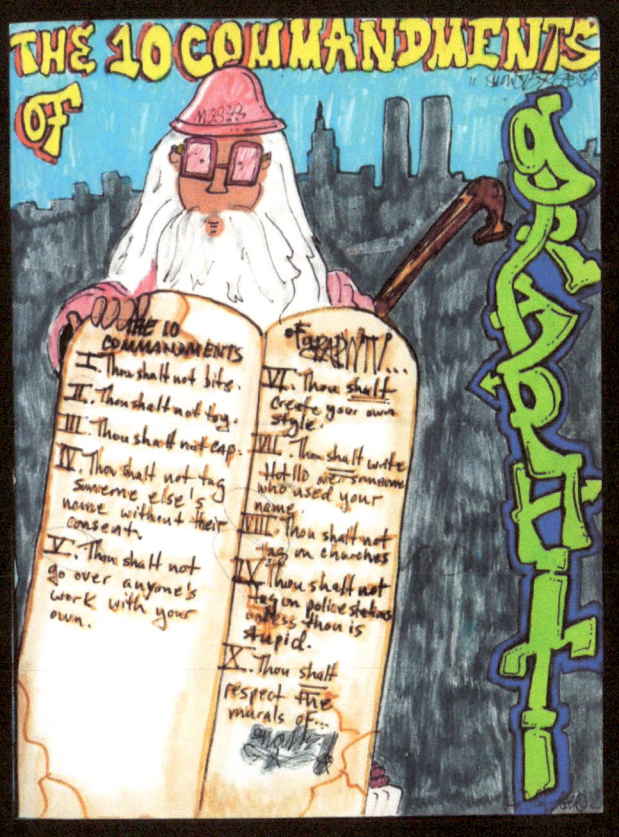

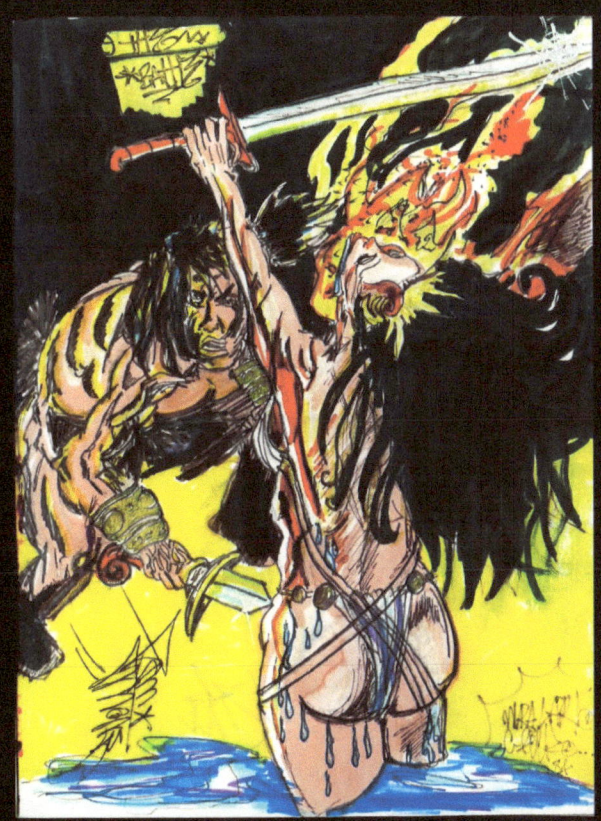

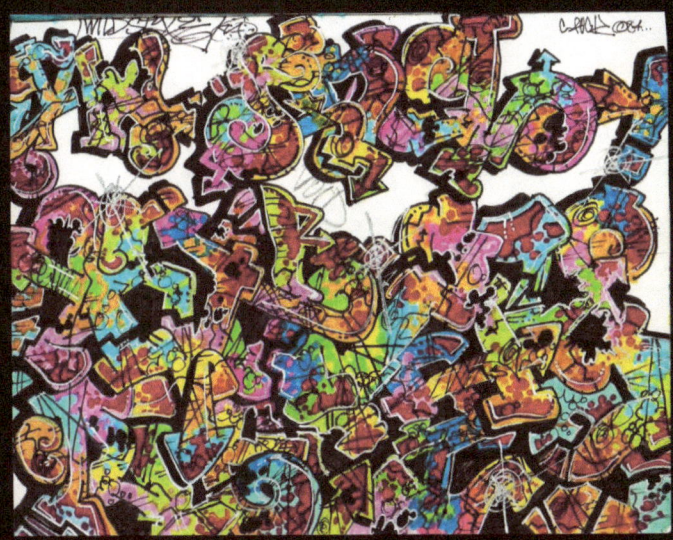

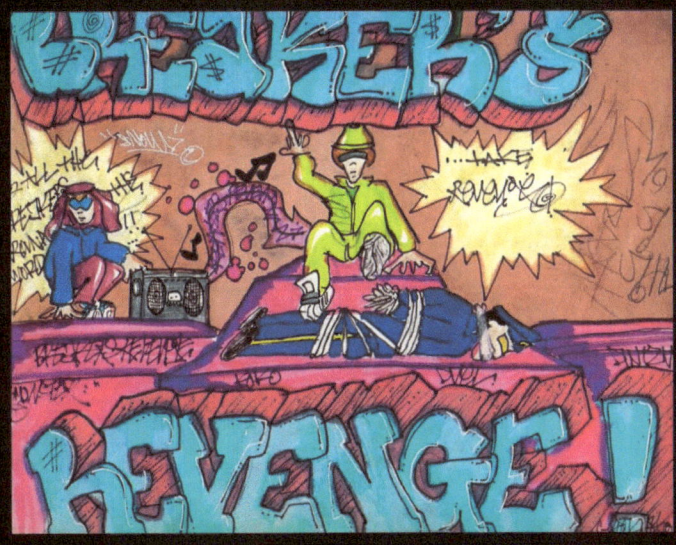

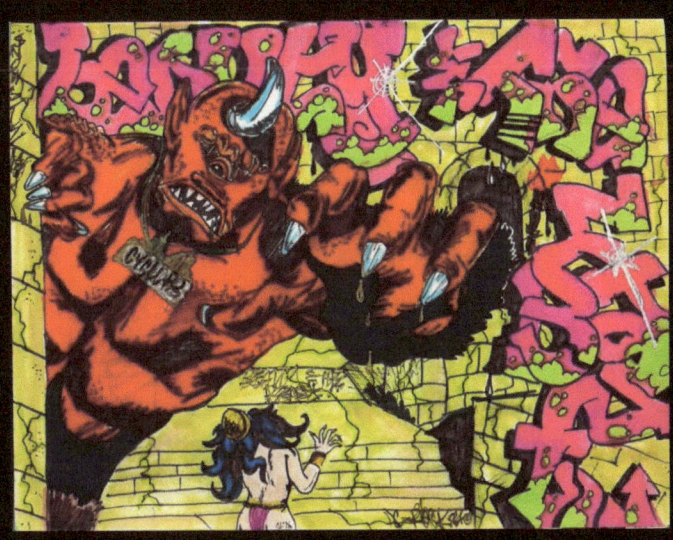

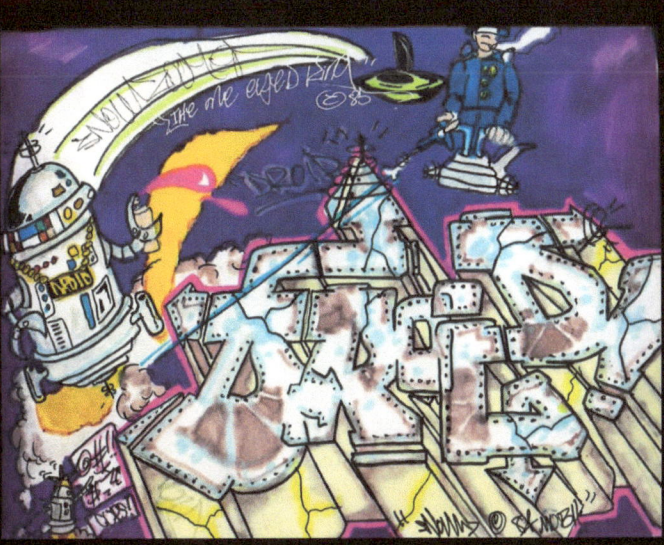

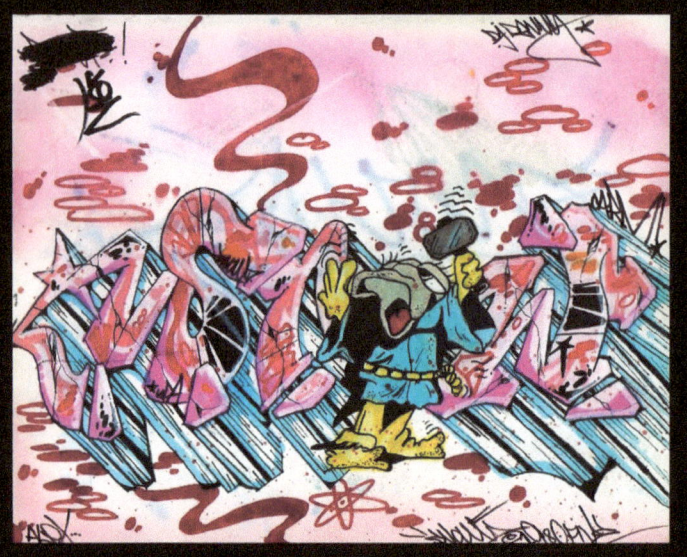
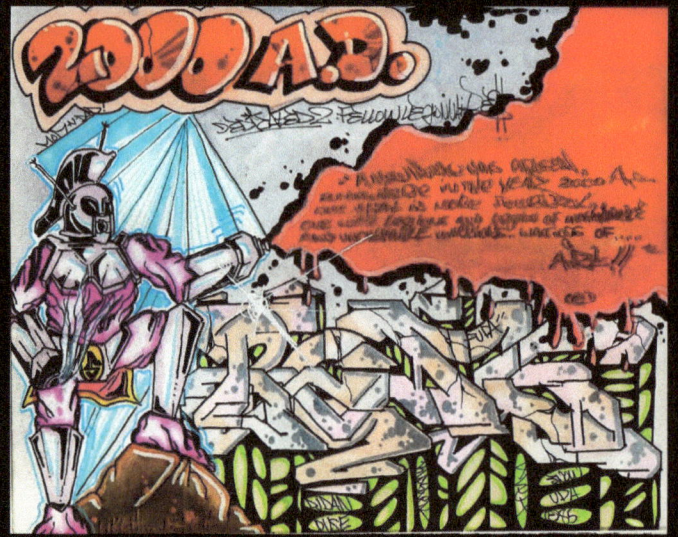
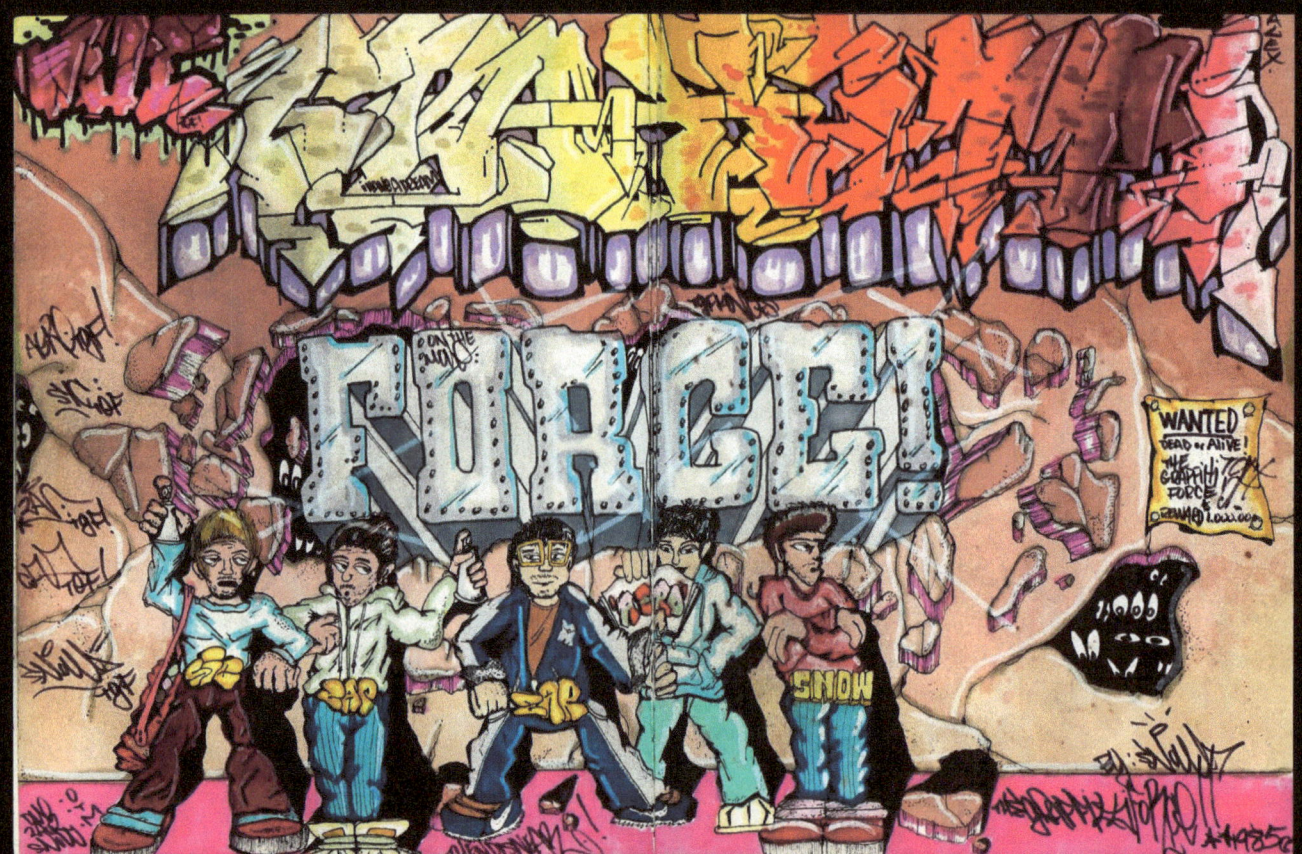
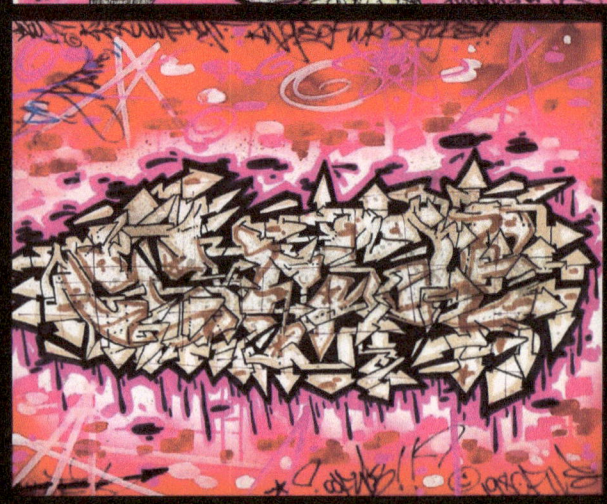
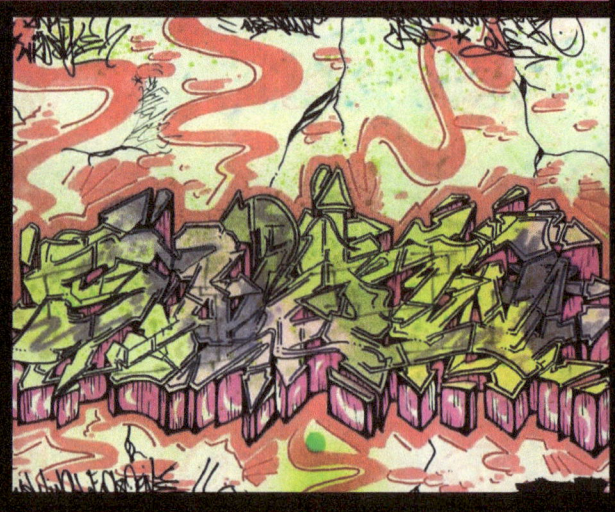

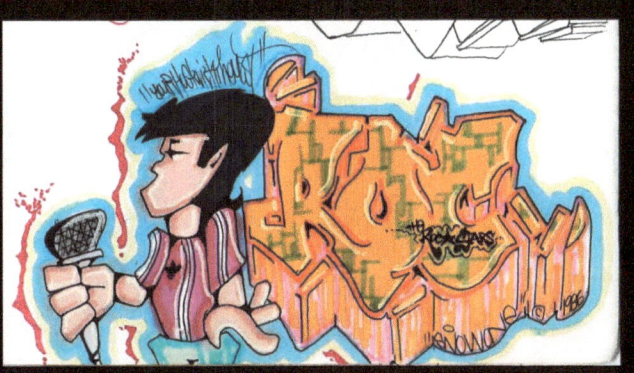
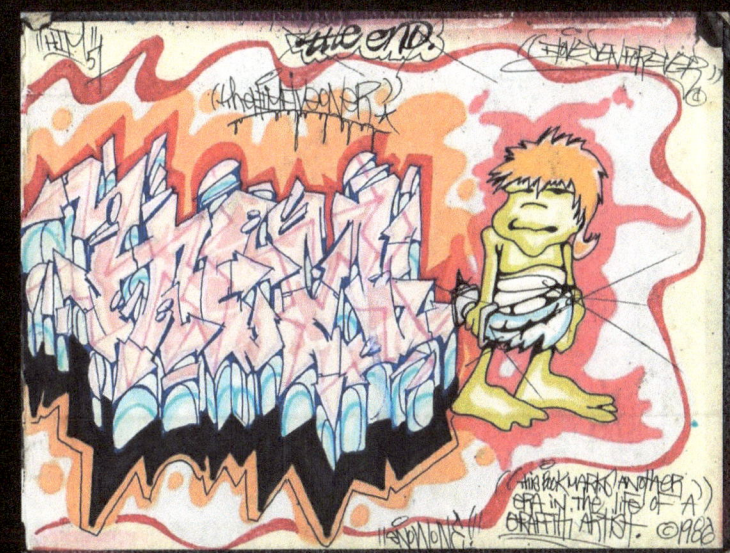
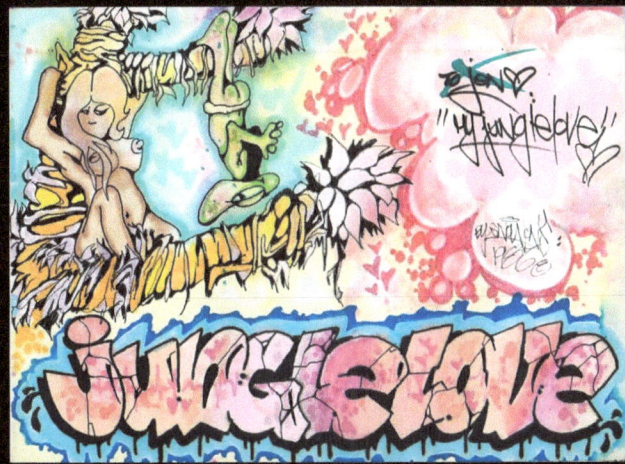
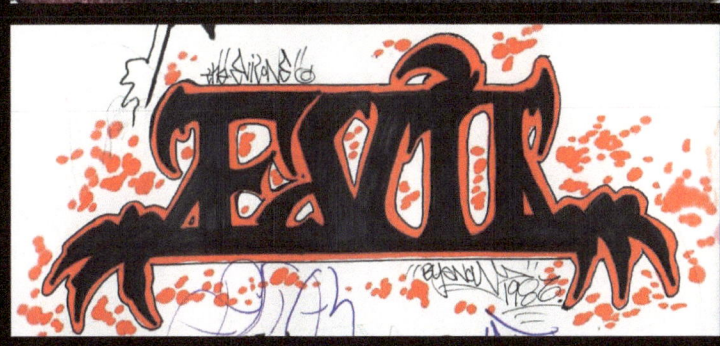
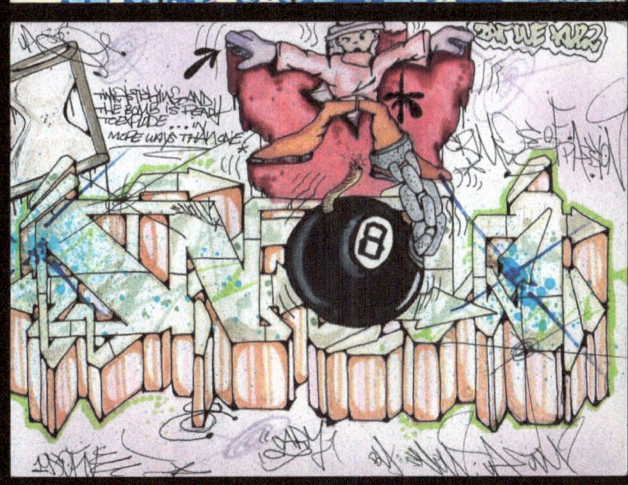
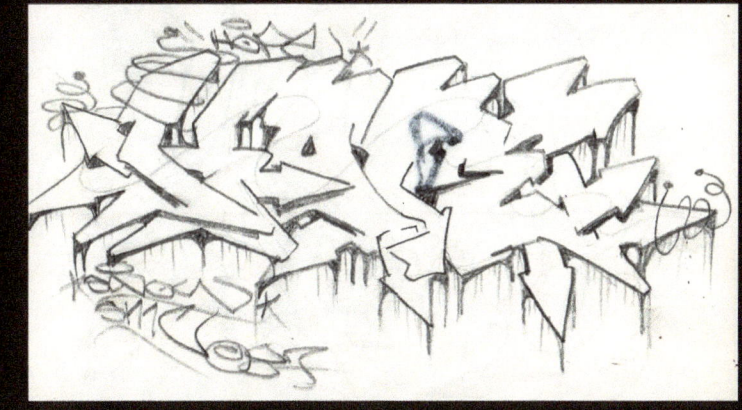
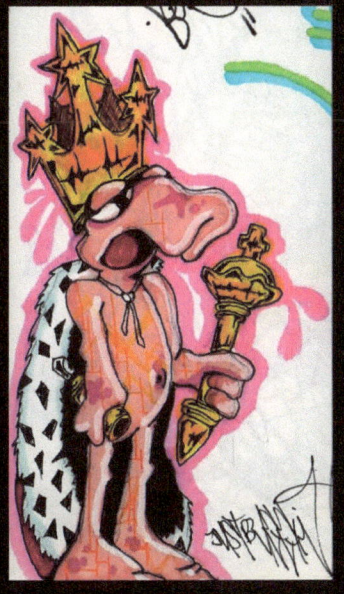
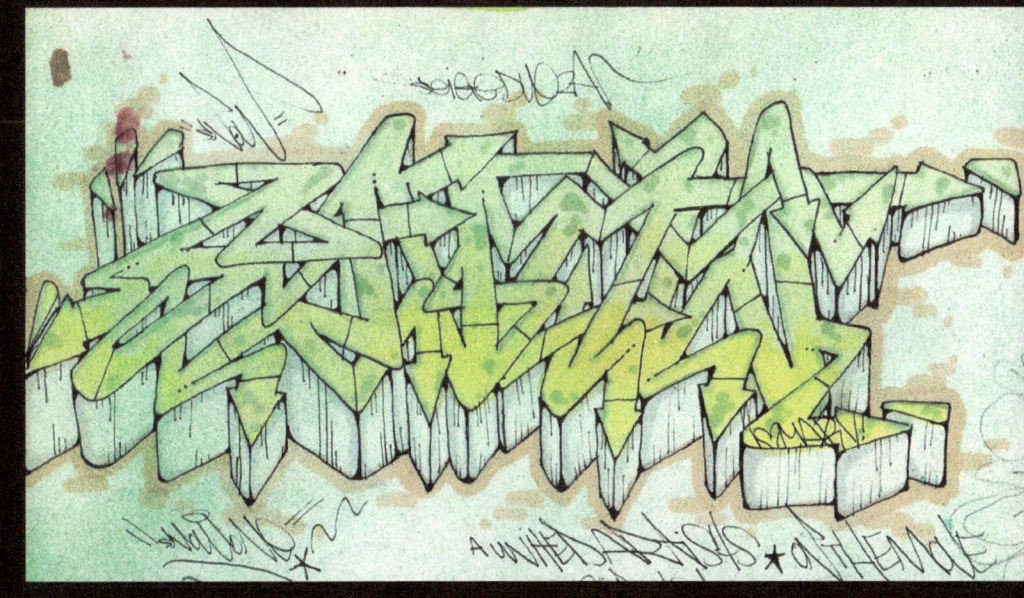

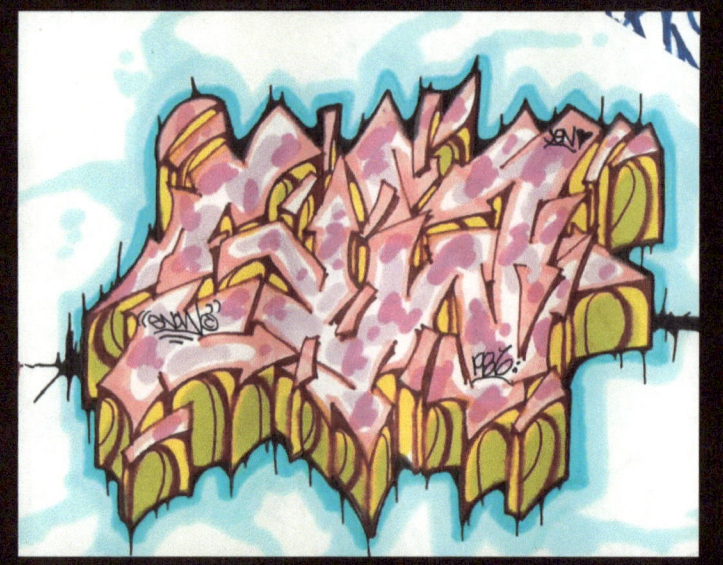

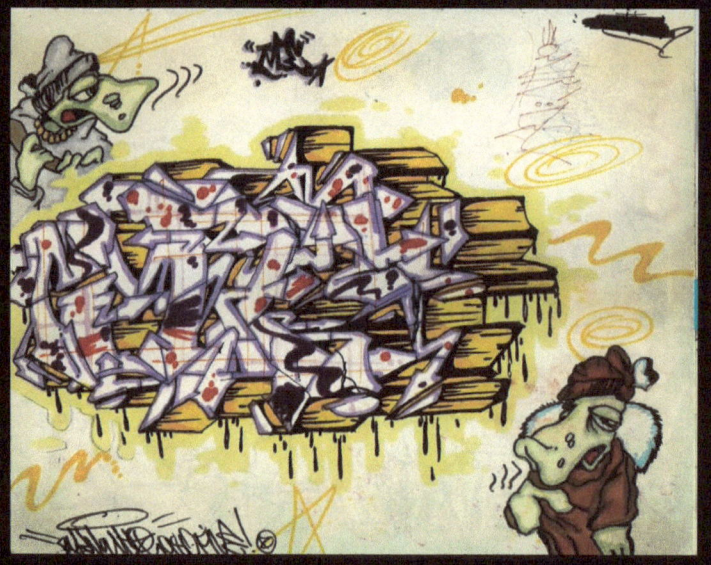

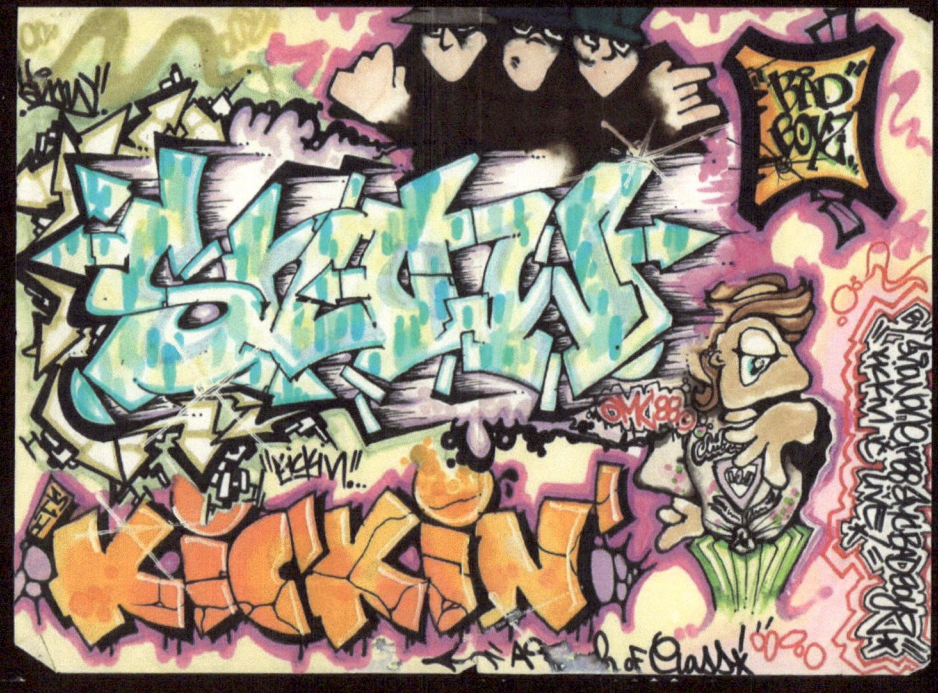

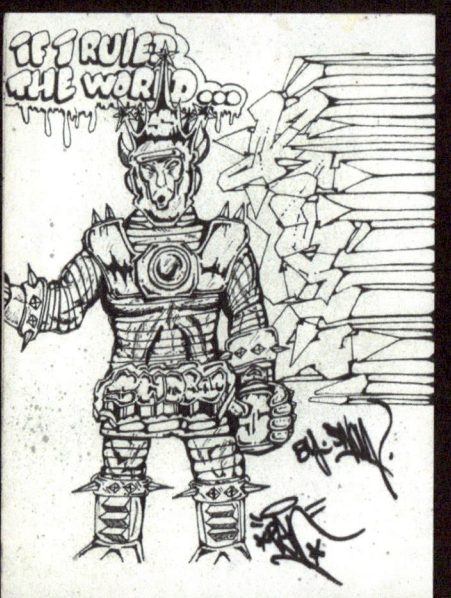

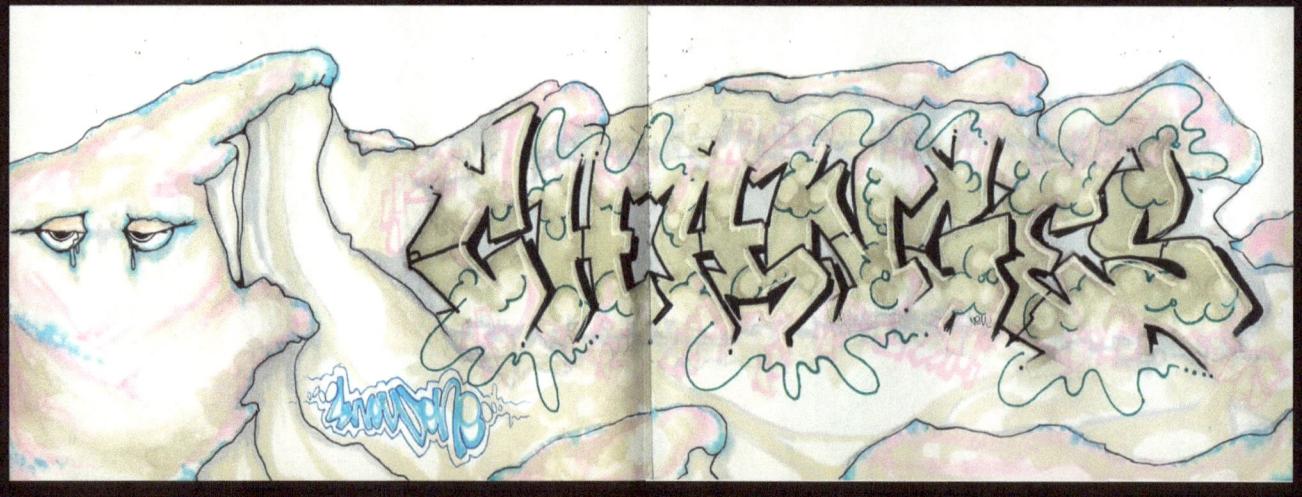

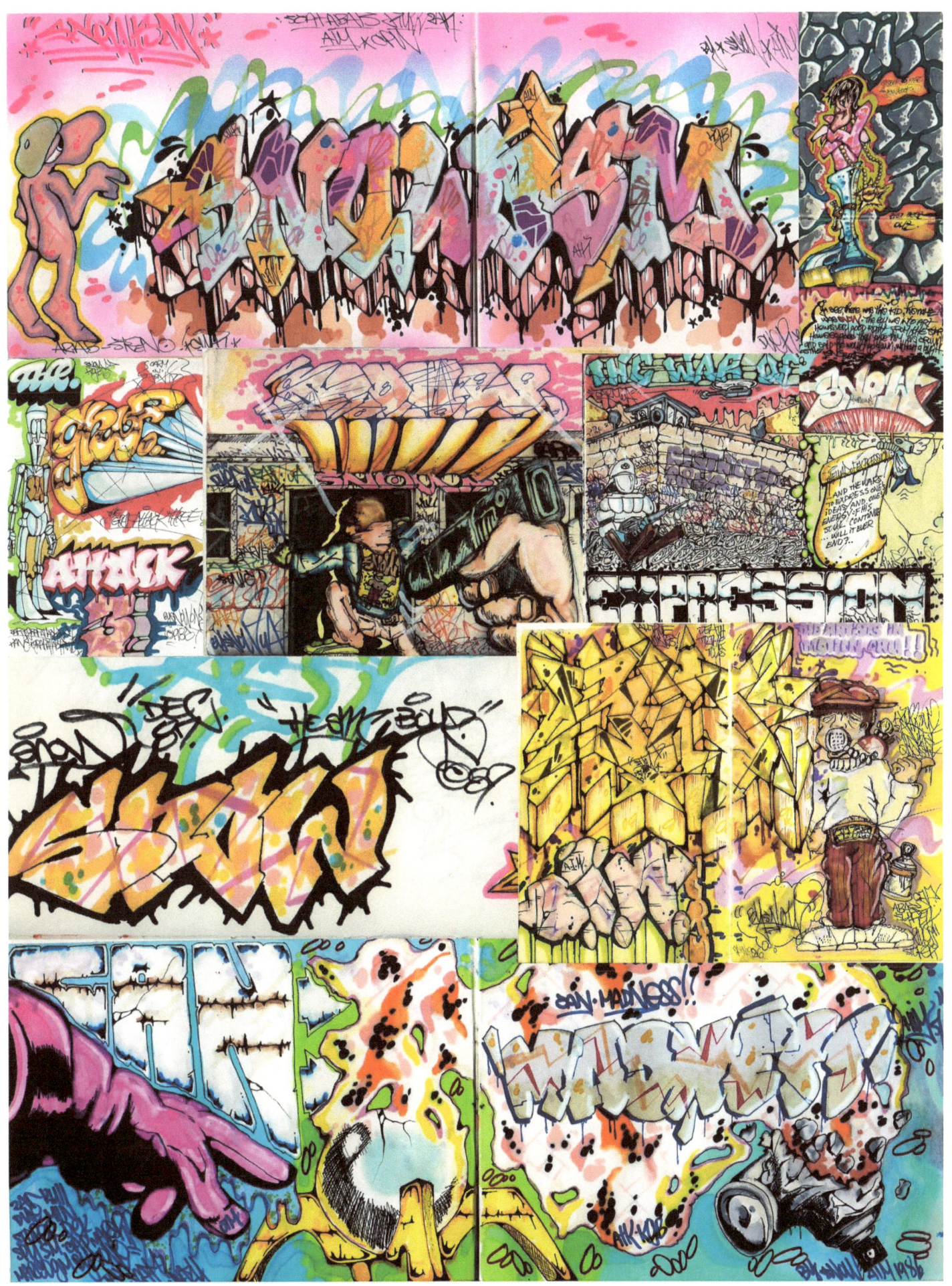

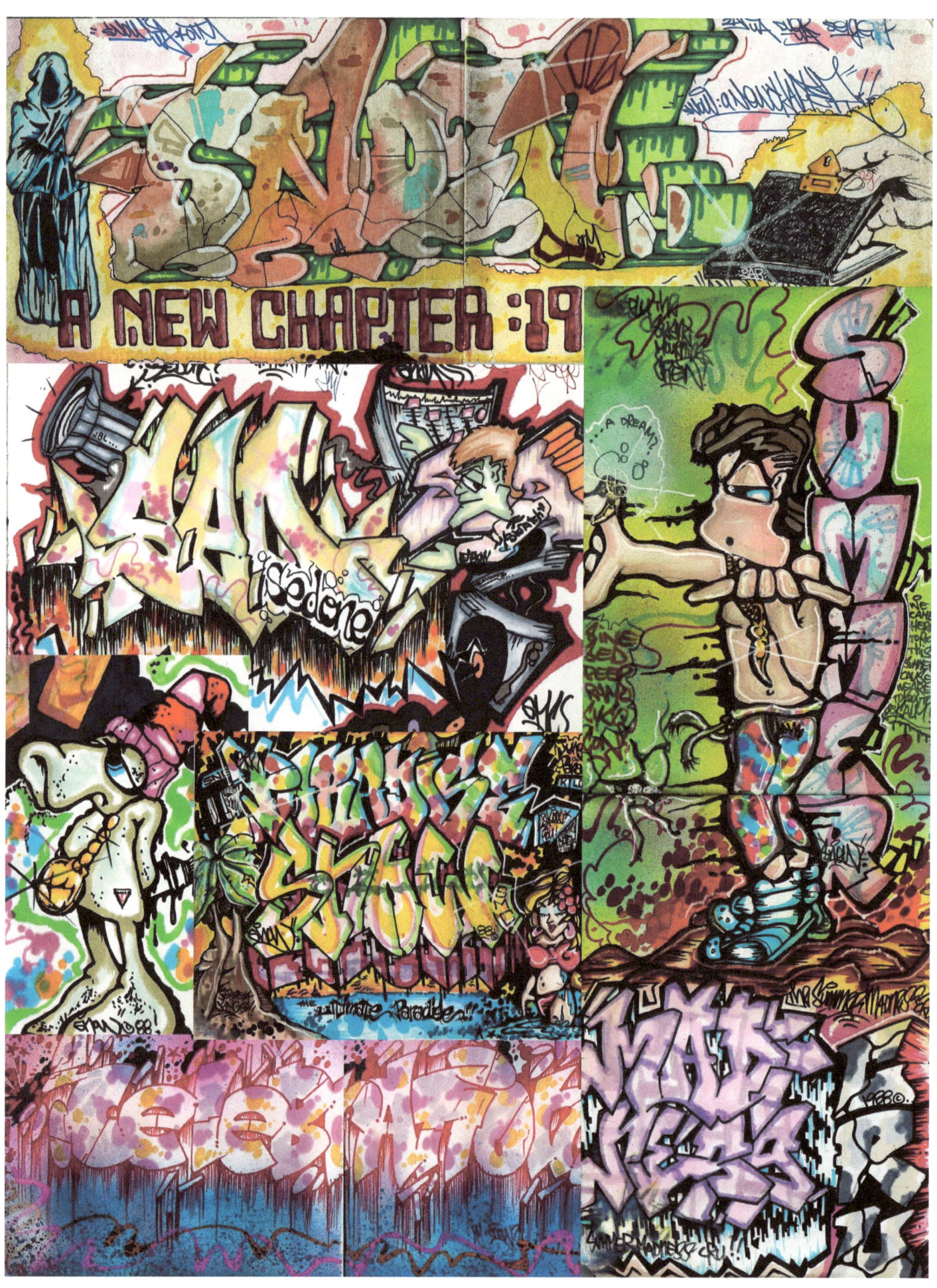

TAGGED!

Cops nab graffiti 'artist' blamed for $1M in damage

Spray-painters get 'canvas'

A paint disaster or art?

City cracks down on graffiti, but not all want it g

STAFF PHOTOS BY CARMINE GALASSO

itzgerald walking near where police say three of North Jersey's most notorious graffiti artists were arrested.

GRAFFITI: Arrests

A 16   The North Jersey Herald & News   Monday, April 6, 19

Paterson police crack down on 'bombing'

GRAFFITI

THURSDAY, JULY 22, 1993   2★P   PASSAIC

GRAFFITI: One man gets jail   graffiti

Getting tough on graffiti at a public school

Would-be policeman is spared state graffiti charge

Artful effort turns walls into gallery

COLLEEN MANCINO   gained notoriety king of graffiti and

TUESDAY, APRIL 20, 1993

Totowa graffiti arrests hailed

'Major hitters,' detective says

Judge: Graffiti king hasn't been reformed

City worker guilty of criminal mischief

Saying no to graffiti

Paterson to b   in whitewash eff   ts

NORTH JERSEY '9

A CLOSE-UP LOOK AT OUR REGION

Cops' graffiti expert tracks 'disease running rampant'

By JUSTO BAUTISTA   vacation to find every room in their home

who entered through a second-story window. During that same time, another home on the block was burglarized, police   A pregnant woman is lucky to be alive after a traffic light fell on the sunroof of her car as she drove by a construction site

pregnant driver unscathed

— RITA MALLEY

Writing on wall can tell cop plenty

Onetime graffiti king back in Paterson

By BRUNO TEDESCHI   The new charges come less than two weeks after Santiago was ar-

Staff Writer   Juan "Mitch" Santiago, the self-

described   rested for allegedly spraying graffiti.

Denies defacing 4 more sites

erald & News

GRAFFITI/ Con

olorful but more dama

ng, the spray paint

Paterson seeks to quell graffiti

Writers of Graffiti, Vow In Turnabout, A Cleaner Paterson

seum, ZM

e Paters
St "A lot

February

welcome to

other
omotes
said.
unger

Donald Ko

them."
Anothe
iti arti

Graffiti Reward

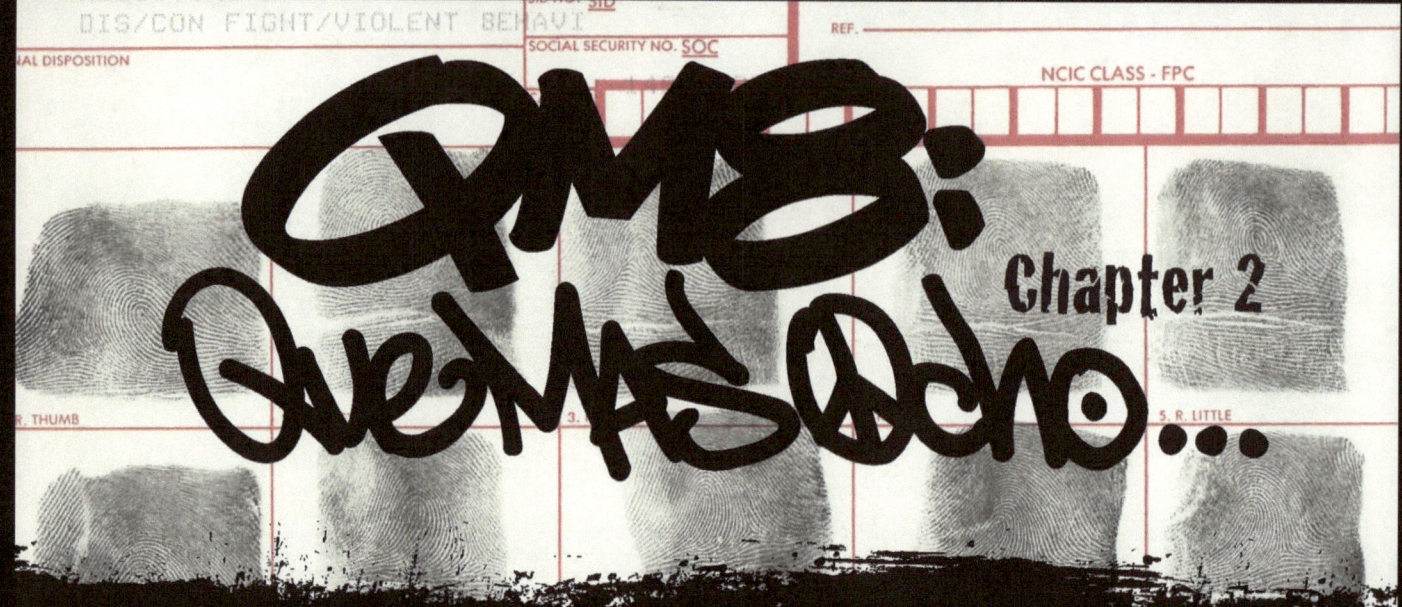

QMB:
Que Mas Ocho...
Chapter 2

By late 1987, Snow was living on his own, working for Elite Graphics and learning the printing trade. He pumped gas and delivered pizza part-time as well. All the funds contributed to buying his art supplies, most especially his spray paint. His days of "racking" (shoplifting) were "mostly" behind him at this point, and the money helped to soften the 19 year old's adjustment to the reality of being independent. Snow's family had relocated to Pennsylvania and then ultimately to Florida. He had no real financial safety net' and did all that he could to work and hustle himself an income. During this time, with his family at such a great distance, he often did whatever he had to in order to survive and put food in his belly.

Elite Graphics
Fairfield, NJ
1987

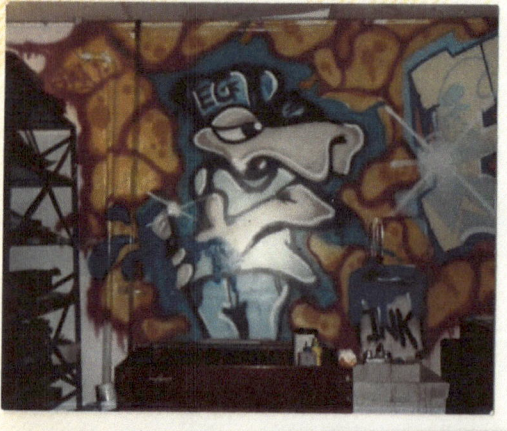

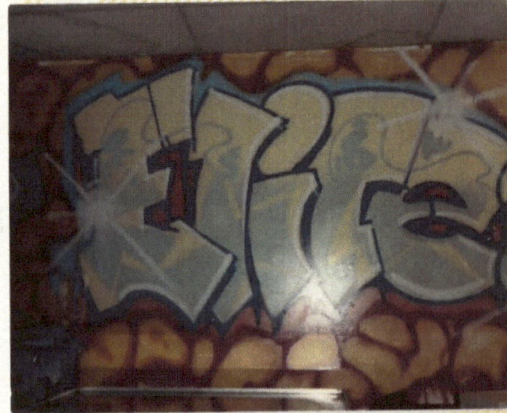

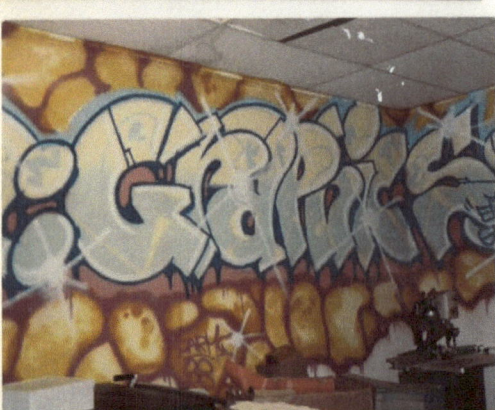

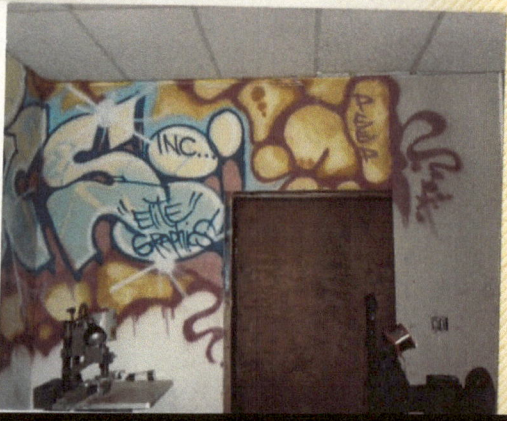

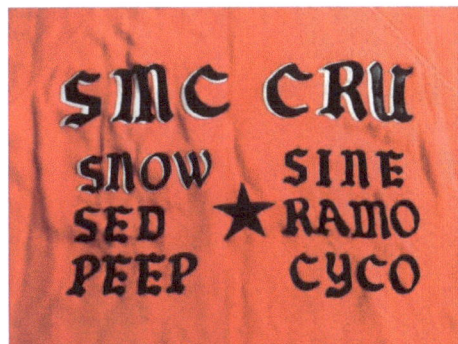
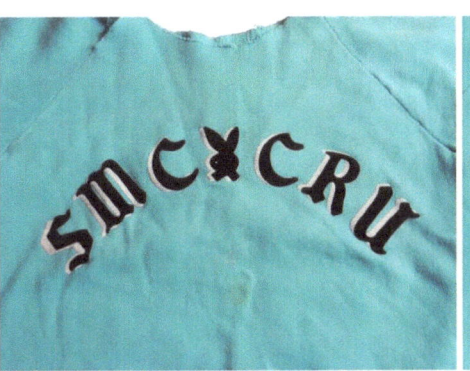

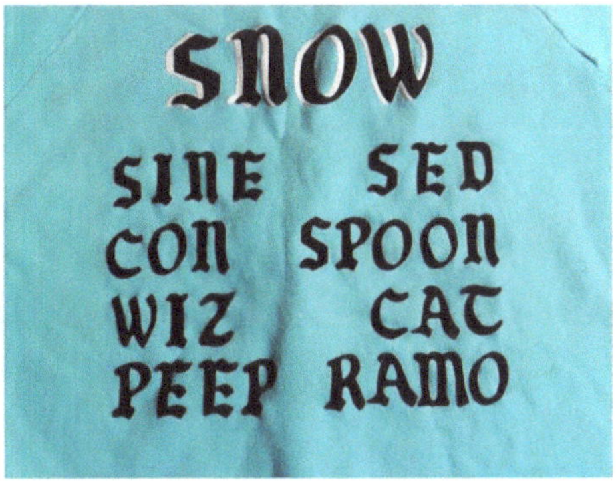

He didn't get much sleep as he was usually up till the wee hours of the morning pursuing the struggle for graffiti fame. He ran with a group out of Essex County: The SMC Crew. Along with Snow, the SMC (Summer Madness Crew; Silent Mourning Crew) was comprised of: SED, SINE, RAMO, CON, SPOON, PEEP, and CYCO. They most especially did a lot of damage to the Jersey Shore area, hence the name Summer Madness Crew.

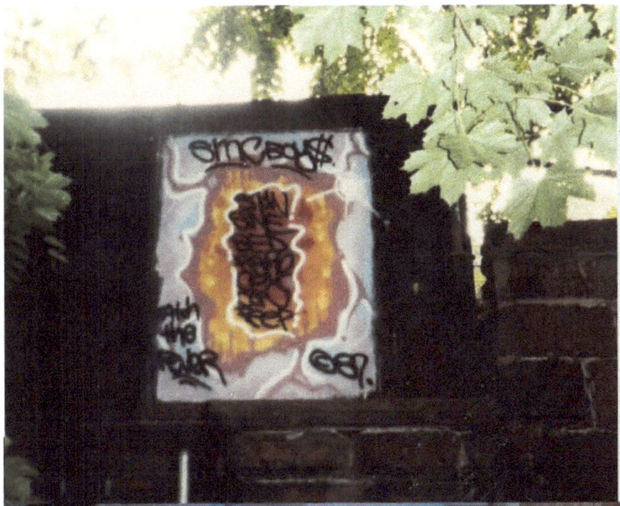

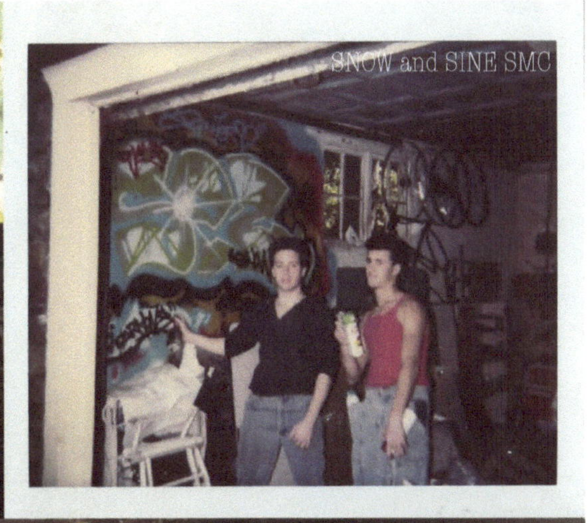

SNOW and SINE SMC

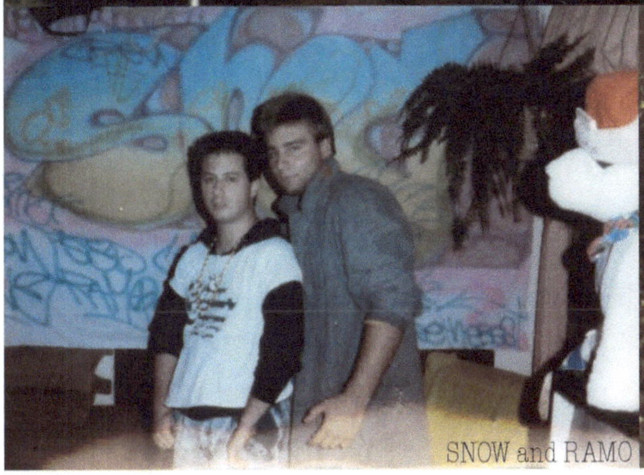

SNOW and RAMO

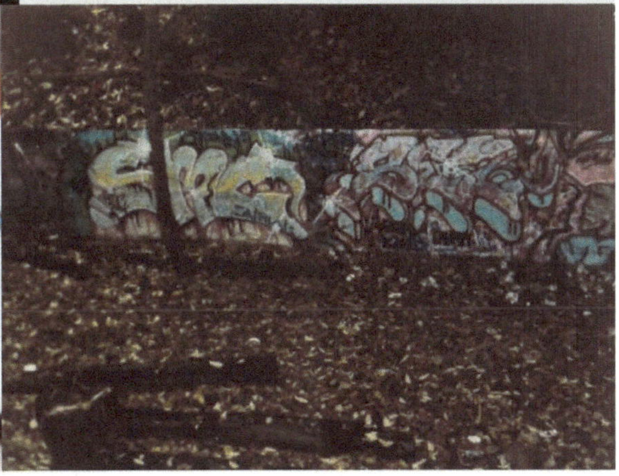

Snow was clearly the leader of the group, both in experience and in talent. He was from the hood, he traveled, and he had been writing graffiti more than the younger, fledgeling crew members. Snow was living as a graffiti outlaw of sorts. His nocturnal exploits were attracting the continued interest of law enforcement and bringing him infamy as one of NJ's most notorious vandals. His high profile name could be found mostly everywhere across northern NJ and even throughout parts of NYC, southern NJ, and in Philadelphia.

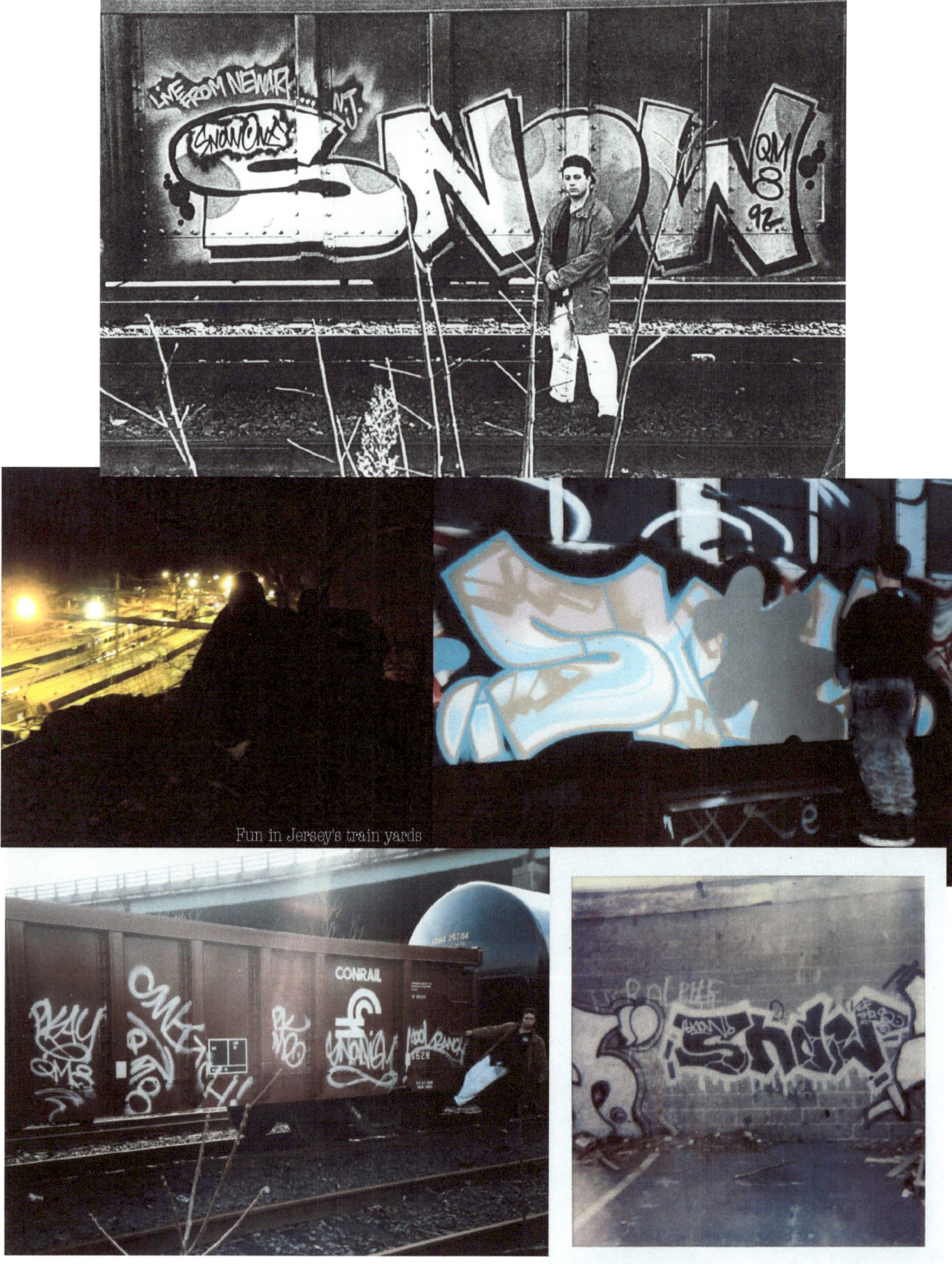

Fun in Jersey's train yards

Most graffiti writers and artists welcomed him into their neighborhoods and territories. Ironically, it was in his own home city of Paterson where Snow faced the most adversity. In 1991, Snow had reconnected with his old partner ZAR of TGF Crew. They decided, once again, to go "all city" in Paterson. This time they were starting to work with another graffiti veteran of Silk City who ran a crew called TMD: Toys Must Die. TMD was started by an individual in Paterson named Juan "MITCH" Santiago. Juan went by the name of MITCH (not to be confused with the NYC legendary MITCH77 UA of LATIN ARTISTS from the Bronx). Paterson had always been a battleground for turf amongst its graffiti denizens. But in 1993, there were an excessive number of graffiti arrests. It was close to election time and graffiti was being used as an easy political platform to "clean up" both the cityscape and *with* voters. Turmoil was brewing in Silk City. Politics, informants, police, and disloyalty were all in abundance.

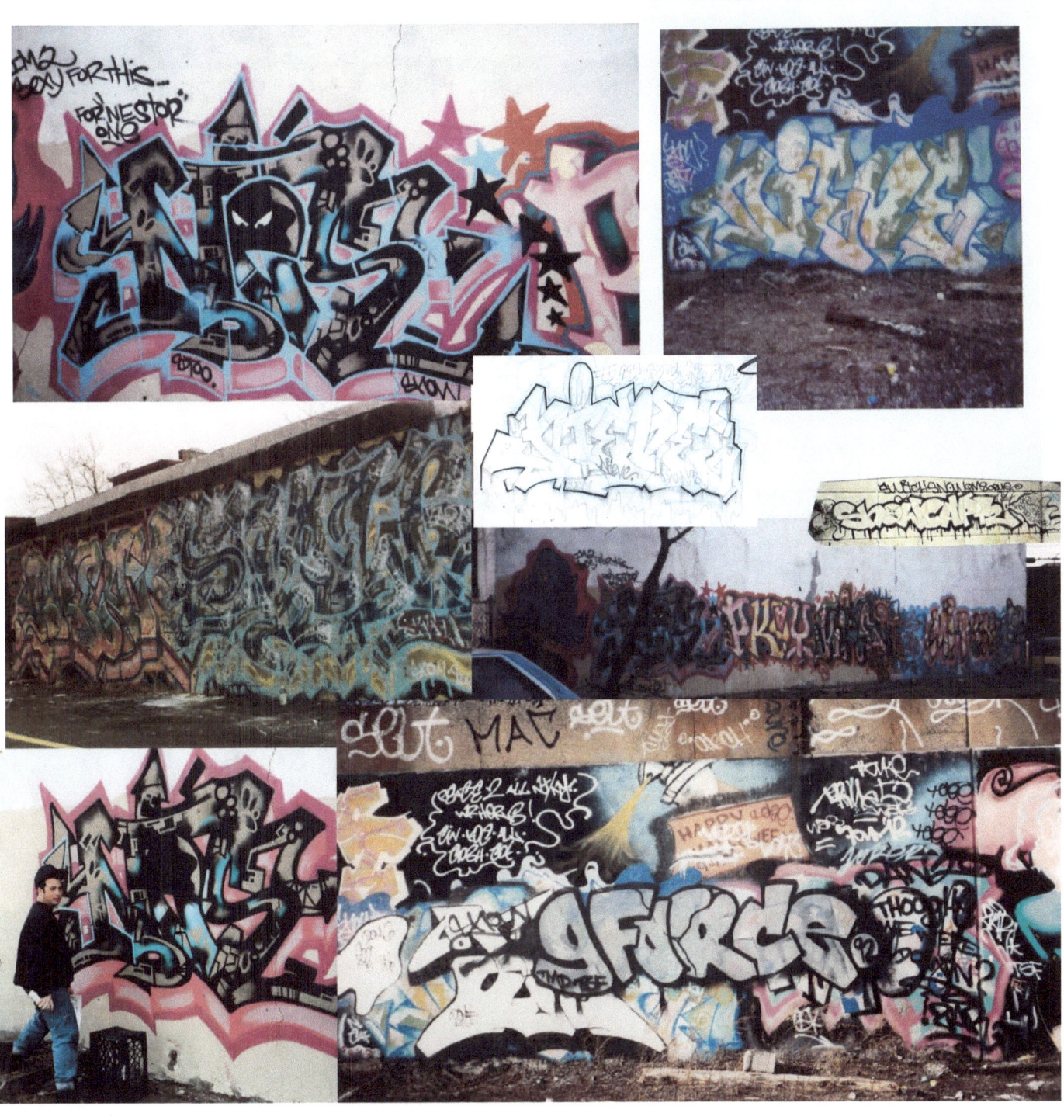

WANTED !!
GRAFFITI

$500.00
Reward

For information leading to the arrest and conviction of a Graffiti Vandal

For more information, watch
"Paterson's Most Wanted"
Saturday & Sunday at 7pm & 11pm

Call 278-TIPS

"Paterson's Most Wanted" Hot Line!

After SNOW and ZAR went "all city", they decided to leave TMD. There were differences of opinions on how to guide and nurture the once-thriving graffiti scene, and there was an uncomfortable level of mistrust, even amongst the vandals themselves. As his fame and talent were on the rise, so was the hate, envy, and jealousy that followed Snow and his newly-formed crew: QM8. Snow had moved on to create yet another crew. It was formed in PKAY's kitchen in Dover, NJ with PKAY, SELF, NEK, DJ SATONE (from Philly), and advised by KRENZ AM7 (from California). The meaning of QM8 took on a more philosophical connotation. It meant "Que Mas?... Ocho". Que Mas means "What more?" or "What else?" in Spanish. The numeral eight, or Ocho, symbolizes infinity. So it basically meant: What else or what more could one want but to rock graffiti art for all of infinity? Snow recruited SWITCH, SAIN, TEZ, and TOPAZ from Paterson. PKAY and SELF, living in Morris County, recruited RELEK and FUZE and branched out to PHILLY with PRAEZ, ENDE, and JESC. Later, the crew expanded with CERS FUA (from Brooklyn) and PALE and BOX (from the west coast). Other members were MESK from DC, PRE and KARE AFU from Philly, NACE and CHILD (RIP), with BRUE 152, XPOE, MASE BNS, EZRA, and MC TAME LTD from the Brick City of Newark, NJ. There was YES2, TORE, WAE, KAZ3, RAZE, and PASE BT from the Bronx. SEDES, SOE, CUS, URGE, from Paterson, came next, with HITMAN LEEN, 2TEK, RIC BT, DEMER, THENONE, LEAN, MR. MUSTART, GENT, RAIN (VS Crew), and NIZ joining the crew much later in the 2000's.

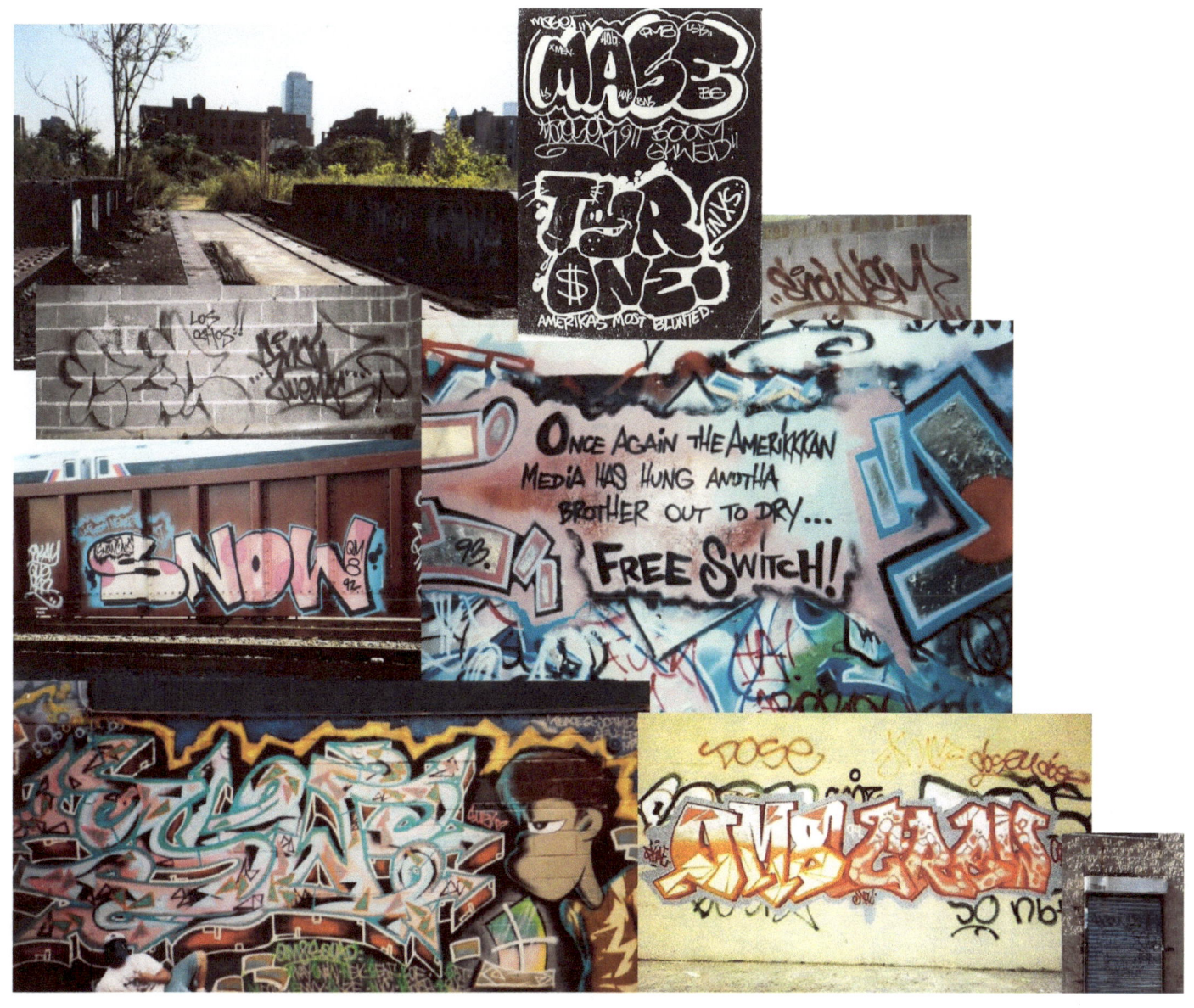

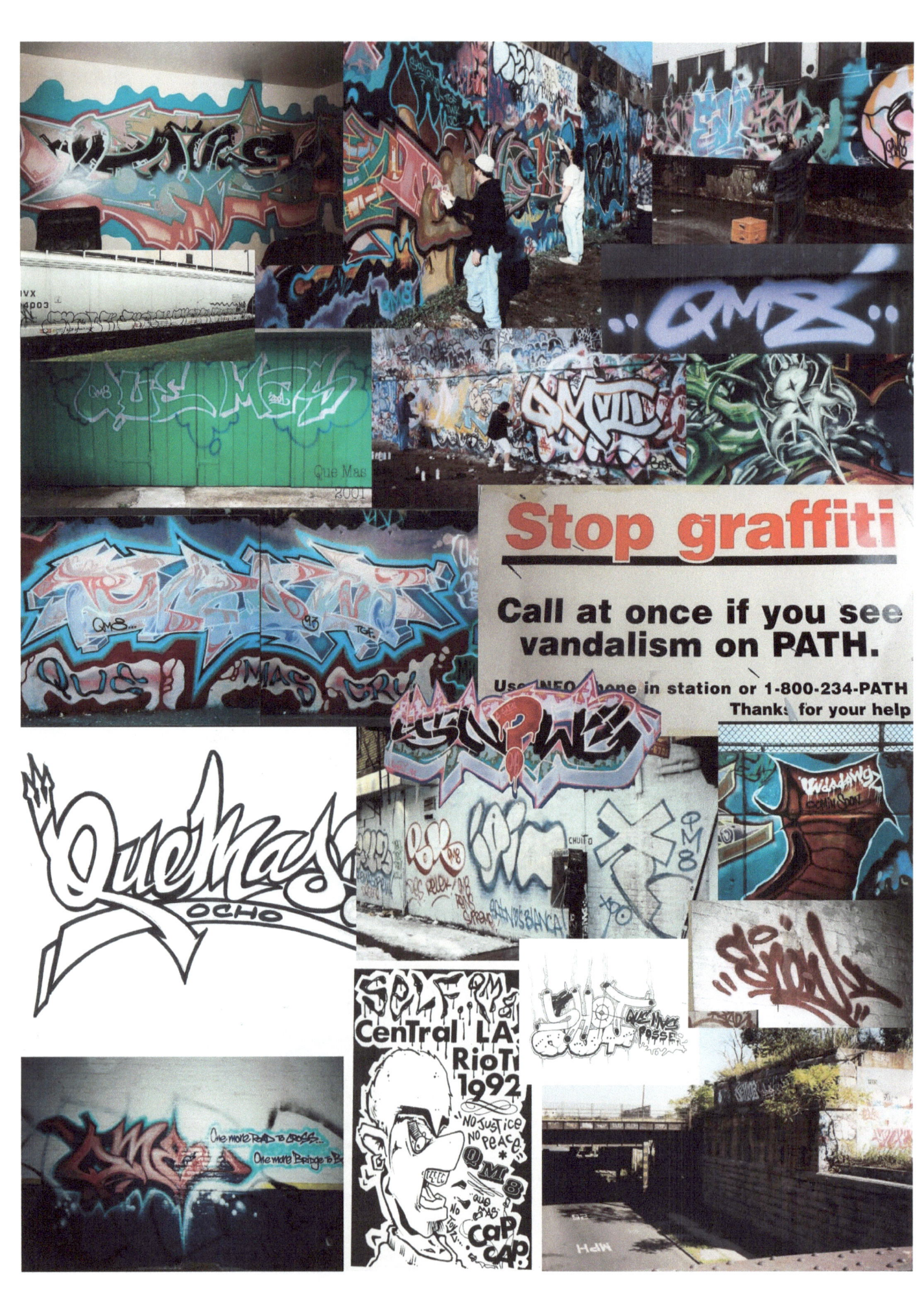

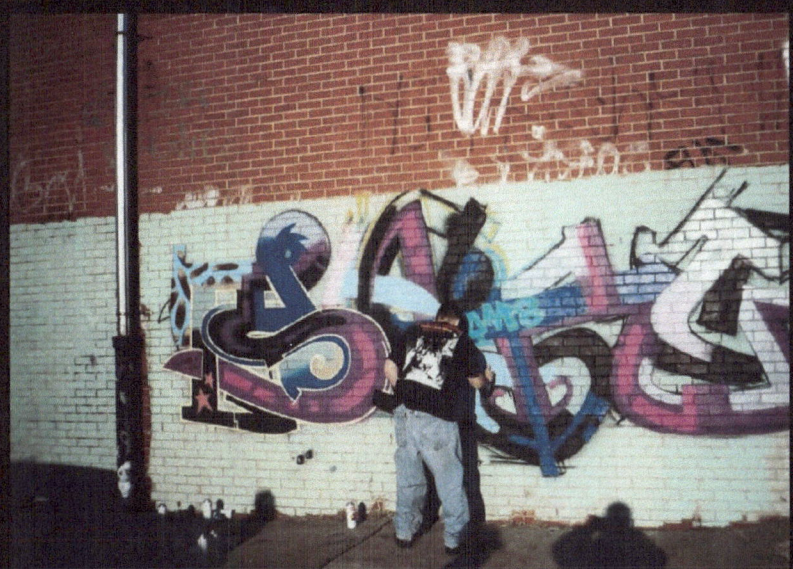

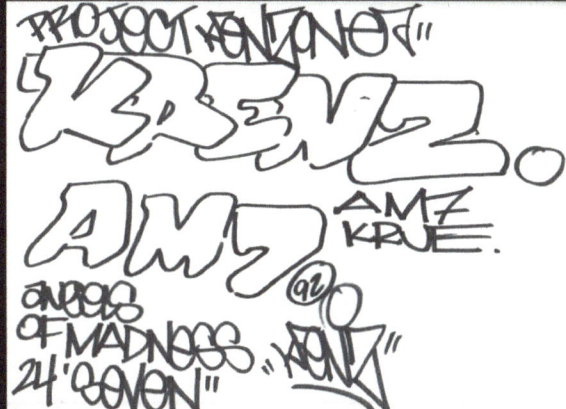

KRENZ AM7 helped to form QM8

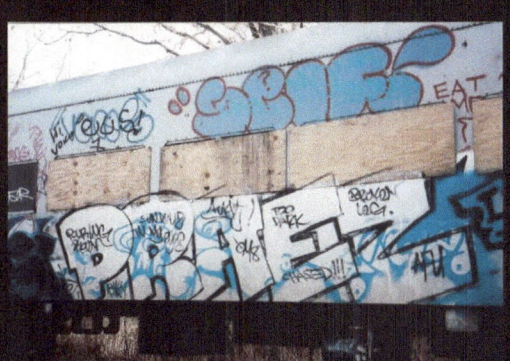

PRAEZ QM8
1992

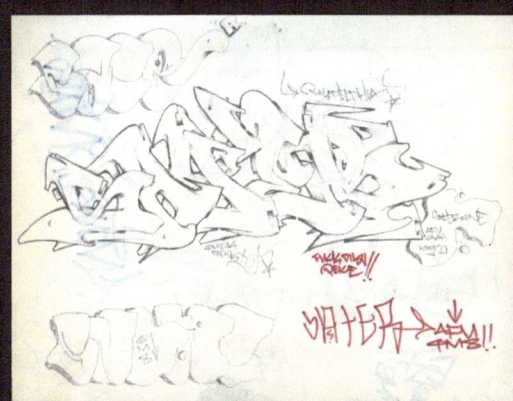

"Snow is one of the best on the planet; A true style master!"
DJ SAT-ONE QM8

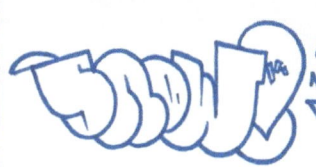

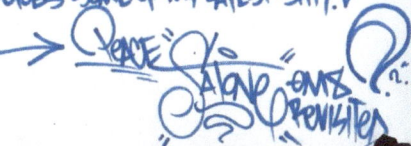

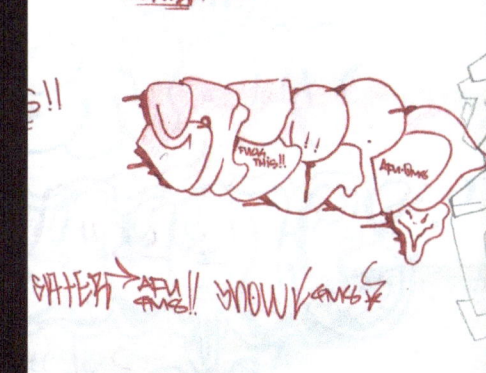

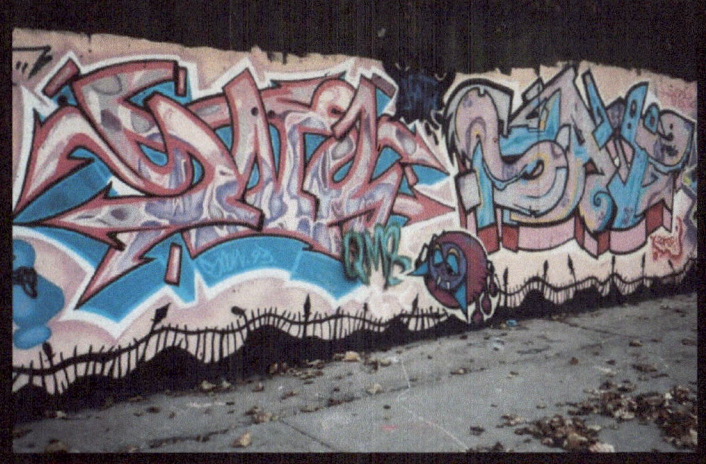

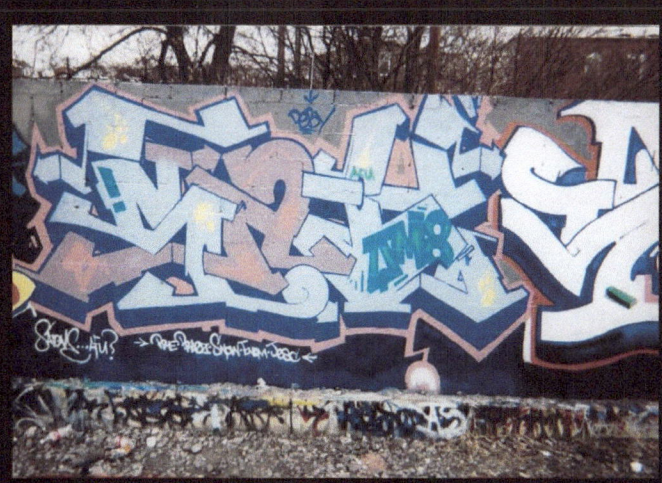

"Back then, it was rare that writers from different graffiti scenes would hook up with each other. The internet wasn't a tool. My brother Sat-One is the reason that Snow was introduced to Philly. Actually, there was a point when writers thought he was from Philly. Snow is a highly respected artist to this day in Philly, mainly for what he does best... bad ass burners!!!

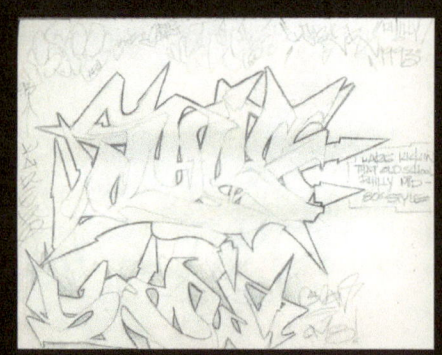

"Snow's talents are definitely organic, original, and spontaneous. Snow was the first artist that I saw approach graffiti style like I do; the next masterpiece had to be different than the previous one. If you have been writing for years and years, it's tough to reinvent your style, along with trying to evolve with it. Snow amazes me each time with a new outline, production, design, or canvas, as well as his creative ideas. I always use Snow's work for inspiration to help drive my style to different levels. Talent is respect and inspiration from your peers in this game, and Snow holds the throne.

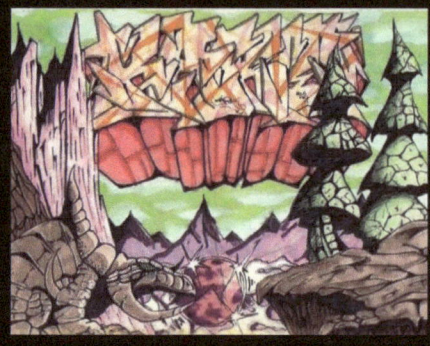

"When QM8 made its way out to Philly, it was more of a brotherhood/family than a standard graf crew. So saying that, QM8 just grew roots from the ground work laid by Snow, Sat-One, and the other artists. Once they started killing walls all over Philly, Jersey, and NY, QM8 became a household name. As an old-head, I thought what Sat and Snow were doing in Philly was the best thing that could have happened to our graf scene. Both of them raised the bar in the '90s. The scene needed a steroid shot, and that's just what they gave it. A lot of the old-heads I know totally give respect to QM8, especially Snow and Sat. They helped the younger writers develop and understand the true essence of graffiti.

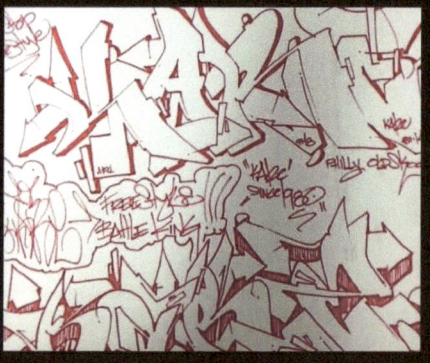

"Snow's reputation here in Philly is nothing but positive; it's not like Snow stopped by one day, did a piece, and then left. At times, I think he was in Philly more than NJ. He was always crashing at our house. His body of work is definitely tied to Philly and is impossible to list. Snow's legacy still stands tall, and it isn't over."

Jim KING KARE Thorpe

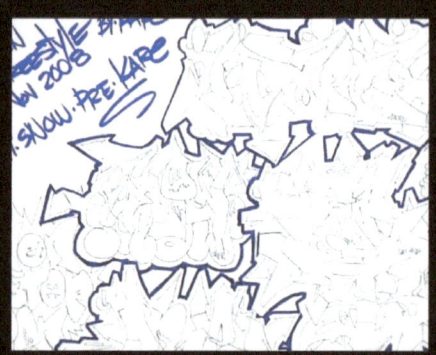

"SAT and KARE are like family to me. They've always been a huge inspiration for me."
SNOW

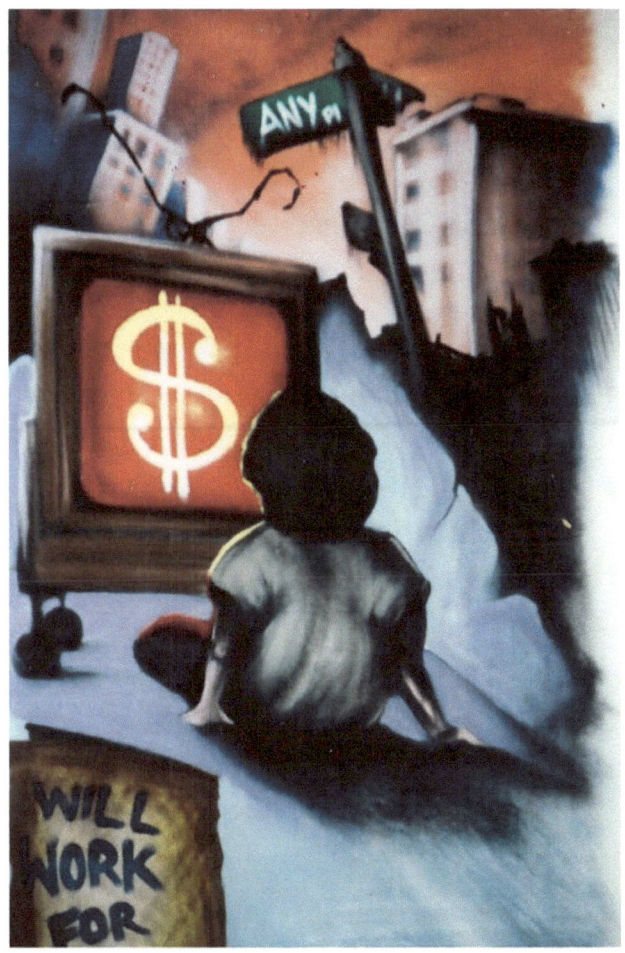

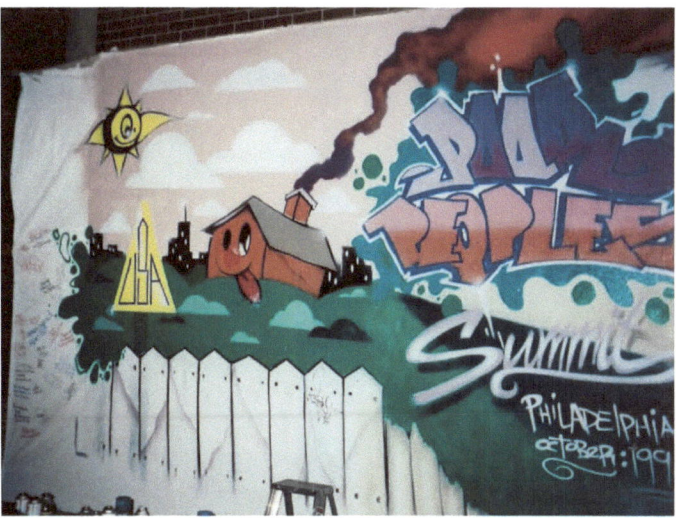

Poor People's Summit at Temple University
1998

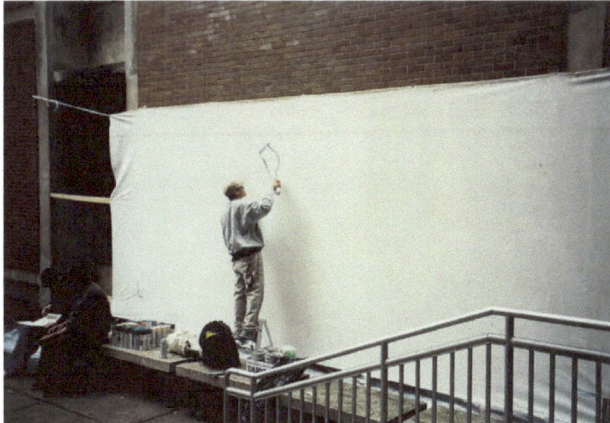

SAT and SNOW collabo at the Summit

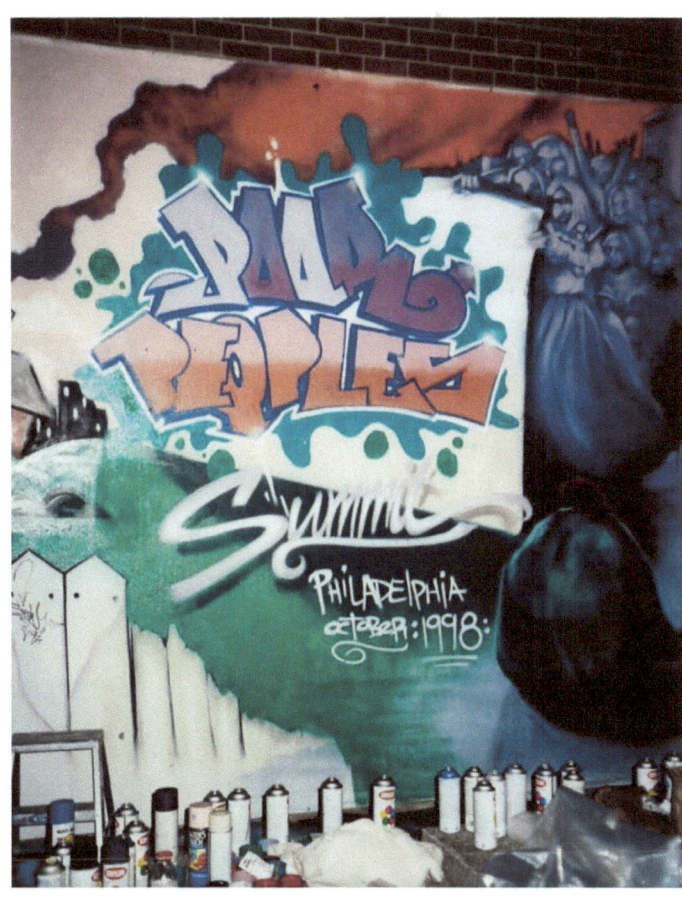

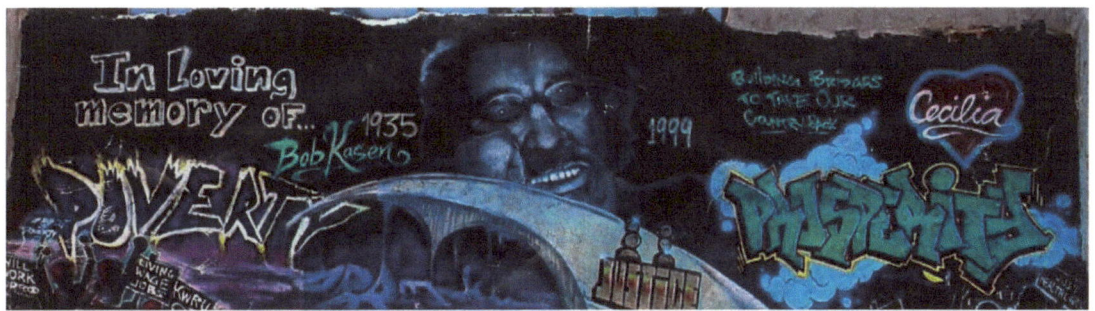

Memorial in Philly for Bob Kasen, founding member and organizer of the Labor Party by SAT and SNOW
1999

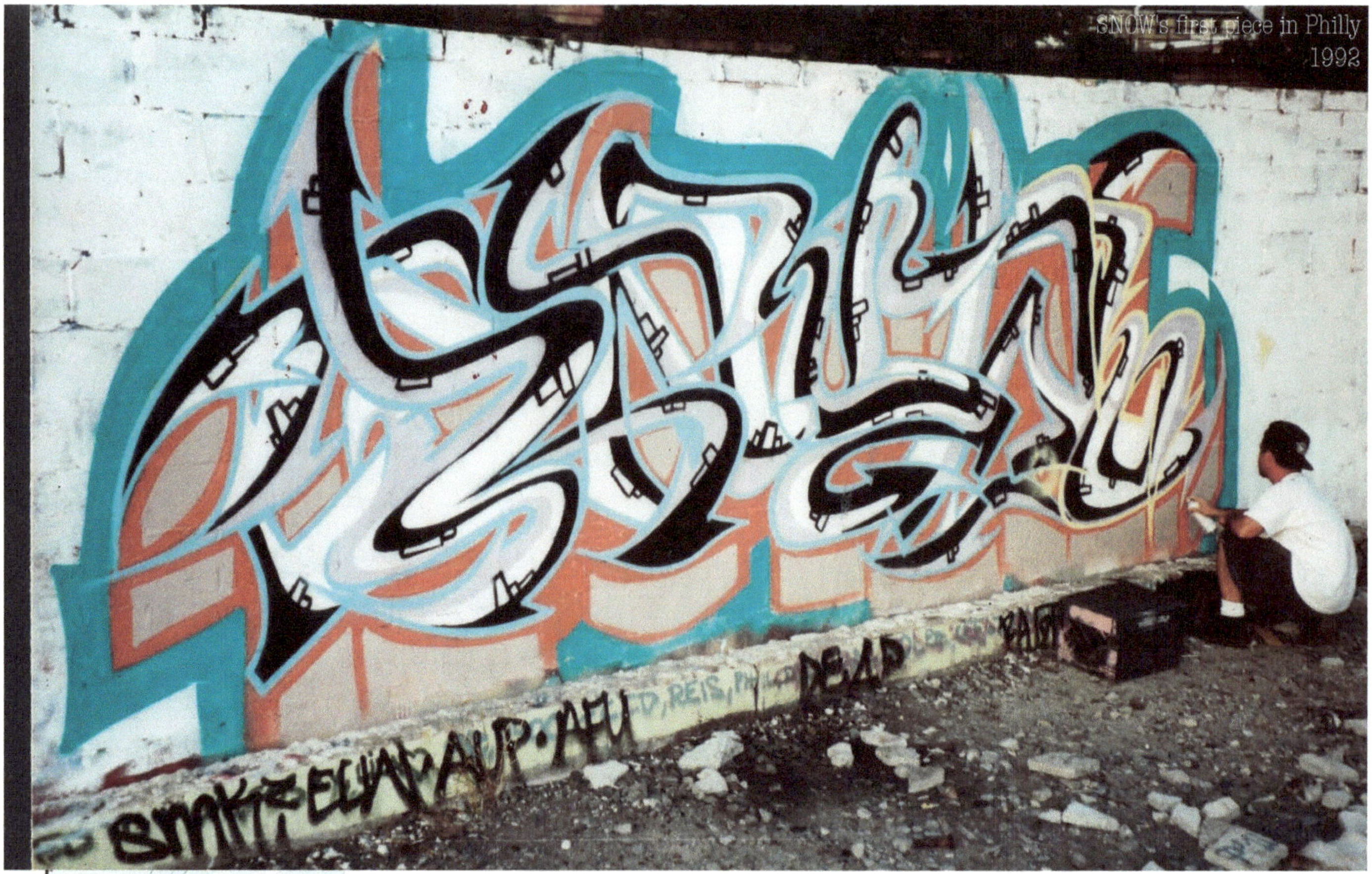

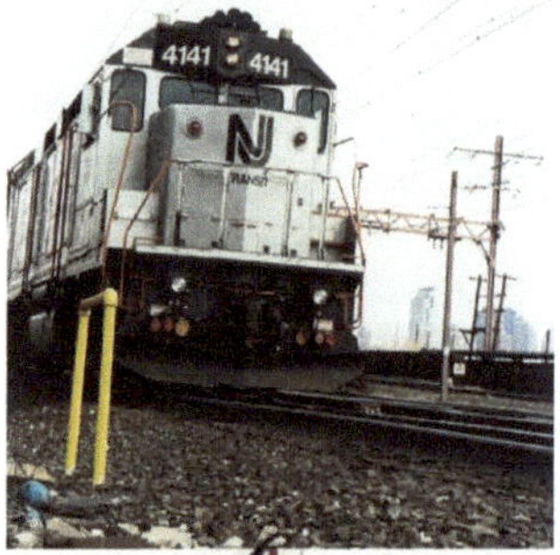

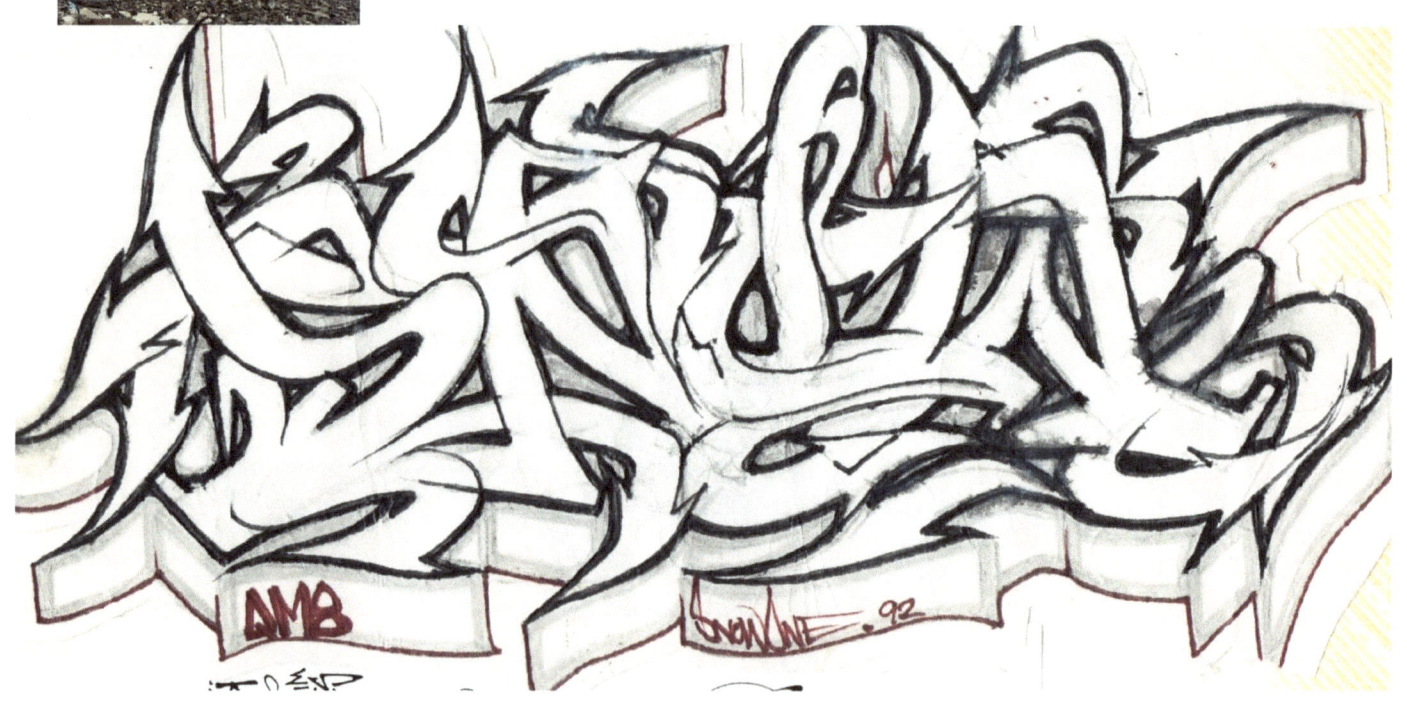

"We were the first crew that made frequent trips from NJ down to Philly. QM8 definitely brought a new flavor to Philly, and Philly in turn influenced QM8. It was a pipeline of style, and we were the trailblazers laying the path."

SNOW

Graffiti and QM8 were both transcending way beyond what any of these youth had envisioned at its onset. QM8 opened Paterson's first Hip Hop store in 1992 called The Burning Point. The Grand Opening featured live painting from popular artists: SUB and KAWS DF, ROM, TKID, PER, CLARK, CES, YES2, TDEE, and NOMAD (Snow's favorite writer), with performances by the Newark-based rap group, The Artifacts. At that same time, Mitch Santiago was hosting Paterson's first Graffiti-a-thon at School #15 (the Paterson Graffiti Hall of Fame). These two events were coinciding with the expansion of the graffiti scene worldwide. Artists from NYC, LA, Philly, DC, Puerto Rico, Connecticut, Chicago, and even Europe were attending the events at both the store and the schoolyard. *

Snow's part in all this was interesting enough. In the early '90s, law enforcement had reached a boiling point with Snow. Snow managed to always stay one step ahead of the police. But with loyalties running thin and rival graffiti crews (the media called them "gangs") at war with each other, and the city, the QM8 Crew was "served up" on a silver platter for law enforcement. Informants had been giving the police tips and leads on the crew's activities.

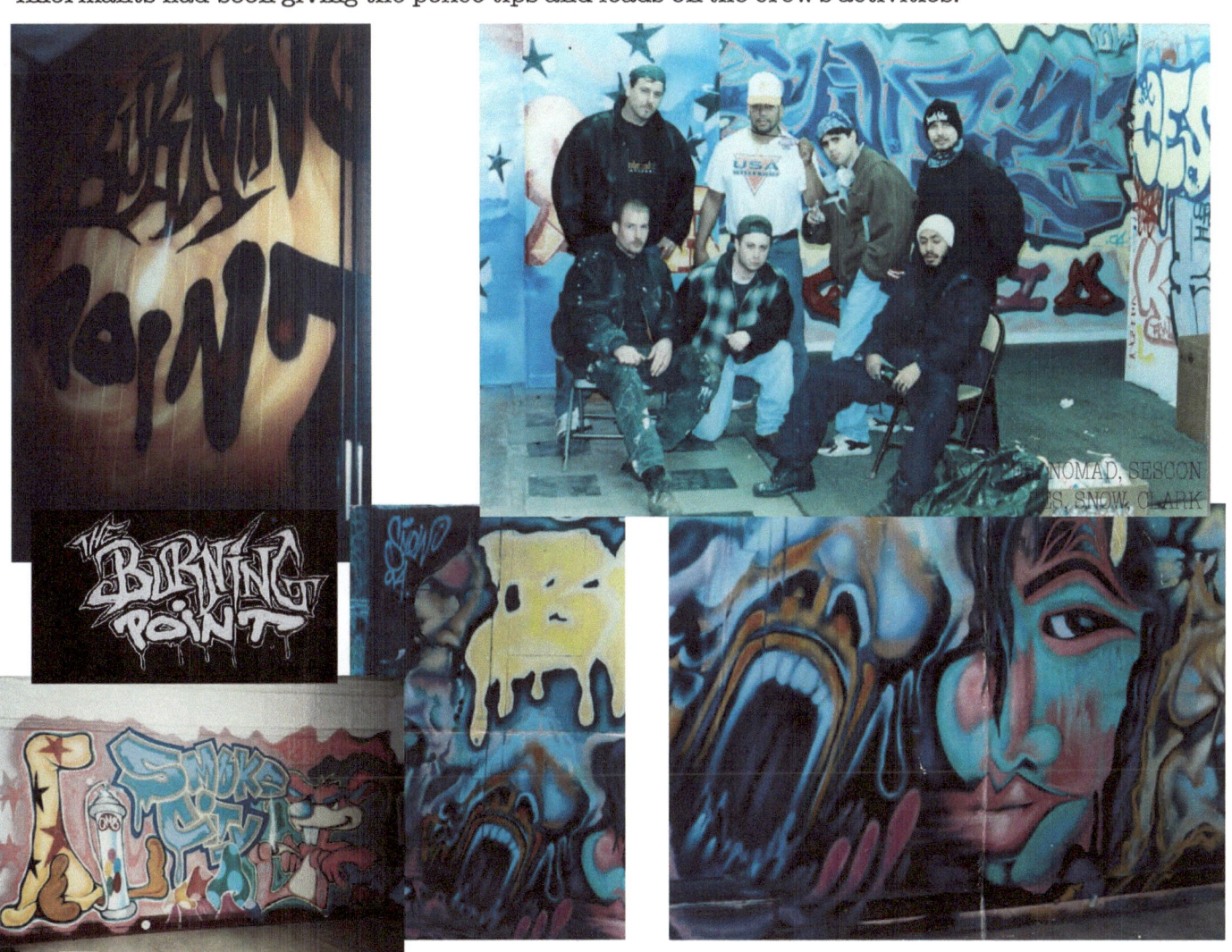

NOMAD, SESCON ... S, SNOW, CLARK

* **Author's note**: It is important to note that this part of Snow's story has many twists and turns. The scandal that followed destroyed, or at the very least, significantly impaired the graffiti scene in Paterson for many, many years thereafter. Many people are quick to pass judgement and listen to lies and hearsay without knowing what really happened back then. The spirit of this book is more of a celebration of Snow's work than a documentary of that scandalous era. Perhaps in a future book we will discuss this era in further detail.

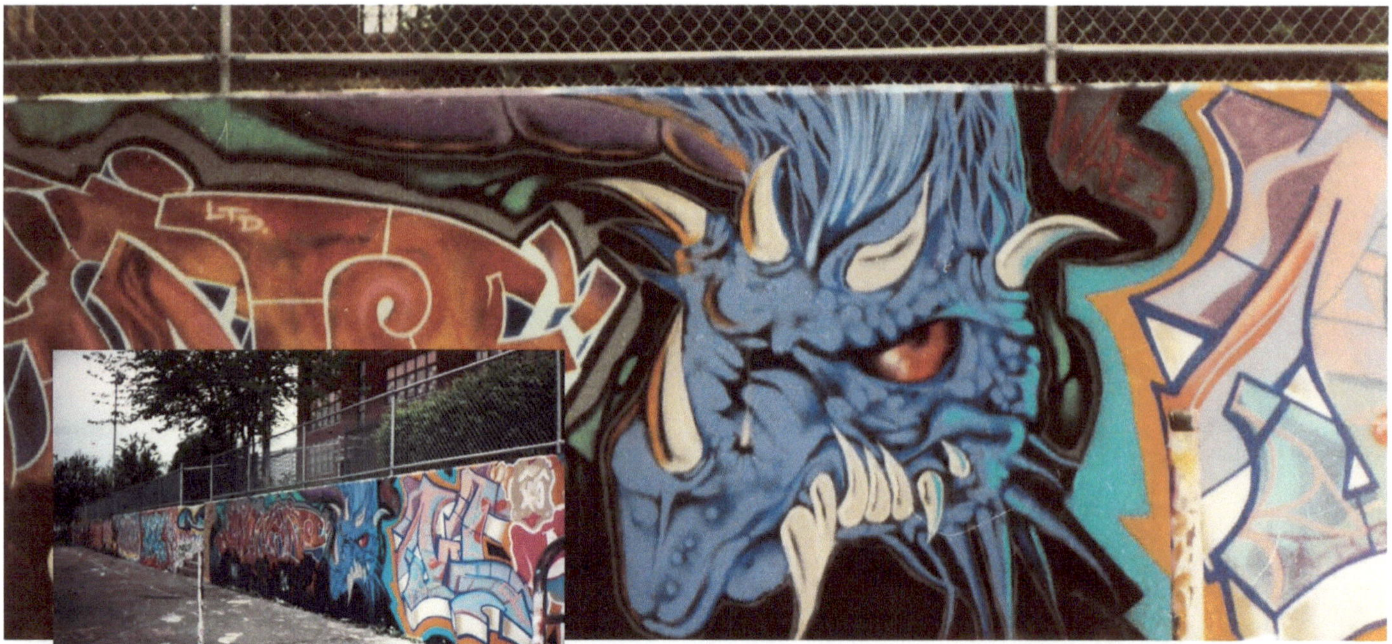

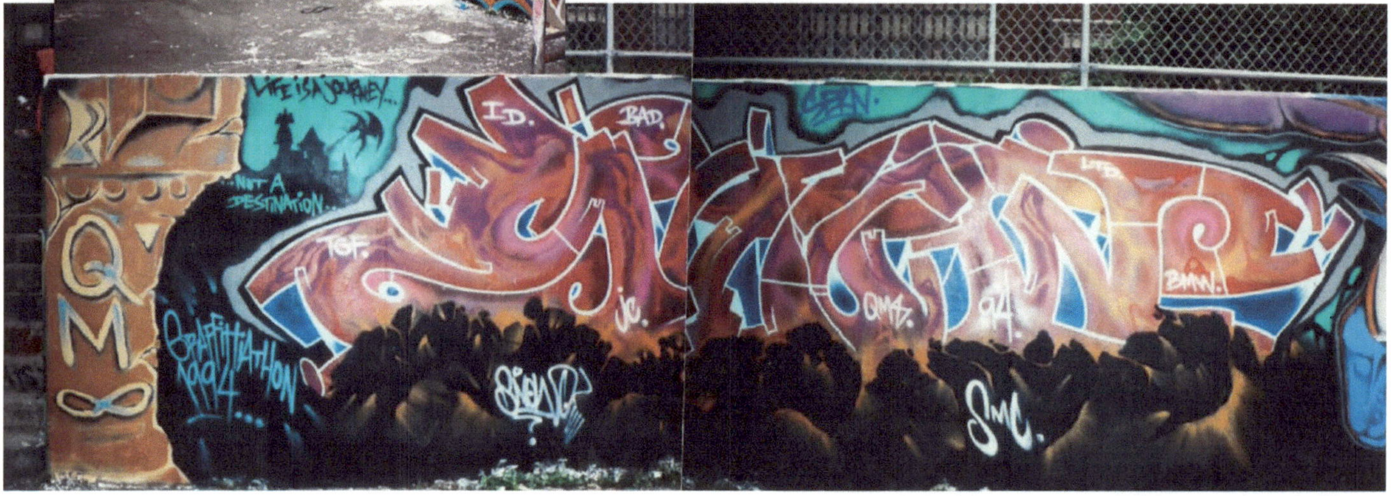

"School 15 in Paterson has always served as a Graffiti Hall of Fame. So many pieces done there; artists from all over the world have come to rock on those hallowed walls. There is a lot of history buried under those layers of paint."

SNOW

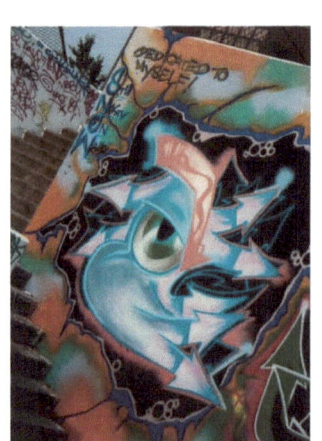

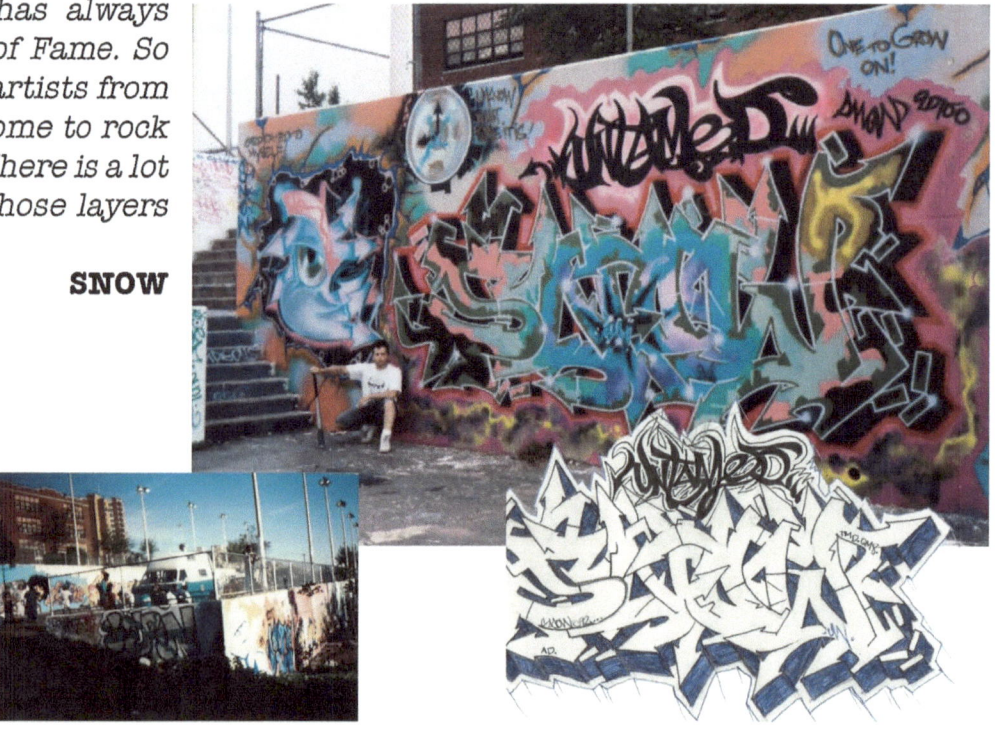

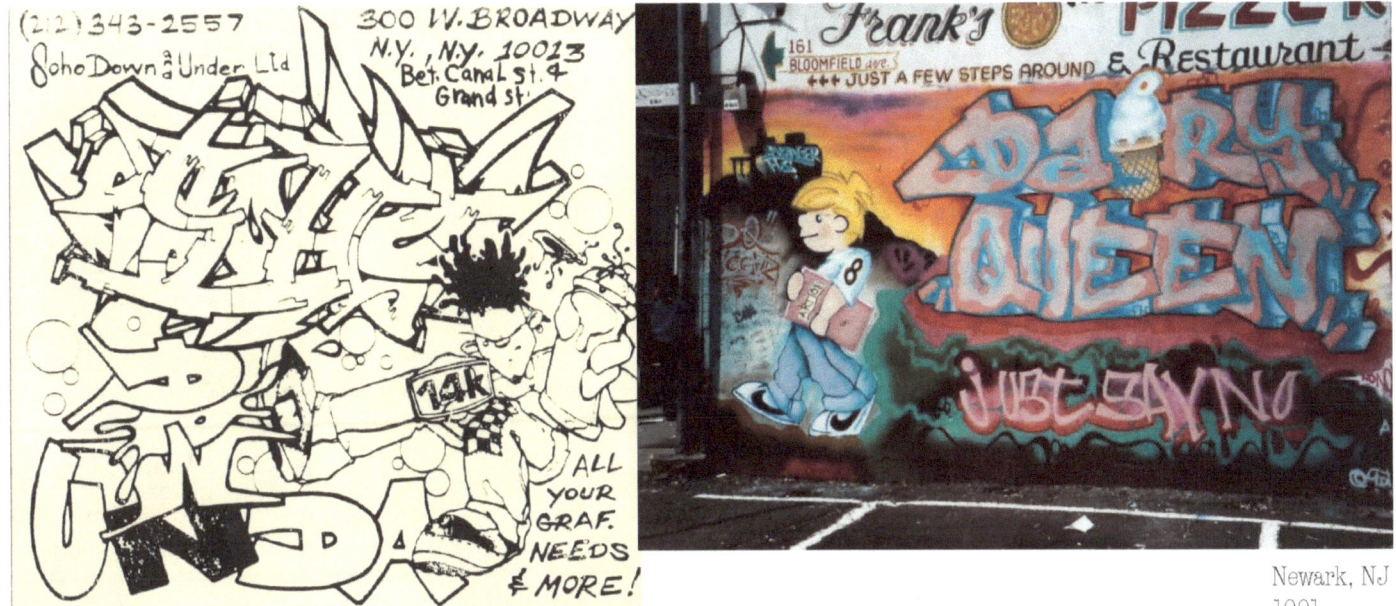

(212) 343-2557
Soho Down a Under Ltd

300 W. BROADWAY
N.Y., N.Y. 10013
Bet. Canal St. 4
Grand St.

14k

ALL YOUR GRAF. NEEDS & MORE!

161 BLOOMFIELD ave.
+++ JUST A FEW STEPS AROUND

JUST SAY NO

Newark, NJ
1991

Original logo design for Soho Down N
Unda, now known as Scrap Yard NYC;
done by PKAY and SNOW
1992

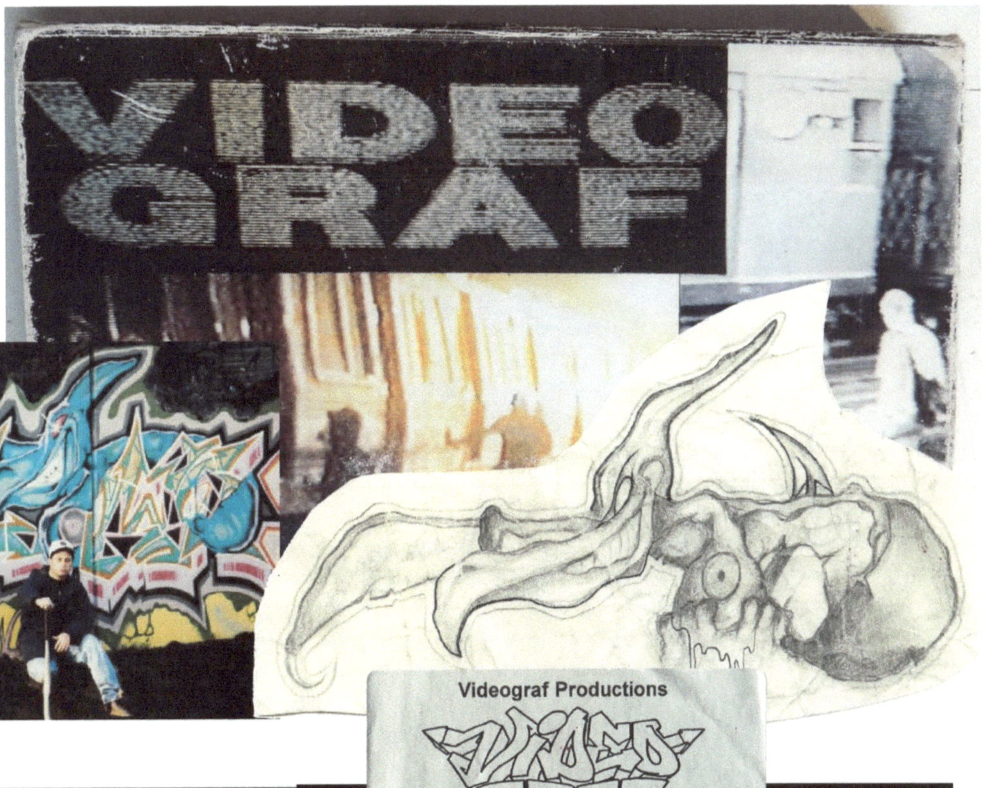

Piece for Videograf 7

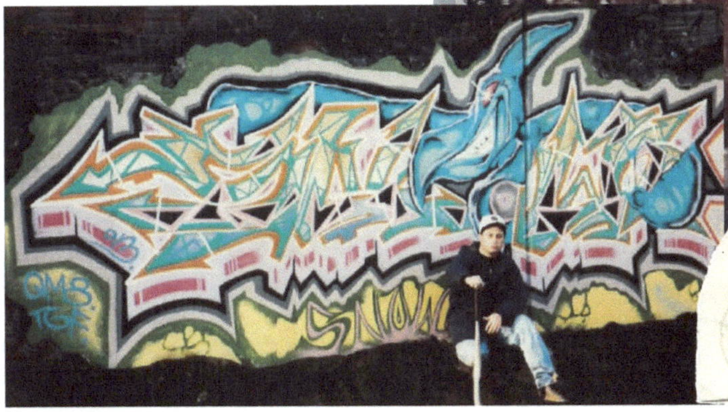

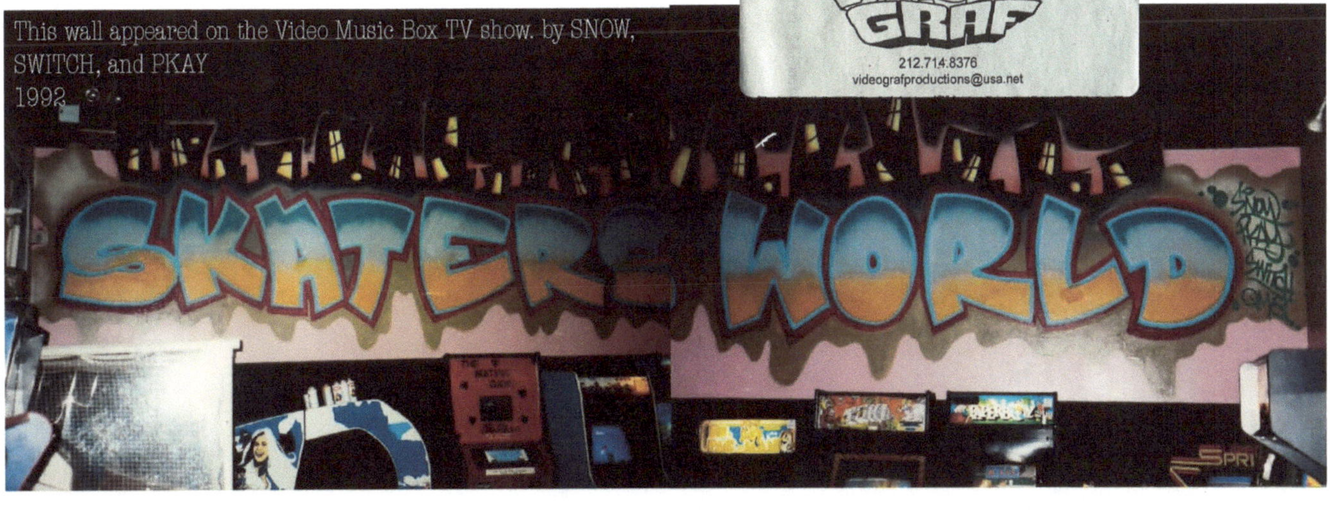

Videograf Productions

212.714.8376
videografproductions@usa.net

This wall appeared on the Video Music Box TV show. by SNOW,
SWITCH, and PKAY
1992

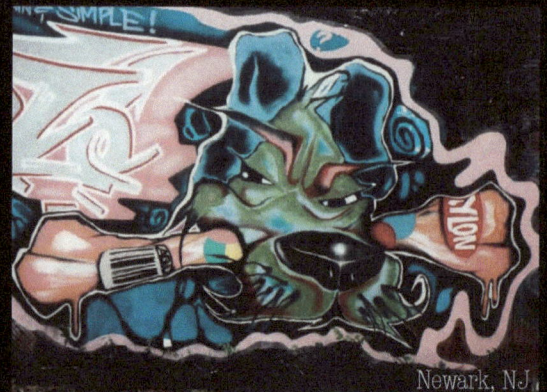

Newark, NJ

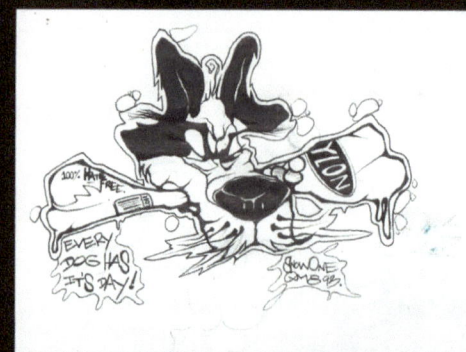

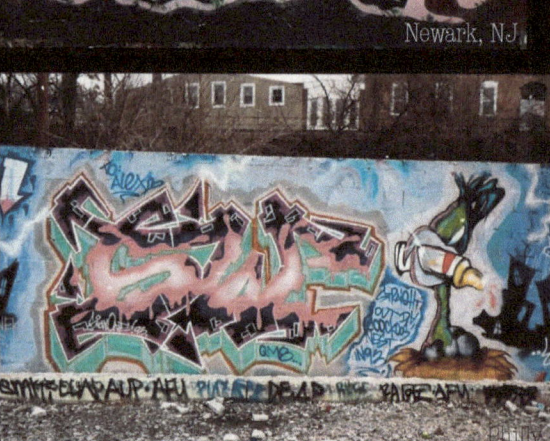

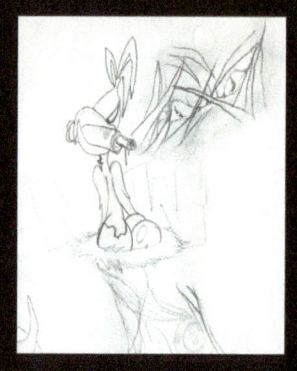

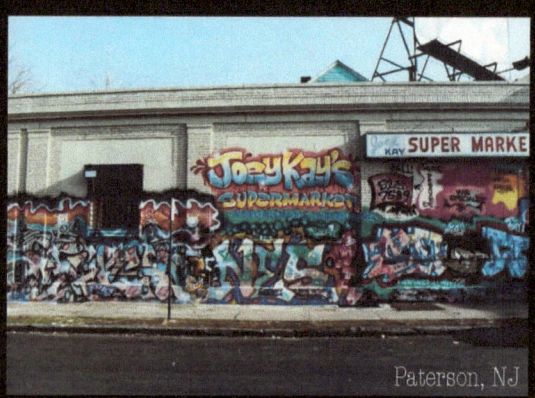

Paterson, NJ

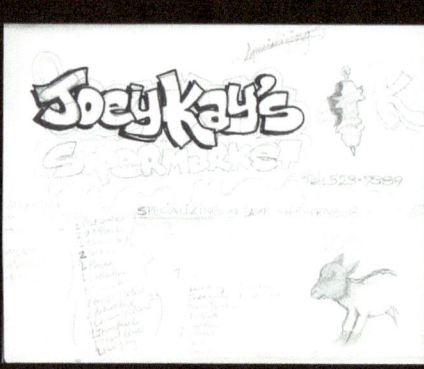

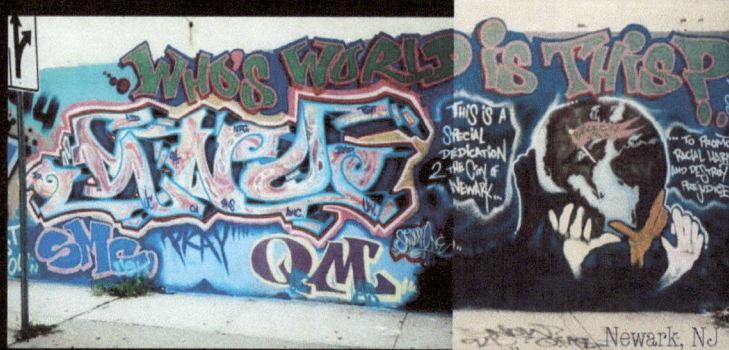

Newark, NJ

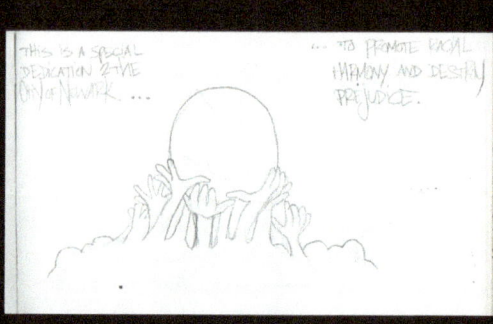

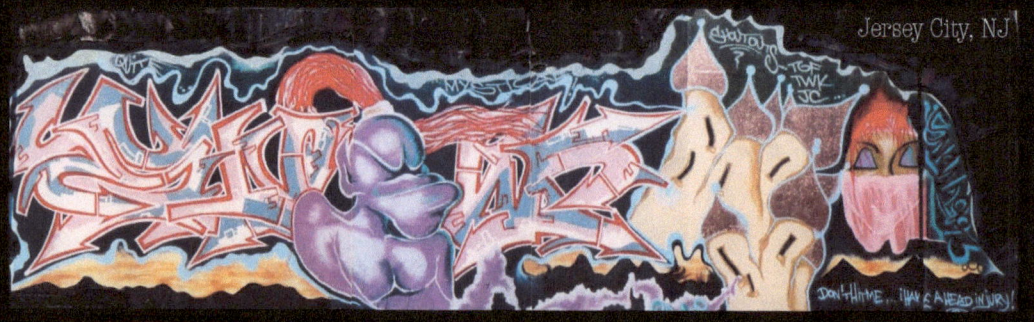

Jersey City, NJ

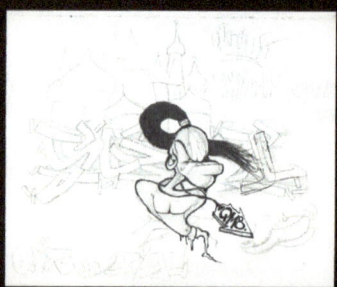

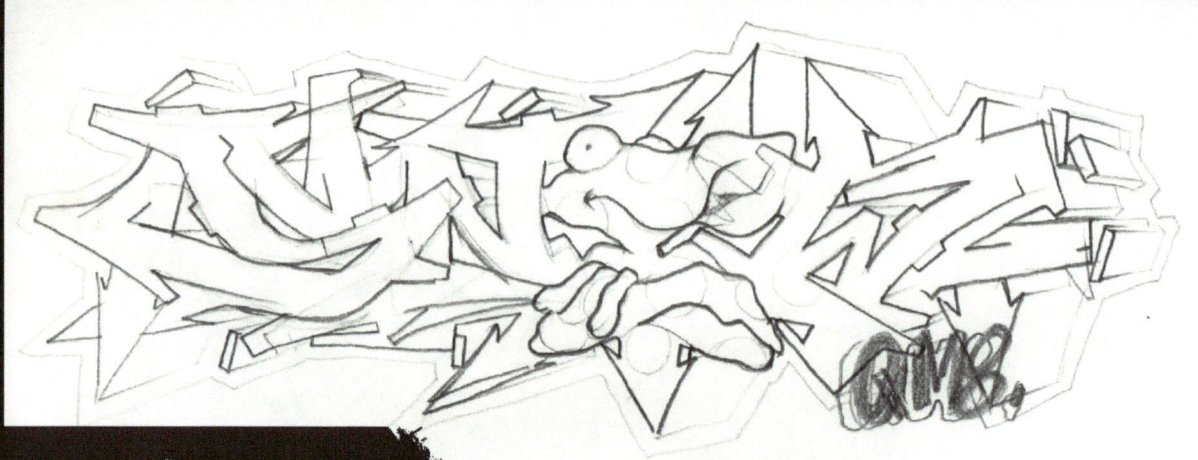

Some Sketches

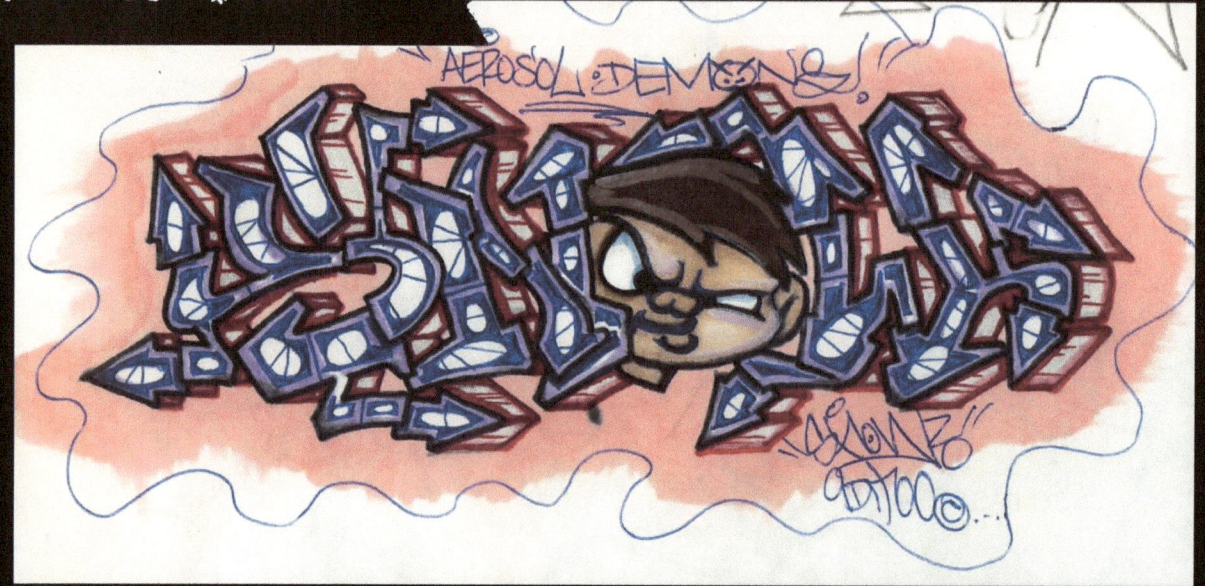

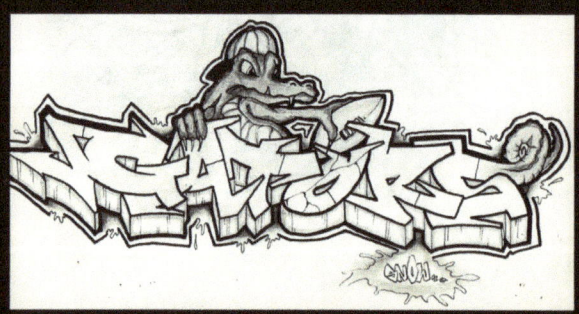

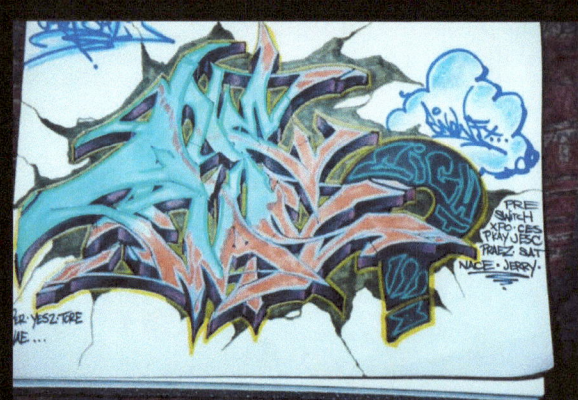

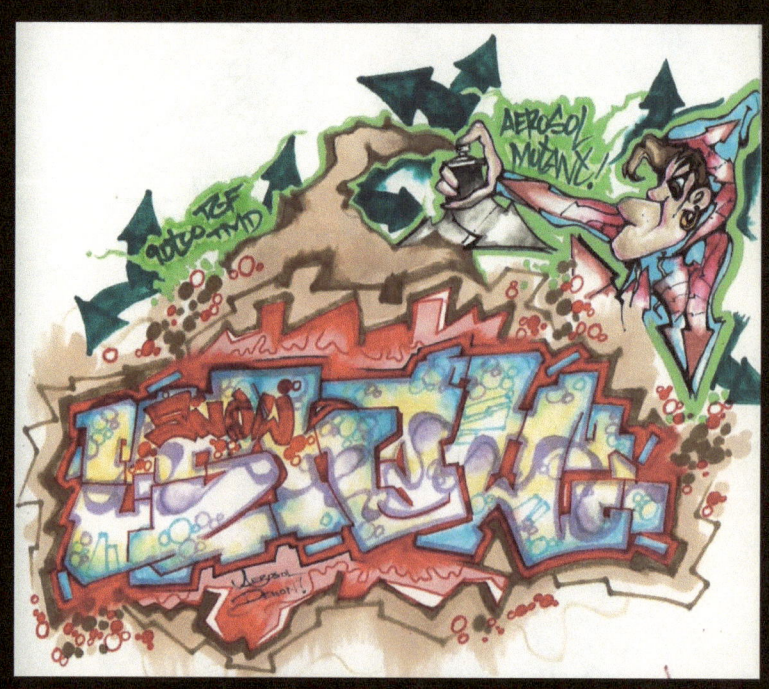

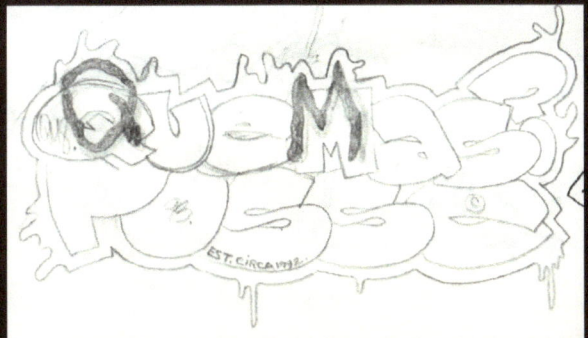

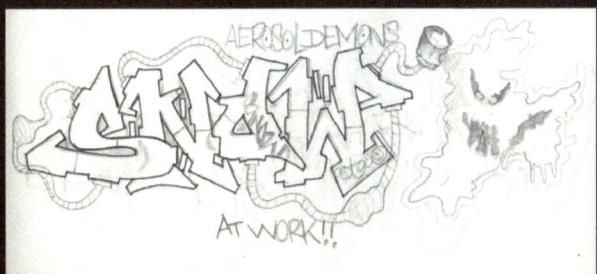

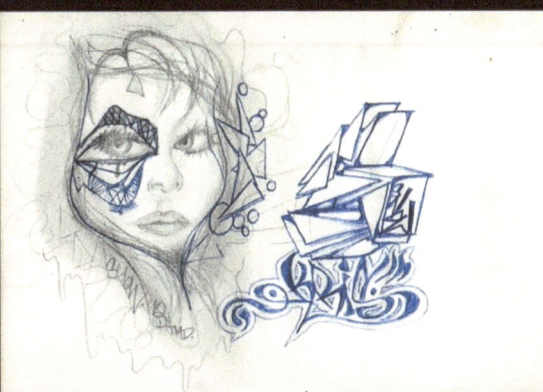

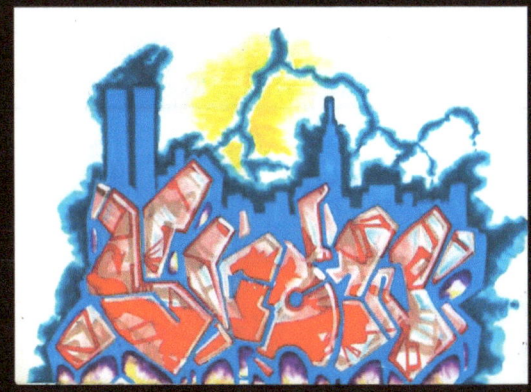

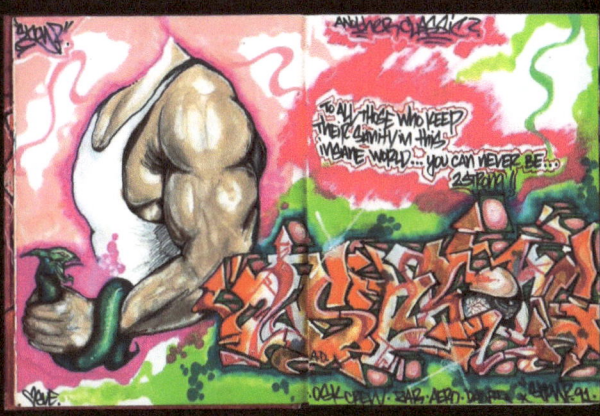

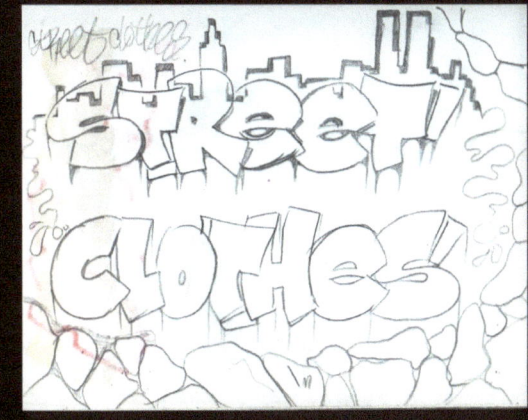

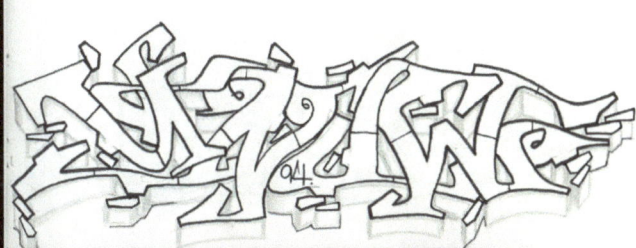

and illustrations

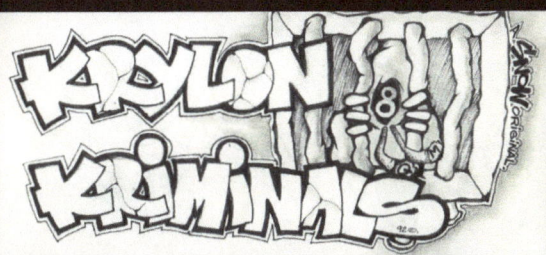

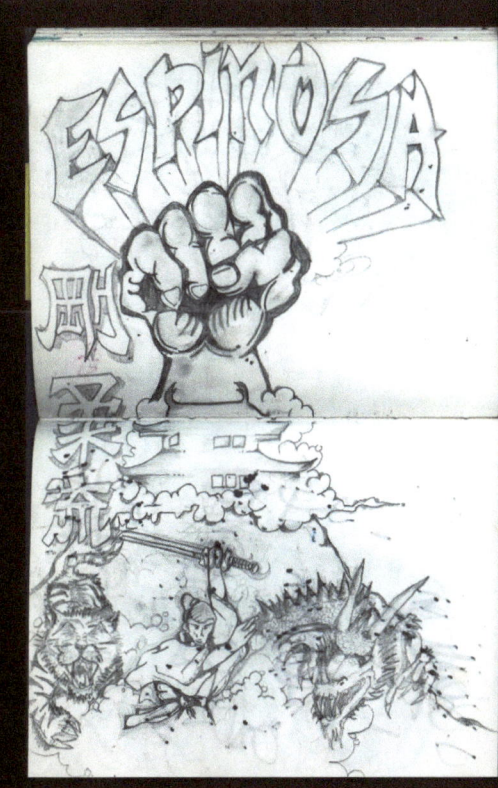

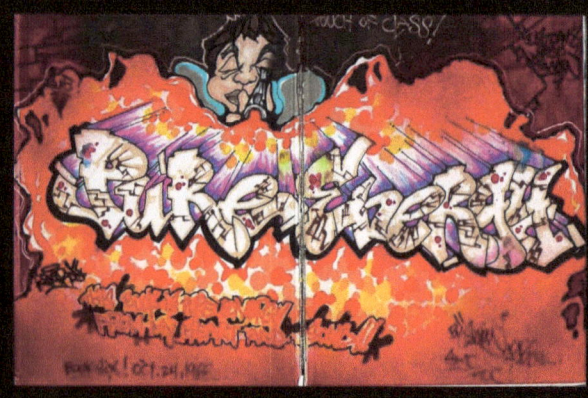

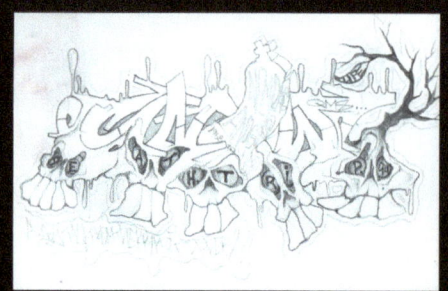

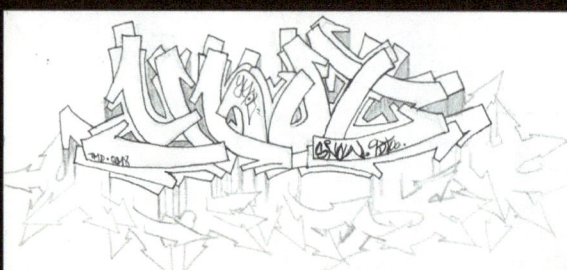

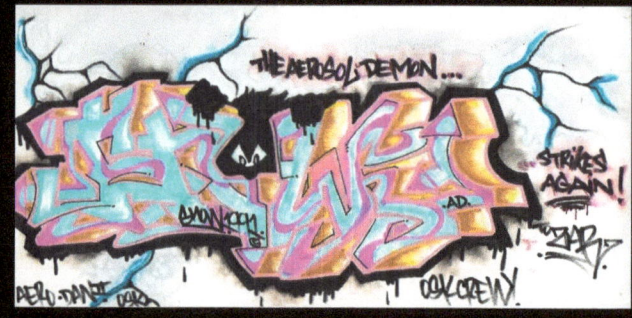

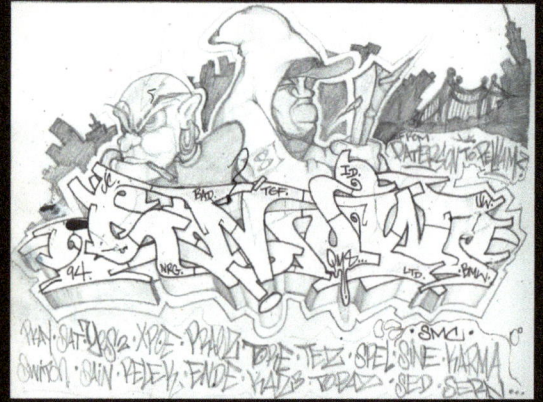

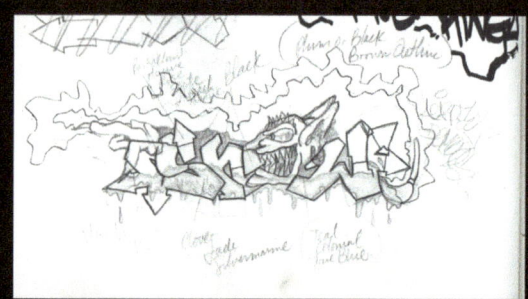

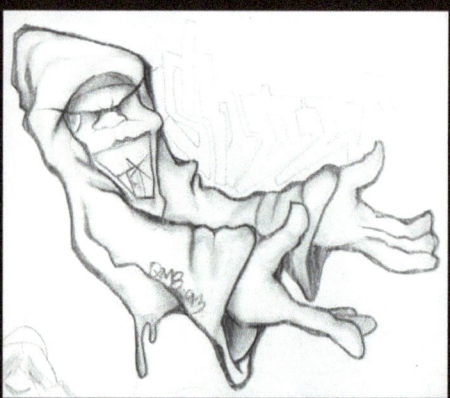

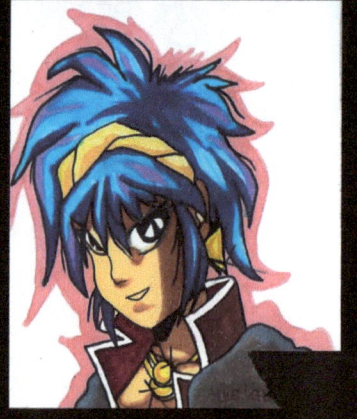

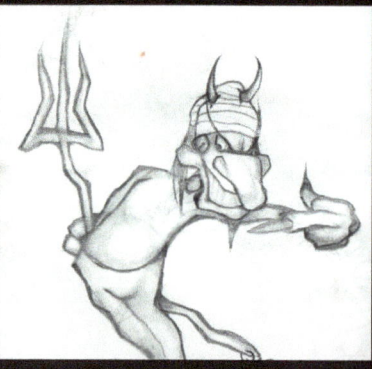

1988-1995

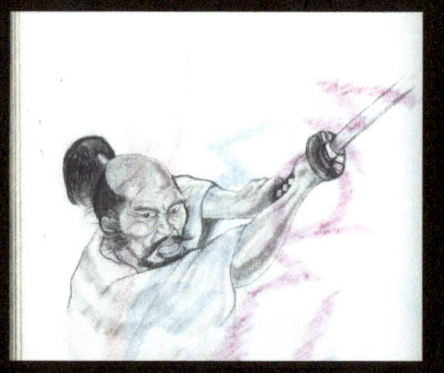

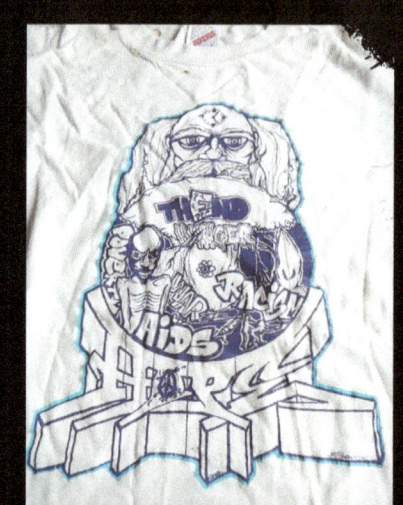

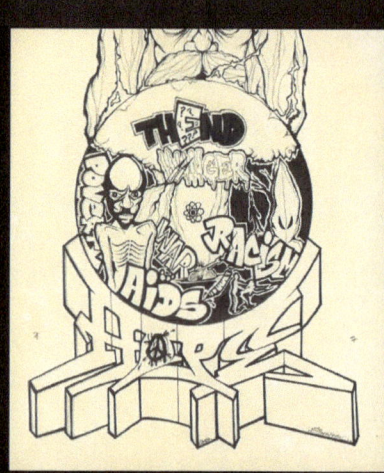

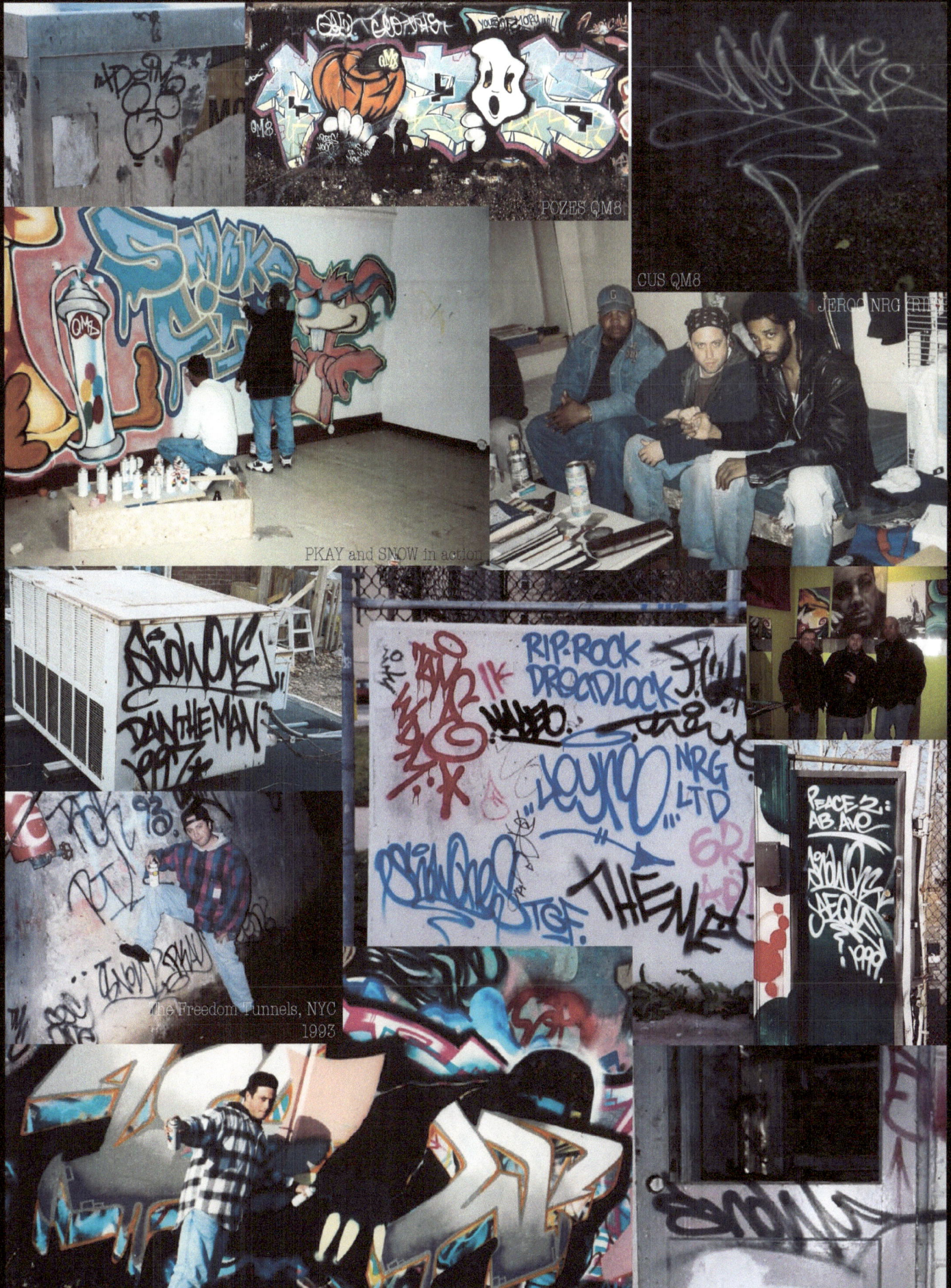

POZES QM8

CUS QM8

JEROC NRG TRIBE

PKAY and SNOW in action

the Freedom Tunnels, NYC
1993

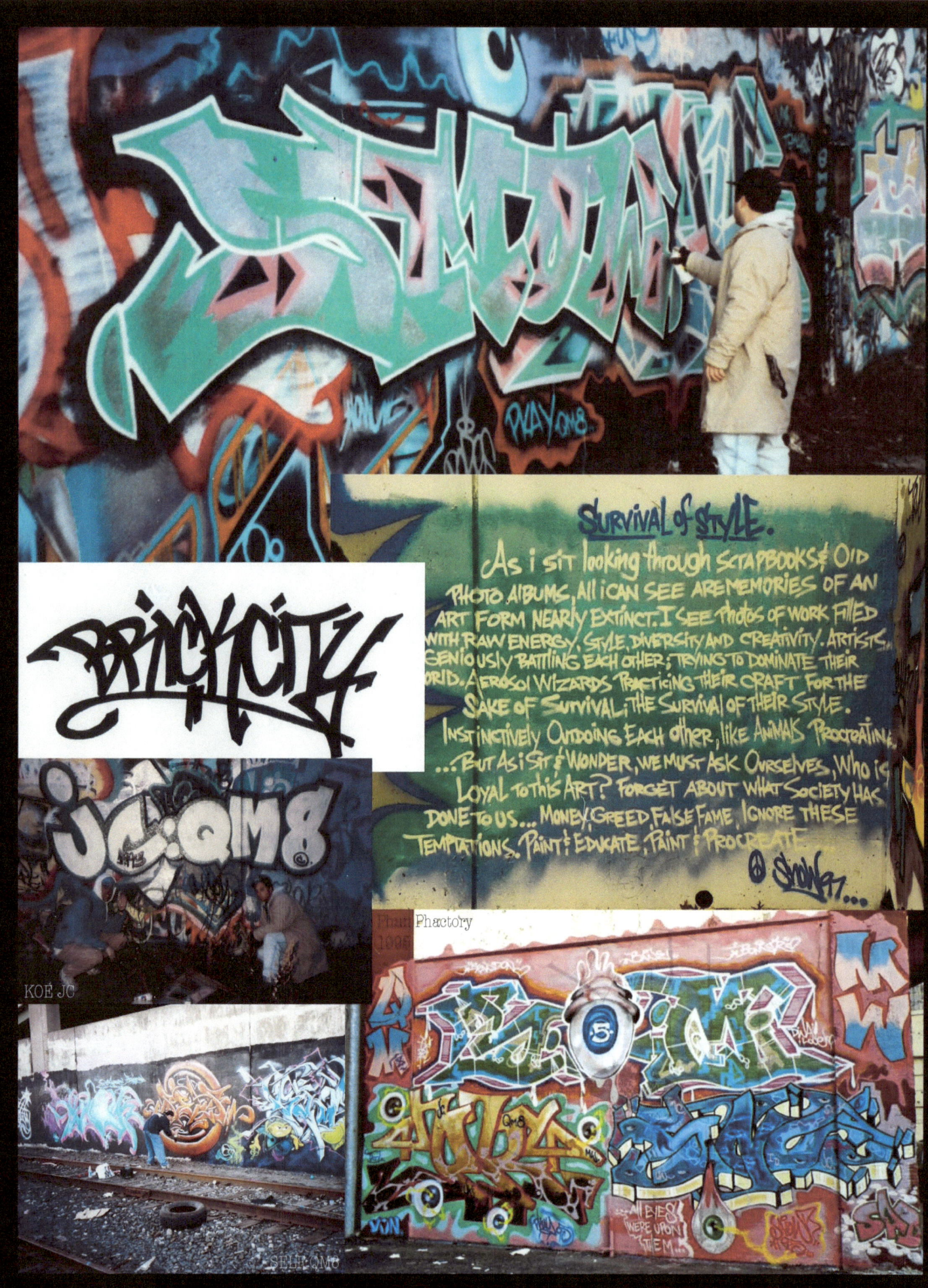

BRICKCITY

JC:QM8

KOE JC

Phactory

SURVIVAL of STYLE.

As i sit looking through scrapbooks & old photo albums, all i can see are memories of an art form nearly extinct. I see photos of work filled with raw energy, style, diversity and creativity. Artists geniously battling each other; trying to dominate their world. Aerosol wizards practicing their craft for the sake of survival; the survival of their style. Instinctively outdoing each other, like animals procreating... But as i sit & wonder, we must ask ourselves, who is loyal to this art? Forget about what society has done to us... money, greed, false fame, ignore these temptations. Paint & educate, paint & procreate...

SNOW 97...

The events and tensions of the early '90s culminated with the arrest of SNOW, SWITCH, SELF, and later, SAIN and TOPAZ. This was during an election year and the then mayor, Bill Pascrell, along with law enforcement officials, celebrated the capture of these notorious vandals by putting their arrests on the front page of North Jersey's newspapers. The trio was convicted and made an example of, as an attempt to deter future graffiti writers. If you travel throughout NJ in the present day, you will see the visual evidence that this campaign was, and still is for the most part, unsuccessful.

The dream of every Paterson graffiti writer enjoying a thriving graffiti scene with live painting events, art shows, media exposure, and a retail store was quickly smashed and short-lived; Not by the expected and traditional foes of law enforcement and politicians but by the lack of integrity amongst the graffiti writers themselves. The personal agendas and selfish motives of some of the graffiti crew leaders helped to bring on the premature demise of graffiti in Paterson.

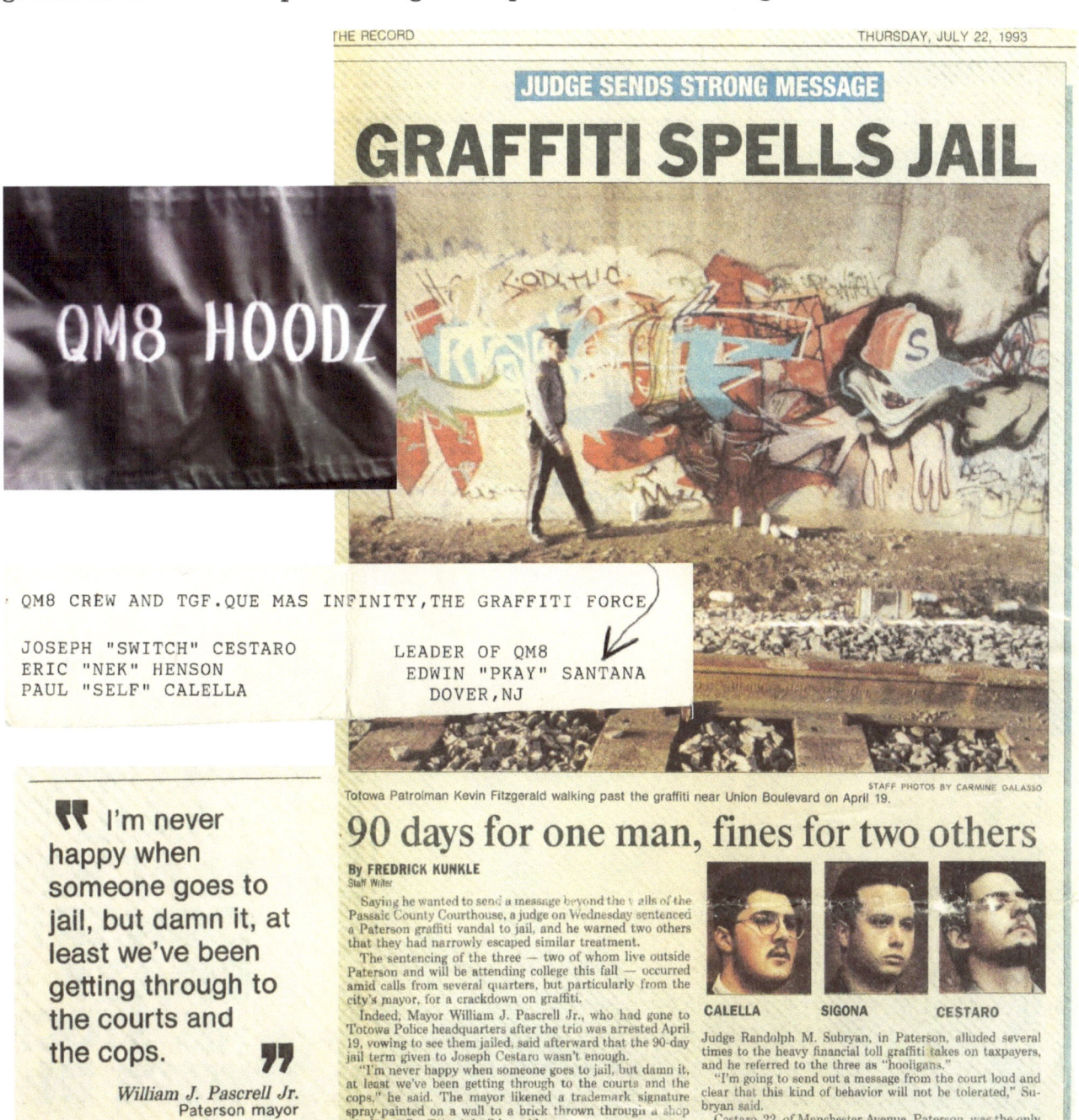

QM8 HOODZ

THE RECORD

THURSDAY, JULY 22, 1993

JUDGE SENDS STRONG MESSAGE

GRAFFITI SPELLS JAIL

QM8 CREW AND TGF.QUE MAS INFINITY,THE GRAFFITI FORCE

JOSEPH "SWITCH" CESTARO
ERIC "NEK" HENSON
PAUL "SELF" CALELLA

LEADER OF QM8
EDWIN "PKAY" SANTANA
DOVER,NJ

STAFF PHOTOS BY CARMINE GALASSO

Totowa Patrolman Kevin Fitzgerald walking past the graffiti near Union Boulevard on April 19.

90 days for one man, fines for two others

By FREDRICK KUNKLE
Staff Writer

Saying he wanted to send a message beyond the walls of the Passaic County Courthouse, a judge on Wednesday sentenced a Paterson graffiti vandal to jail, and he warned two others that they had narrowly escaped similar treatment.

The sentencing of the three — two of whom live outside Paterson and will be attending college this fall — occurred amid calls from several quarters, but particularly from the city's mayor, for a crackdown on graffiti.

Indeed, Mayor William J. Pascrell Jr., who had gone to Totowa Police headquarters after the trio was arrested April 19, vowing to see them jailed, said afterward that the 90-day jail term given to Joseph Cestaro wasn't enough.

"I'm never happy when someone goes to jail, but damn it, at least we've been getting through to the courts and the cops," he said. The mayor likened a trademark signature spray-painted on a wall to a brick thrown through a shop window. "Graffiti stinks," he said.

Without mentioning Pascrell by name, Superior Court

CALELLA   SIGONA   CESTARO

Judge Randolph M. Subryan, in Paterson, alluded several times to the heavy financial toll graffiti takes on taxpayers, and he referred to the three as "hooligans."

"I'm going to send out a message from the court loud and clear that this kind of behavior will not be tolerated," Subryan said.

Cestaro, 22, of Manchester Avenue, Paterson, was the only

See **GRAFFITI** Page **B-5**

❝ I'm never happy when someone goes to jail, but damn it, at least we've been getting through to the courts and the cops. ❞

William J. Pascrell Jr.
Paterson mayor

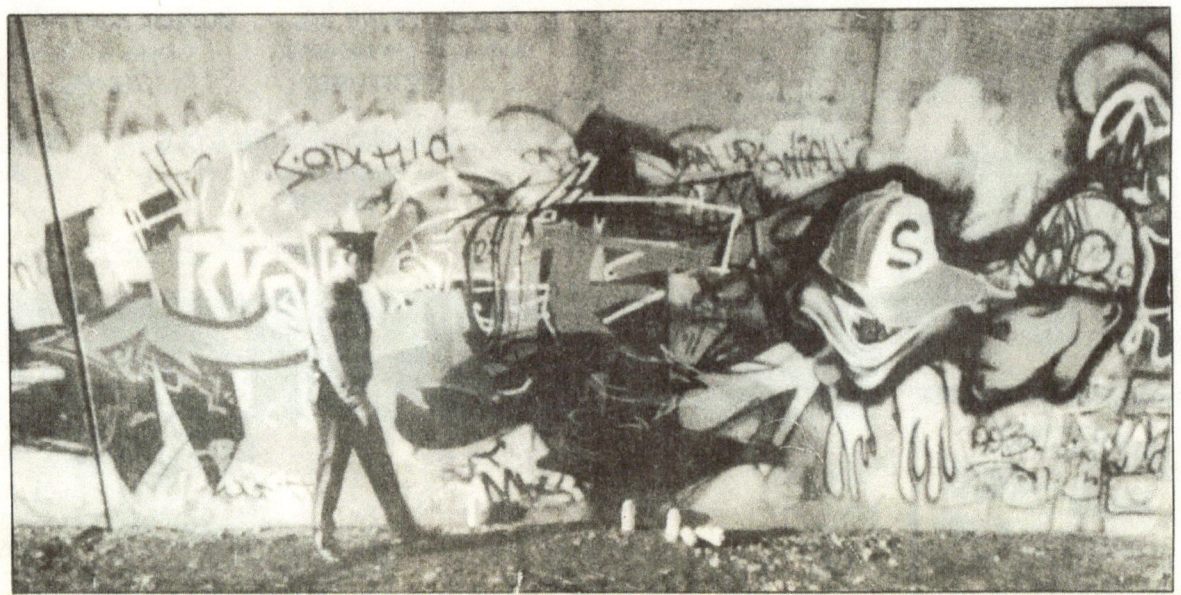

Totowa Patrolman Kevin Fitzgerald walking near where police say three of North Jersey's most notorious graffiti artists were arrested.

GRAFFITI: Arrests

From Page A-1

one-man crusade against graffiti ever since he became mayor.

"I assured the guys who got arrested today I am not backing off," Pascrell said. After he was notified about the arrests, the mayor rushed to Totowa police headquarters with Paterson Detective Donald Reddin, a graffiti expert.

Cestaro, 22, of Manchester Avenue, Paterson; Sigona, 25, of Cedar Grove; and Calella, 20, of Randolph, were described by Reddin as "major hitters" in a graffiti gang known as "TGF" (The Graffiti Force), whose works appear all over North Jersey.

"They hit 50 to 100 buildings every night," said Reddin, with the "art" usually amounting to their *noms de plume*.

Totowa police confiscated 100 cans of spray paint at the scene, as well as cars belonging to Cestaro and Calella. Totowa Detective Lt. Robert Coyle said the suspects apparently replaced the original nozzles on the spray cans and were using their own custom-made nozzles to paint the mural. Two backpacks and a duffel bag, apparently used to haul the spray cans from the car to the railway tunnel, also were found at the scene, Coyle said.

In Totowa, Cestaro was charged with two counts of criminal mischief over $500, an indictable offense, and Sigona and Calella were charged with criminal mischief, Coyle said.

Bail for Cestaro and Sigona was set at $1,000 each, bail for Calella at $1,500.

Reddin said the suspects will face several counts of criminal mischief in Paterson, and their arrests could lead to the arrests of 15 to 20 more graffiti artists, all members of "TGF."

The graffiti problem in Paterson is so severe that Pascrell recently wrote county and municipal judges to suggest that jail time was needed to stem the plague.

"We romanticized graffiti in the Eighties, and it got us nowhere," Pascrell said.

"This is not an honorable profession," the mayor said. "It is only a matter of time before the problem spills over into every community. It's happening with drugs, and with graffiti, unless we work together and battle this."

Reddin said there are about 25 gangs of graffiti artists in the city.

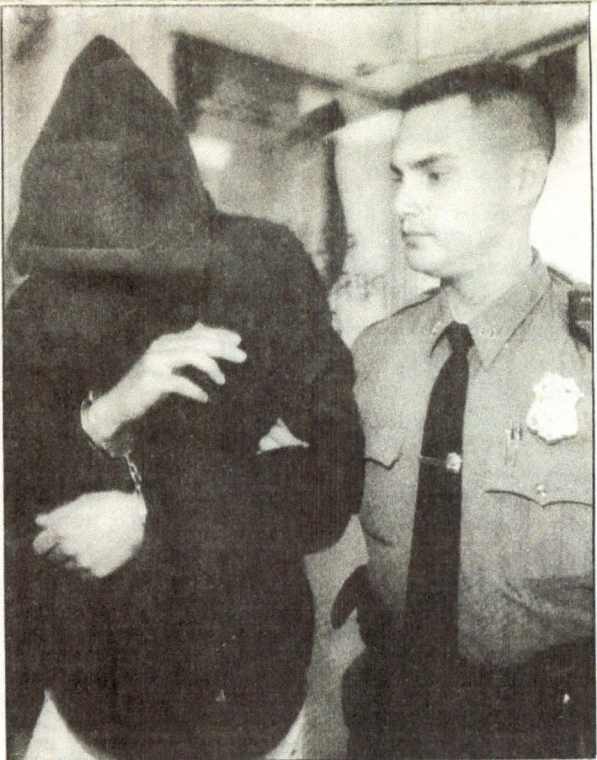

Joseph "Switch" Cestaro being led into court in Totowa. Cestaro and two others were arrested while painting a mural, police said.

All the while, Snow had been investigated and shadowed by Detective Donald Reddin. The hard-nosed Reddin earned the nickname "Detective Dirt" for being an extremely street smart individual and having a knack for deciphering the graffiti language of the streets of Paterson. He was the go-to cop when the city decided it was time to put an end to the graffiti epidemic plaguing its streets and neighborhoods. Snow was at the top of his list of targeted priority vandals. It would not take Det. Dirt that long to discover Snow's true identity. There was no internet, and with limited access to technology and resources, Reddin did it the hard and old fashioned way: by canvasing the streets and flipping informants to get the information he wanted.

PATERSON POLIC...

JUVENILE

TIME 10:41 AM

PATERSON

SUPPLEMEN

DEPARTMEN

PATERSON POLICE DEPARTMENT

...REPORT

MUNICIPAL COURT
CITY OF PATERSON
NEW JERSEY 07505

111 BROADW
PATERSON,

Writing on wall can tell cop plenty   Cops' graffiti expert tracks 'disease running rampant'

In order to understand what he was getting himself into, Reddin spent several years playing cat-n-mouse with the numerous graffiti vandals of Passaic County. He claims to have enjoyed his time and to have taken his responsibility to clean up Paterson very seriously. He was the type of cop to help you out if you were being honest. However, he was also the grimy detective who would "stick it to you" if you crossed him. He was the first cop in NJ to acquire a search warrant for graffiti. By the time he made the full-time switch from narcotics to gangs and juvenile, he had compiled a list of more than 750 graffiti tag names and aliases. He created a database that was ultimately used by the NJ State Police in an effort to thwart the growing vandalism issue in the Garden State. Reddin's massive, and diverse, experiences had helped him to finely tune his natural ability of figuring people out; A nice gift to have while trying to decode street names and street language in the inner city. He was the first and foremost expert on vandalism in NJ. While investigating Snow, Reddin noticed that Snow was different from many of the other graffiti writers. Snow was extremely sharp and highly intelligent. Reddin had implemented several tricks to gather evidence and catch vandals. One of these was to collect and match the discarded caps and spray paint cans usually left behind by other reckless youths. With Snow, there was no evidence left behind. A long way from the kid dubbed "walking evidence" by his father. This impressed Reddin. He was growing curious about this young man and tried to anticipate his next moves.

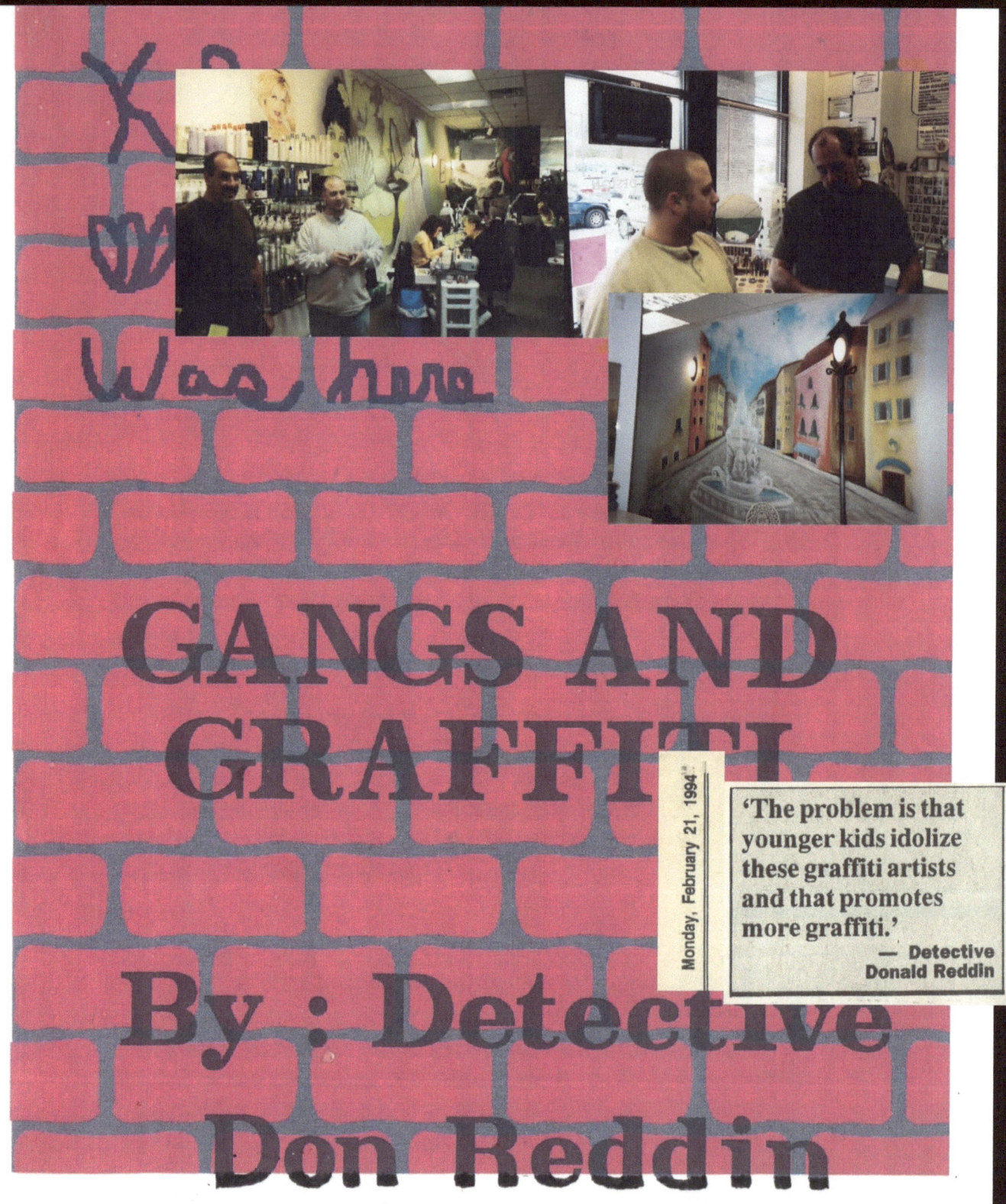

GANGS AND GRAFFITI

Monday, February 21, 1994

'The problem is that younger kids idolize these graffiti artists and that promotes more graffiti.'
— Detective Donald Reddin

By : Detective Don Reddin

Upon Detective Dirt and Snow's first encounter (at a legal wall the crew was painting, on Straight Street in Paterson), there was a bit of a shock for the elusive graffiti writer. He found out that Reddin had not only known who Snow was but had prior knowledge of his current and previous addresses. Constantly moving was how Snow had managed to stay one step ahead of the authorities thus far. You can imagine how this unnerved Snow by finding out that this veteran detective had very private information, details only known by Snow's closest friends and crewmates.

"Hello my name is The Hitman Leen, aka Leen One; originally of Crazy Kings and TMD, but now a loyal lifetime member of QM8. I have had the honor and opportunity to be involved with QM8 for many years now and have come to see the evolution of an incredible artist, mentor, brother, and dear friend, Snow. He has been an ongoing staple of graffiti, both in the NJ area and world wide. He has always been a brother before anything and I would fight till the end to support and defend him from all the ignorant haters that have become bumps in the road on his journey to be a street art master. In our circle we consider him the Golden Child, but dont tell him I told you that. Haha.

"When I first saw him, I knew he was gifted and had the determination that was going to make an impact in society and its cultural movement. The man has painted with some of the best artists in the world and has had the honor of getting and giving respect to all those he has come in contact with. I was inspired by not only his ability to be a great artist, but also because he is an amazing individual and has persevered through some very ignorant adversity. The art and the streets have given him the platform to go even harder at all the haters and find his ability to be the best at what he does. QM8 is, and has always been, a significant crew since the early '90s and has gone on to make a legacy for itself in the streets. With incredible masterpieces and killing all the spots, the crew has always been indestructable, while always us fans of the art are amazed with their ability to maintain a strong name in the graf world."

LEEN QM8

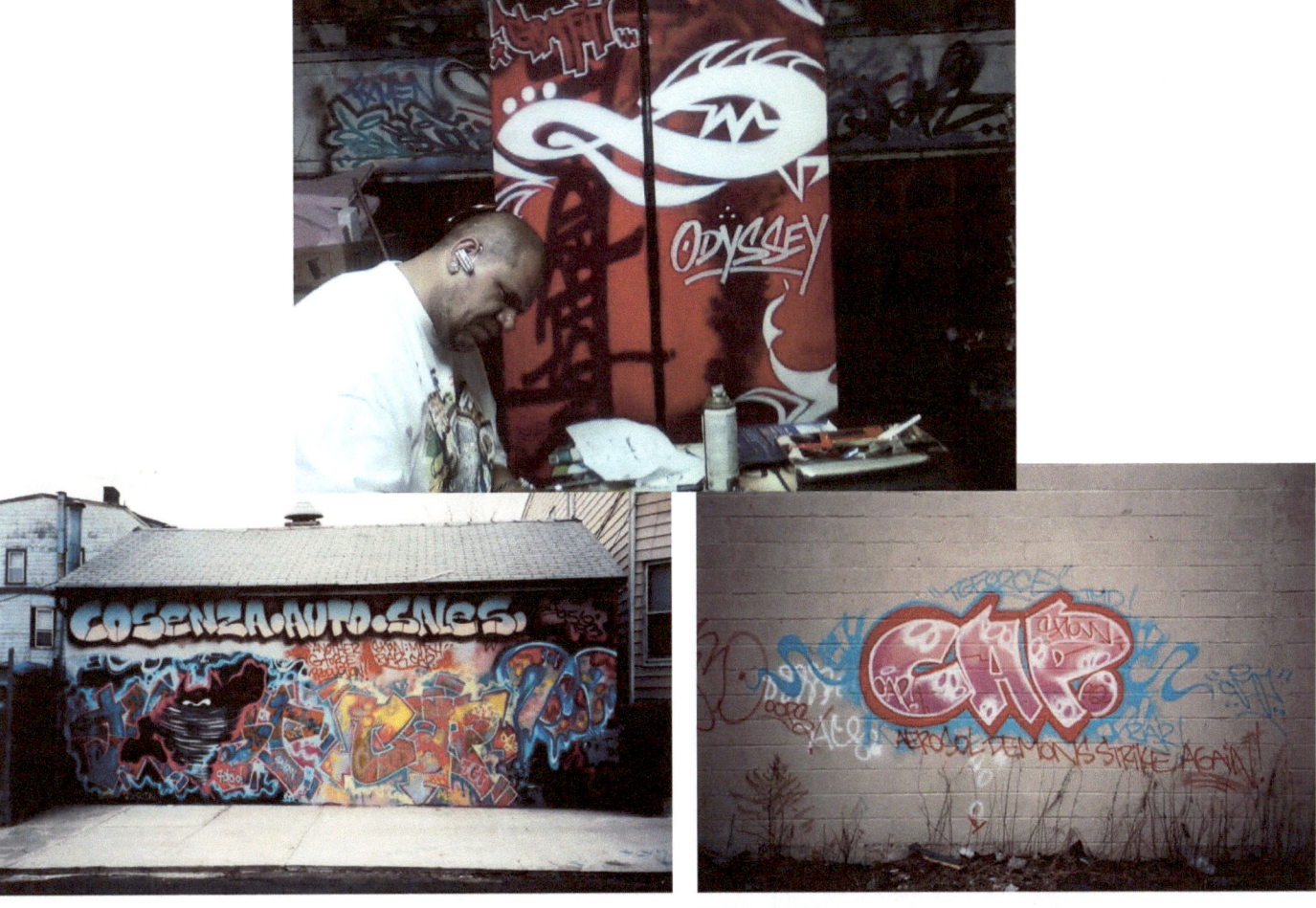

TWIST by SNOW, CAP by ZAR, and 7UP   CAP by SNOW

"Snow is one of the most dangerous graf heads out there. His skills are the sickest. His whole style and flow is just amazing. He is a stand up guy; honest, hard working, very creative, very focused, and a true brother. For many years, at least twice a month, we had detectives at our houses trying to get us to slip up. They basically started the graffiti task force in Paterson because of us (the QM8 Crew). Snow always stood up to beef with knowledge and respect, and was always ready to battle on walls or with hands. But most never wanted to battle him, because his skills have always been the sickest around."

SWITCH QM8

MATT RAINEY:The Herald & News

...ph A. Cestaro no longer vandalizes property with his art.

"We met at School 15 while I was having trouble on a wall. This was my first time during a mural and some certain bitch ass that talked me into doing it said he would help me do my outline and show me how to blend, etc. Well that punk ass left me like a fool, and I was getting mad and started to throw cans and was packing up to leave. Then out of the blue, a dude (Snow) walks up to me and asks me if everything's all good. I told him the situation, and he just started to help me. I did not know Snow at this time, but I knew of him. This was a big event, with people from NY and all over NJ there, and he did not have to take the time to stop and help me out. We've been brothers ever since."

SWITCH QM8

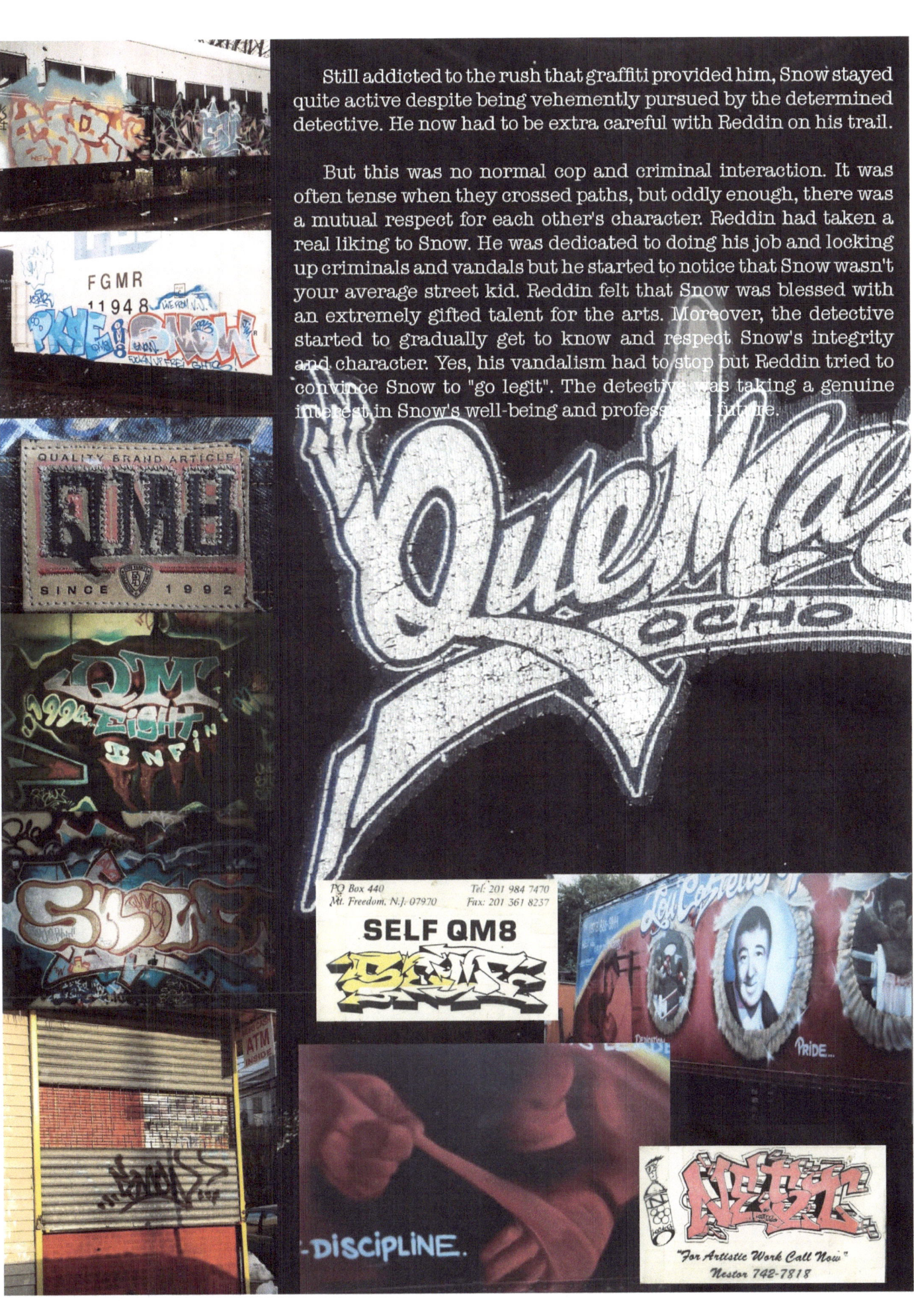

Still addicted to the rush that graffiti provided him, Snow stayed quite active despite being vehemently pursued by the determined detective. He now had to be extra careful with Reddin on his trail.

But this was no normal cop and criminal interaction. It was often tense when they crossed paths, but oddly enough, there was a mutual respect for each other's character. Reddin had taken a real liking to Snow. He was dedicated to doing his job and locking up criminals and vandals but he started to notice that Snow wasn't your average street kid. Reddin felt that Snow was blessed with an extremely gifted talent for the arts. Moreover, the detective started to gradually get to know and respect Snow's integrity and character. Yes, his vandalism had to stop but Reddin tried to convince Snow to "go legit". The detective was taking a genuine interest in Snow's well-being and professional future.

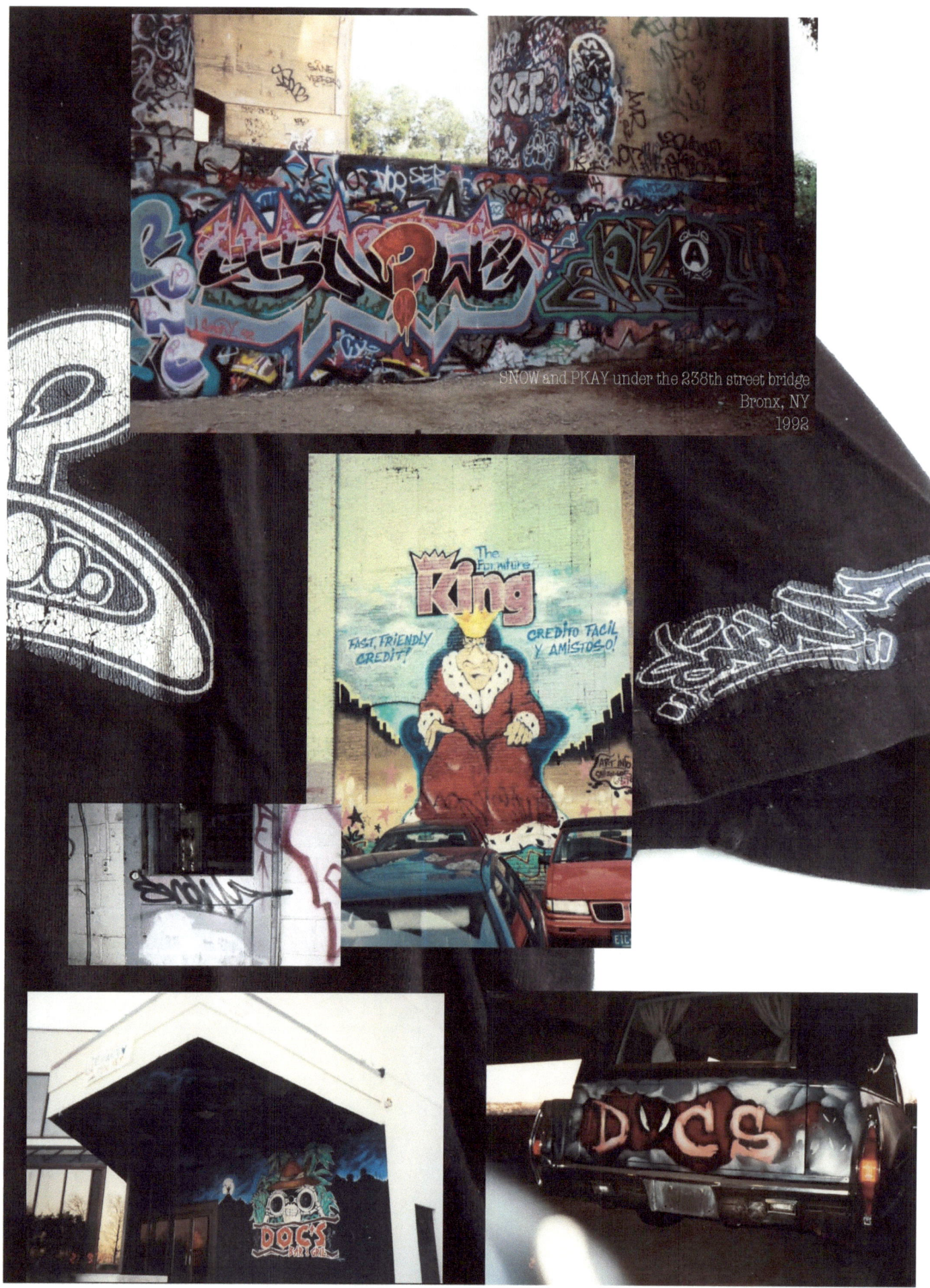

SNOW and PKAY under the 238th street bridge
Bronx, NY
1992

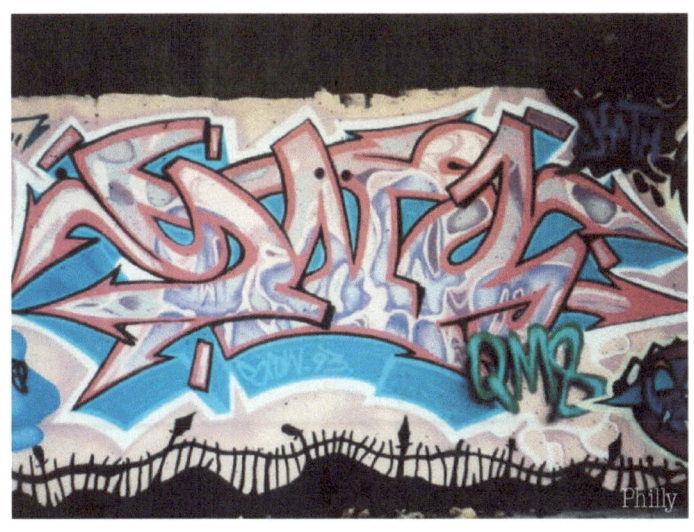

Philly

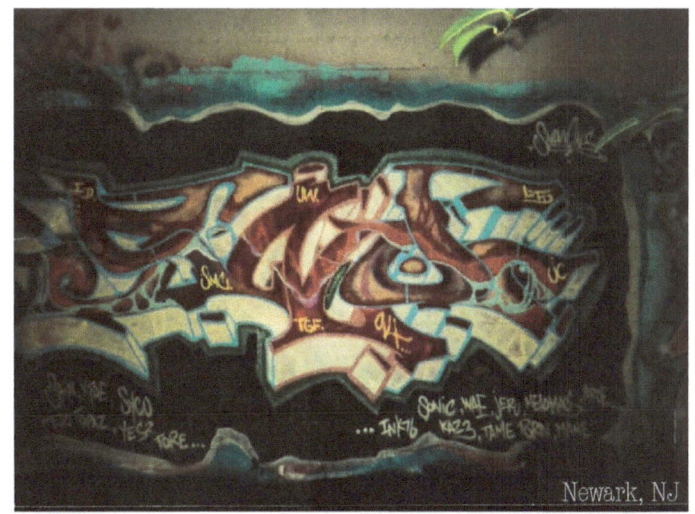

Newark, NJ

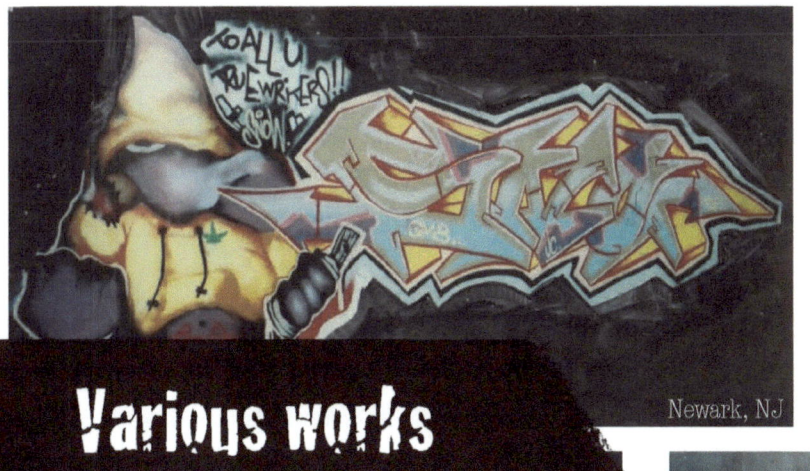

Various works

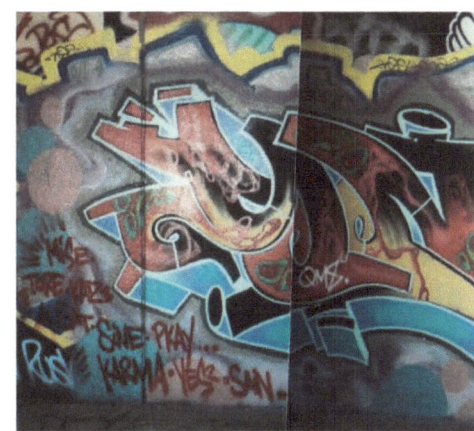

Newark, NJ

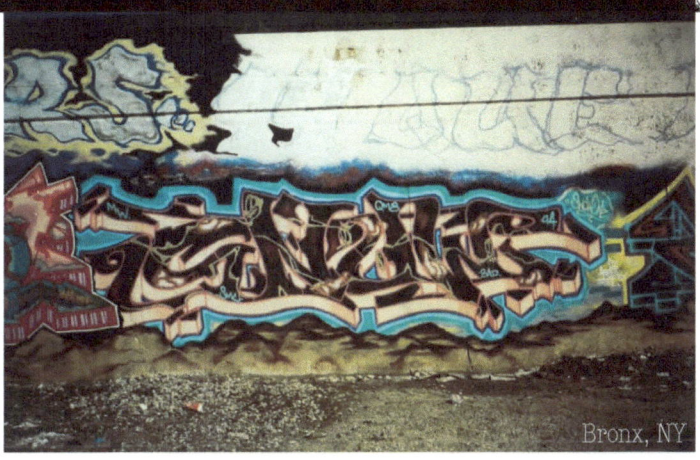

Bronx, NY

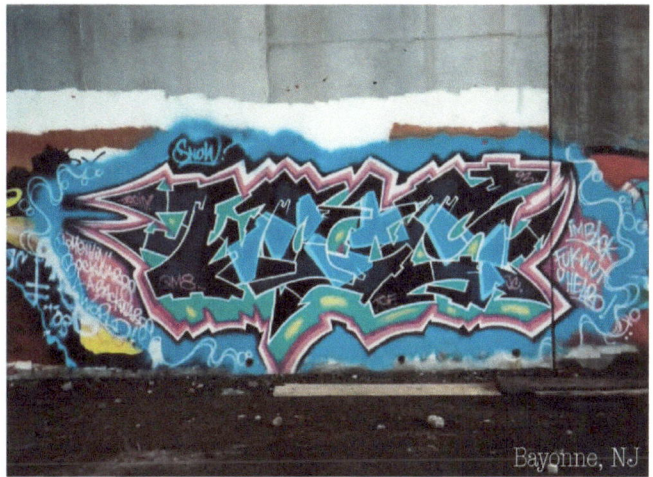

Bayonne, NJ

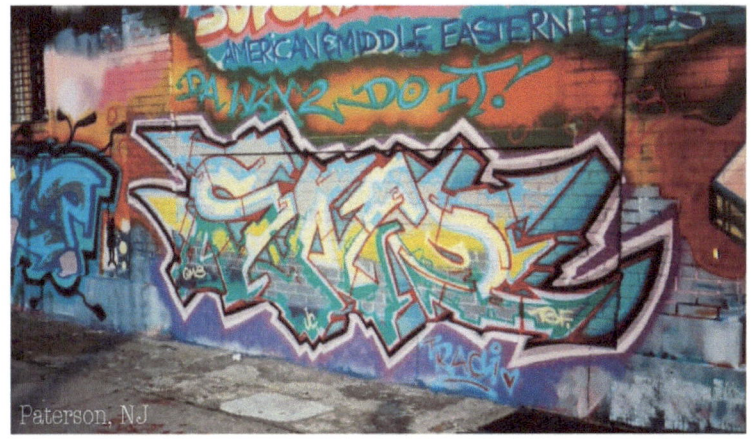

Paterson, NJ

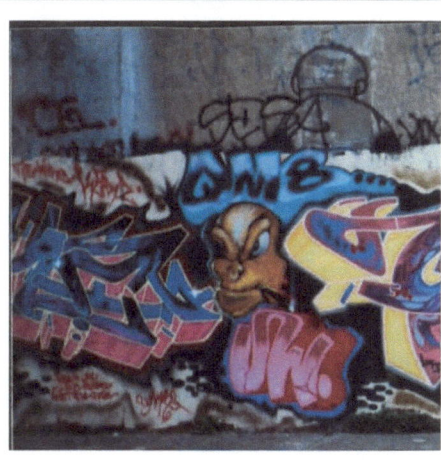

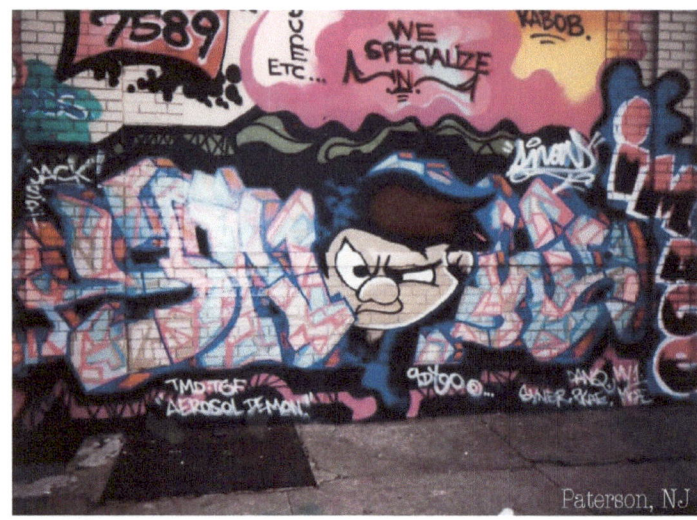

Paterson, NJ

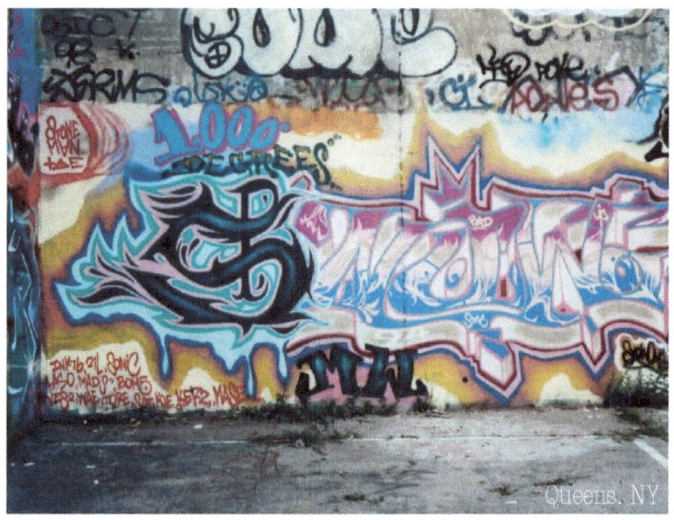

Queens, NY

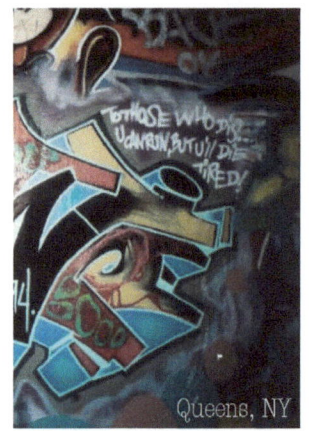

Queens, NY

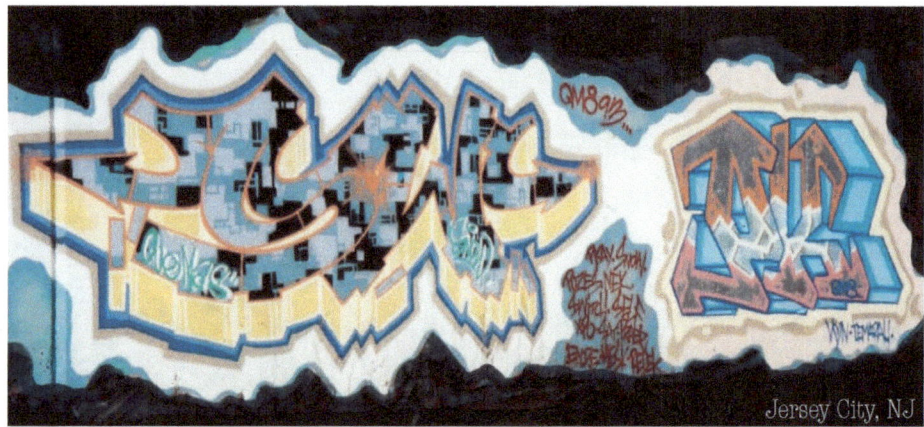

Jersey City, NJ

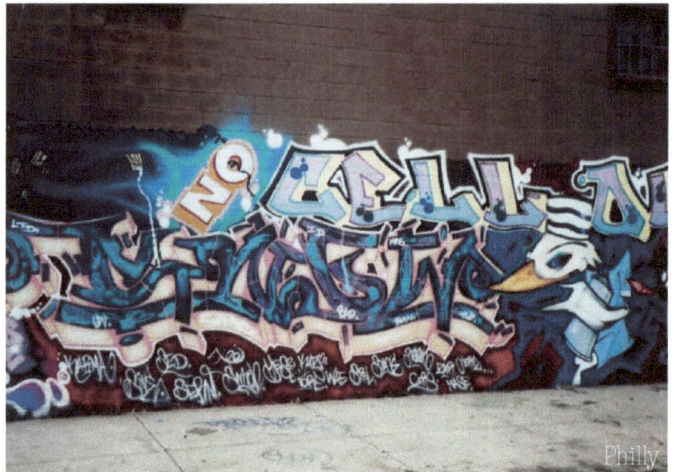

Philly

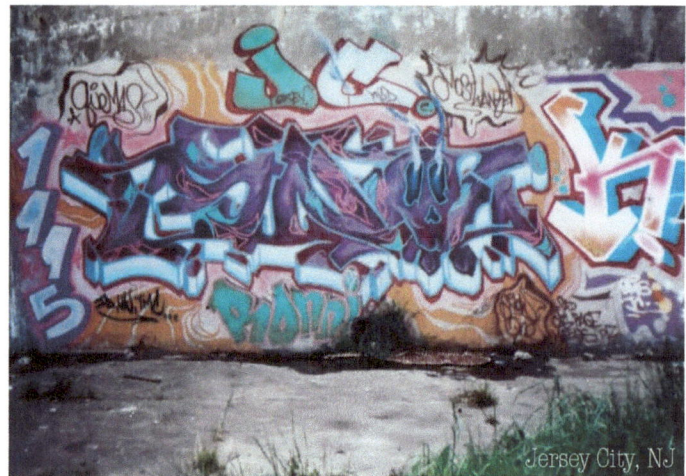

Jersey City, NJ

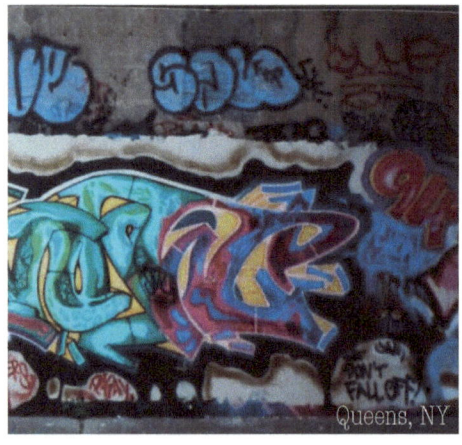

Queens, NY

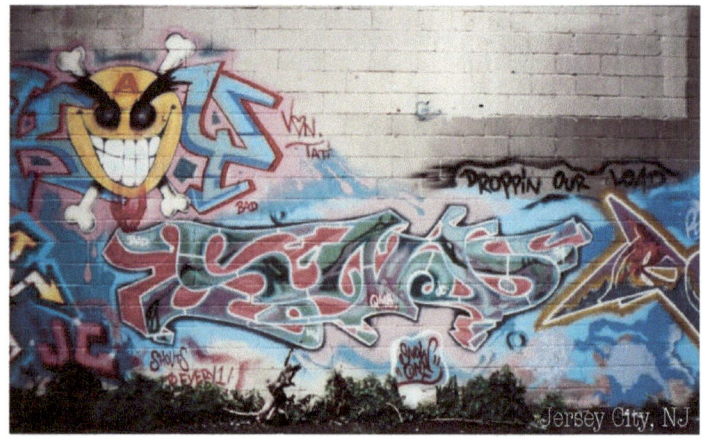

Jersey City, NJ

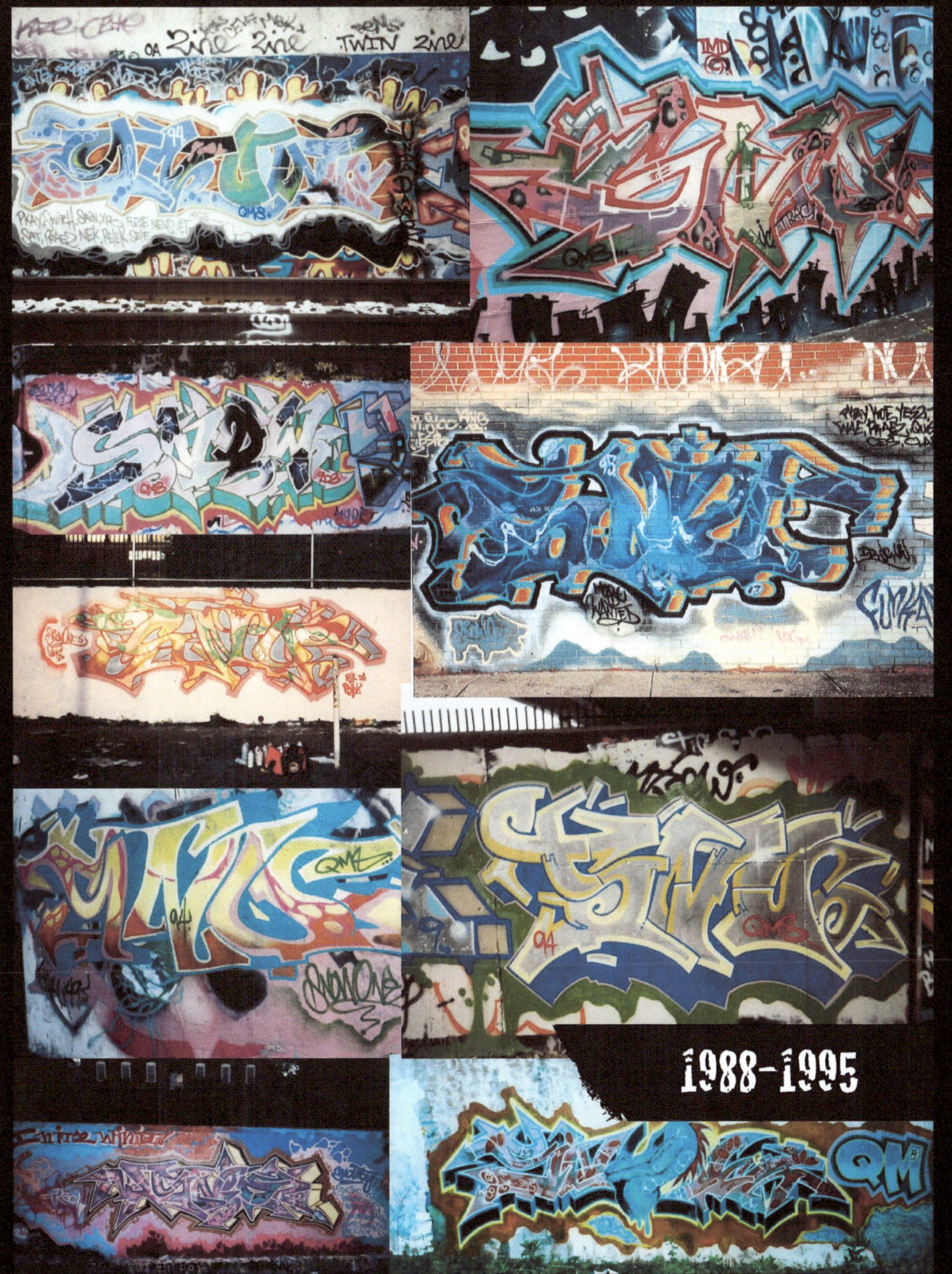

1988-1995

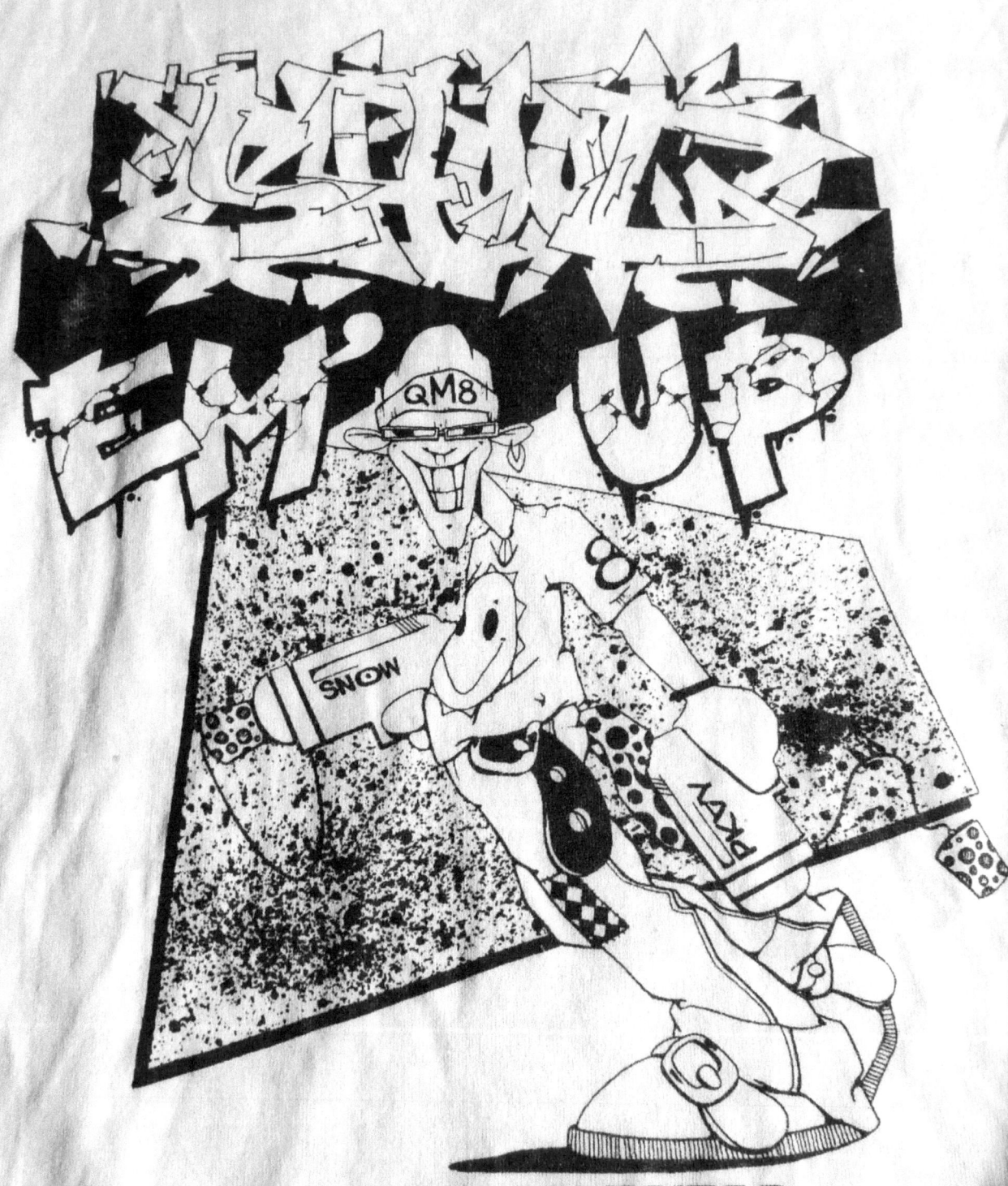

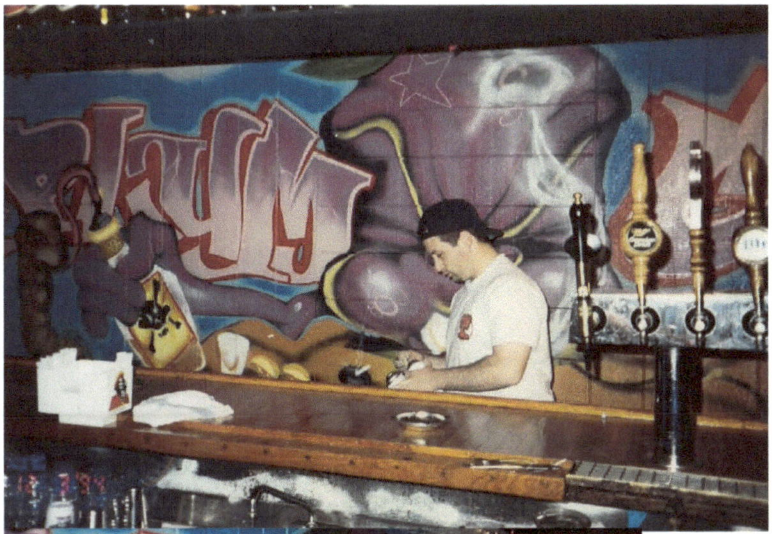

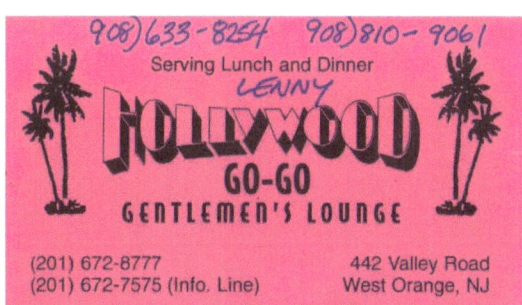

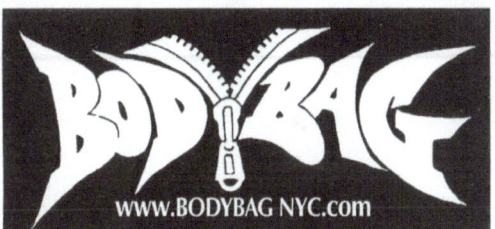

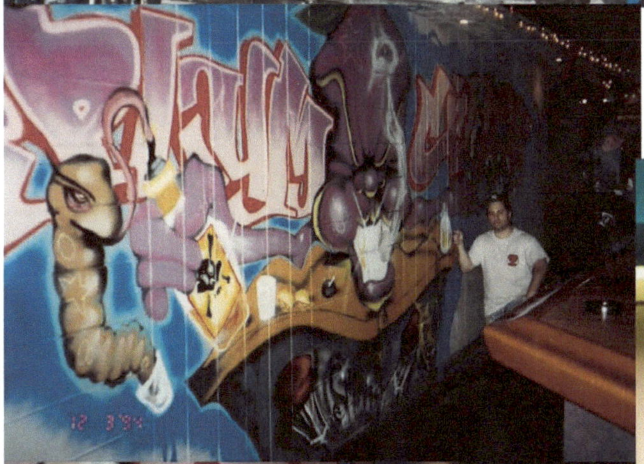

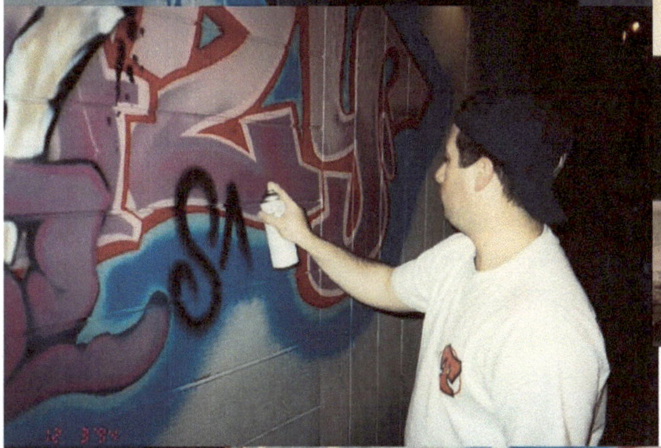

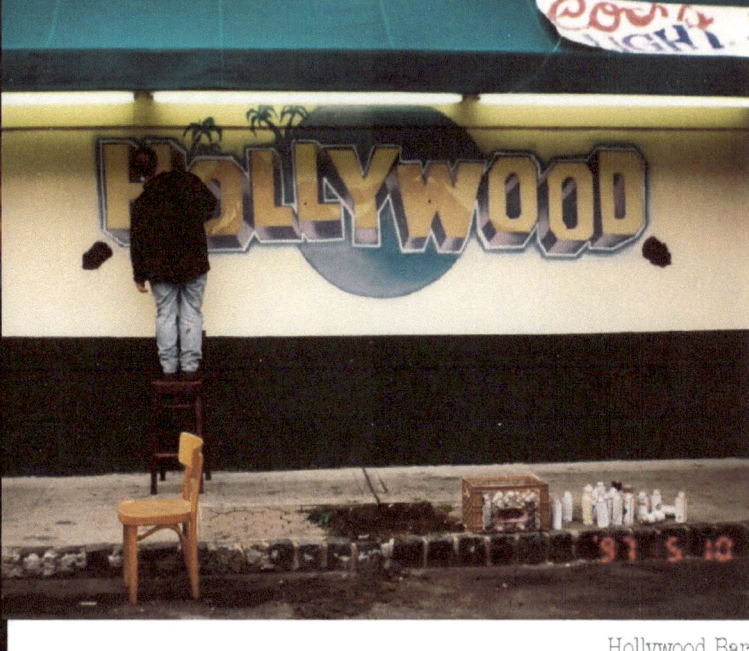

Hollywood Bar
West Orange, NJ
1997
Lenny Schilizzi (RIP)

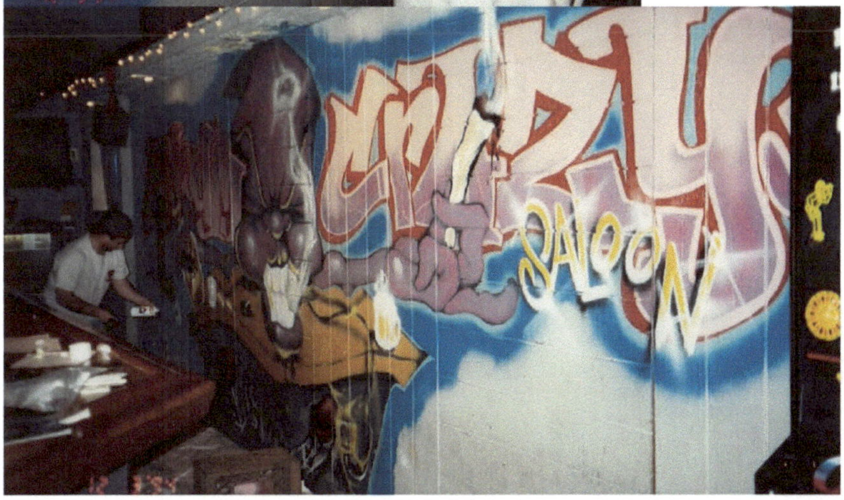

Plum Crazy Saloon
Clifton, NJ
1994

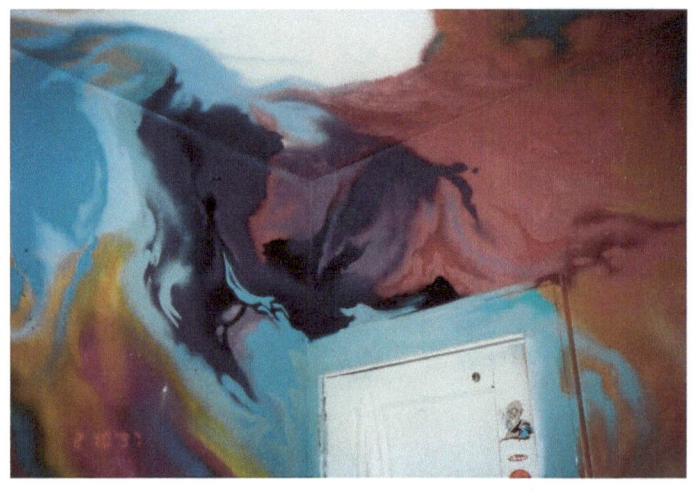 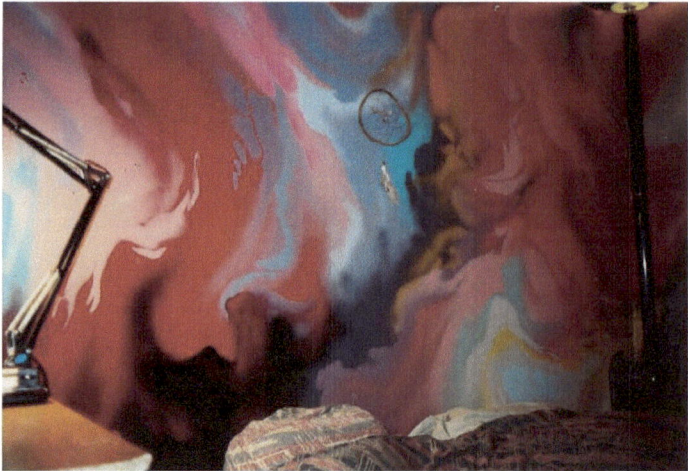

Abstract room
1997

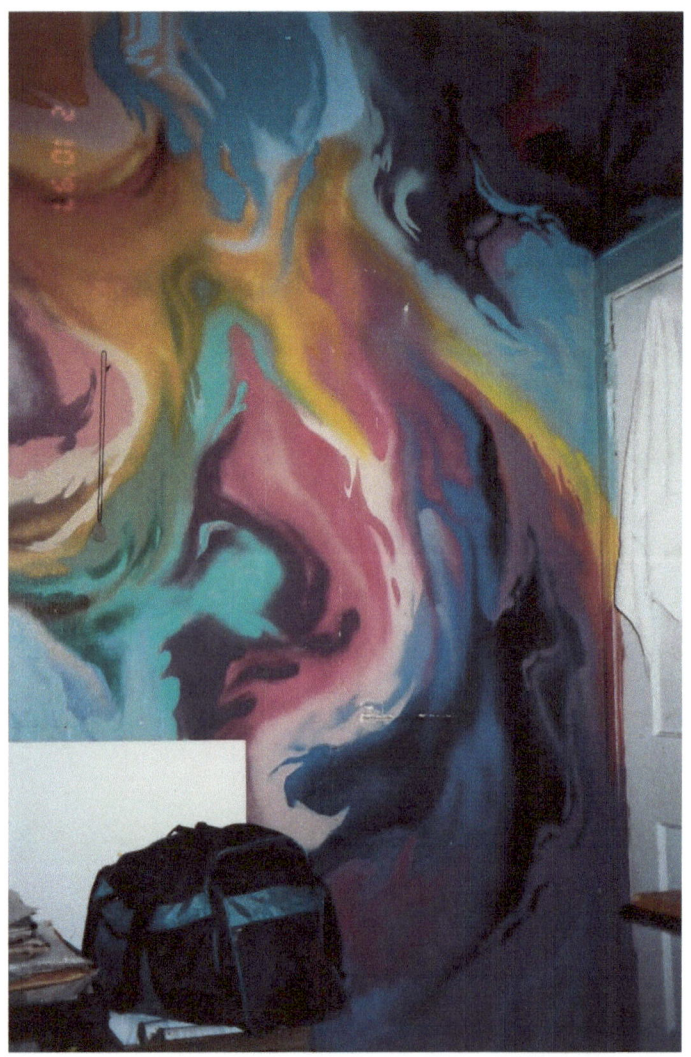

"This was a very experimental period in my life. There was a lot of growth during this time. I was exploring many different creative outlets and modes of thought. Different processes, different mediums, and different mindstates were the norm during this tumultous but productive chapter of my life."

SNOW

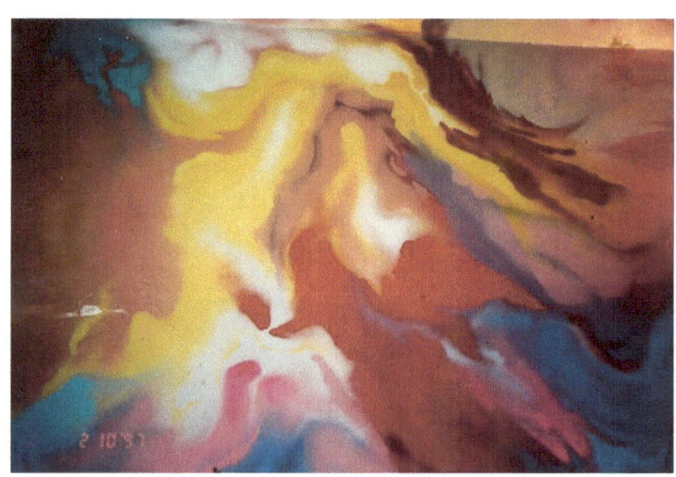

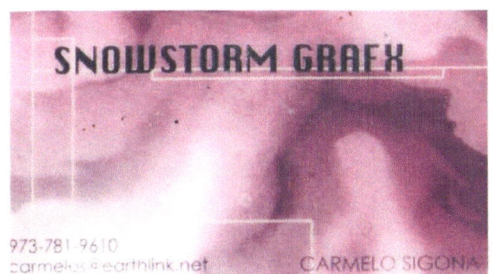
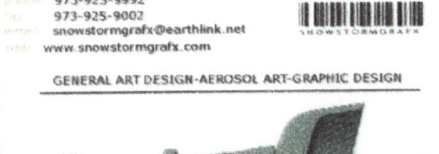
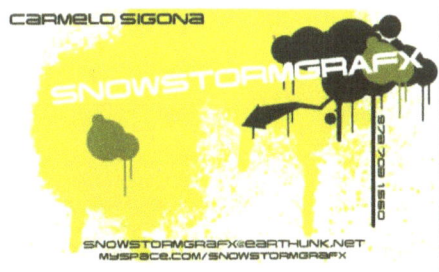

SNOWSTORM GRAFX
973-925-9992
973-925-9002
snowstormgrafx@earthlink.net
www.snowstormgrafx.com
GENERAL ART DESIGN-AEROSOL ART-GRAPHIC DESIGN
973-781-9610
carmelos@earthlink.net
CARMELO SIGONA
CARMELO SIGONA
SNOWSTORMGRAFX
SNOWSTORMGRAFX@EARTHLINK.NET
MYSPACE.COM/SNOWSTORMGRAFX

"Snowstorm Grafx LLC was officially started in 1996. Throughout the years, I changed the look and feel of the logo and the brand while trying to stay relevant with the times. It was my dream to own and operate my own commercial art studio, and I recall these times with fondness and deep sentiment."

SNOW

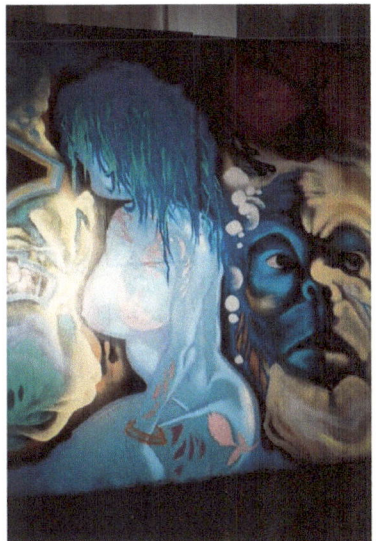
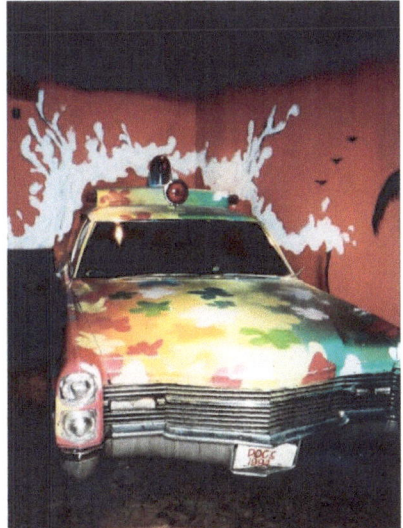
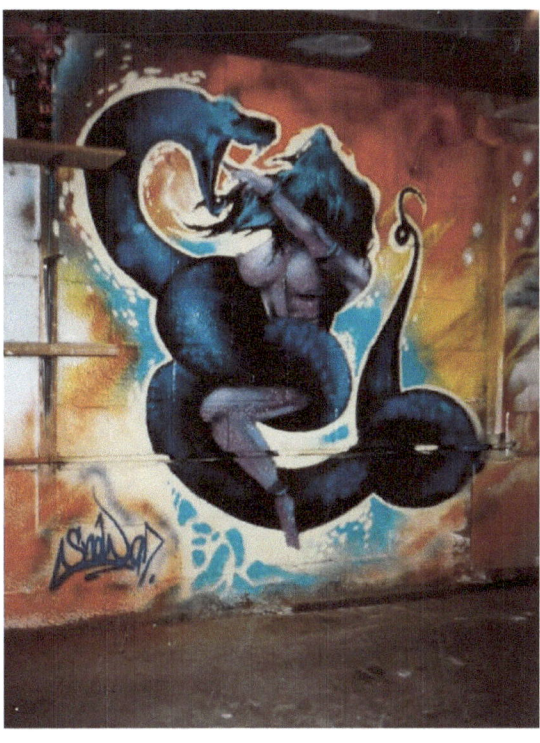

First mural done at the Ringside Pub
Caldwell, NJ
1994

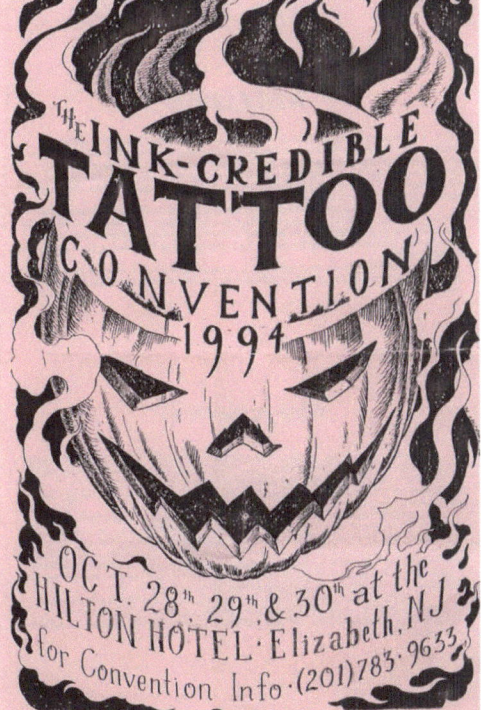
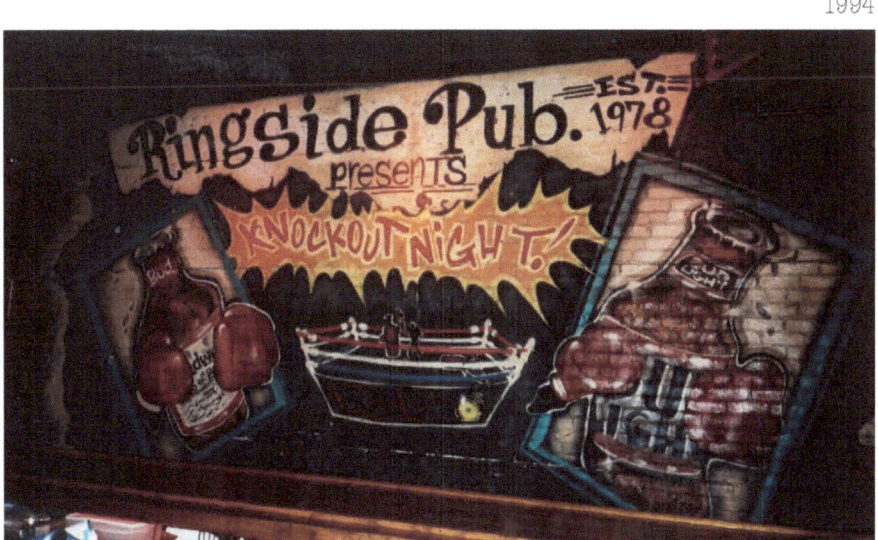

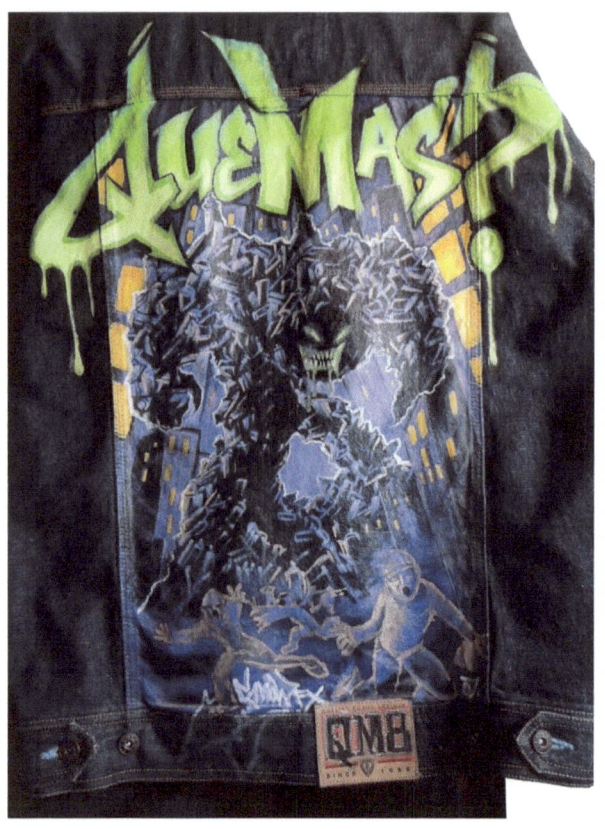

After Snow's arrest, Reddin told Snow he thought that he could be financially successful if he would just channel his energy and talent in a more positive and productive direction, echoing the words uttered so many times previously by his parents. Reddin took personal responsibility by offering to find Snow projects where he could be paid for his talents. The street art and graffiti culture was growing across the globe, and with all the treachery and hatred Snow was dealing with in the streets of Paterson, along with the legal and financial mess he had brought upon himself, Snow started to seriously consider the advice of Detective Donald "DIRT" Reddin. He started to see the futility of his path and was opening his mind to begin anew and move his life in a more positive direction. Reddin told Snow, "You are on a journey, and your talents can bring you prosperity instead of stress and strife. Your art will make you rich; you just have to give it a shot and take the first step." Snow asked, "Who would hire me?" Reddin "answered" by finding Snow more and more work. Reddin stayed true to his word. The two men formed a strong bond and have a friendship to this very day. It was the genuine words of wisdom, the mutual respect, and admiration that got through to Snow. Snow started believing in himself and set out to build a career as a professional artist.

After a brief period living on City Island in the Bronx where he started to paint more and more in the borough dubbed "the mecca of Hip Hop", he decided to consolidate his three jobs and was fortunate to take a position with Dun and Bradstreet, a fortune 500 company. Snow worked nights and weekends as a mural artist. Thanks to the foundation his parents had instilled in him and the guidance of Don Reddin, Snow was gradually starting to place his troubled past behind him. He continued his love of street art but channeled it in a more positive direction, as he ceased *most* of his late night missions. He truly started to flourish and made a more conscious effort to consider the consequences of his actions.

All the while, graffiti and street art were growing worldwide...

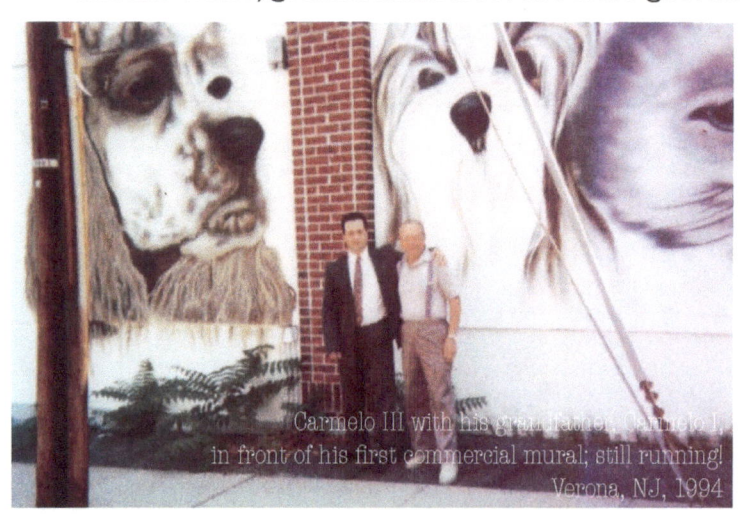

Carmelo III with his grandfather, Carmelo I,
in front of his first commercial mural; still running!
Verona, N.J. 1994

Carmelo A. Sigona
Sales Support Specialist
Small Business Services

**Dun & Bradstreet
Information Services**

a company of
The Dun & Bradstreet Corporation

Three Sylvan Way
Parsippany, NJ 07054
201-605-6879

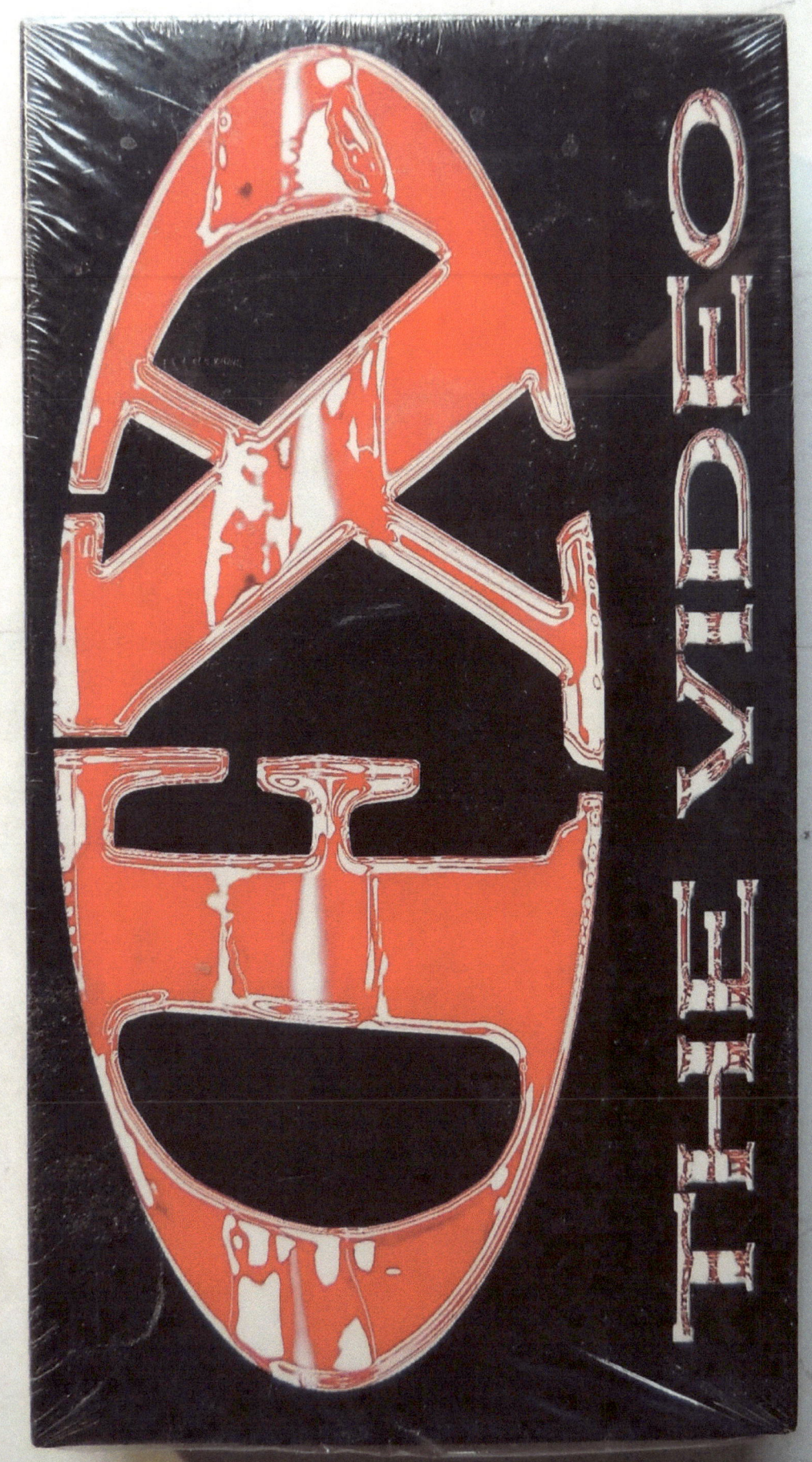

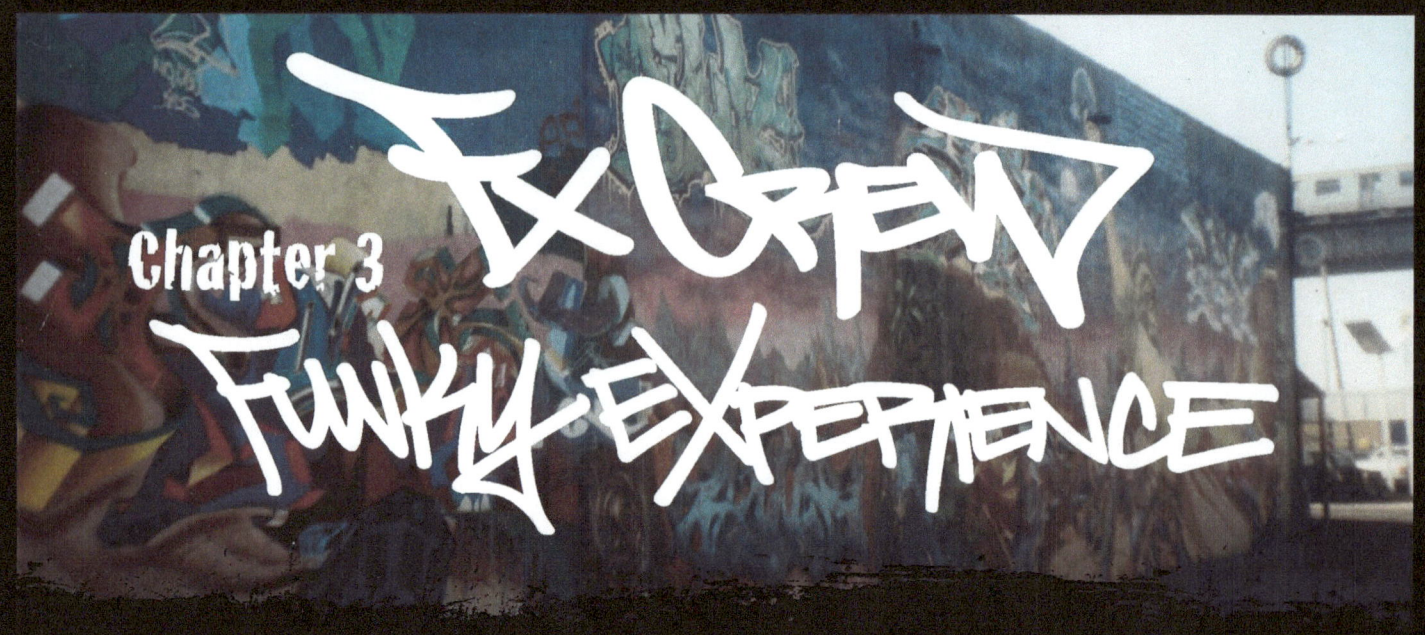

Chapter 3
FX Crew
Funky Experience

By 1994, Snow was really getting a hold on his life. He began to control that lack of structure that his father was so concerned about earlier in his life. He was employed full-time at Dun and Bradstreet Corporation. His art was also providing a steady income stream for himself. He started to work with McFarlane Toys as well. Snow's life was "snowballing" in the right direction. But it was his graffiti art and name that was about to reach a whole new level. He had already achieved graffiti "King" status in New Jersey, capping it off with his infamous and storied run with the QM8 Crew.

Stepping back a moment to 1993; the future graffiti legend was living on City Island in the Bronx. There, he spent much time painting with graffiti style masters, legends, and subway pioneers. He would prove himself worthy to hang and keep pace with graffiti's elite writers. He continued to turn heads in the Bronx as the "kid from Jersey". He did eventually move back to his side of the Hudson River. And though in New Jersey, he still traveled to the Bronx regularly to paint with his contemporaries. Though still a member of his NJ based crews, Snow was shifting his focus more and more into pursuing a solo career.

In 1995, Snow was approached by his dear friend CES and his partner PER of the FX Crew to join, what many say, was the most talented graffiti roster of all time. They invited Snow to get down with their crew and like the 27 Yankees, they were a virtual All Star squad of graffiti artists. Though many have come and gone, the crew had once boasted an impressive lineup of the following members: PER, POEM, POSE2, CES, SUB, COPE2, SERVE, TKID 170, NOMAD, CLARK, YES2, EAZ, KERZ, KINGBEE, VASE, DAIM, HESH, LOOMIT, TOAST, SKE, REK, KENT, DARE, and SEW. Each with a unique set of talents and skills, each with his own style and extensive history. This contributed to the crew's excellence and notoriety.

RIZE, CES, YES2, SNOW, SUB, PER, POEM
1997

Many years later the crew would once again expand with a whole new generation of international and top tier talent: HEF, PEETA, DUCK, HEX, MEK, MUSE, PASE, KAIS, ABE, INFA, JEW, SUCH, DECK, YES1, KES, WIKED, PILOT, GORE, and BELIN.

It takes the best to recognize the best. This happened when Snow received a call from YES2, telling him that he had just been riding on the 6 train near Castle Hill Avenue. As the train was slowly moving, YES2 explained that he was looking down at the freshly painted *3 Horsemen* wall that PER, CES, and SNOW had just done. It was a pleasant surprise to watch SEEN UA posing with his wife in front of the new FX Crew wall. This was a positive sign that the crew was doing big things, but more attention was to come.

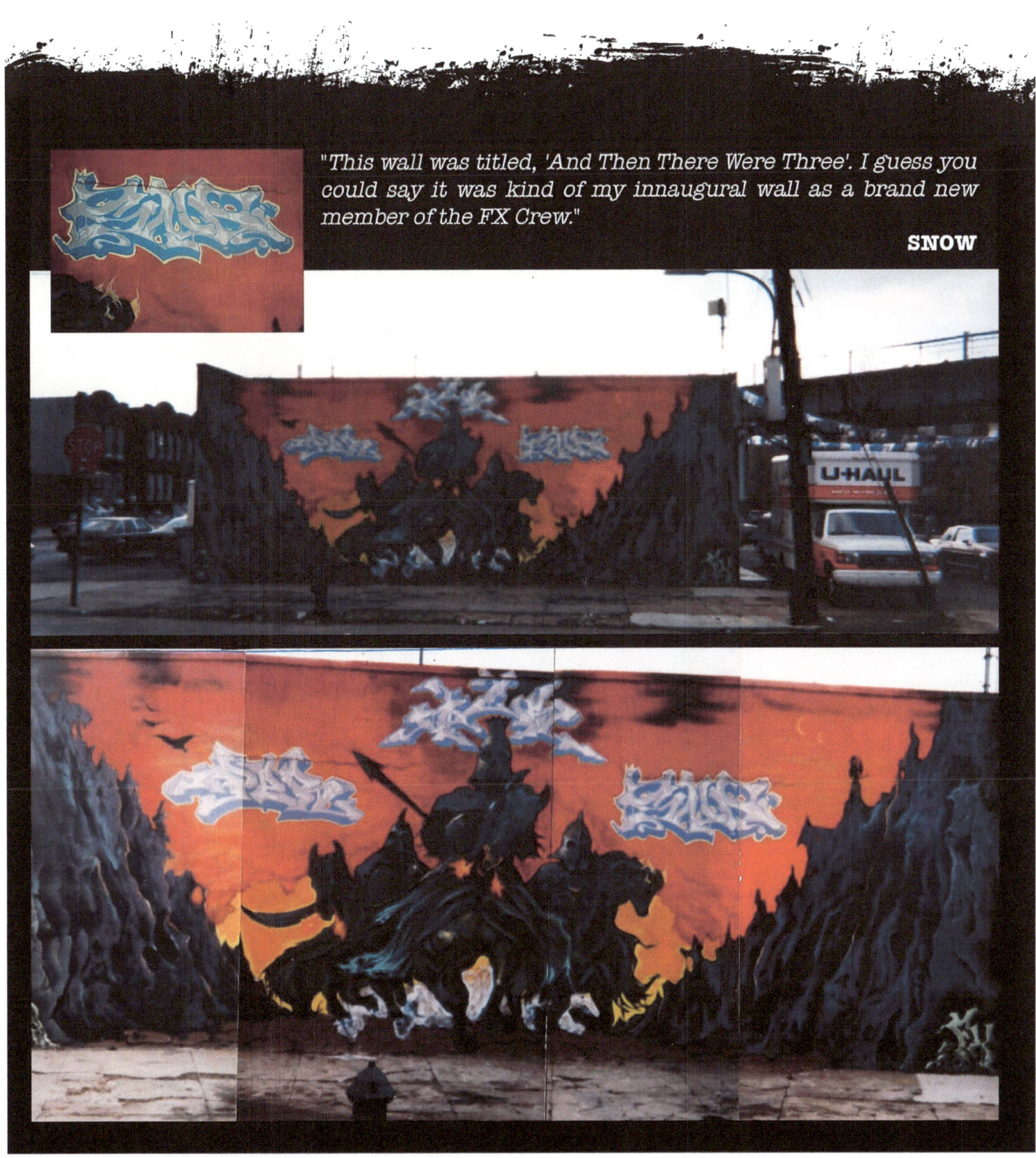

"This wall was titled, 'And Then There Were Three'. I guess you could say it was kind of my innaugural wall as a brand new member of the FX Crew."

SNOW

By 1996, the FX Crew was regularly being featured in the graffiti art videos and magazines like The Source Magazine, XXL, Rap Pages, etc., and the crew was flourishing as one of the best in the world.

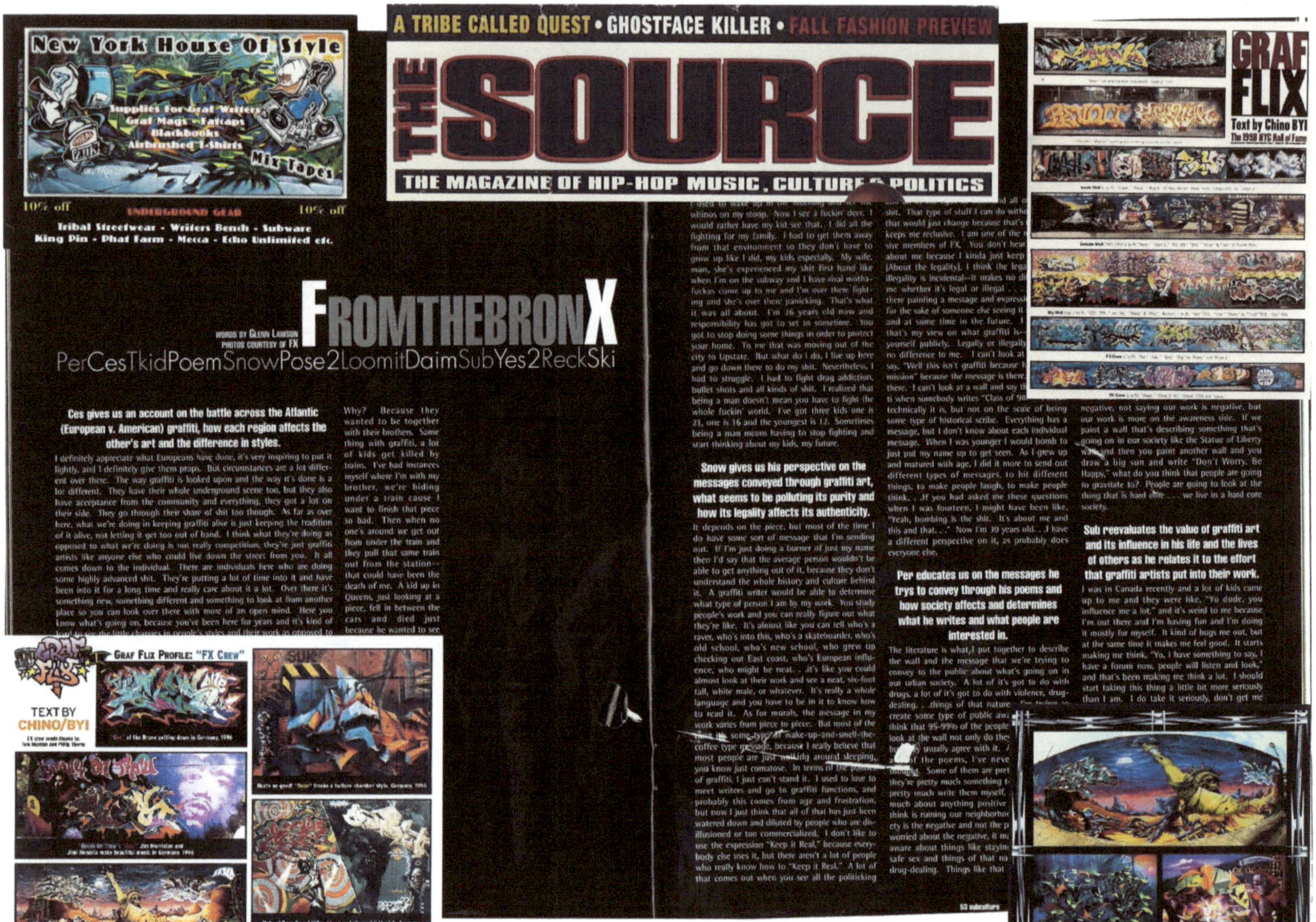

A TRIBE CALLED QUEST • GHOSTFACE KILLER • FALL FASHION PREVIEW

THE SOURCE

THE MAGAZINE OF HIP-HOP MUSIC, CULTURE & POLITICS

GRAF FLIX

Text by Chino BYI
The 1996 NYC Hall of Fame

FROMTHEBRONX

WORDS BY GLENN LAWSON
PHOTOS COURTESY OF FX

PerCesTkidPoemSnowPose2LoomitDaimSubYes2ReckSki

Ces gives us an account on the battle across the Atlantic (European v. American) graffiti, how each region affects the other's art and the difference in styles.

Snow gives us his perspective on the messages conveyed through graffiti art, what seems to be polluting its purity and how its legality affects its authenticity.

Per educates us on the messages he tries to convey through his poems and how society affects and determines what he writes and what people are interested in.

Sub reevaluates the value of graffiti art and its influence in his life and the lives of others as he relates it to the effort that graffiti artists put into their work.

Graf Flix Profile: "FX Crew"

TEXT BY CHINO/BYI

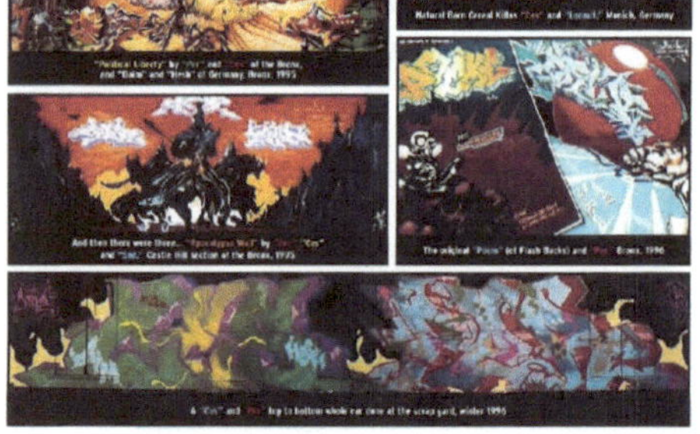

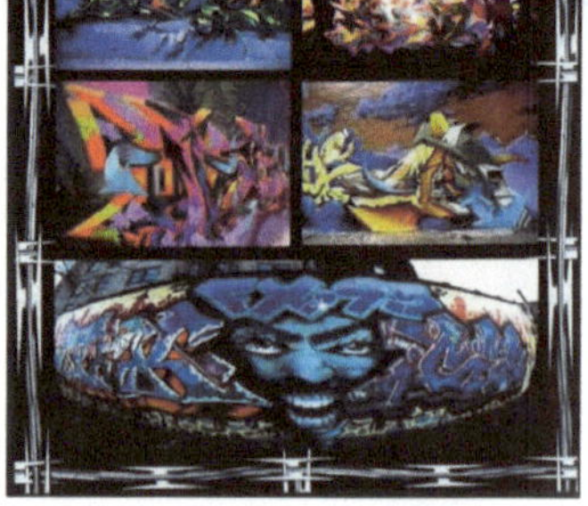

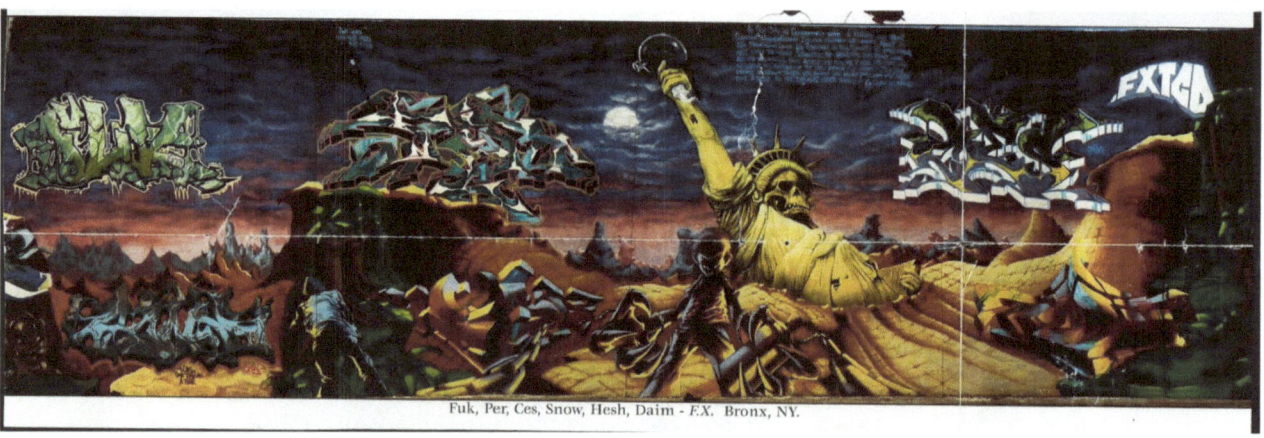

"My mom called me from Florida and told me that my sister showed her which Hip-Hop magazines our works appeared in. My mom was so proud."

SNOW

Fuk, Per, Ces, Snow, Hesh, Daim - F.X. Bronx, NY.

Early in the wee hours of the morning of March 9, 1997, SNOW, SERVE, and PER were getting ready to get an early start on a commercial project they had planned to work on. Snow had taken off time from work, again, to participate in the job. While loading the van, they heard on the radio that Notorious BIG had been tragically shot to death. They paused with sadness and then briefly discussed, while quickly agreeing, to scratch the plan to paint the job and pay tribute to the fallen rapper instead. The trio was met at the wall in progress by CES, HEF, and SIENIDE of the Bronx. Together, the crew painted a colorful memorial and cultural commentary on violence in Hip Hop. The wall was quickly given an overwhelming amount of press, and the media swarmed the artists as they finished the wall. *The NY Post*, *Time* and *People magazine*, *The Village Voice*, and numerous TV news channels all covered the story and the mural. Even Bad Boy Records sent the crew a thank you card for the talented artwork. Incidentally, not only did Snow's family, now in Florida, see the newscasts, but it also caught the attention of Snow's boss at Dun and Bradstreet, who watched the story on the news.

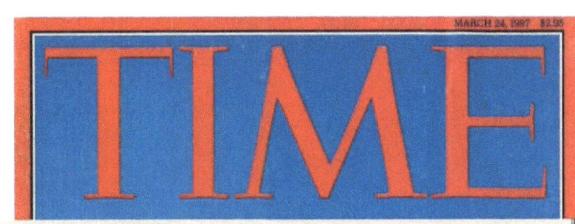

MARCH 24, 1987 $2.95

TIME

14 ★★R   NEW YORK POST, MONDAY, MARCH 10, 1997

RAP WAR

Violence stalks world of gangsta rappers

By DEVLIN BARRETT

The violent world of gangsta rap is full of deadly real-life feuds between competing labels and stars who act out much of the vicious street-gang violence they rap about.

Notorious B.I.G., whose real name was Christopher Wallace, is the second titan of the gangsta rap world to be killed in the past year, but the industry has a long, sordid record of violent crime.

In the past few years, many of the attacks on rappers have been blamed on a vicious feud between the two industry powerhouses, the Bad Boy label on the East Coast and Death Row Records on the West Coast.

The rap sheet for rappers includes:

■ The murder of Tupac Shakur in a drive-by shooting last September in Las Vegas while riding with Death Row exec Suge Knight. He died seven days later as a result of his wounds.

It was the second time Shakur had been shot in less than two years.

In a 1994 attack, Shakur was shot five times and robbed of $40,000 worth of jewelry in the lobby of a Midtown Manhattan recording studio.

He lost a testicle in the attack, which he said was executed by men taking

orders from Bad Boy.

■ Murder charges against Snoop Doggy Dogg of Death Row in 1995. He was later acquitted of the charges.

■ The 1995 slaying of rapper Stretch Walker, who was killed in what police believe was an execution.

■ The fatal crushing of nine people at a celebrity rap basketball game at City College sponsored by Sean "Puffy" Combs, founder of Bad Boy.

Some of rap's brightest stars are former gang members with long criminal records, and acts of brutal violence follow them even after selling millions of records.

Ice T, who caused a furor in 1992 with the release of a song titled "Cop Killer," was a member of an L.A. gang and served hard time in California prisons before becoming a recording star.

Knight, another former gang member, was convicted of robbery and assault in 1994 after becoming one of the most successful executives in the rap world.

Just last month, he was sentenced to nine years in prison for violating probation on that charge.

And Wallace, murdered yesterday, was a teen-age crack dealer in Bedford-Stuyvesant before he hit the big time.

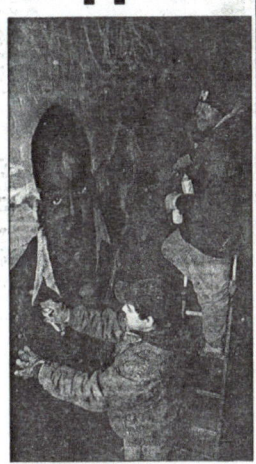

IN MEMORIUM: The FX Crew pays tribute to slain rapper Biggie Smalls with a mural at Westchester and Wards avenues in The Bronx.   *Post* Gary Miller

...ays the FBI is trying... ...ween East Coast... 'Whether we accept... ...ups are a move... ...is serving a 60-... ...prison in Atlanta... ...d-car robbery in... ...government has... ...ap industry."

...MUSIC WAS OF-...sed on such...-intrigue, gang-...naraderie, killers'...wait. On his new...e even raps about...onitored by the...t while in inter-...is felonious past,...yed a loathing for...the song *Some*-...new CD, he hunts...ver, as he shoots...holding a child...of his own.) The...pirer, director of...entary *Rhyme &*...thing I ever had to...cing the transition...g nigger to, like, a...

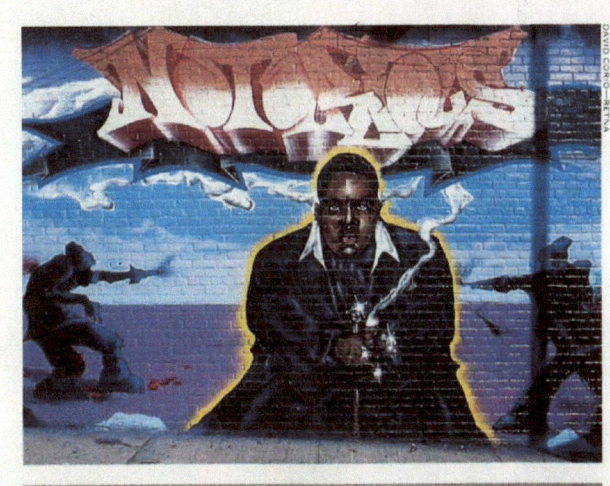

■ VIEWPOINT ■

Farai Chideya

All Eyez on Us

...the hip-hop generation to get real

...RATION ALL ABOUT VIOLENCE AND DEGRADATION? ARE ...ed to go the way of Tupac Shakur and Biggie Smalls? ...m a member of that generation. In the weeks to come, ...se of the death of two of the youngest, richest, best-...erica, we'll probably succumb to a natural temptation ..." from the "hip-hop kids." I'm not buying it. I grew ...In elementary school I tuned my radio to the techno-

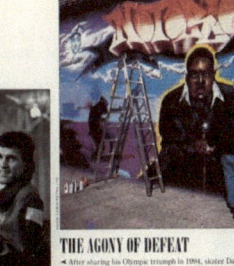

People weekly

March 24, 1997
Vol. 47, No. 11

THE AGONY OF DEFEAT
◄ After sharing his Olympic triumph in 1994, skater Dan Jansen's wife is reeling over the split. "I still love him," says Robin (with Dan and daughter Jane that March). **61**

BAD RAP
▲ Fans remember gangsta rapper Notorious B.I.G., shot down in L.A. **69**

COVER STORY
▼ With her parents in seclusion and the police on the defensive, questions about JonBenét Ramsey's brutal murder grow more complex. **108**

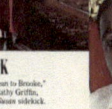

FAST TRACK
▲ "It's fun being mean to Brooke," says acid-tongued Kathy Griffin, *Suddenly Susan* sidekick. **91**

MAIL • 4
PICKS & PANS • 15
THE INSIDER • 17
STYLE WATCH • 95
PASSAGES • 116
FIRST LOOK • 123
PUZZLER • 130
CHATTER • 142

STAR TRACKS • 6
Matthew McConaughey tops himself. Prince Charles and Princess Diana do double duty for the kids. Whitney Houston goes to the circus, and more

UP FRONT
48 • A quarter-century after Marlon Brando, Al Pacino and others gave us *The Godfather*, some of the stars look back on the movie and their lives

56 • His sixteenth-year-round illness is recounted in *DEW former Rep. Pete Peterson is recounted*

CLONES • 72
Screen newcomer Skeet Ulrich (*Scream* and *Truck*) insists he's no Johnny Depp-elginger

DISCOVERY • 75
On a routine run across the River Almond, Scottish ferryman Robert Graham caught the eye of a rare—and long submerged—Roman sculpture

INTRODUCING • 88
Australian-reared Jorge Rademacher stirs Slatkin in his U.S. TV debut on *General Hospital's* Ice

ON THE MOVE • 91
As Brooke Shields's sparring partner on NBC's *Suddenly Susan*, Kathy Griffin finds a prime-(time) outlet for her acerbic wit

SCREEN • 97
Like most overnight sensations, *Sling Blade's* double-Oscar nominee Billy Bob Thornton struggled for years before lightning struck

UPDATE • 105
Despite haunting memories of his years in Viet-...

J.C. Watts Jr. takes his plays to Washington, scoring points as a hard-hitting conservative

TO THE TOP • 145
In a bestseller, Dr. Jason Theodosakis says he has found *The Arthritis Cure*: He feels it in his bones

JOCKS • 148
If Caltech's basketball team ranks as the smartest in the NCAA, their numbers on the court are more than a bit lower

On location: The making of the Selena movie

MARCH 24, 1997

People weekly

NOTORIOUS B.I.G.: Another rap victim

JENNIFER LOPEZ as the slain singer

JonBenét's unsolved murder

WHAT'S

March 25, 1997 • Vol. XLII No. 12 • America's Largest Weekly Newspaper • $1.25

the village VOICE

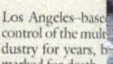

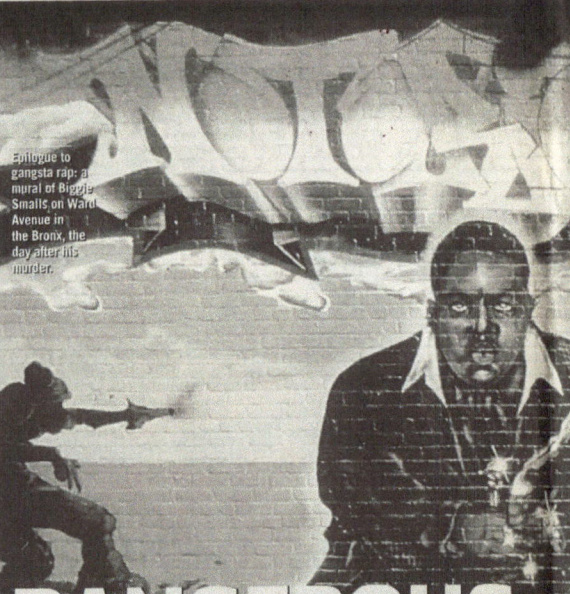

Epilogue to gangsta rap: a mural of Biggie Smalls on Ward Avenue in the Bronx, the day after his murder.

DANGEROUS GROUND

THEY FINALLY GOT BIGGIE IN L.A., AFTER AN ABORTED HIT IN ATLANTA

BY PETER NOEL

Los Angeles–based control of the mult dustry for years, b marked for death.

Neither Biggie heavily armed people in the two c the Atlanta concert to get an autograp artists were passeng on their way back Buckhead.

"Y'all know an guard asked.

"We don't kno said. "We didn't co

Being shadow come an imprima Coast–West Coast 1994 with the atte the lobby of a Mani Death Row rapper, robbed of $40,000 Combs and Biggie they both denied. Death Row Reco Knight, reportedly Atlanta of Death R Combs. Less than Randy "Stretch" W when he was shot a and killed by three

"When they performed down tain clubs, people in the crowd be 'Tupac!' " when he was still alive, the recalls. "One time we was onstage Caesar [of Junior M.A.F.I.A.] heard about Tupac. He said, 'Suck ma cock Tupac.' Biggie cut off his microphon 'Suck ma dick if you bought this shit

According to the bodyguard, squelched the attack, admonishing Little Caesar. "We would like to com and end all that [the East Coast–We

Eight months before he was executed parked Chevrolet Suburban in down Notorious B.I.G., also known as Bigg attempt on his life in Atlanta.

Until now, no one has talked freely about Smalls and several other rappers including Littl managed to avoid an apparent gang-related hit.

FX Crew Incorporated
c/o Carmen Sigona
254 Bloomfield Avenue
Apt. 3L
Caldwell, New Jersey 07006

March 19, 1997

Dear Bad Boy Entertainment,

Enclosed is a photo of the Notorious B.I.G. Memorial Wall, that we at FX Inc., painted in the Bronx on March 9th & 10th. The wall is located at Ward and Westchester Avenues. We hope you like our tribute to Biggie and the message (One coast, One culture) that we conveyed to the Hip Hop community. We are big fans of both Biggie and Bad Boy Entertainment. We would like to extend our support and condolences to the Bad Boy and Wallace Families.

Please contact us if we can be of any help artistically, or otherwise. Once again, we send our deepest sympathies for this tragic loss.

Sincerely,

The FX Crew Inc.

FX Crew Inc.
254 Bloomfield Avenue
#3L
Caldwell, N.J. 07006

The Bad Boy Family
extends gratitude & love
for your kind thoughts and sympathies
on behalf of our artist
Christopher "Notorious B.I.G." Wallace

Snow was trying to maintain a balance between his job, his artwork, and his passion for graffiti. The one thing that had changed was that he found more and more an increasing demand for his work. By 1997, he started to feel that he would have to make a choice as this juggling act would prove to be too much for Snow. He made his choice. He decided to leave his job and courageously pursue his art career. His critics and even some of his friends and family thought he was crazy for leaving his job.

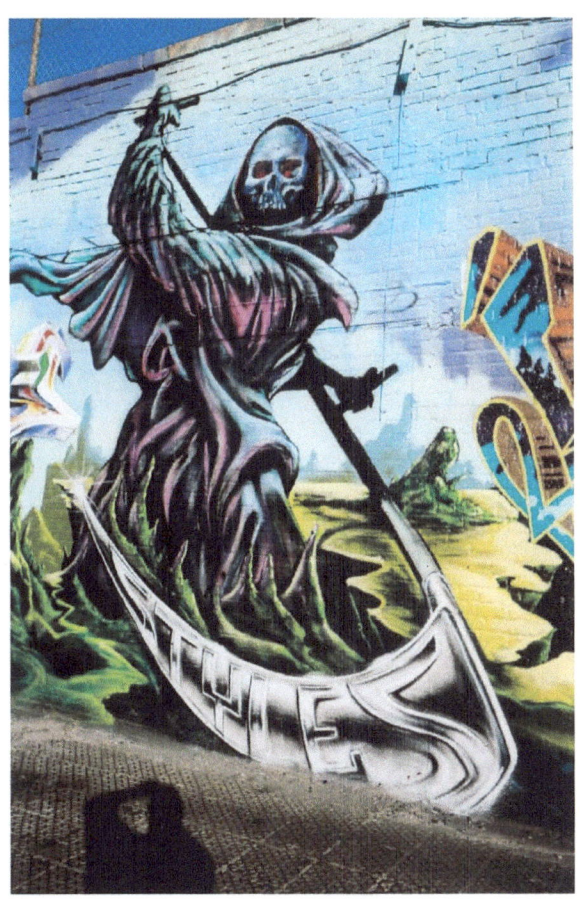

"In addition to being a close friend and crewmate, Snow has been a huge inspiration to myself and many others around the world. He paints with a loose, yet hard approach that illustrates action and movement in his letters, while still embracing his classic style and technic! He does it with ease, and believe me, it's not easy! Some of the best tips I learned, and still use today, are ones I picked up from him many years ago. To evolve as any artist, you cant be afraid of failure. You have to experiment, sometimes creating way outside of your comfort zone. It's not an easy thing to do as a graffiti or street artist because when you fail, people see it! But more importantly, writers see it! For that reason, most continue to create what works for them and what they have perfected because it's safe and easy. Snow is consistent in exercising this change and evolution yet, even at a glance, you'll always know it's a Snow piece. I think that's the type of quality that allows an artist to stand out above the masses.

"He's a pioneer of style, and at a time before you could Google graffiti, and web based media platforms didn't even exist, writers were being inspired globally by his works! A loyal crewmate, Snow has always represented what he believes in proudly, and his passion for the art movement is apparent in everything he creates!"

Jamie HEF

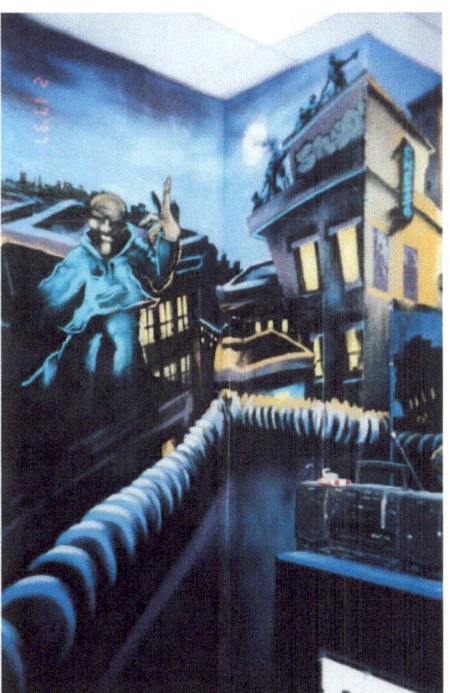

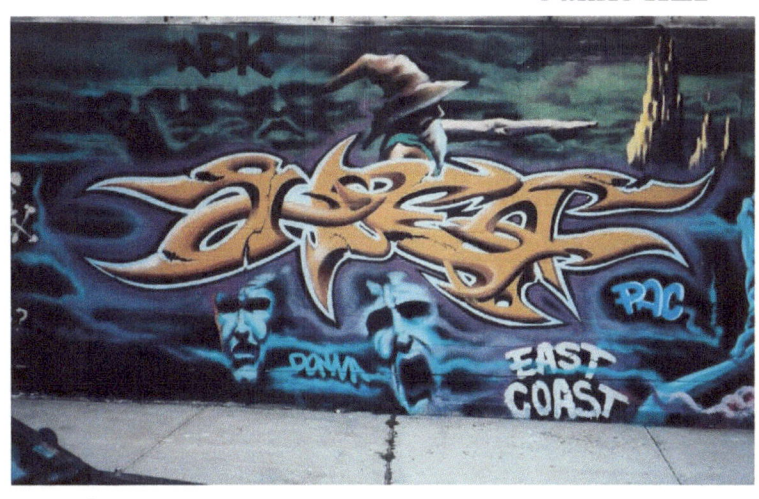

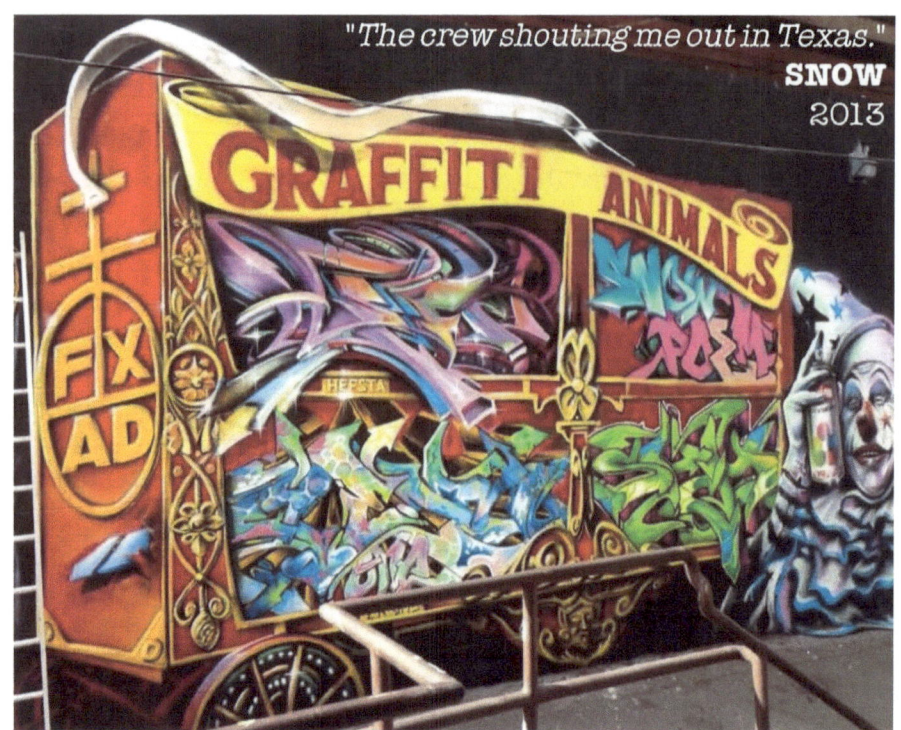

"The crew shouting me out in Texas."
SNOW
2013

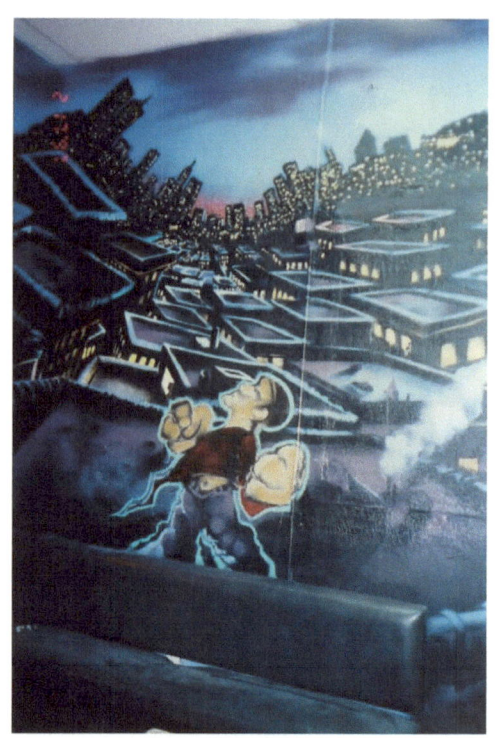

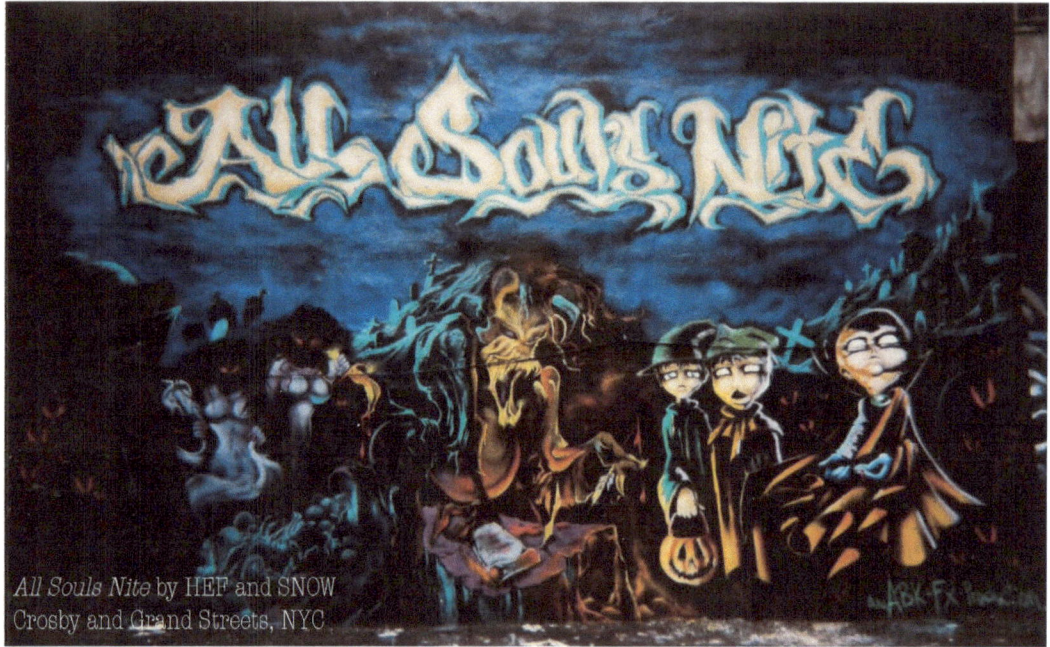

All Souls Nite by HEF and SNOW
Crosby and Grand Streets, NYC

HEF in action

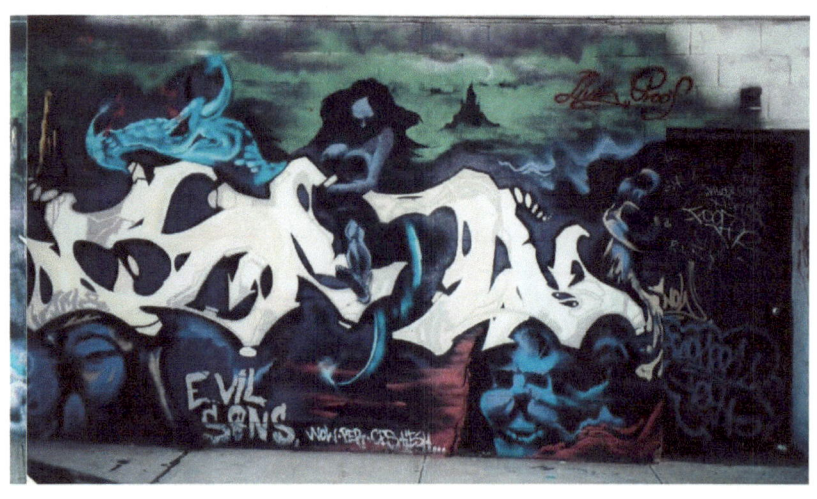

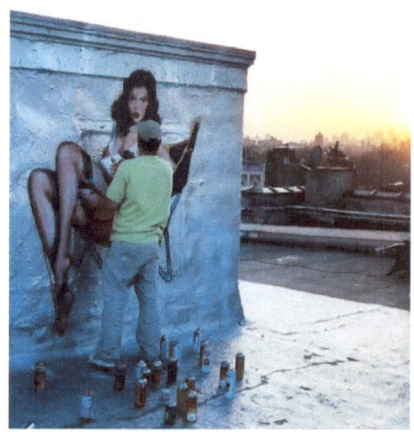

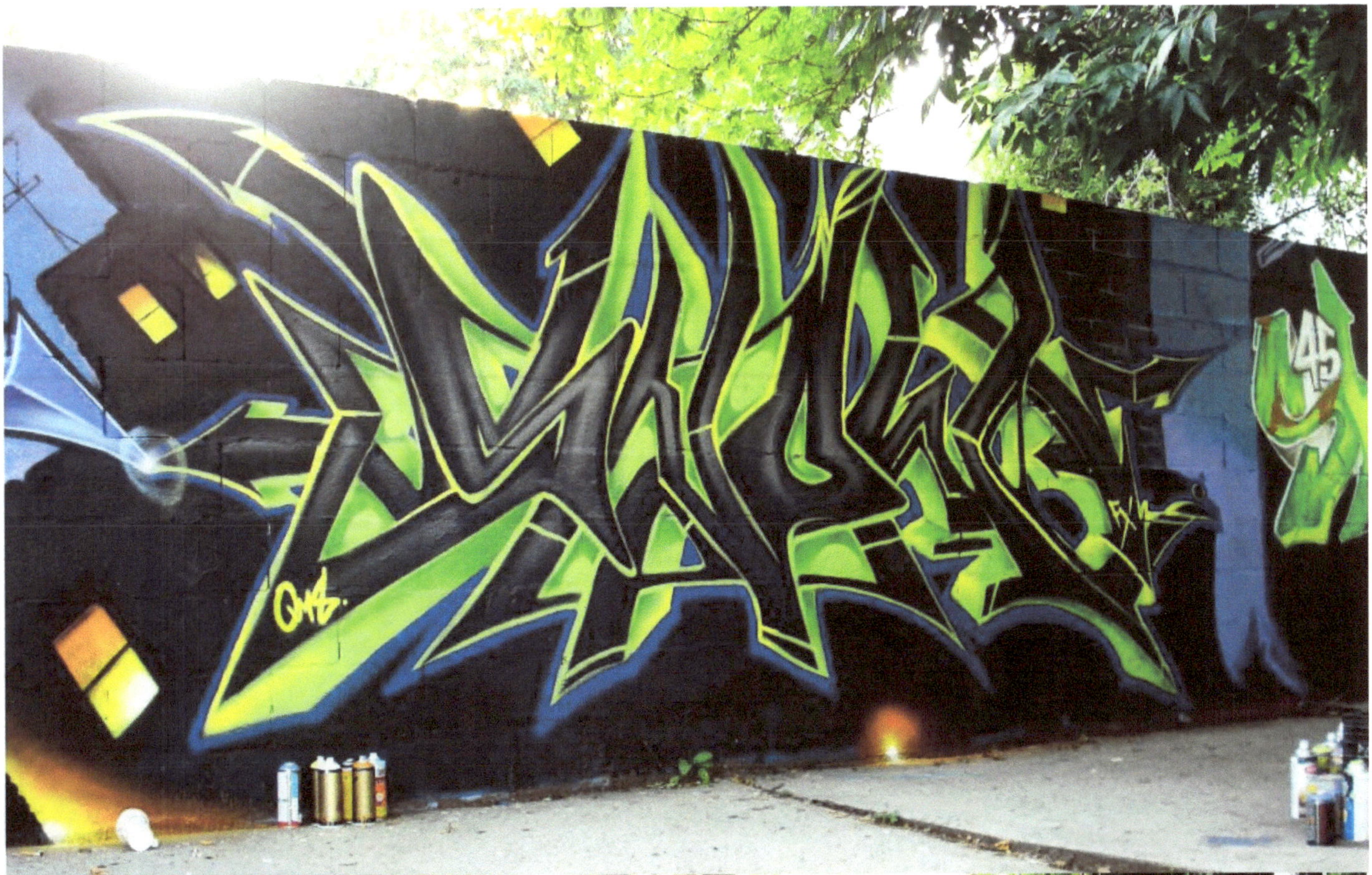

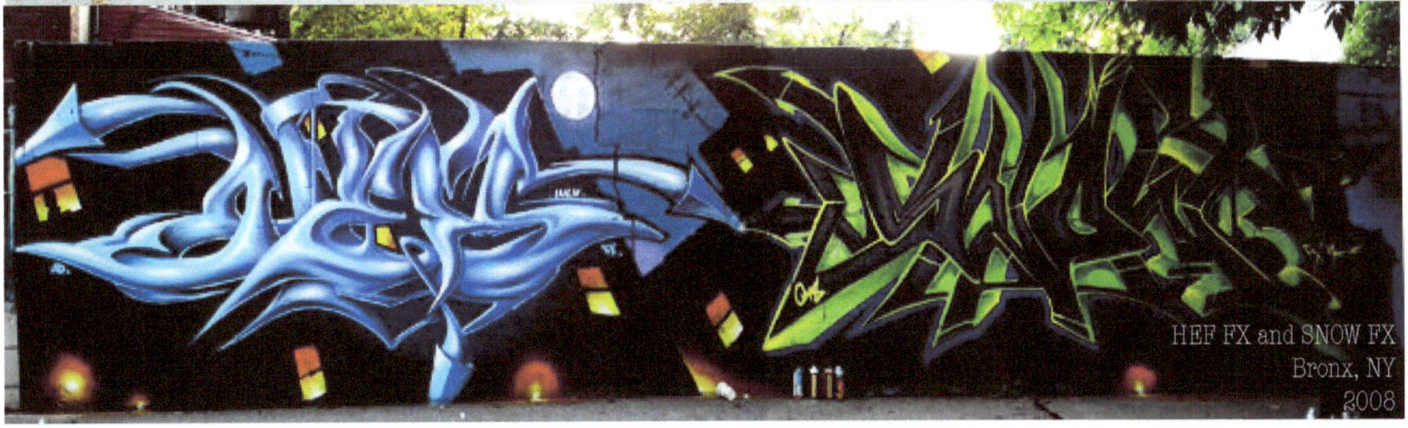

HEF FX and SNOW FX
Bronx, NY
2008

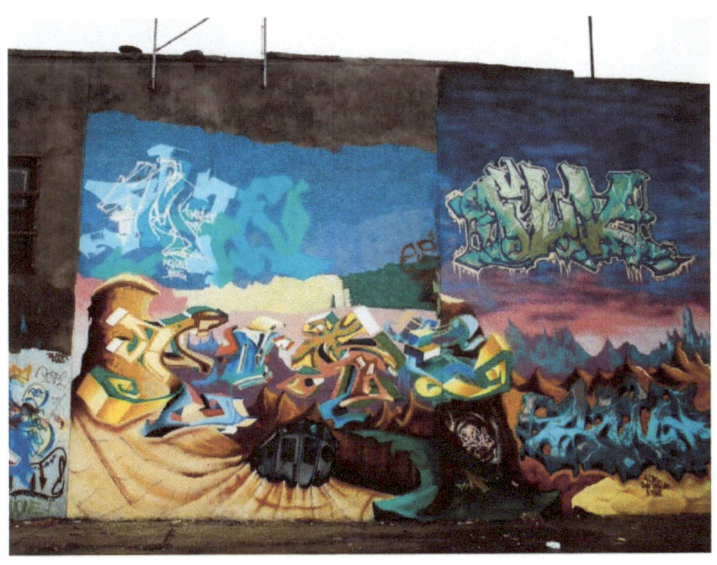

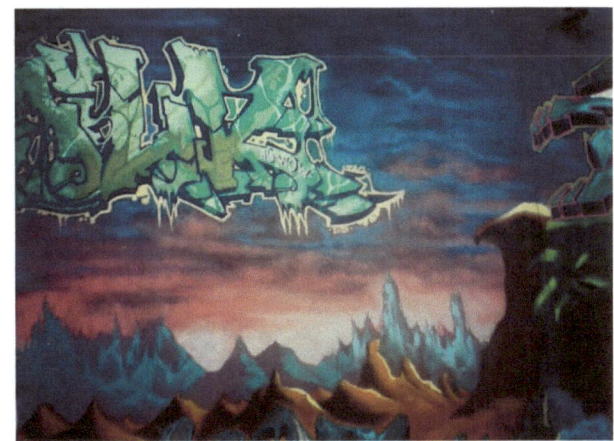

SNO, POSE2, and FUK by WOW123
Bronx. NY
1996

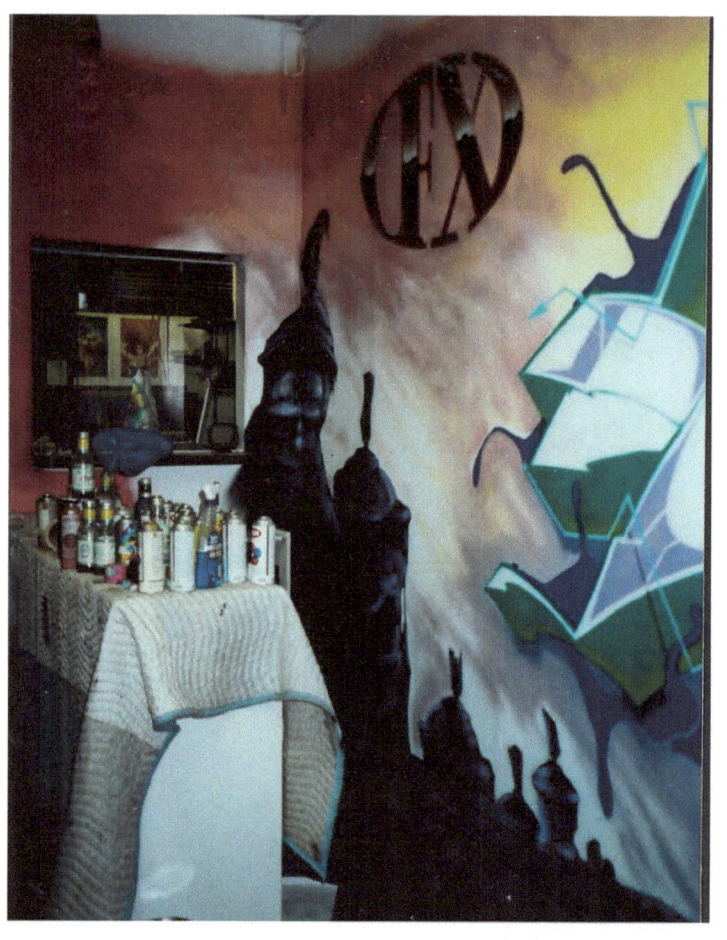

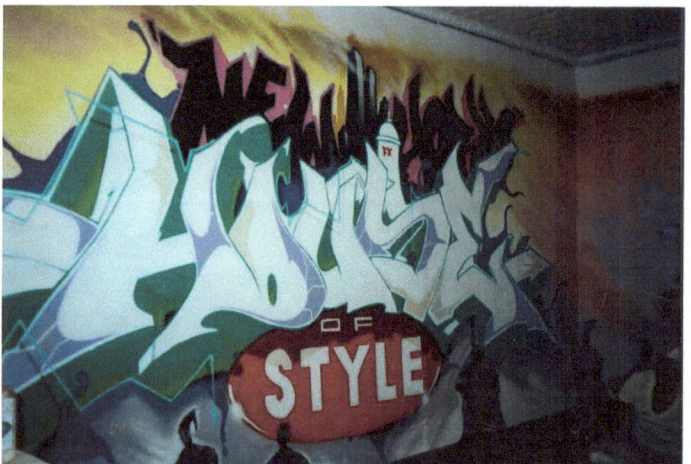

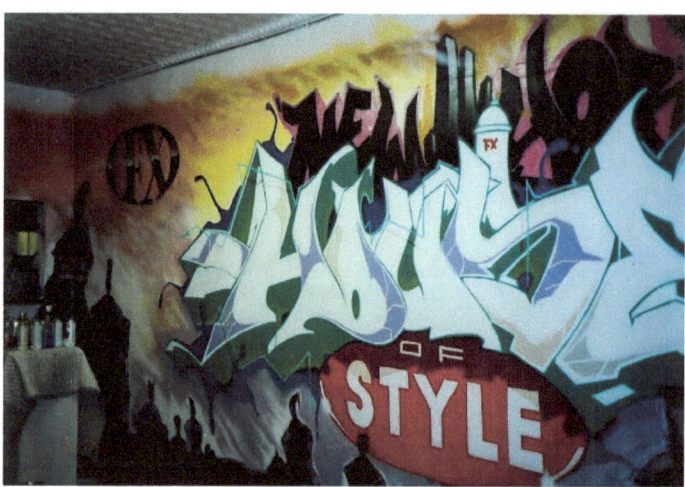

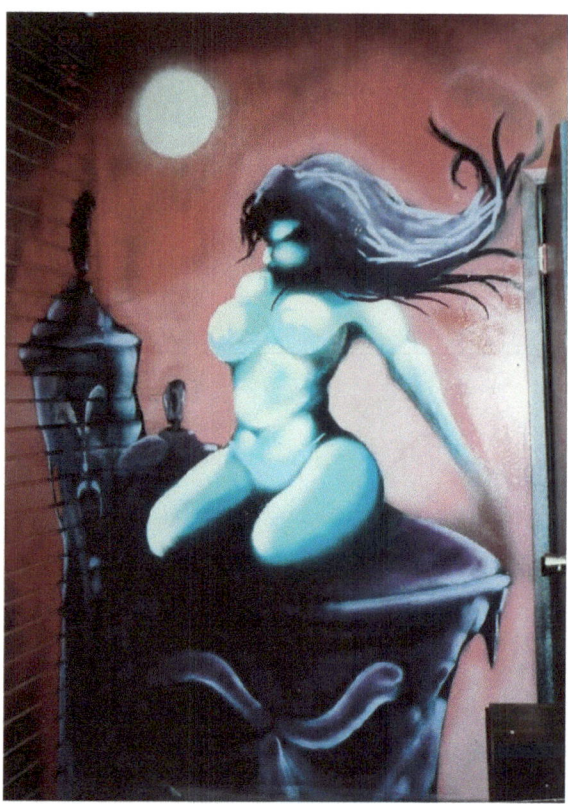

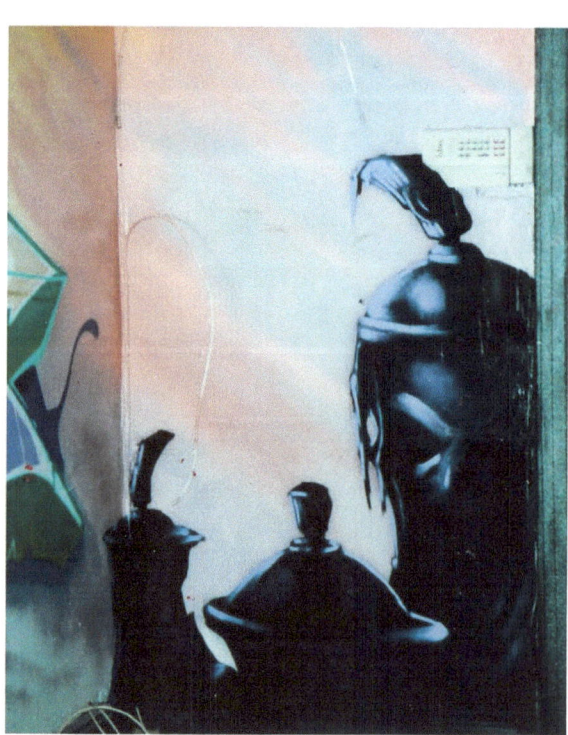

House of Style by CES and SNOW
mid 1990s

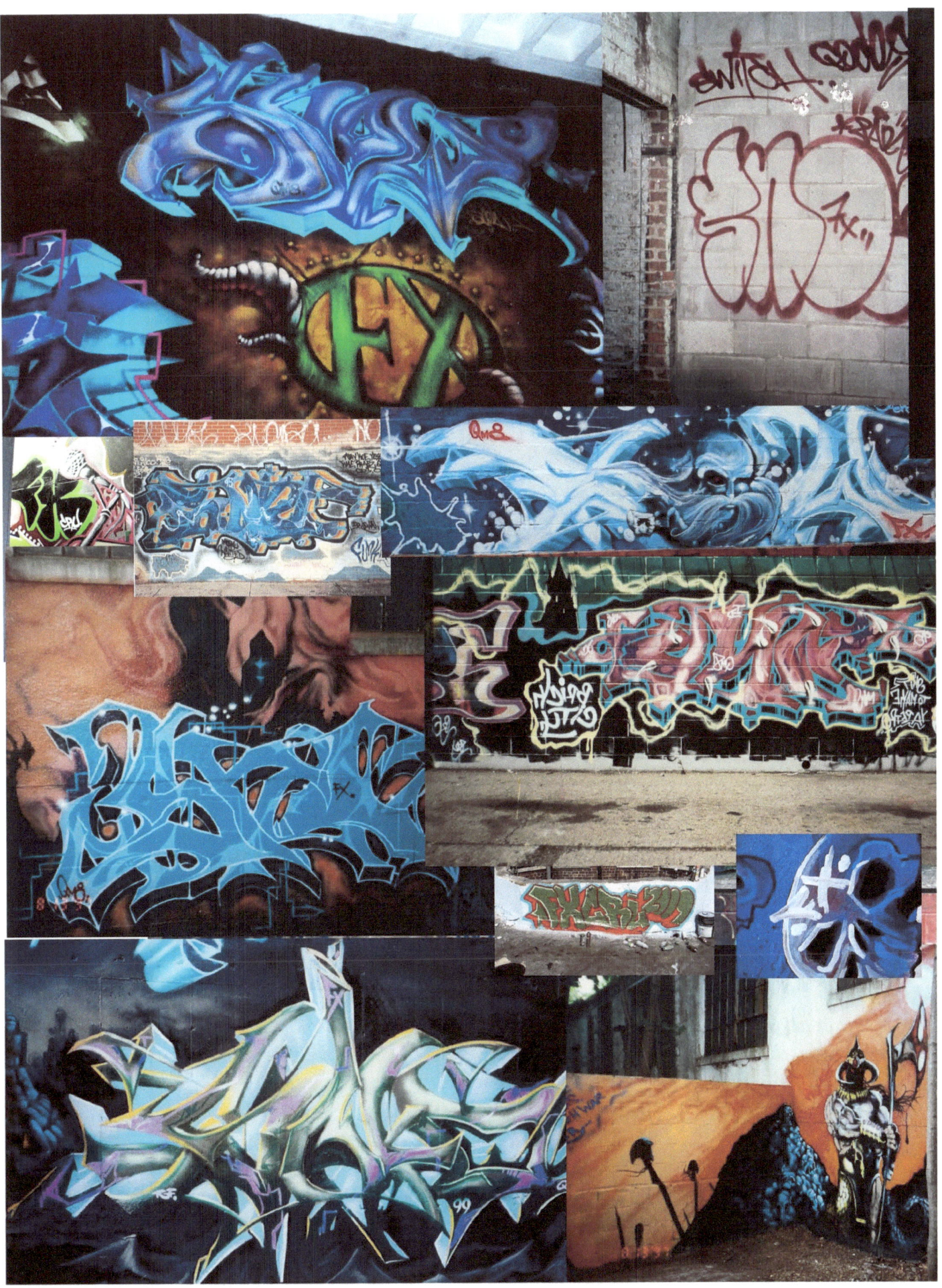

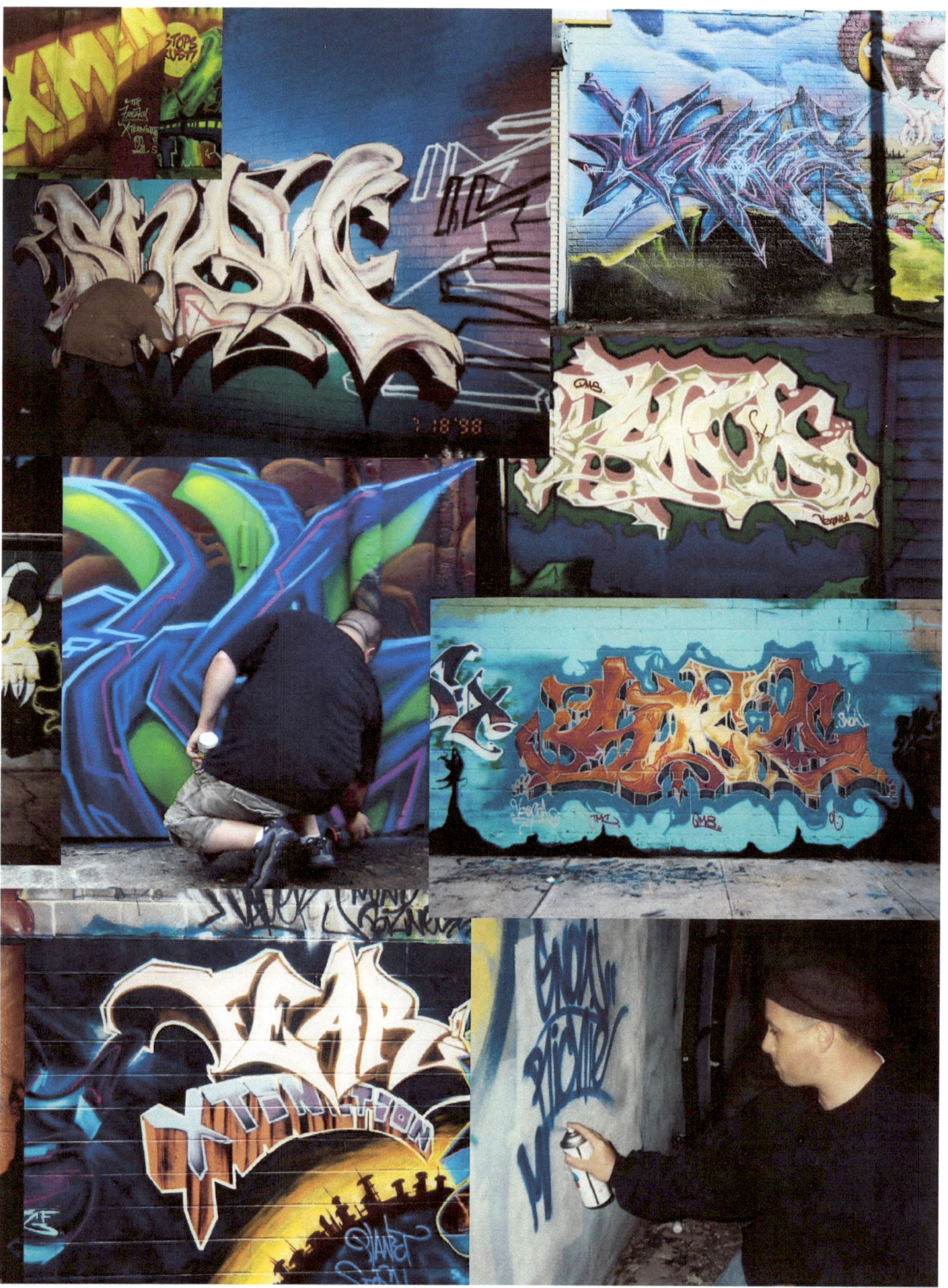

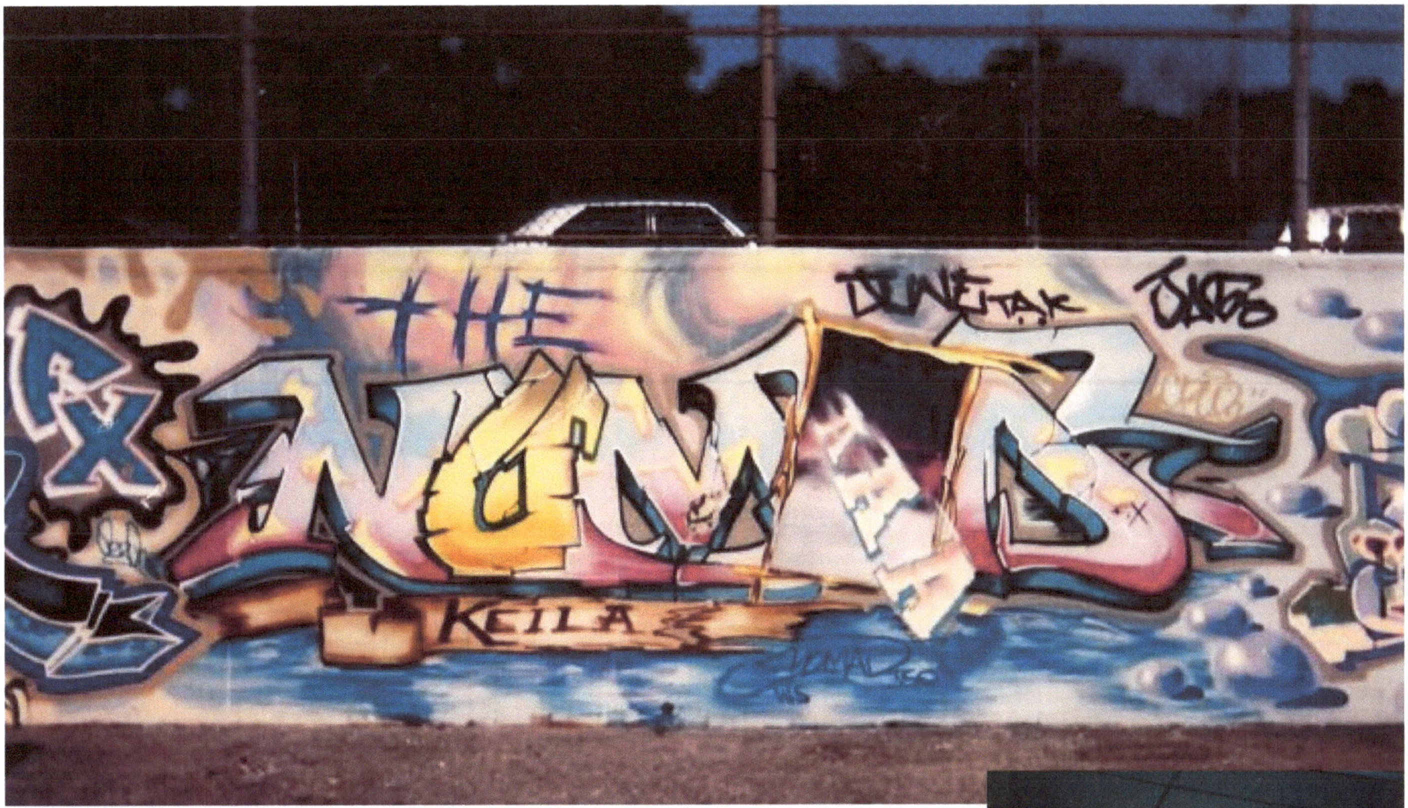

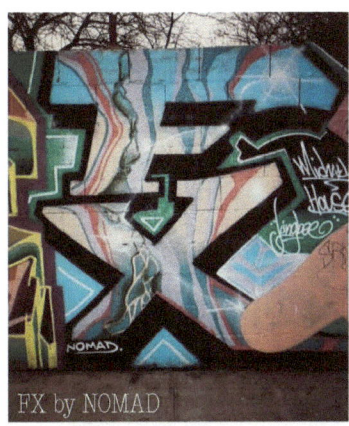

"NOMAD was definitely one of my favorite writers, and this piece was absolutely one of my favorite pieces."

SNOW

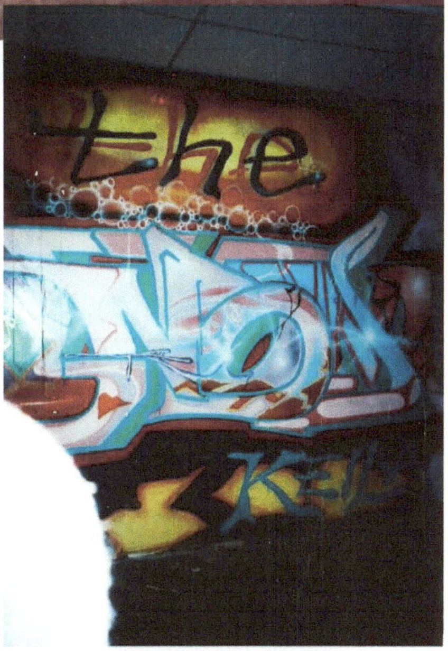

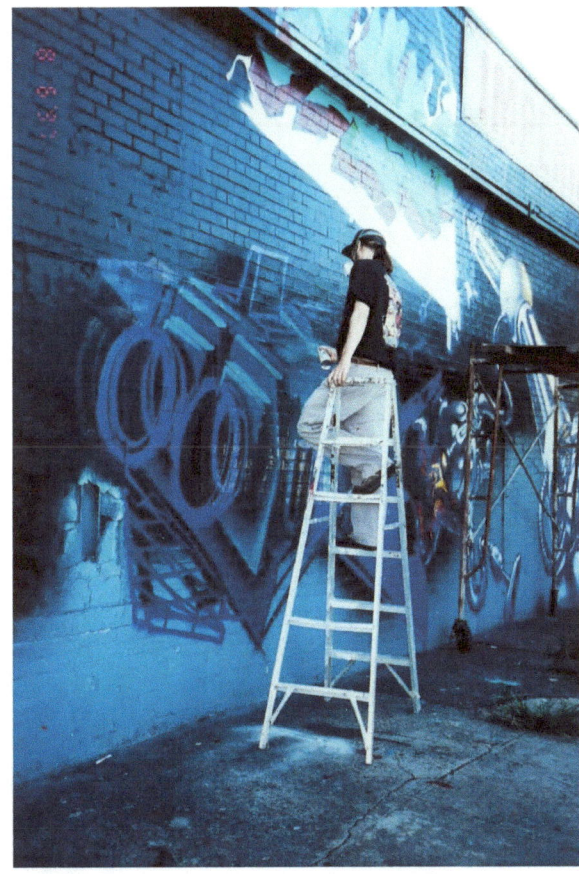

FX by NOMAD

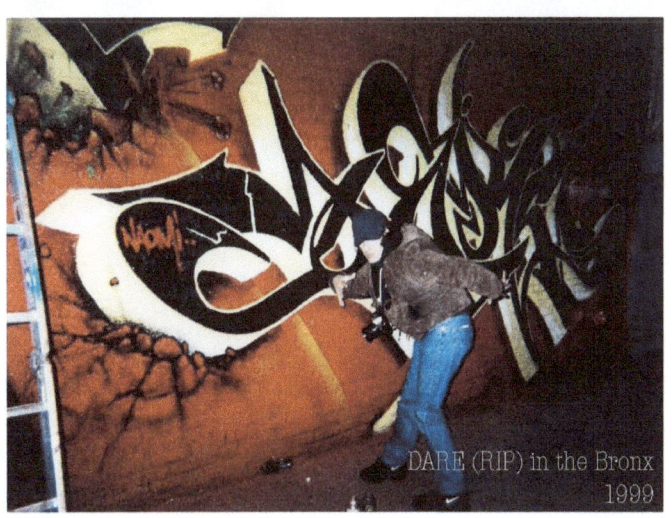

DAIM in action

DARE (RIP) in the Bronx
1999

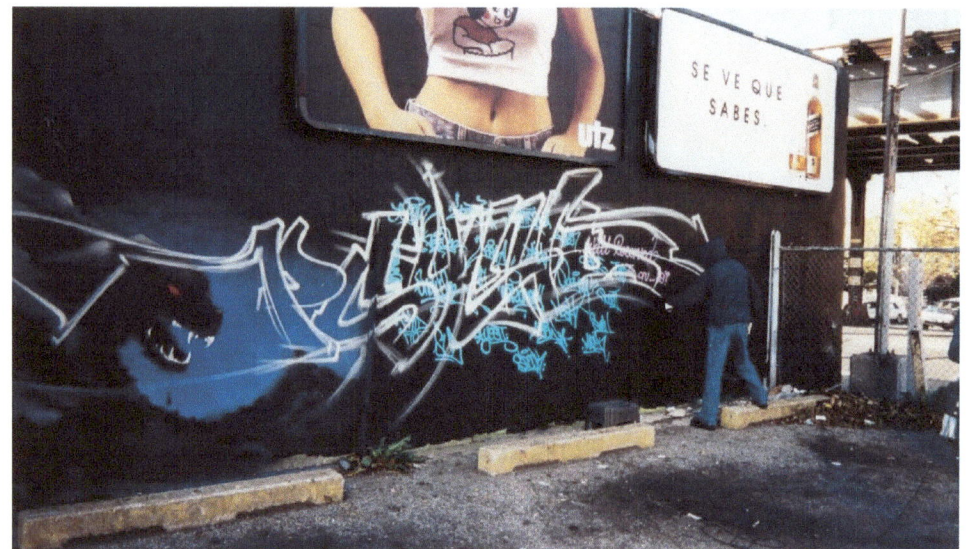

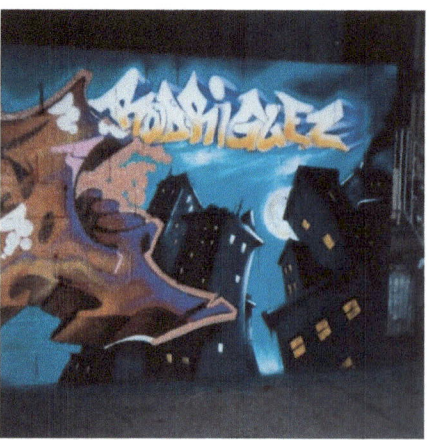

SEEN in action
Bronx, NY
1999

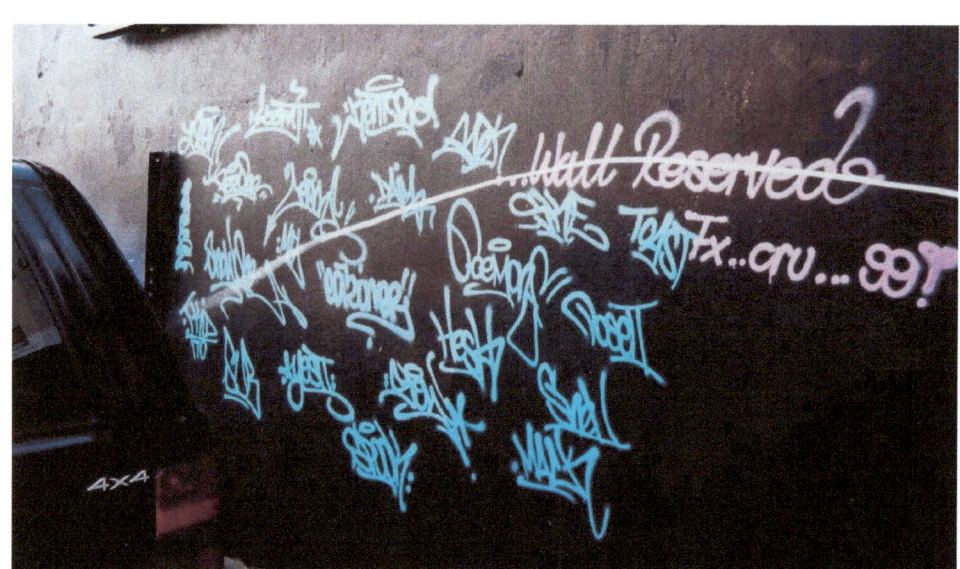

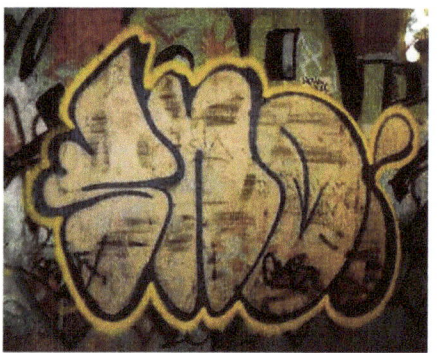

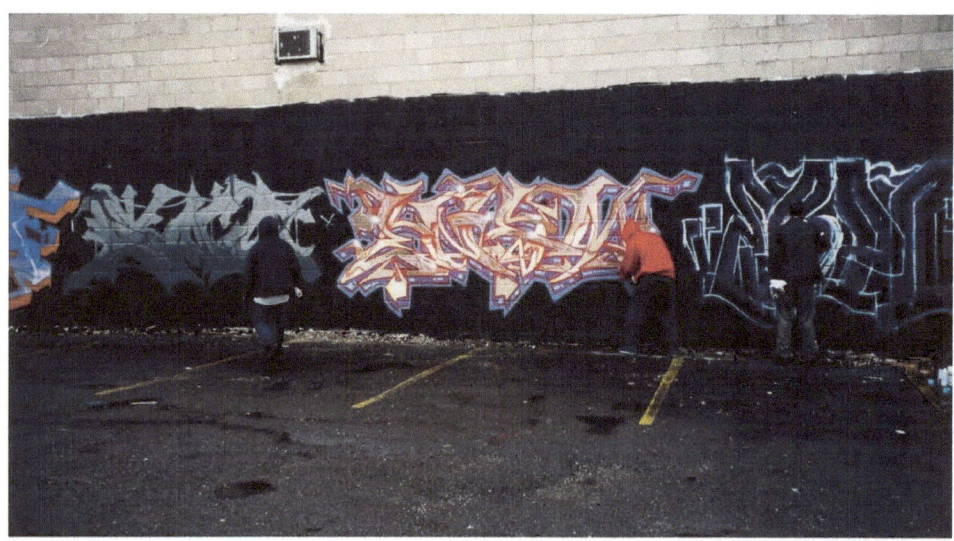
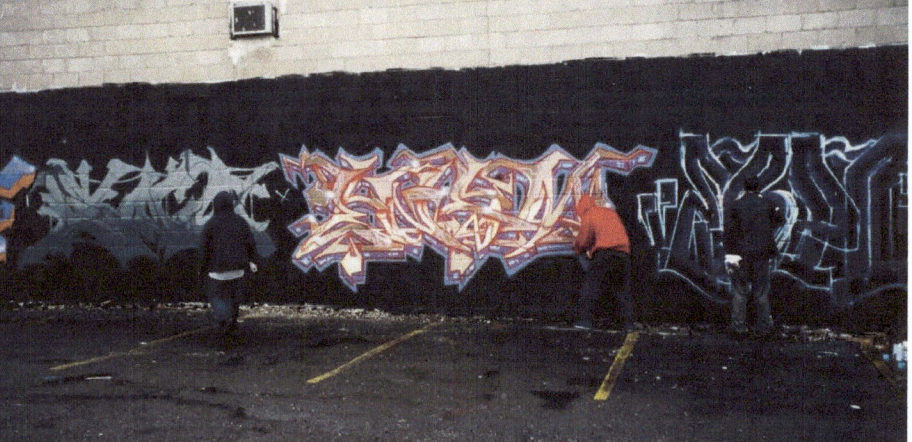

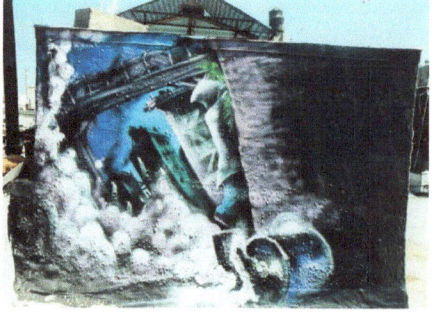

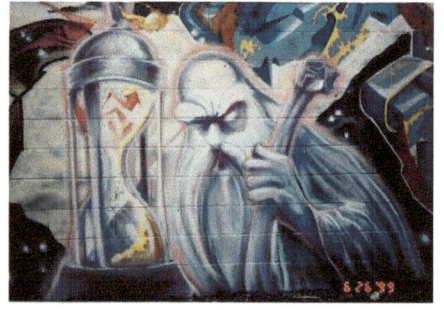

SNOW, ENEM, and ESPO in action
Philly
1997

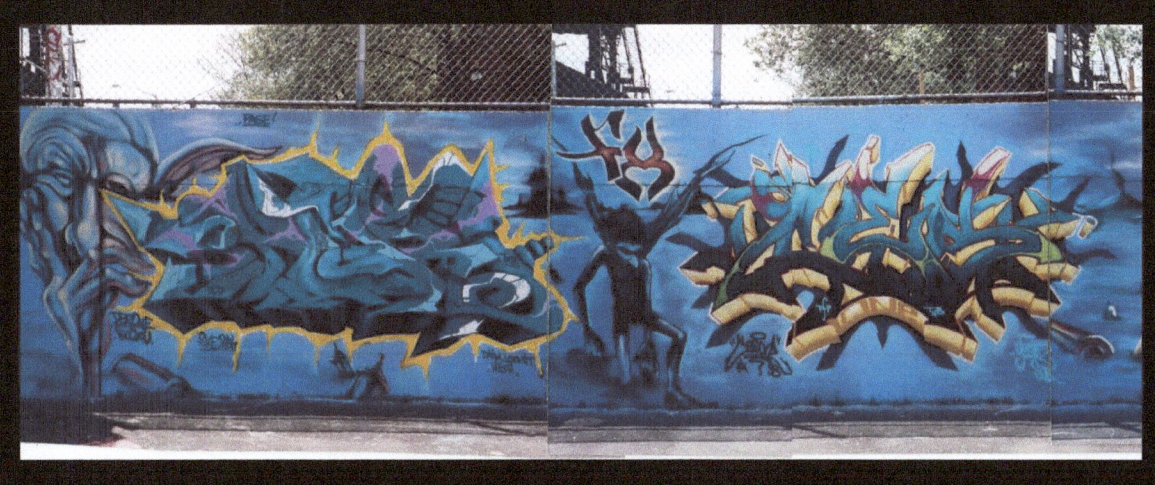

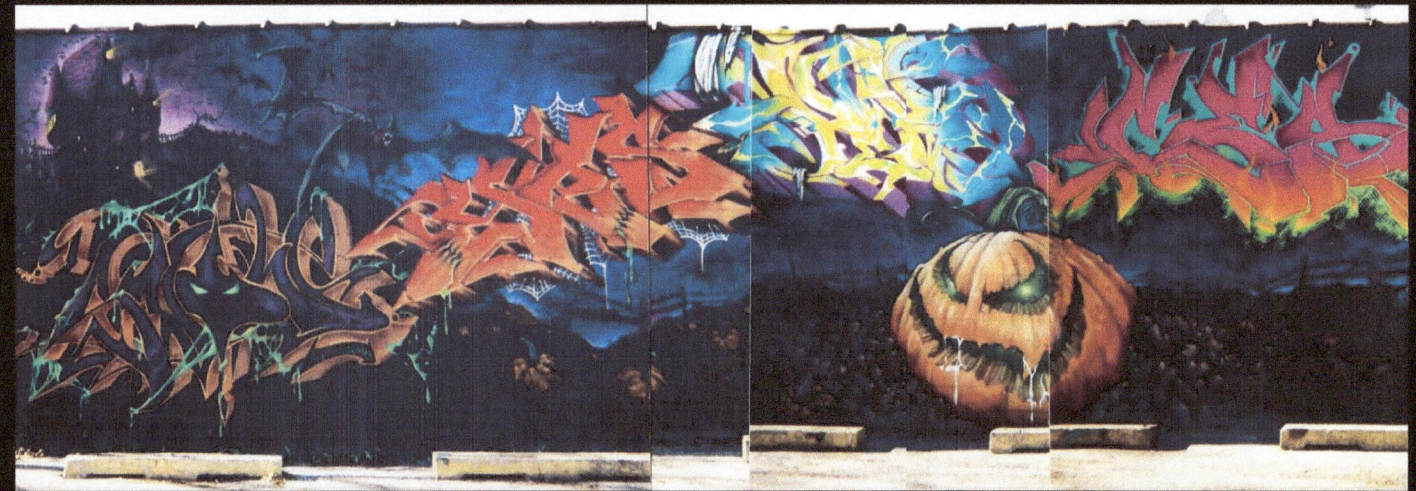

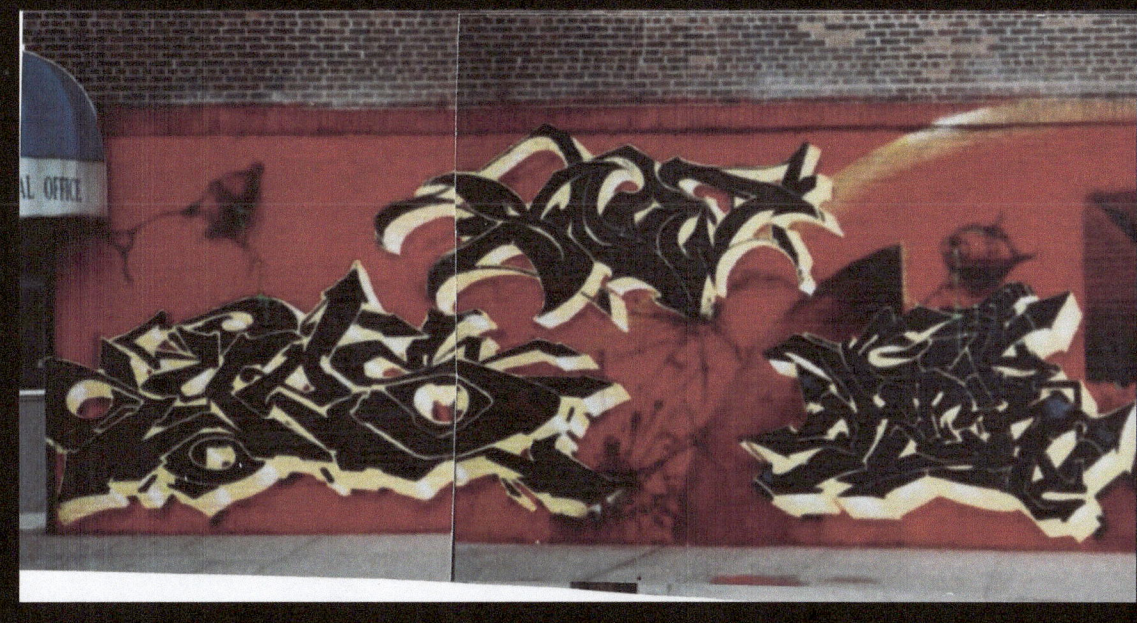

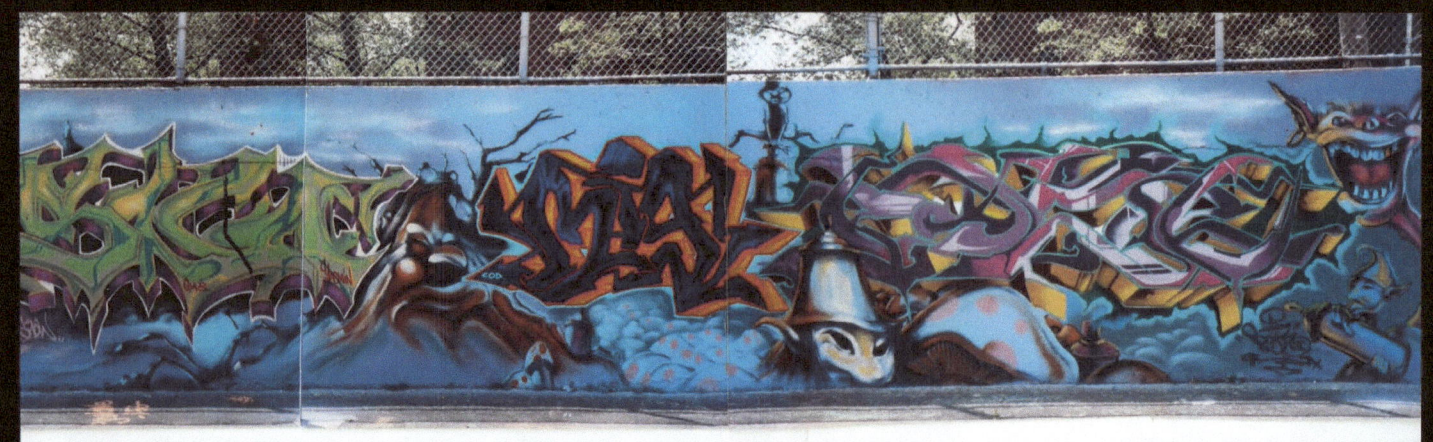

PER, CES, SNO, BIG (by POEM), POSE2
Graffiti Hall of Fame, Harlem, NYC - 1998

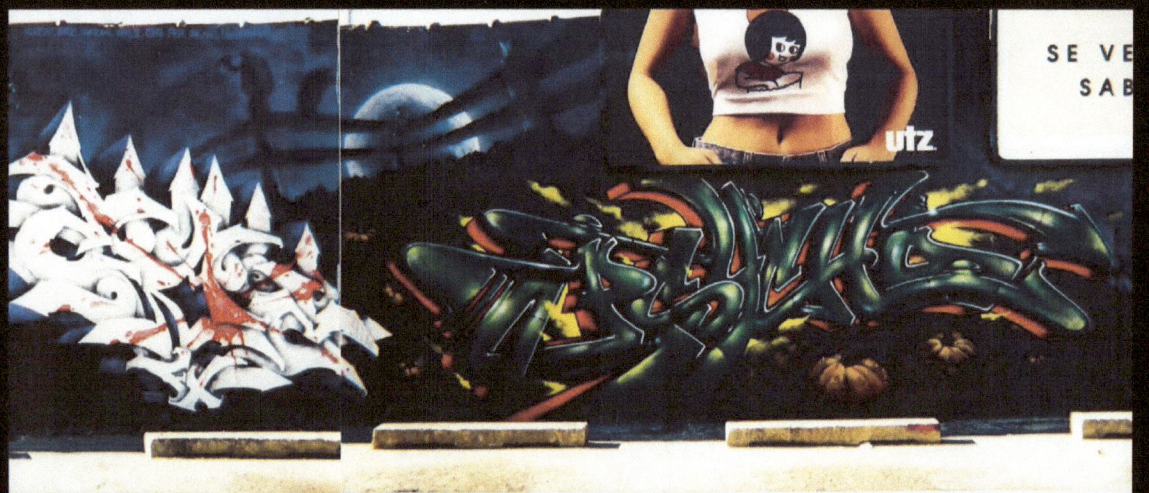

FX Halloween wall   SNOW, YES2, PER, CES, EAZ, PSYCHO (by SEEN UA)
6 line, Bronx. NY - 1999

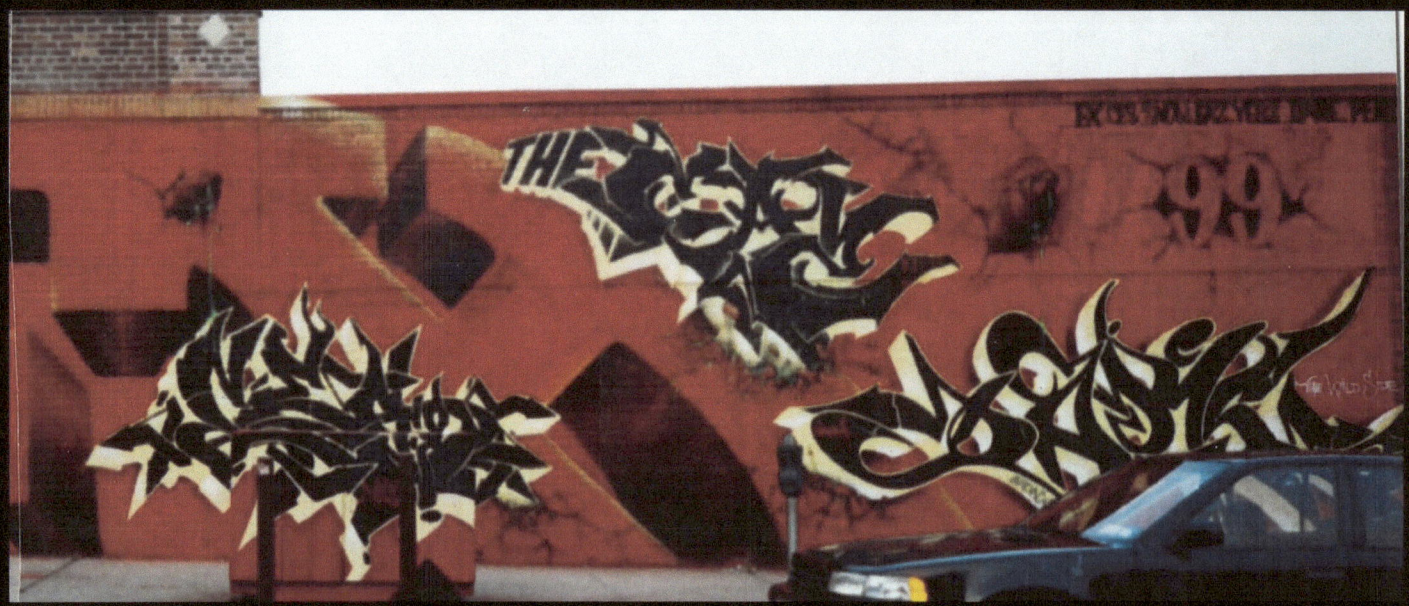

YES2, SNOW, PER, CES, EAZ, DARE TWS (from Switzerland)
6 line Bronx, NY - 1999

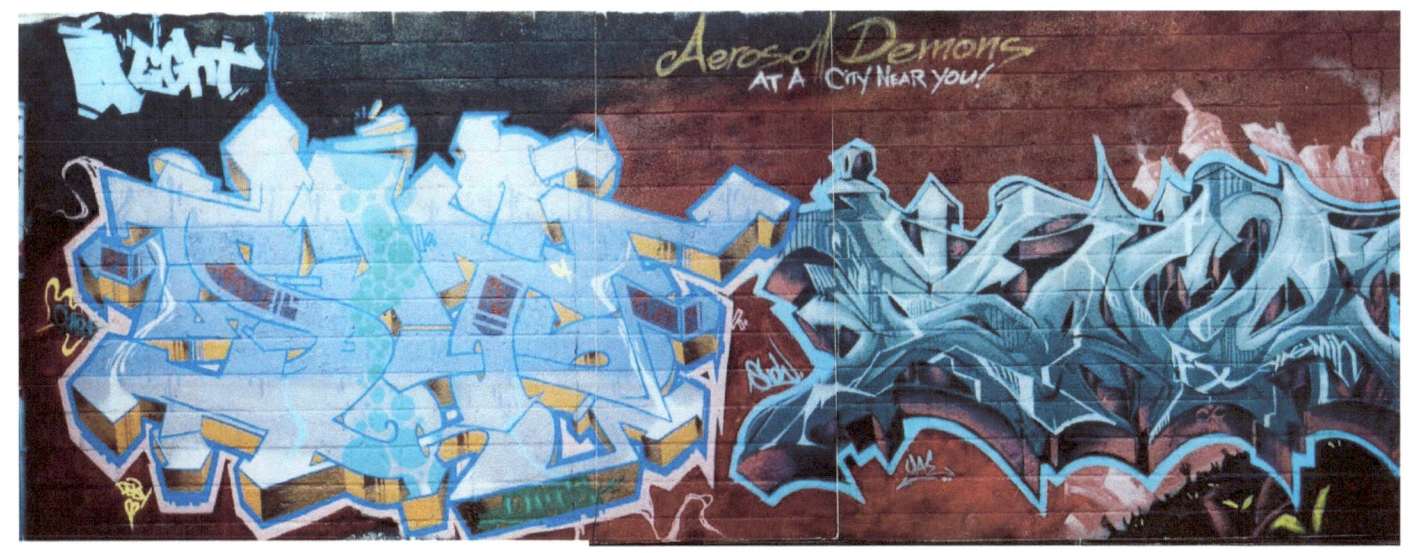

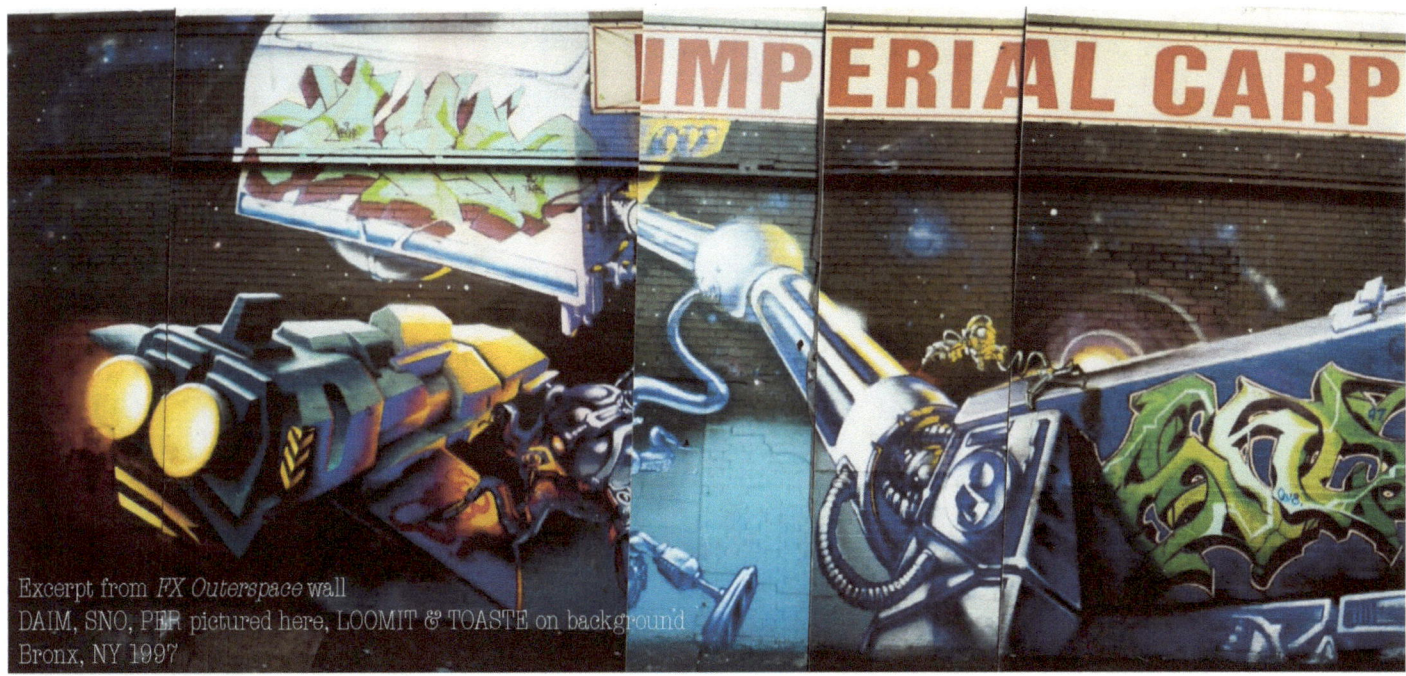

Excerpt from *FX Outerspace* wall
DAIM, SNO, PER pictured here, LOOMIT & TOASTE on background
Bronx, NY 1997

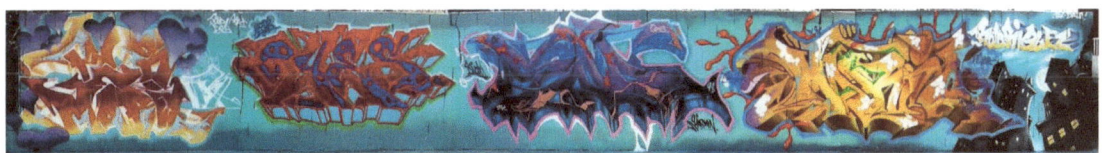

YES2, SNO, PER
1998

REK and SKE
Puerto Rico, 1997

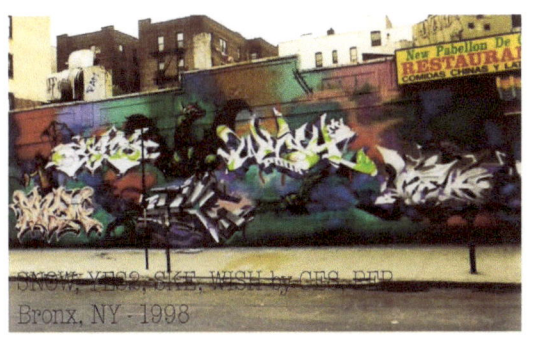

SNOW, YES2, SKE, WISH by CES, PER
Bronx, NY 1998

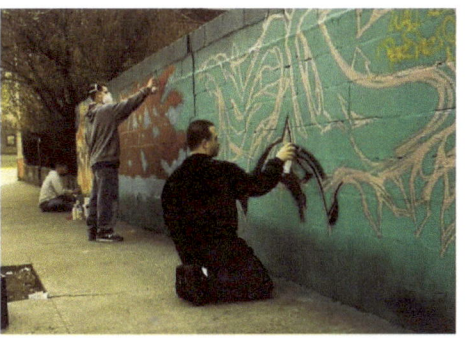

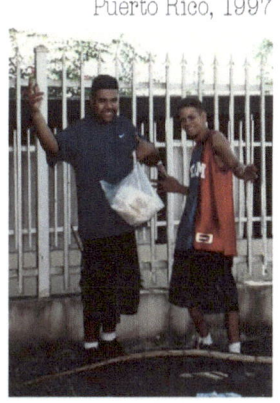

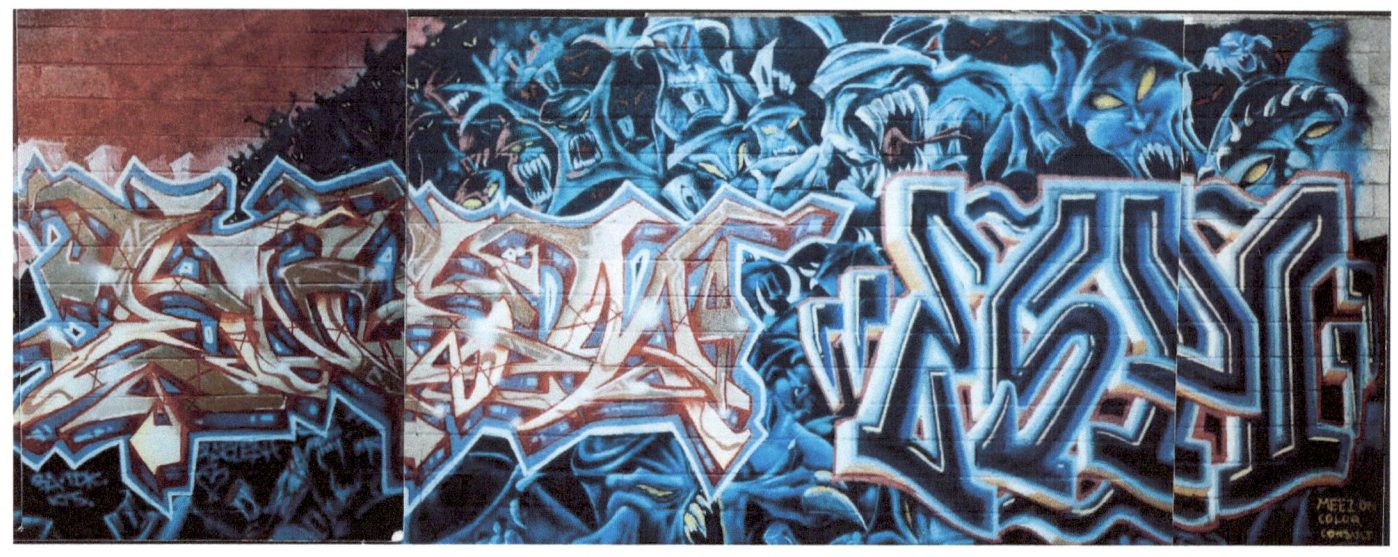

Aerosol Demons wall   SAT, SNO, ENEM, ESPO in Philly

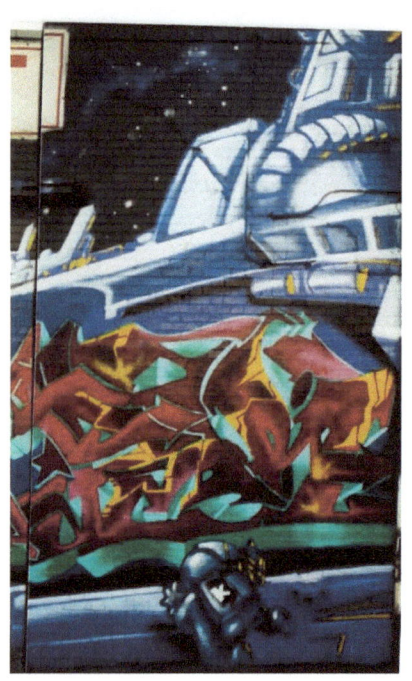

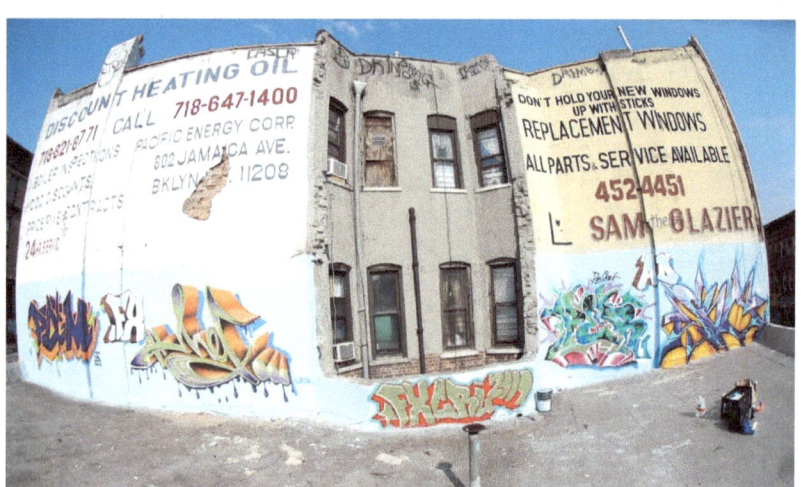

"From its very beginning, Snow was, and still remains, one of FX Crew's most innovative and talented members."

POEM FX

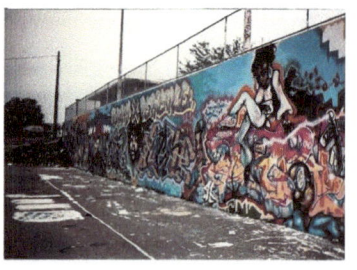

"I remember meeting Snow in 1996 in New York. I have always liked his works, ever since he began in New Jersey. That same year, he, CES, and PER came to Puerto Rico to paint with us for the FX video. Carmelo has always been a great friend, and we had some of the best memories anyone can have."

REK FX TNB

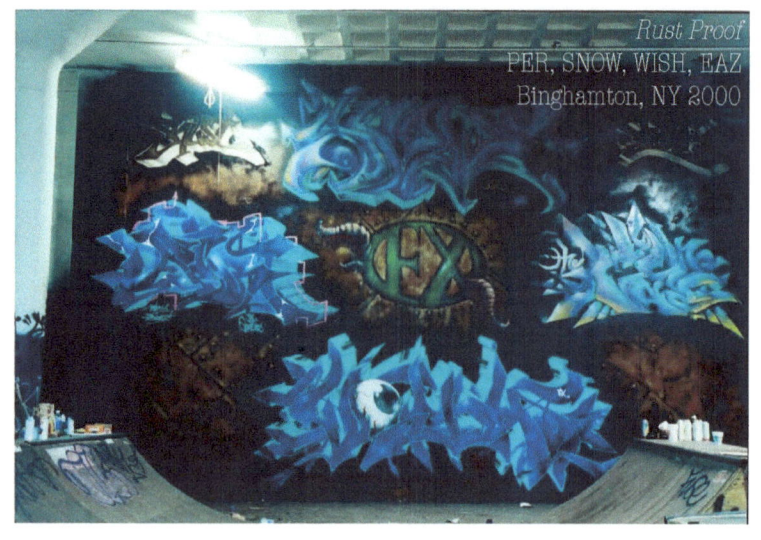

Rust Proof
PER, SNOW, WISH, EAZ
Binghamton, NY 2000

Snow's experiences with FX had allowed him to travel abroad and exhibit his talents and to work alongside greats like SEEN UA and other artists internationally. Aside from art shows in Soho, NYC, Snow traveled to Canada, Puerto Rico, Germany, and Holland. These countries were heavily into Hip Hop art and culture, and had enthusiastically welcomed their American counterparts with open arms. The trips and shows were documented for the Abstract Video project: FX: The Video. The video was released and coveted by graffiti fans across the globe. It became an instant classic and Snow's interview was filmed in the showroom of McFarlane Toys, NYC during the International Toy Fair.

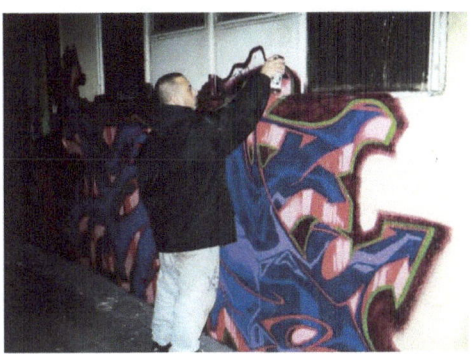

SNOW painting in Munich

"My trip to Europe was an eye opener. I was taken back by their appreciation and knowledge of American Hip Hop. It was the first time I was asked to sign a young child's blackbook. It was really cool."

SNOW

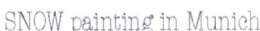
Master LOOMIT in action

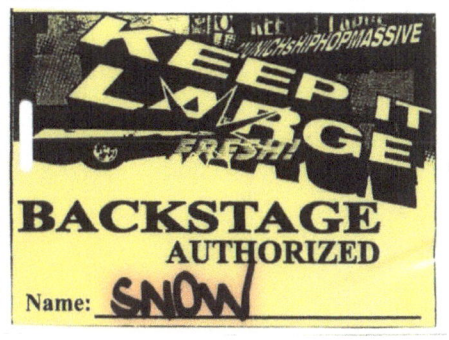

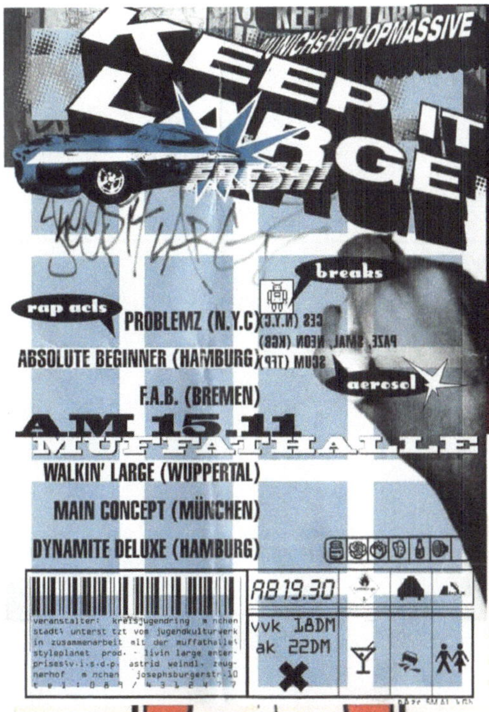

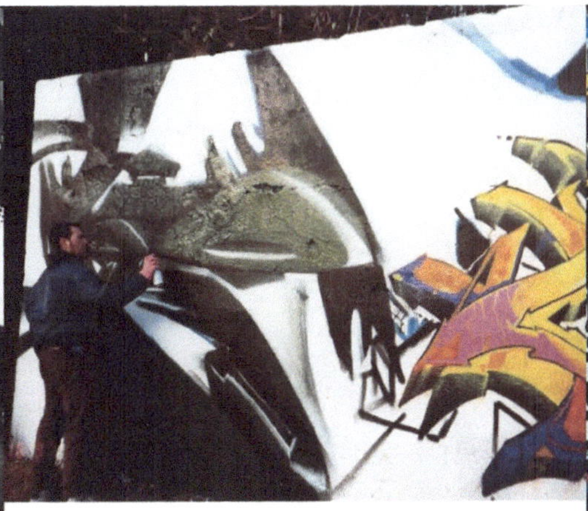

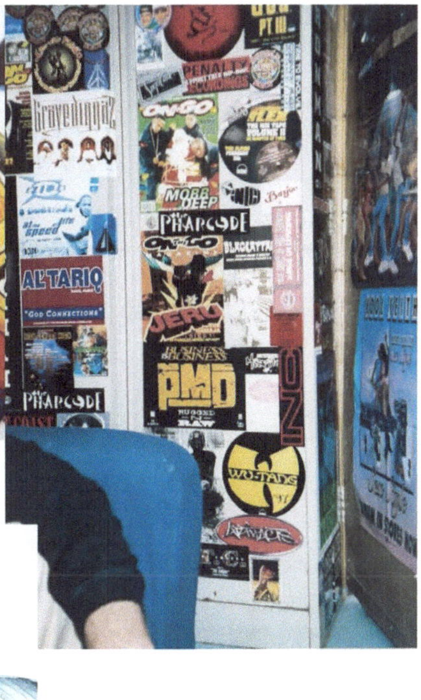

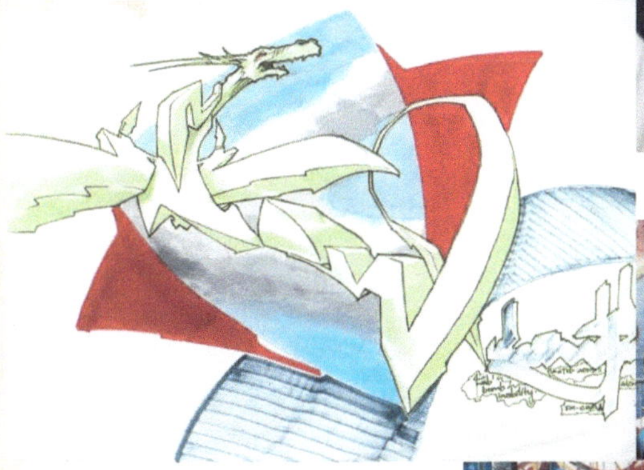

SNOW by LOOMIT
1997

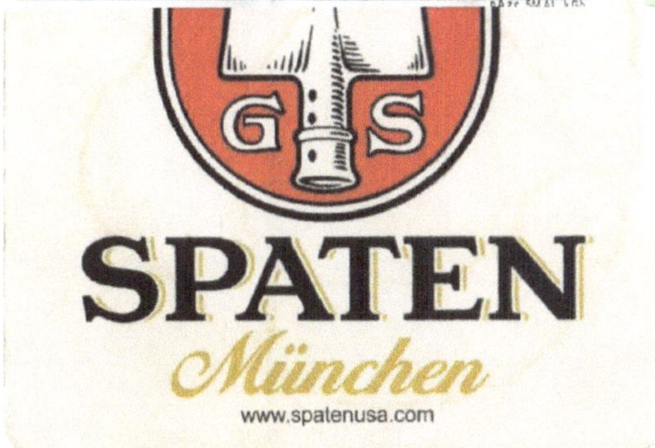

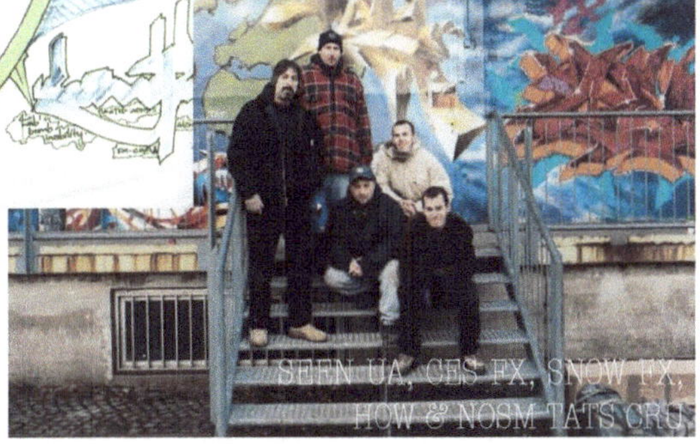

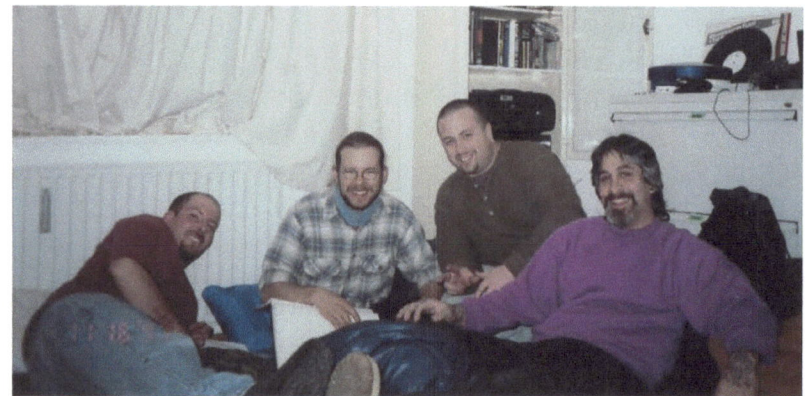

CES, DAIM, SNOW, SEEN
Munich, Germany
1997

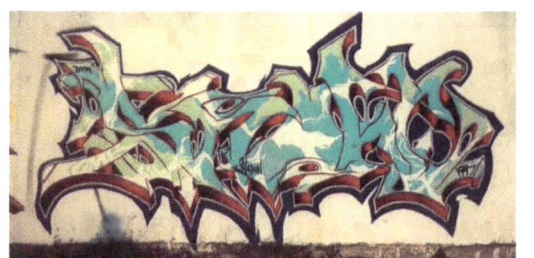

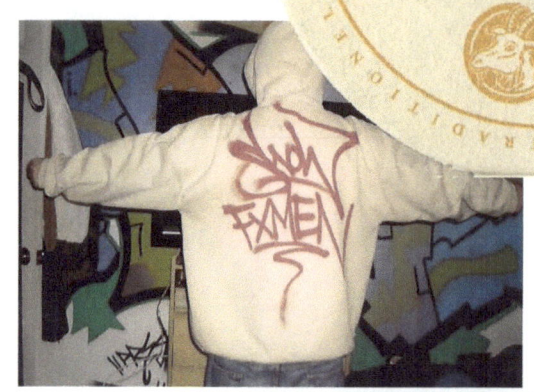

EAZ and SNOW
Under Pressure event
Montreal, 1999

URBAN X-PRESSIONS & ABSOLUT PRESENT

under pressure'99
ABSOLUT X-PRESSIONS
GRAFFITI CONVENTION

b-boys   writers   emcees   turntablists

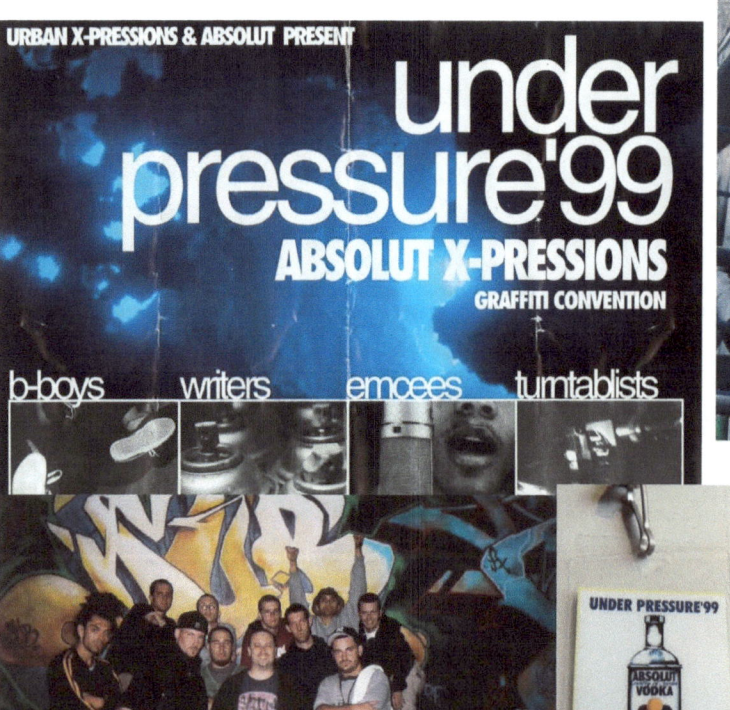

WYS, SHONE 237, CES, CED, EAZ, SNOW, YES2, SEZE,
SUB, SEW, CHILD (RIP)
Montreal, 2000

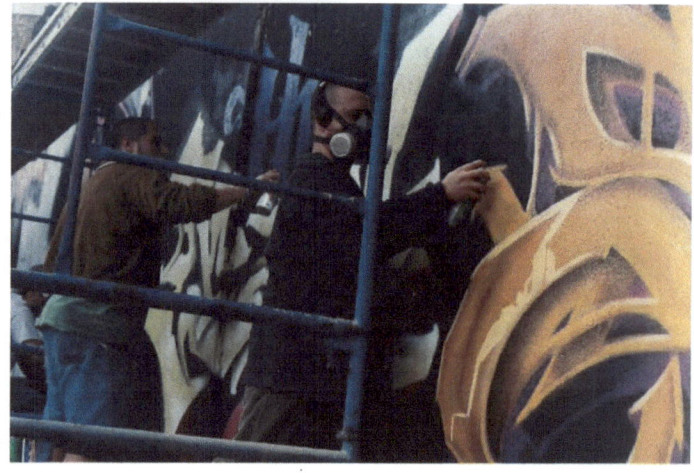

Organized Crime event at East Coast Terminal
Binghamton, NY, 2000

UNDER PRESSURE'99

ABSOLUT VODKA

ABSOLUT X-PRESSIONS.

FOUFOUNES
ELECTRIQUES
Sat. Aug. 7
Sun. Aug. 8
1999

science record shop

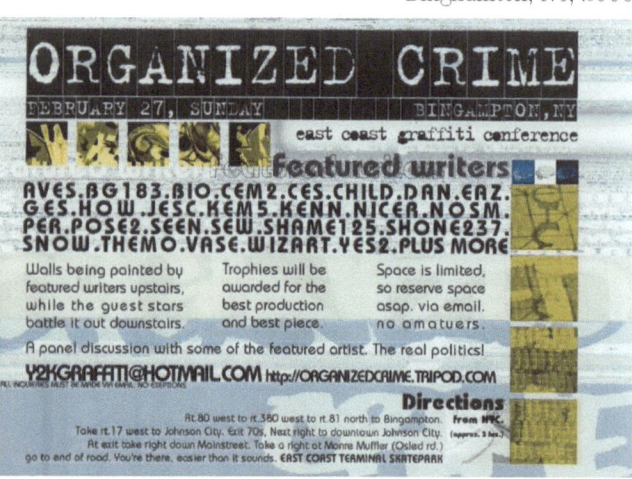

ORGANIZED CRIME
FEBRUARY 27, SUNDAY   BINGAMPTON, NY
east coast graffiti conference

featured writers
AVES.BG183.BIO.CEM2.CES.CHILD.DAN.EAZ.
GES.HOW.JESC.KEM5.KENN.NICER.NOSM.
PER.POSE2.SEEN.SEW.SHAME125.SHONE237.
SNOW.THEMO.VASE.WIZART.YES2.PLUS MORE

Walls being painted by   Trophies will be   Space is limited,
featured writers upstairs,   awarded for the   so reserve space
while the guest stars   best production   asap. via email.
battle it out downstairs.   and best piece.   no amatuers.

A panel discussion with some of the featured artist. The real politics!

Y2KGRAFFITI@HOTMAIL.COM http://ORGANIZEDCRIME.TRIPOD.COM
ALL INQUIRIES MUST BE MADE VIA EMAIL. NO EXCEPTIONS.

Directions
from NYC.

Rt.80 west to rt.380 west to rt.81 north to Bingampton.
Take rt.17 west to Johnson City. Exit 70s. Next right to downtown Johnson City.   (approx. 3 hrs.)
At exit take right down Mainstreet. Take a right at Morris Muffler (Oaled rd.)
go to and of road. You're there. easier than it sounds. EAST COAST TERMINAL SKATEPARK

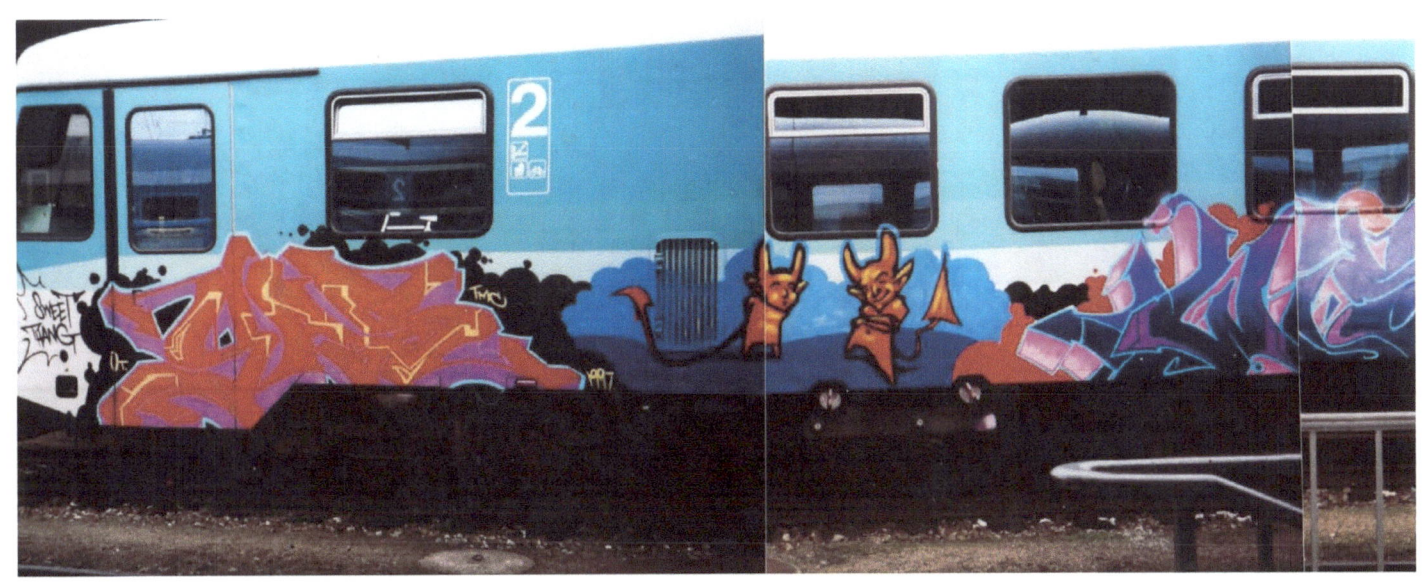

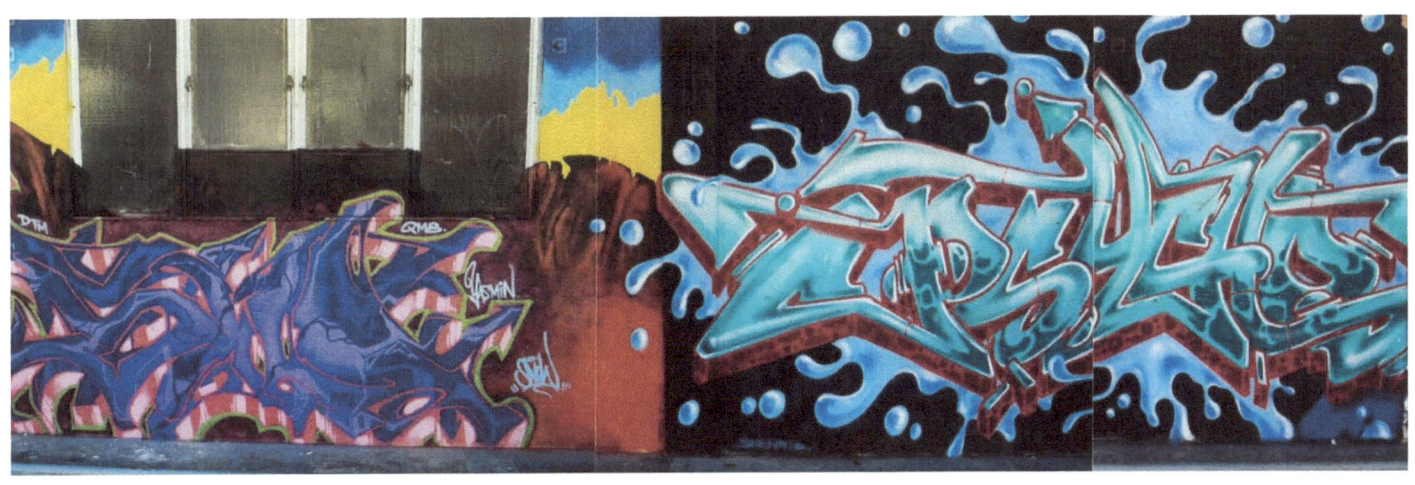

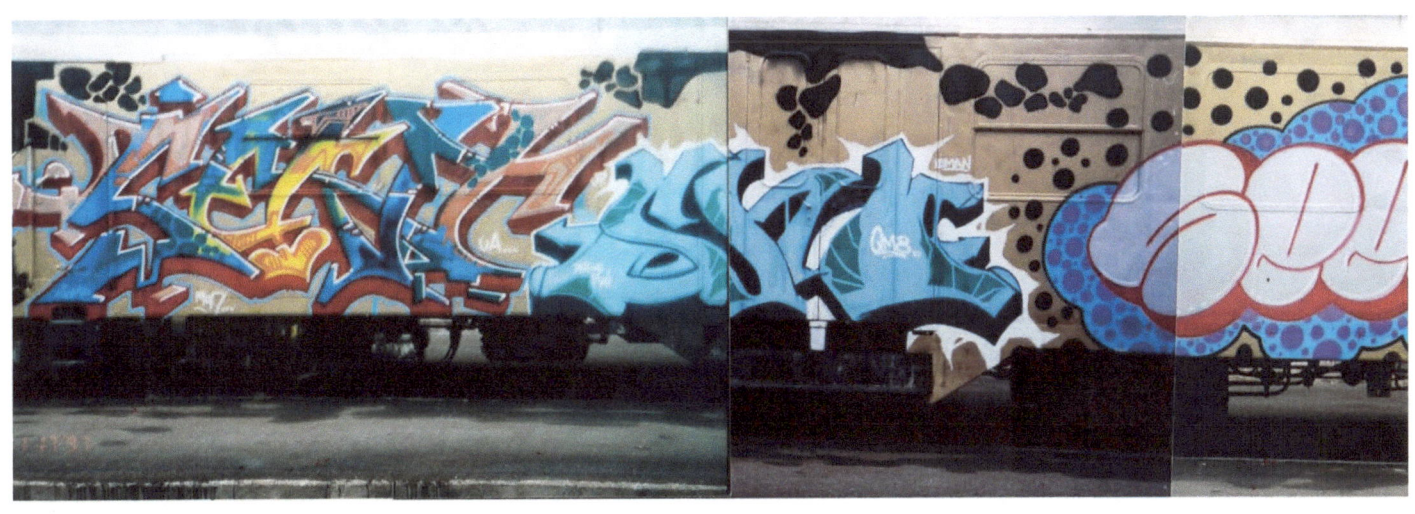

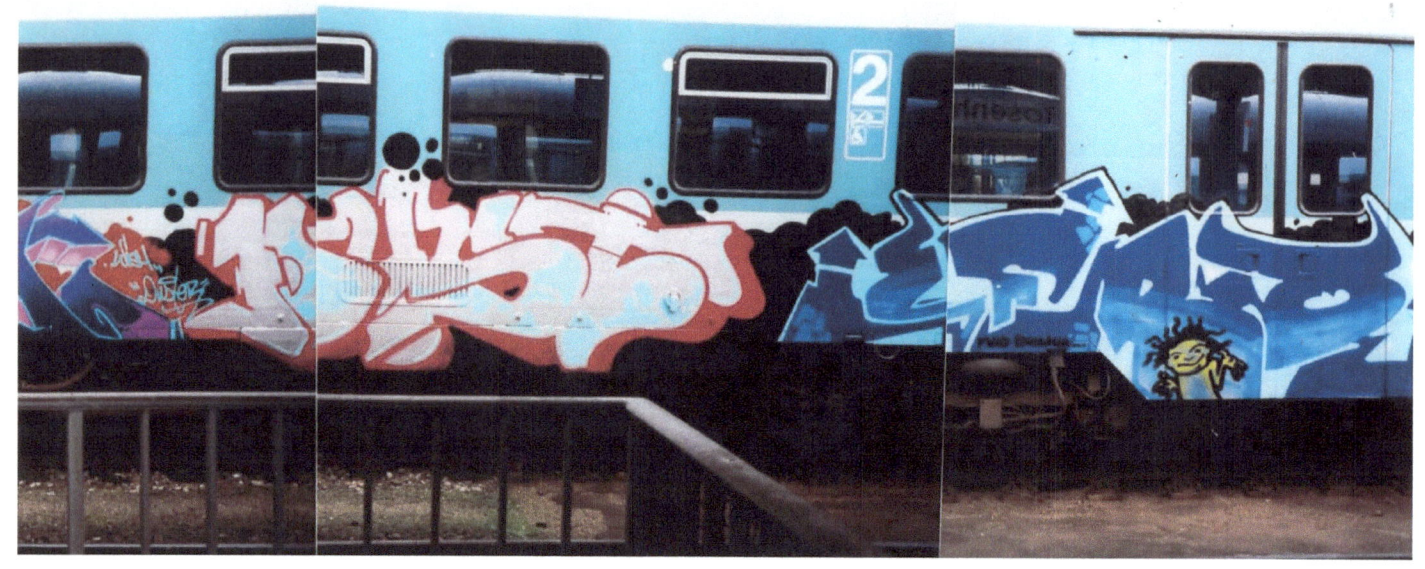

YAS by SNOW, WISH, DUST, and EFRO
Germany
1997

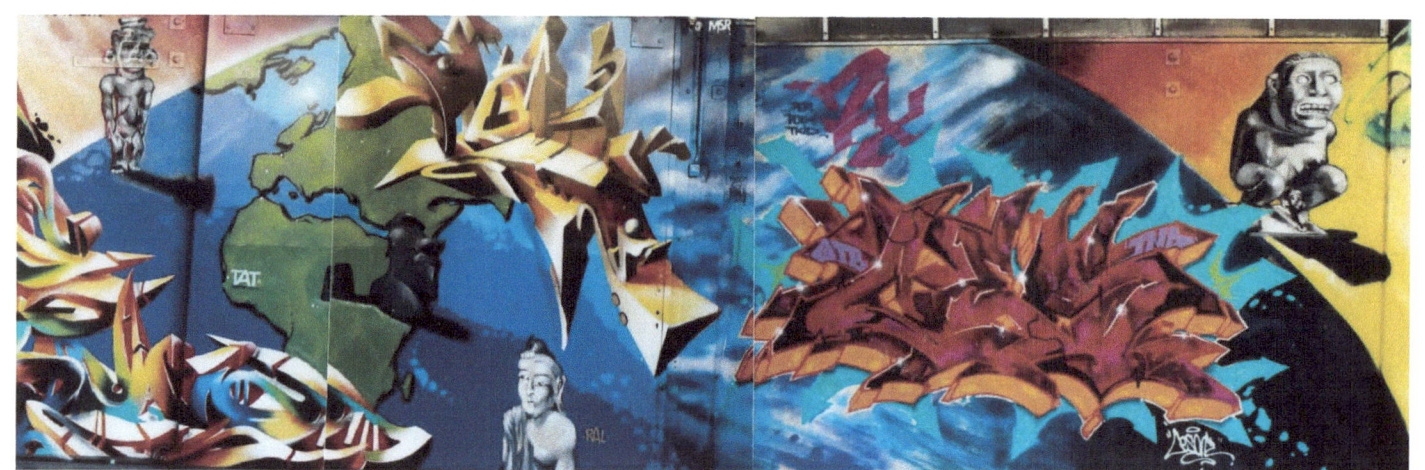

SNO FX, PSYCHO by SEEN UA, NOSM TAT, HOW TAT, CES FX
Kunstpark, Munich
1997

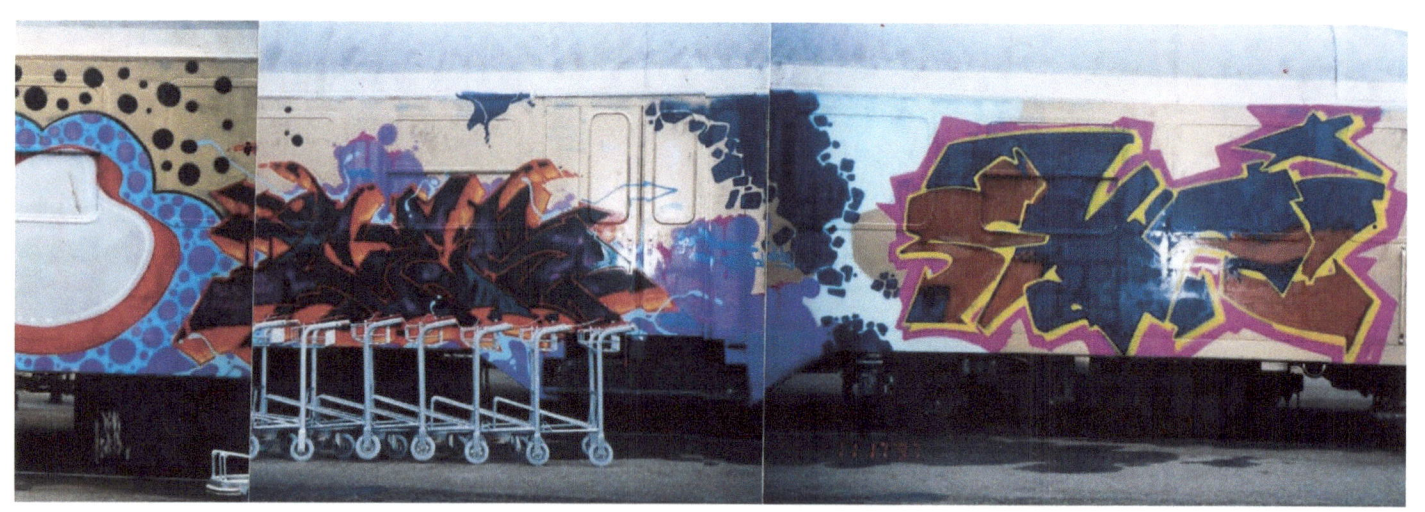

SENT (NEON TFP), SNO FX, SEEN UA, CES FX, LOOMIT

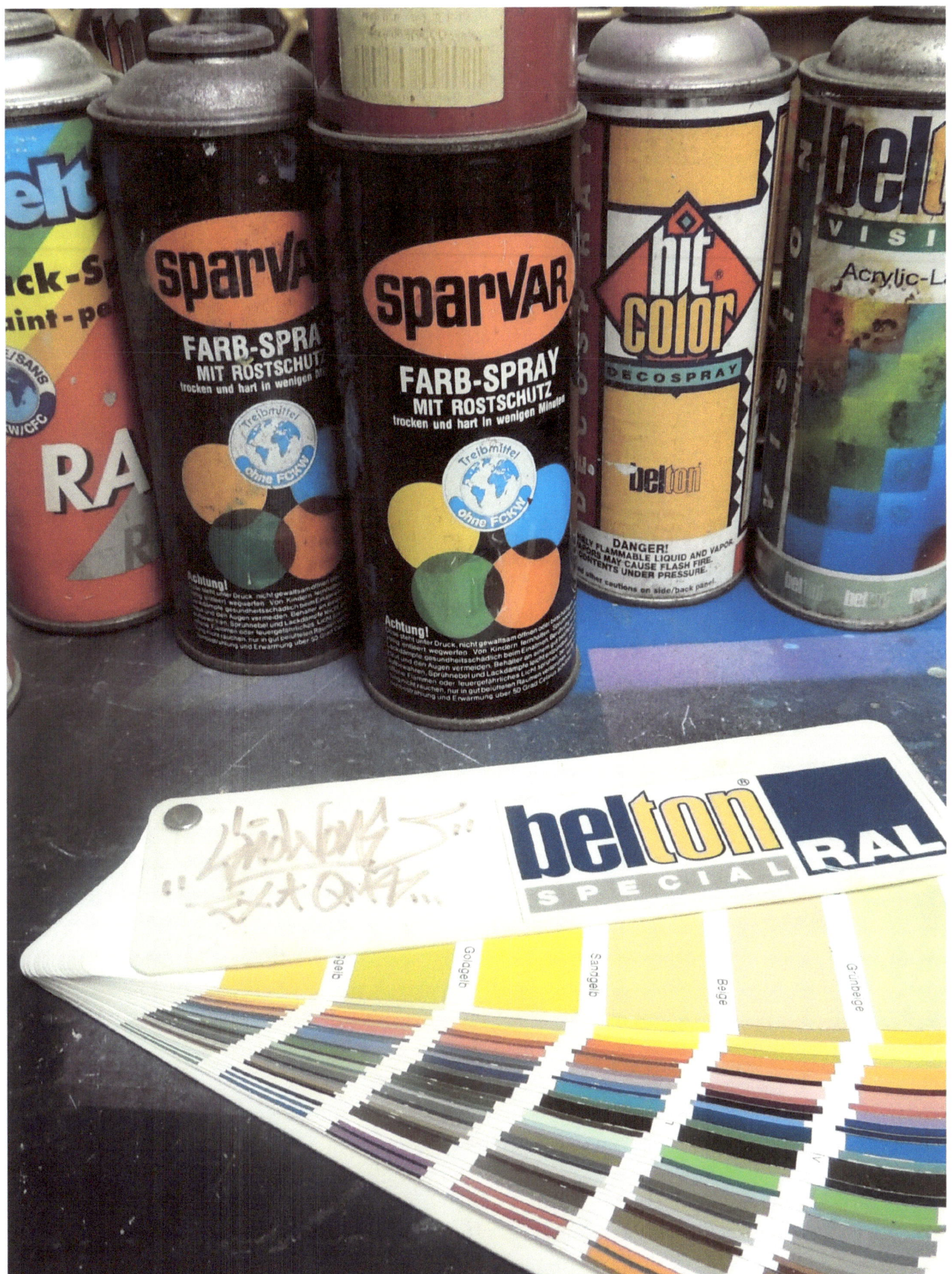

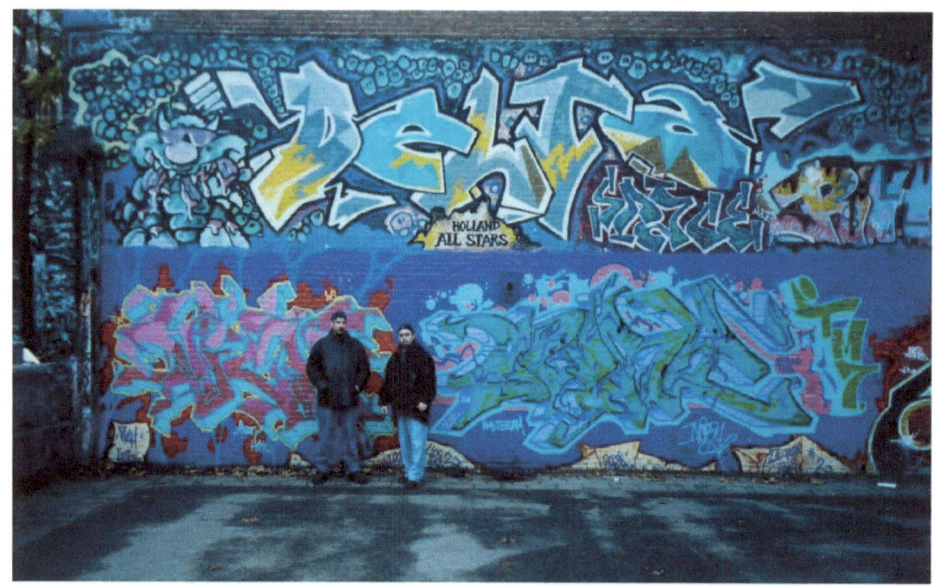

CES and SNOW chilling
Amsterdam, Holland
1997

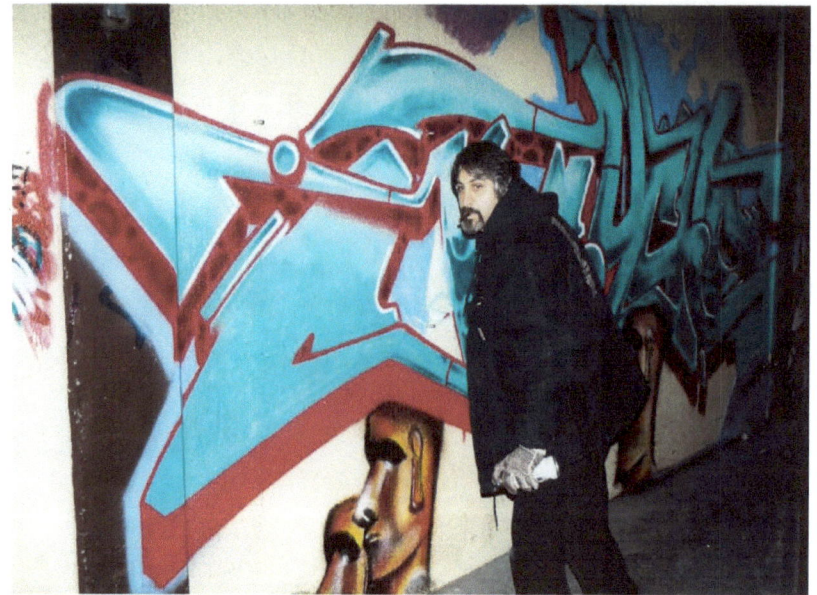

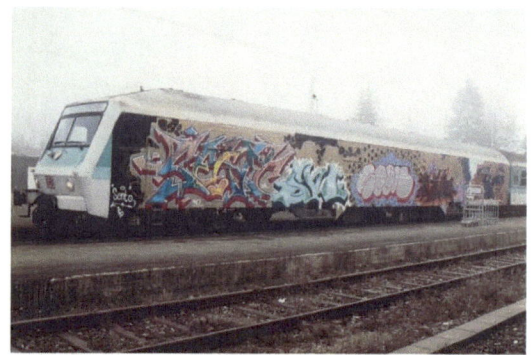

SEEN in action
Munich, Germany
1997

Loomit on background
CES, SNOW, DEMON by SEEN
BMW factory wall
Munich, Germany
1997

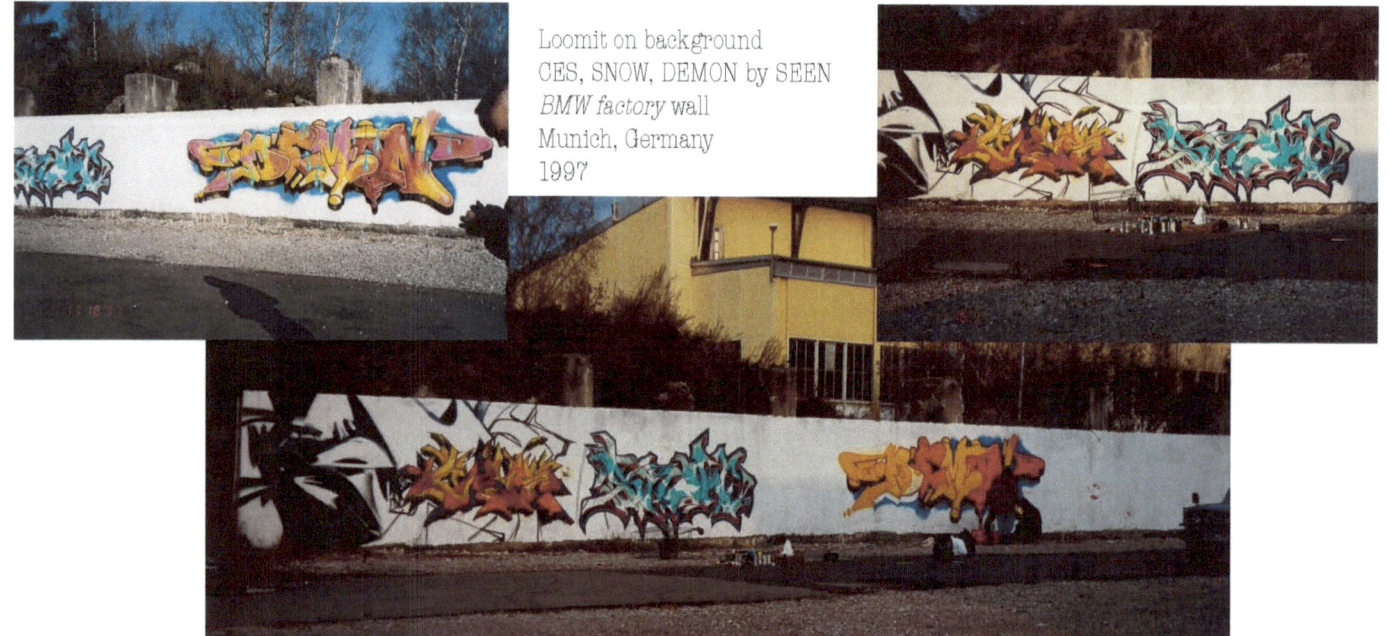

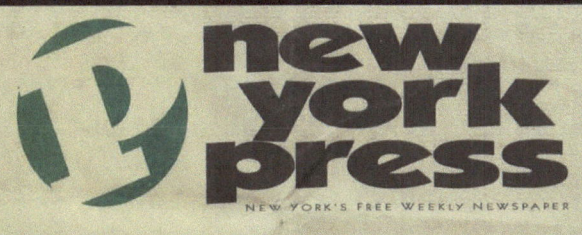

Aerosol Blues 4

Sat. Oct. 4, '97
@ The African Globe Studios
1028 Broad St. Nwk. NJ

installation	Style & Fashion	Beat & Breaks
Pre-Philly	R-36 Apparel	Hard Hittin Harry
Nace-DF	Fashion Show	& Crew
Tame-BS		
PKay-QM8	The 98 Fall	DJ. Rampage DVS
Snow-FX	Collection	Brown Bum
Dezo-TC5,FC		& The Open Mic
2Nasty-AB		Throwdown

so bring your black book, breaking gear & the energy for a true B-boy experience
doors open @ 6pm-until for more info contact Jerry Gant 973. 429.1976 or 510.4743

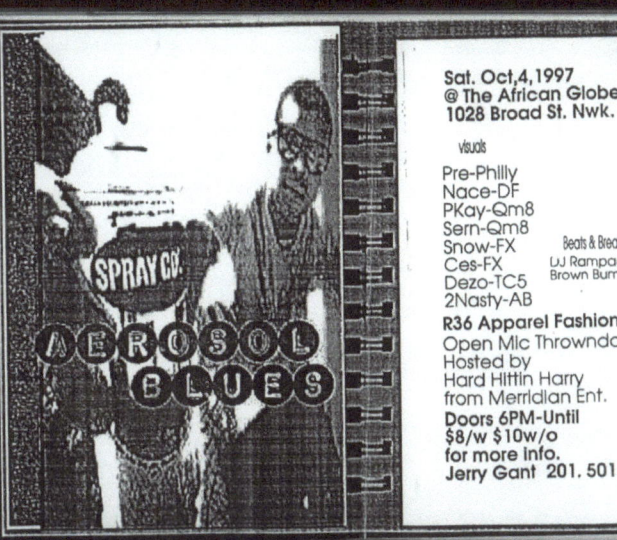

Sat. Oct. 4, 1997
@ The African Globe Studios
1028 Broad St. Nwk. N.J.

visuals

Pre-Philly
Nace-DF
PKay-Qm8
Sern-Qm8
Snow-FX   Beats & Breaks by
Ces-FX   DJ Rampage DVS
Dezo-TC5   Brown Bum & Others
2Nasty-AB

R36 Apparel Fashion Show
Open Mic Throwndown
Hosted by
Hard Hittin Harry
from Merridian Ent.
Doors 6PM-Until
$8/w $10w/o
for more info.
Jerry Gant   201. 501.4743

"The Next Millennium"
Opening Reception:
September 10, 1998

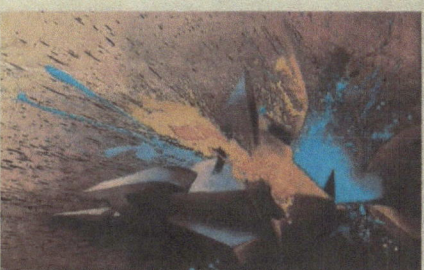

Artists:
CES, DAIM, KENT, LOOMIT, MED,
POEM, POSEII, SEEN, SNOW,
STAK, SUB, T-KID, YES2

Exhibition dates:
September 9-26th

Vincent Louis Galleries
546 Hudson (@ Perry) (212) 462-2709
"in the heart of the west village"

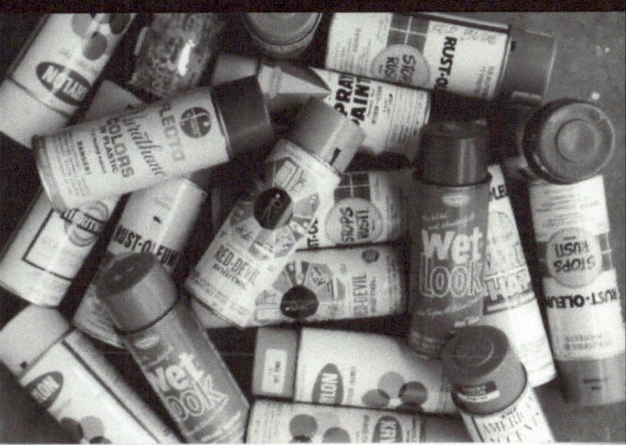

"Spray out the 90's
artworks by

CES, SEEN, MED,
YES II, SNOW, SUB,
POSE II, LOOMIT,
DAIM, KENT.

reception:
6:00 to 9:00 Thur. Sept. 9, 1999
curated by CES
Thursday Sept. 9 - Saturday 9, 1999

PACIFICO FINE ART
546 Hudson Street New York City 10014
Phone (212) 462-2709 Contact Jim Pernotto
Tues.-Sat. 11-6 (between Christopher + Perry)

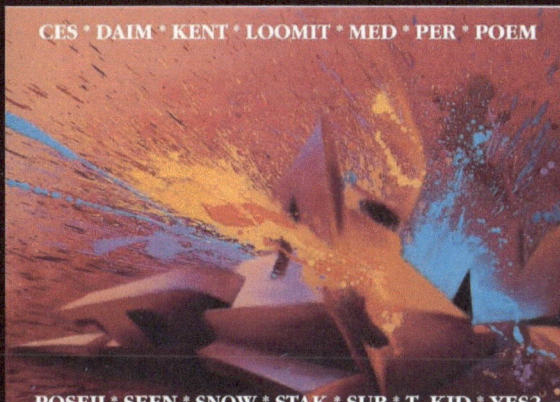

CES * DAIM * KENT * LOOMIT * MED * PER * POEM

POSEII * SEEN * SNOW * STAK * SUB * T-KID * YES2

Vincent Louis Galleries
546 Hudson (@Perry), NY, NY 10014
(212) 462-2709   Fax (212) 462-2646
"in the heart of the west village"

"The Next Millenium"

Artists: CES, DAIM, KENT, LOOMIT,
MED, PER, POEM, POSEII, SEEN,
SNOW, STAK, SUB, T-KID, YES2

Artists' Reception:
September 10th; 6 - 9 PM

Exhibition Dates:
September 9 - 26, 1998

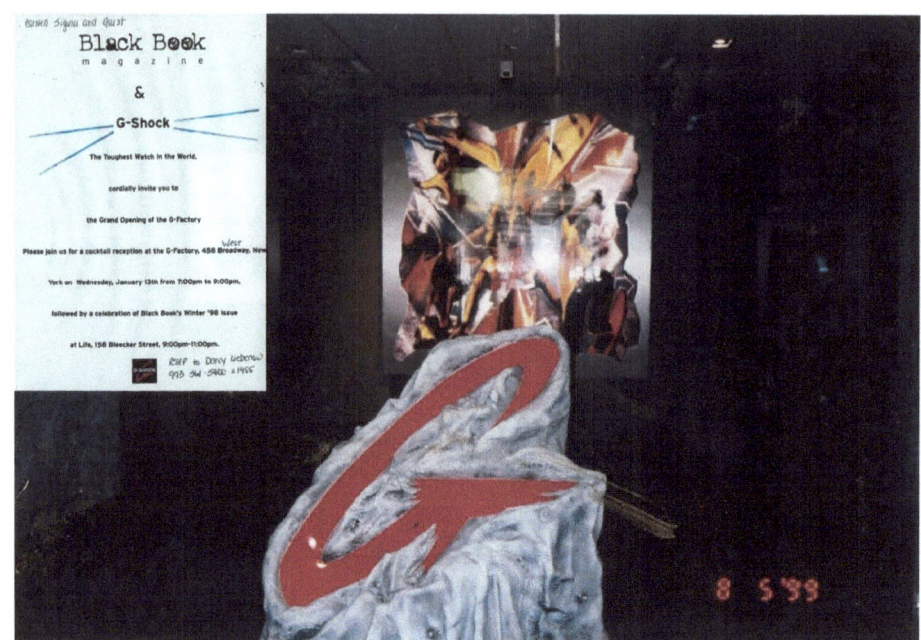

Casio G-Shock / G Factory store design and installation event
West Broadway, Soho, NYC
1999

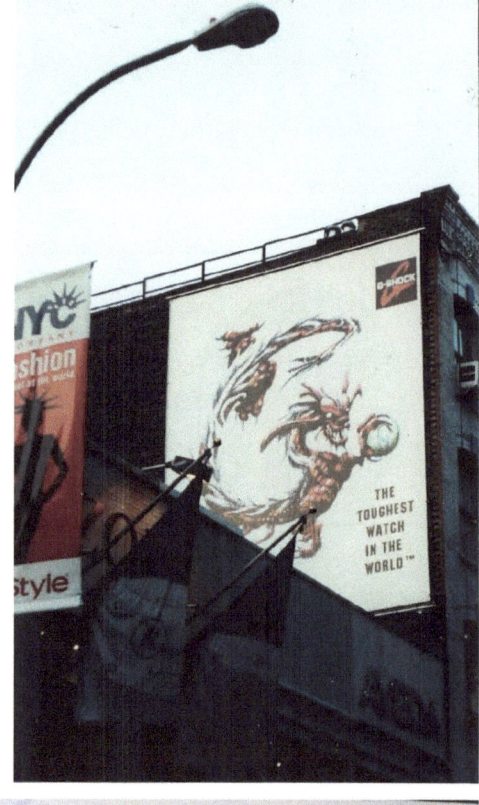

"There's been so many shows and events. The G-Shock project was my favorite. I always promised my mom that my work would be on Broadway, and I'm very happy she was able to see this become a reality before she passed away."

SNOW

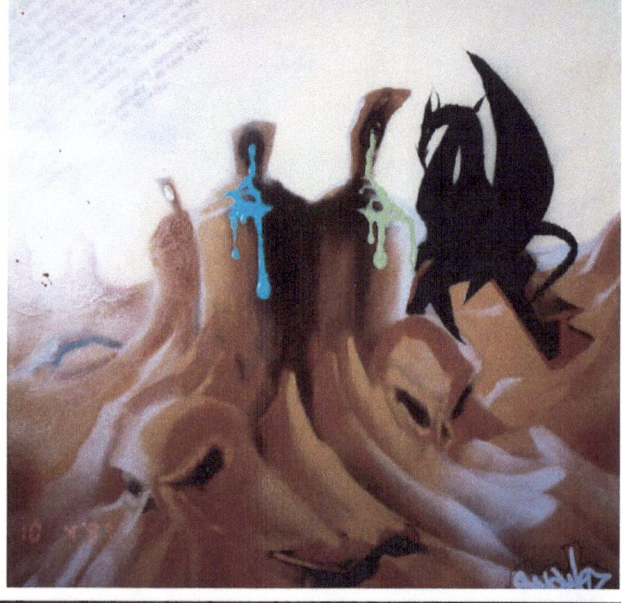

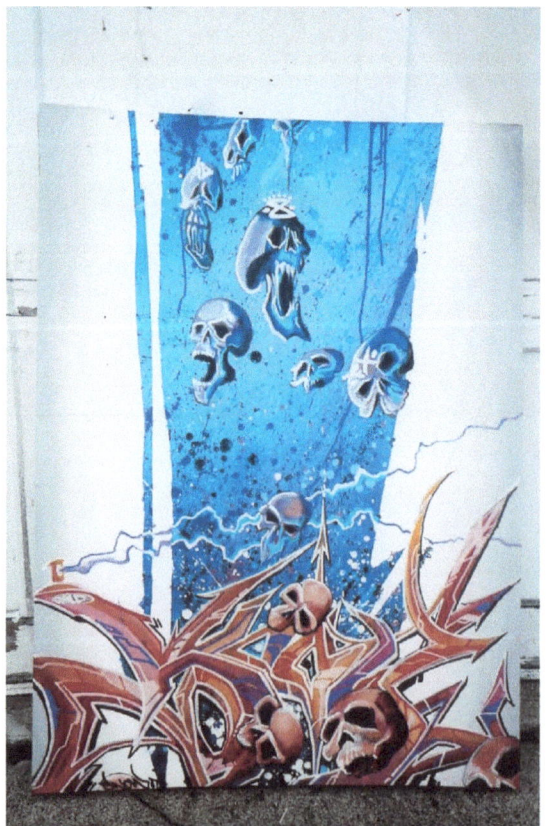

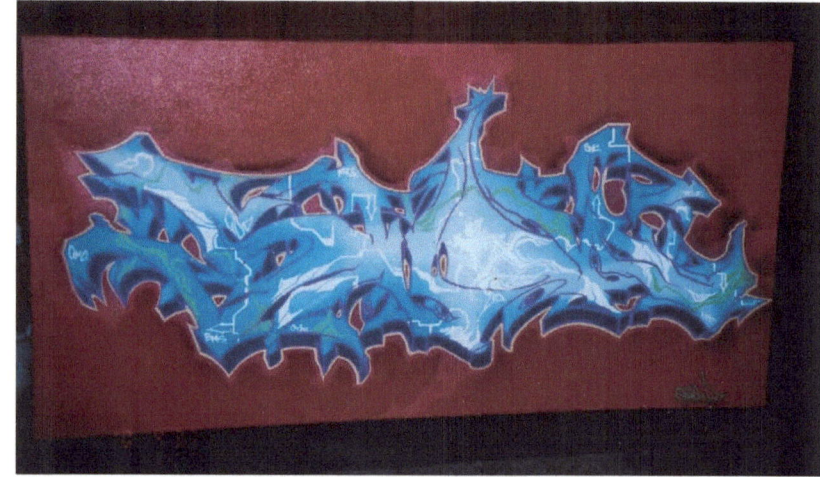

"Snow was not an original member of the FX Crew. However, upon joining the crew, his energy, style, and dedication seasoned the crew with a whole new flavor. His talent and vision influenced the crew in the direction of fantasy art. His ideas were other worldly, and his lettering style was uniquely his own; I think that's why we got along so well: he's a dreamer like me. Armed with mad cans and far out concepts, Carmelo was always willing to travel the distance from New Jersey to New York and all around the world to paint with FX. On a personal note, Snow is just a good dude and a pleasure to be around. He has paid his dues and has suffered the good, the bad, and the ugly that graffiti offers us all. The FX Crew years are indeed a significant chapter in all of our lives. However, I'm certain all the other chapters in Carmelo's life are equally as vivid, rich, and filled with fantasy! Rock on Snow!"

POSE2 FX

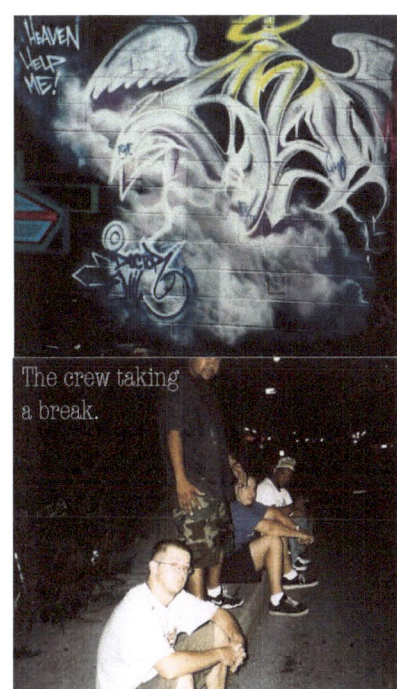

The crew taking a break.

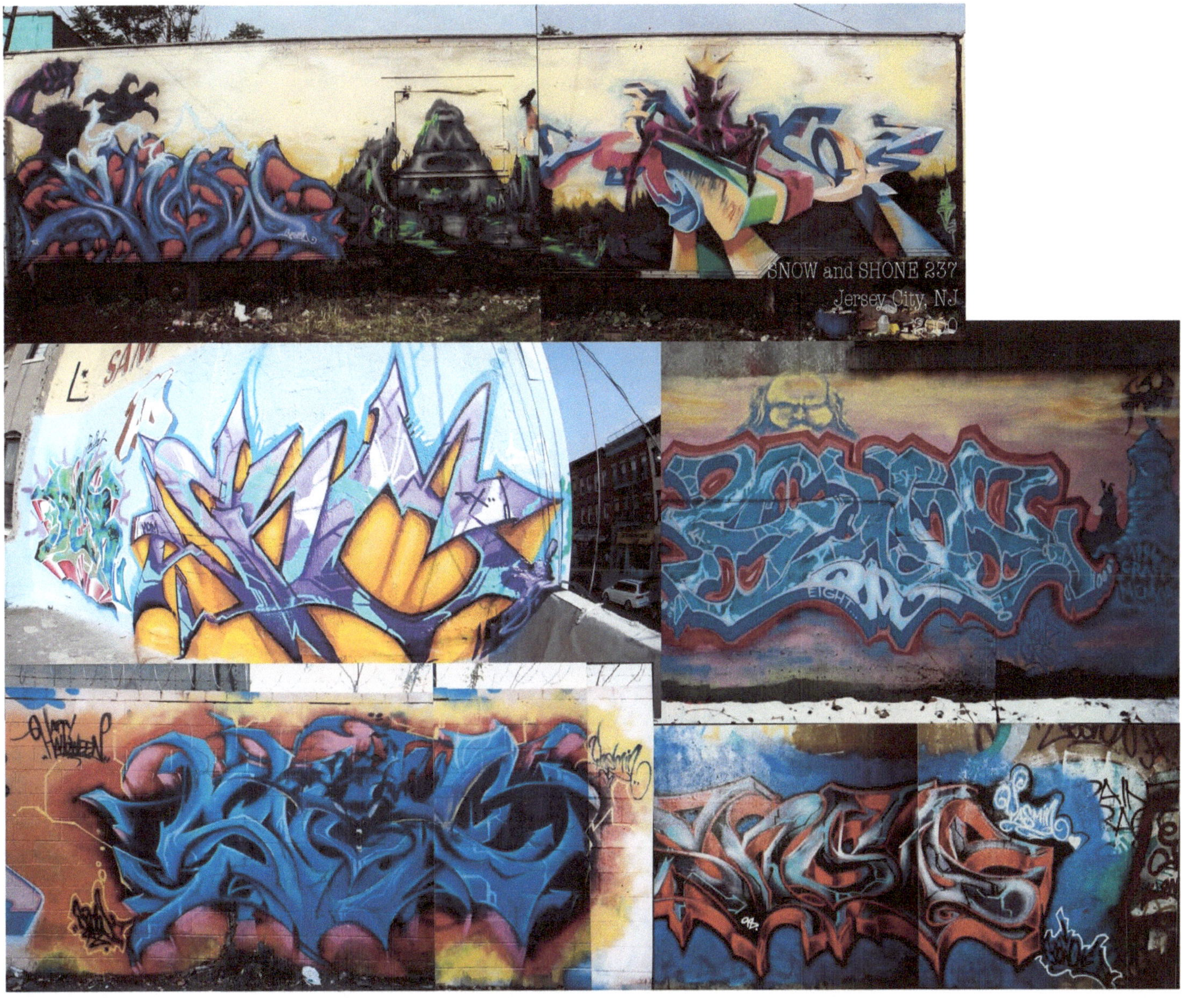

SNOW and SHONE 237
Jersey City, N.J.

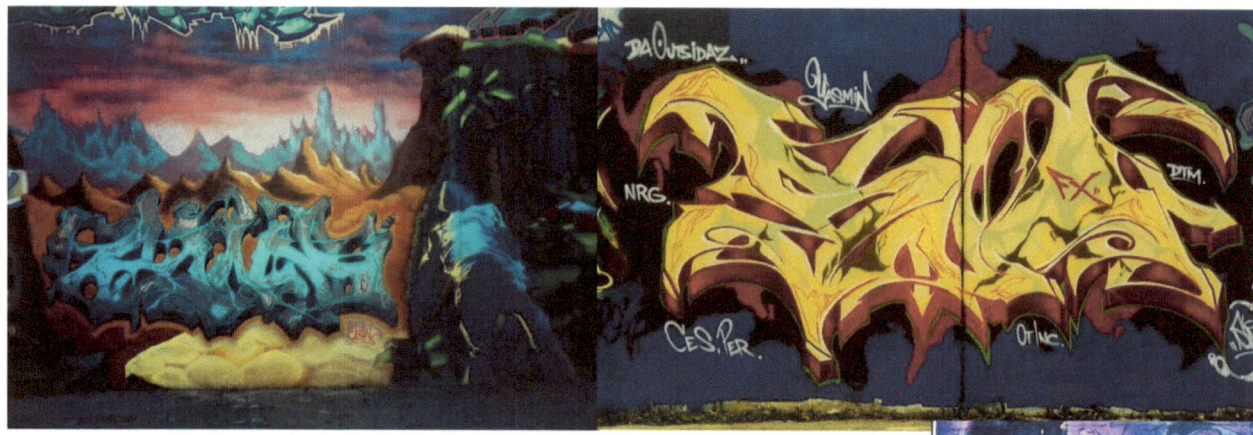

"*Where to begin?! Snow, as far as I'm concerned, embodies the true definition of a writer: well versed in every aspect of the game and constantly pushing himself to progress. When I started writing in the late '90s, Snow was already established and doing his thing with FX. The walls he was doing with those guys at that time completely blew my mind! I would study all the pictures I could find and think to myself, 'How did they do all that with spray paint?!' I met Snow in the mid 2000s, and he was always as cool as they come. We painted a few walls together, and he always told me to keep doing my thing, 'You're gonna be great!', and when he said it, I felt like maybe I could be. Hearing that from someone you look up to really does mean the world. Through all the years he's spent painting, he still had time for the little guys, and I can say wholeheartedly that it's a rarity in the graffiti subculture. Carm is an amazingly talented artist, and I'm proud to call him my brother. One love.*"

MEK

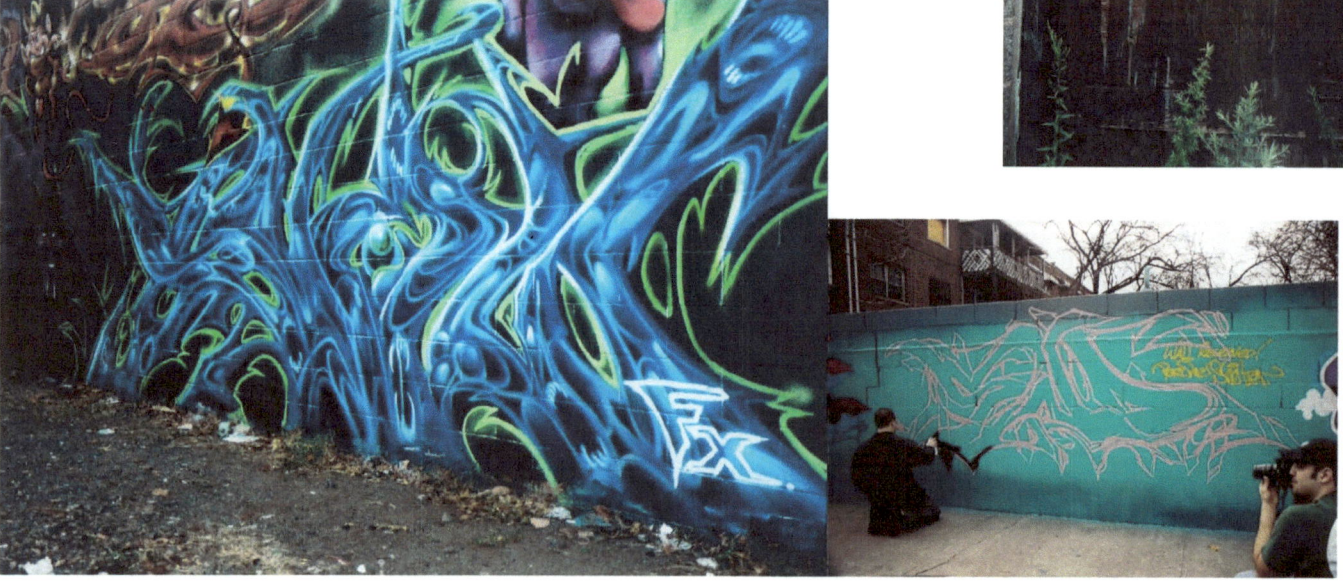

Snow looks back on his FX Crew memories with both fondness and pride. He worked hard through both adversity and opposition to maintain his contributions to the crew and its legacy can still be seen today, inspiring artwork and styles around the world.

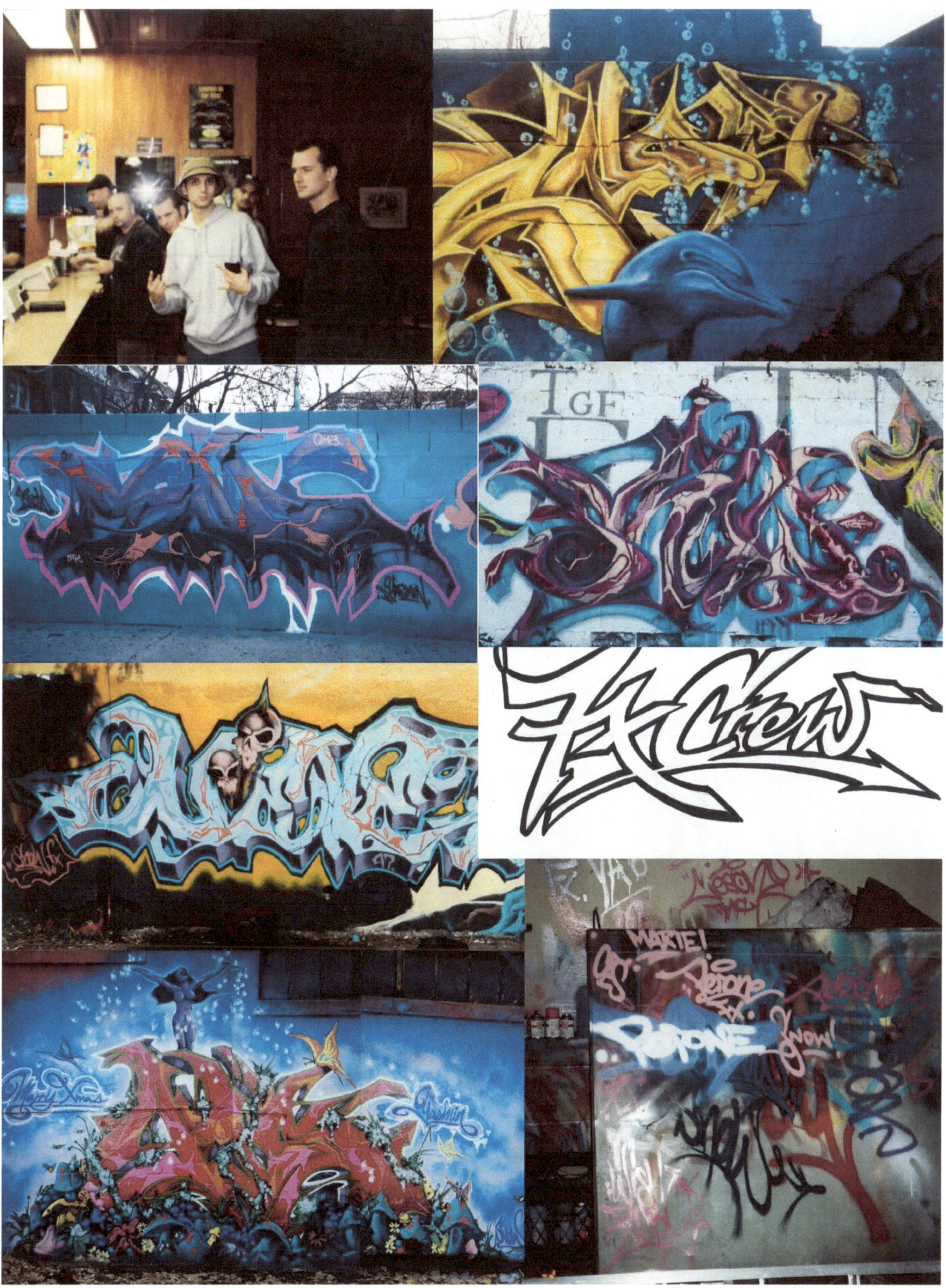

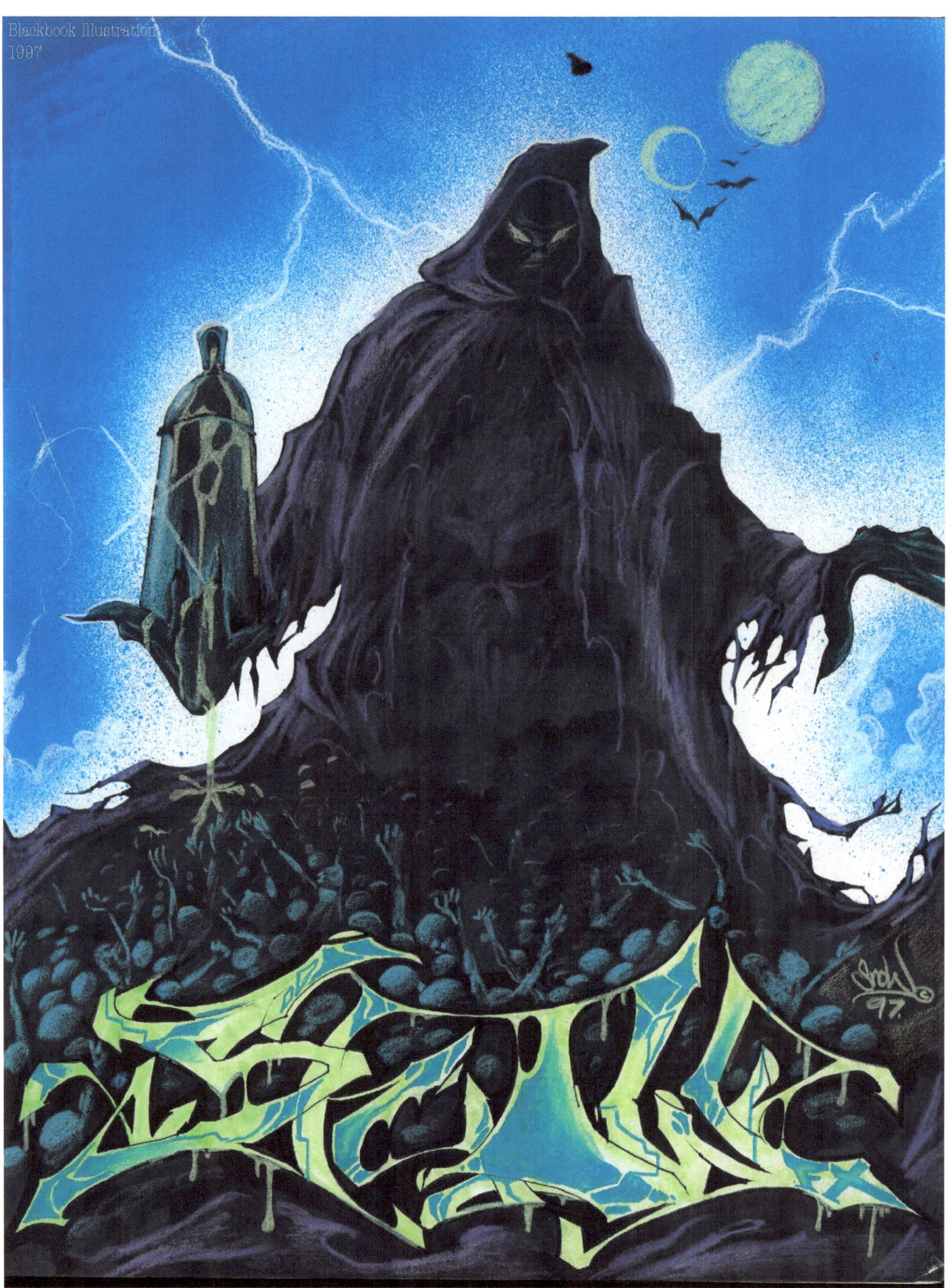

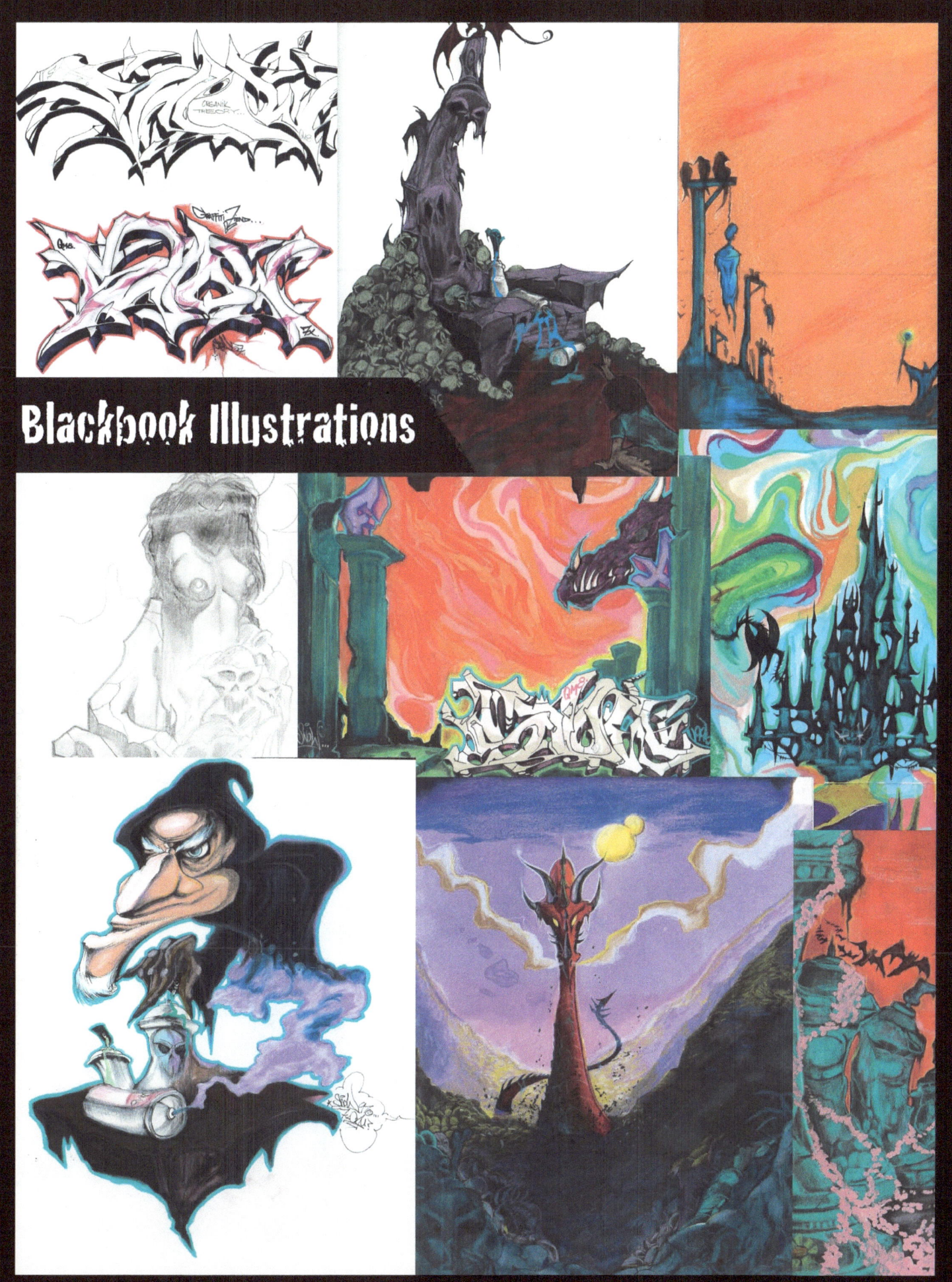

Blackbook Illustrations

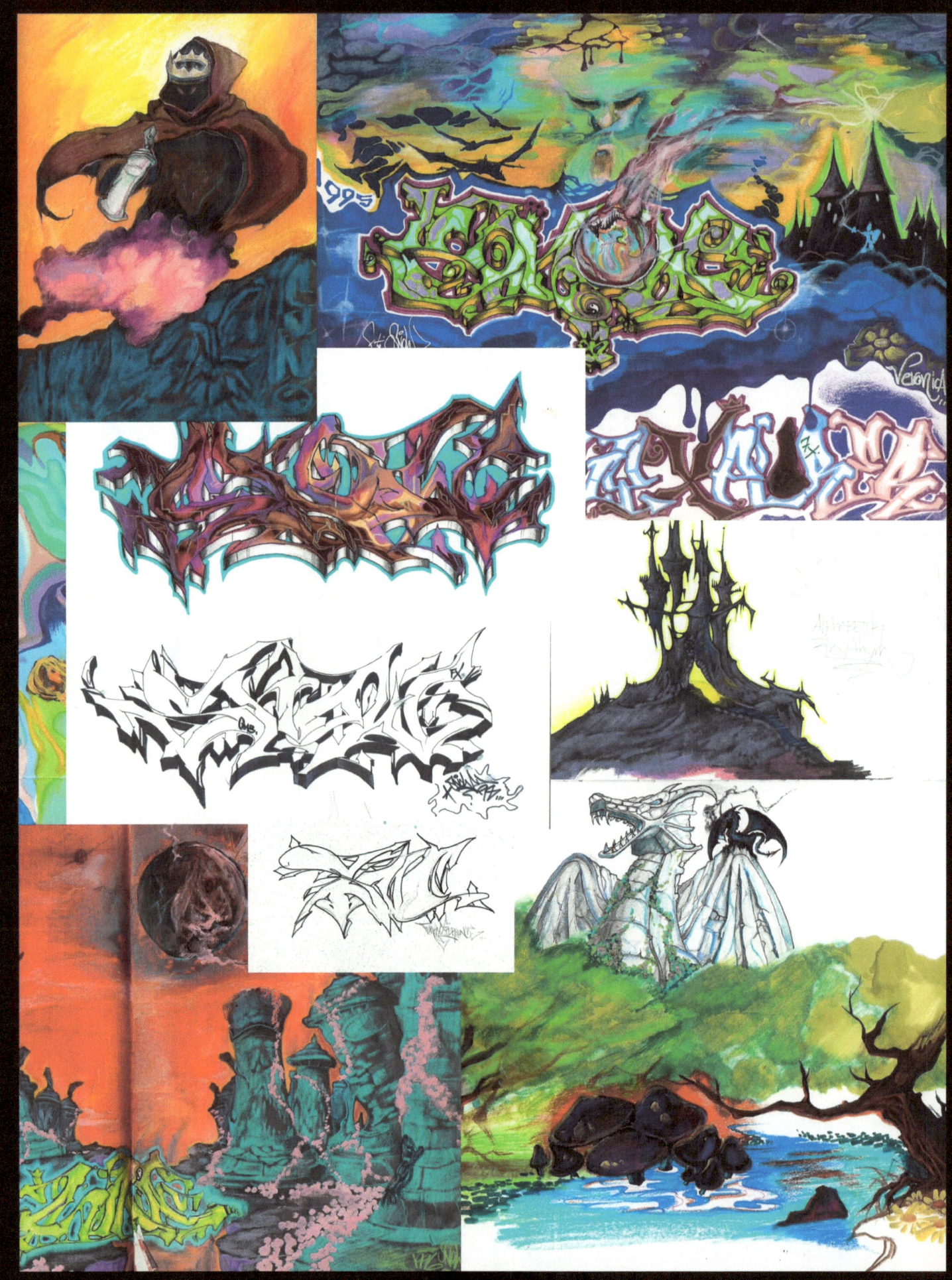

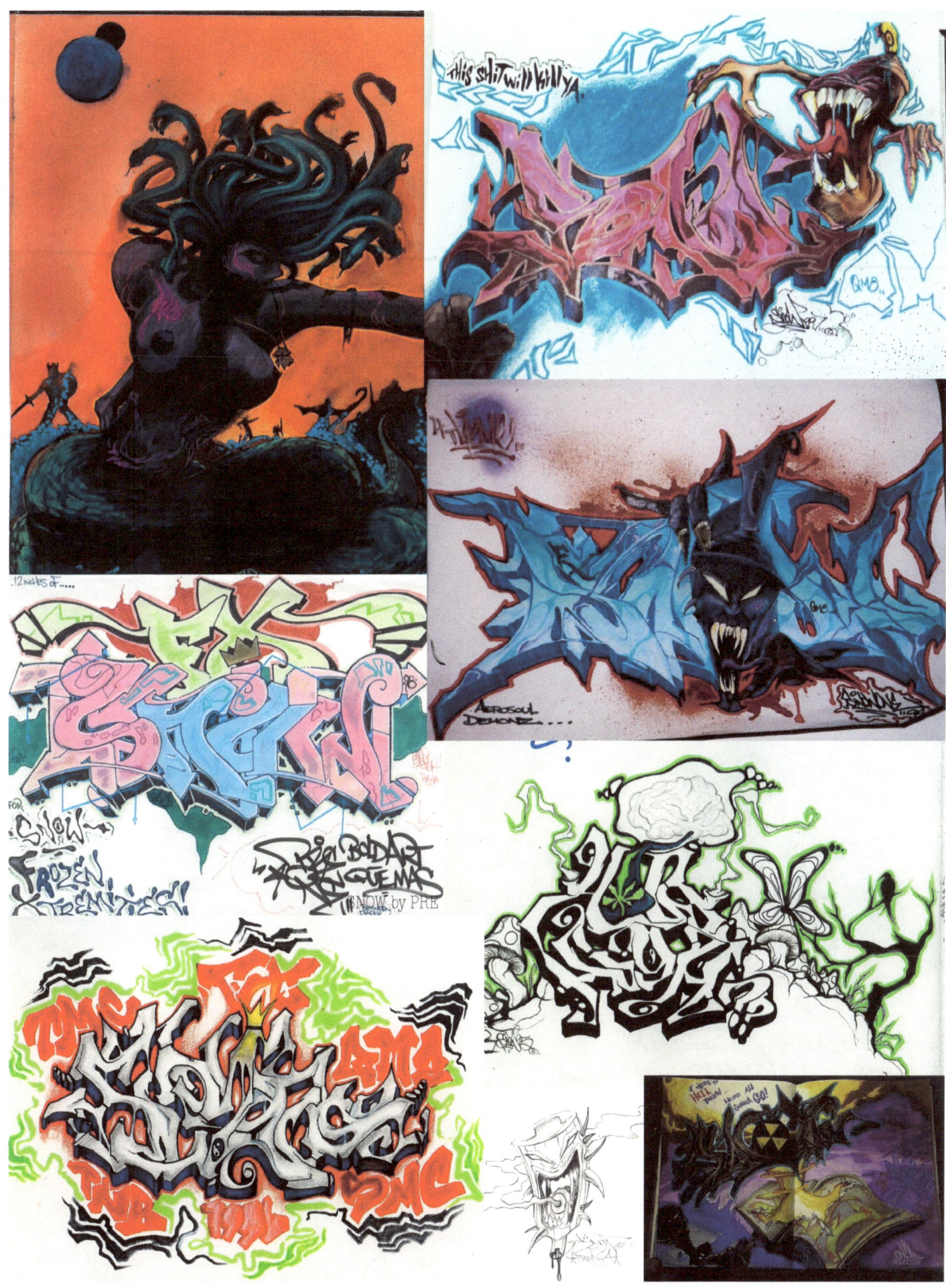

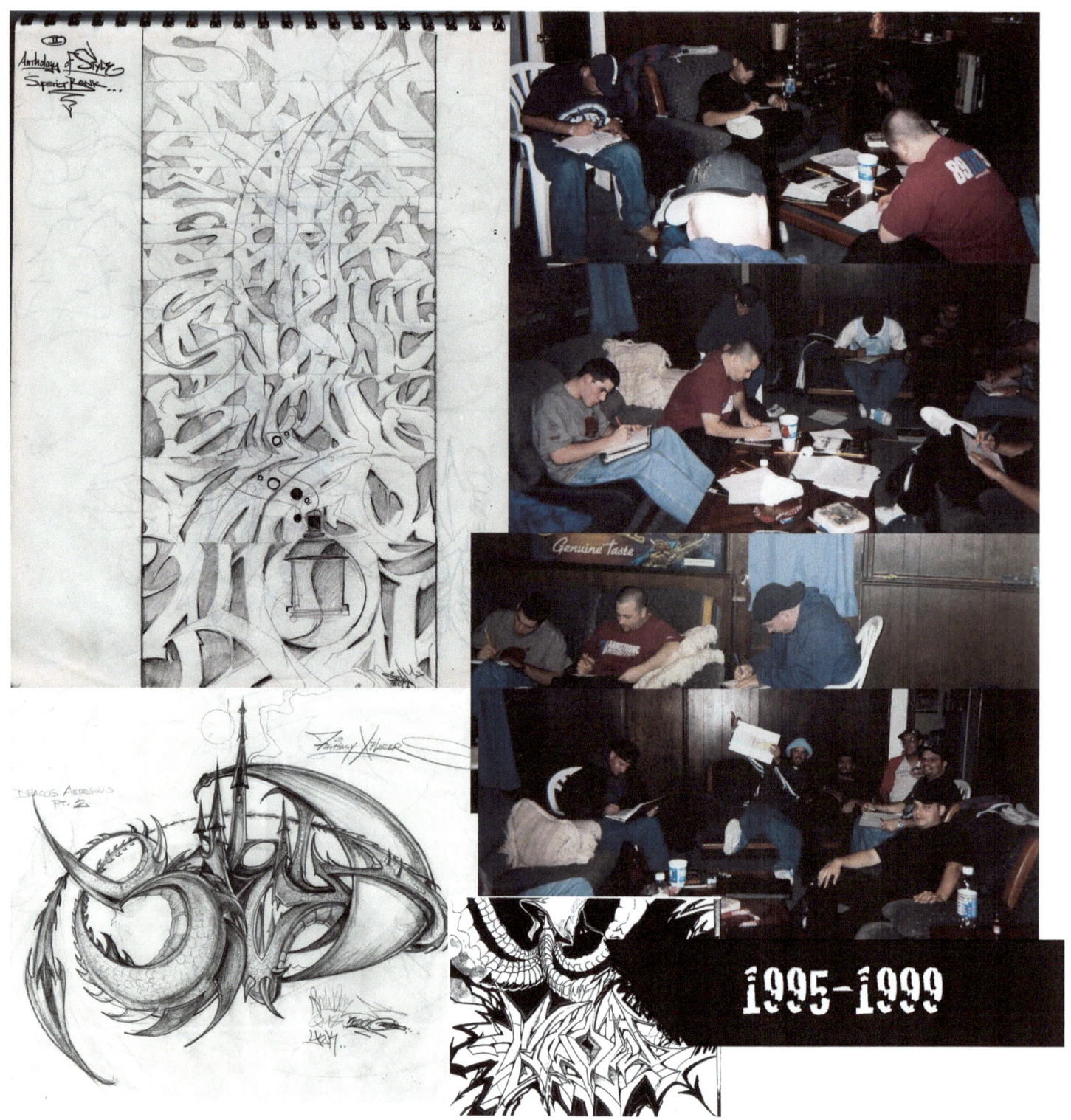

"I really enjoyed our blackbook sessions. I believe it was SWET from Denmark who turned us onto the 5 minute blackbook battle session. it was cool because we would pick a random work, or name, and then you had 5 minutes to rock a freestyle sketch. When time was up, the group would judge who took that round, and the winner got to keep the sketches. One of the more epic sessions we had included myself, CES, PRE from Philly, DJ SAT-ONE, TECK SCW, and ZAR TGF. There was some special guests, including SWET, KENT, and SEEN. It was really a priviledge for me to host these sessions at my home in New Jersey."

SNOW

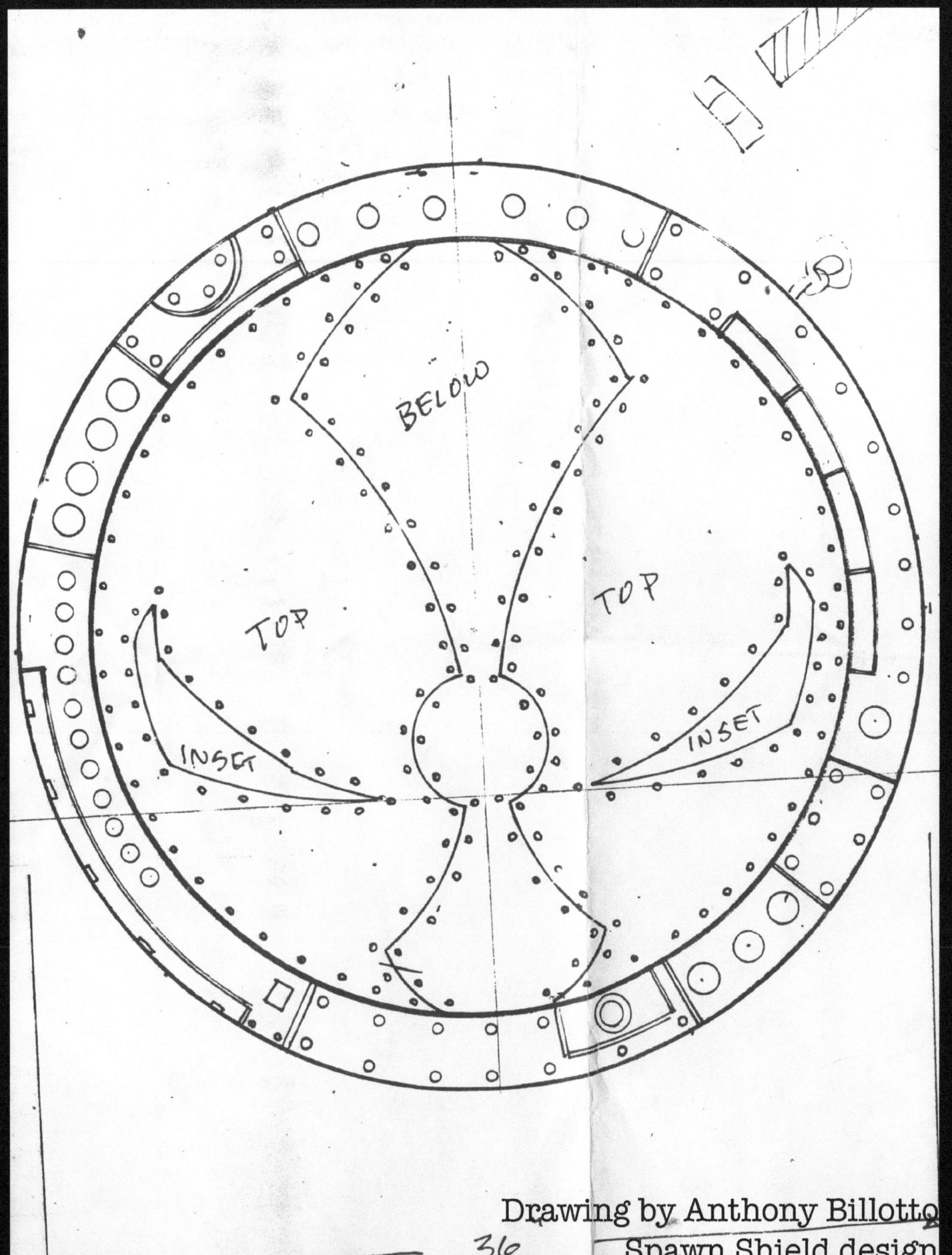

BELOW

TOP

TOP

INSET

INSET

36

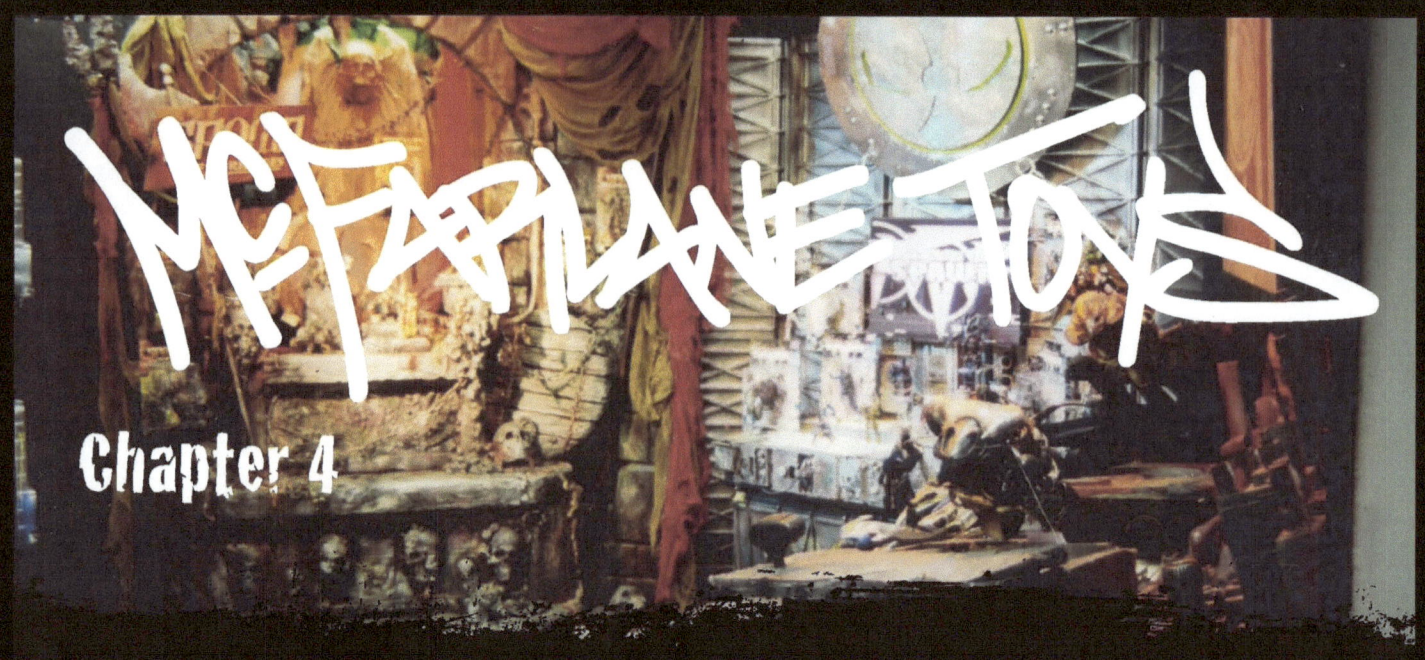

MCFARLANE TOYS

Chapter 4

1994 was really an exciting year for Snow. In addition to the rapidly growing success he was having with FX Crew, Snow's career as a professional artist was also on the rise.

1994 marked the year Snow would meet the then co-President of McFarlane Design Group, Anthony Billotto, through a mutual friend, Steve "The Victim" Hamady. Hamady showed Billotto some of Snow's mural work located behind a local service station adjacent to Snow's apartment in Caldwell, NJ. Billotto, like most, was impressed with Snow's work.

Soon after meeting Snow, Anthony Billotto would offer him a job painting Spawn murals at the McFarlane Toys showroom, located in the toy building on Broadway, NYC. The showroom showcased the new toy designs at the annual International Toy Fair, held at the Jacob Javits Center and the Broadway location of the International Toy Building.

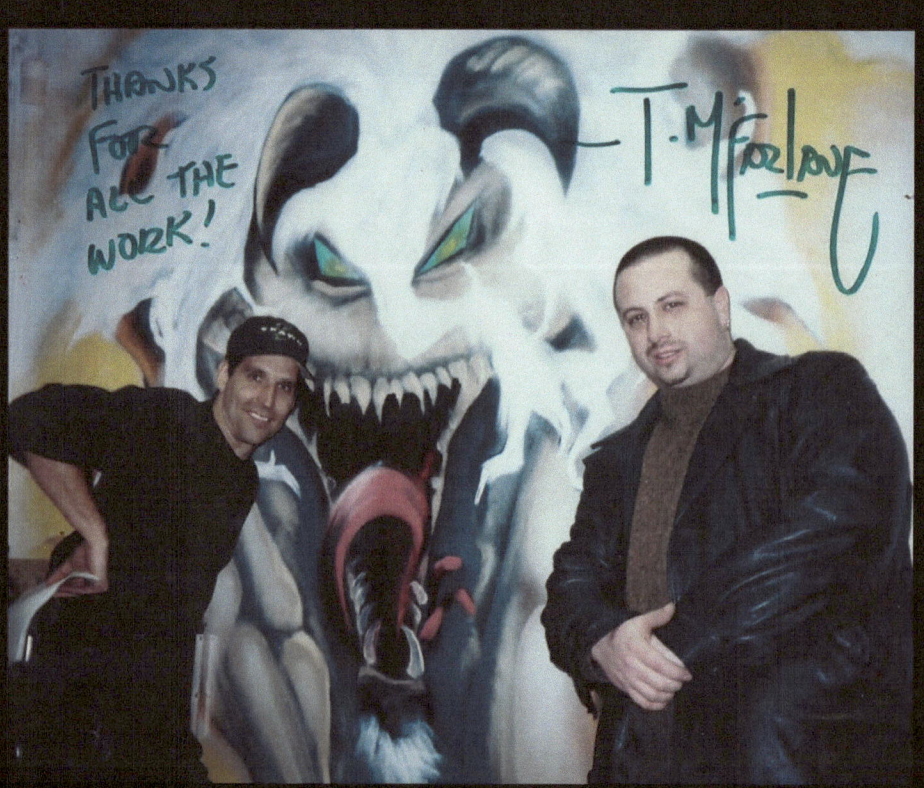

Snow recalls that first experience; feeling a bit out of place as he arrived at the showroom. Donning his typical street painting attire, he made his entrance dressed in with his usual painting jacket, jeans, boots, and backpack, all of which was covered in paint, of course. When the doors of the showroom opened, Snow felt like he had entered the Twilight Zone. The showroom was filled with craftsmen, artists, and contractors, all working on various environments and sets. He recalls, with fond memories, how he felt a bit mesmerized and overwhelmed by the whole scene. Before he could become fully unnerved, he was warmly greeted by Billotto. As Snow started the mural and rendered the original Spawn character, the showroom staff gathered and watch him as he pulled spray cans out of his backpack. He grabbed everyones attention and had an immediate impact on all of them, most especially Anthony (Tony) Billotto. Tony quickly offered Snow more work opportunities. This would launch not only a promising and fulfilling experience with McFarlane Toys, but also start a wonderful friendship between Tony and Snow. Snow also invited his good friend, and crewmate, Jamie HEF to paint in the toy showroom. The tone for Snow's relationship with McFarlane Toys was set with both a positive and promising vibe for the future.

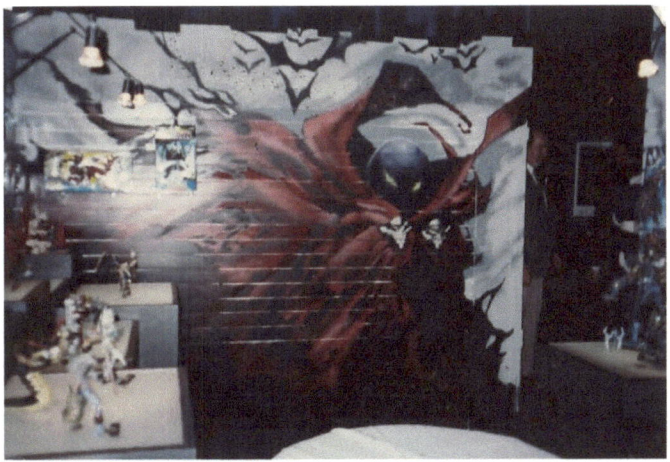
First painting done for McFarlane Toys by Snow

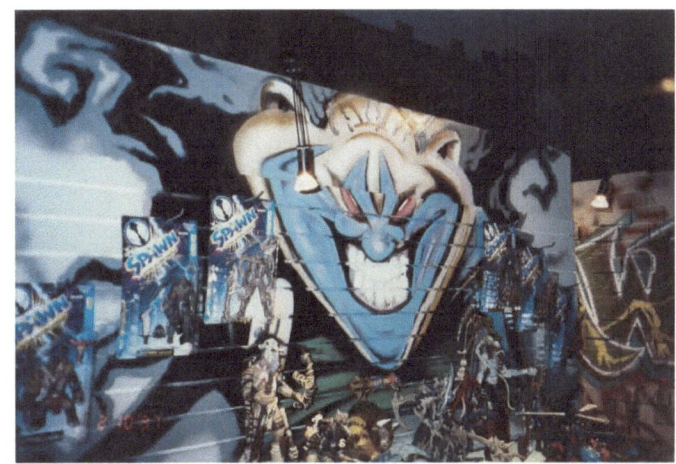
Clown painting by Jamie HEF

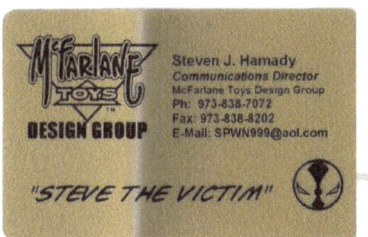

"Steve was the one who introduced me to Tony, and hooked me up with the Spawn gig."
SNOW

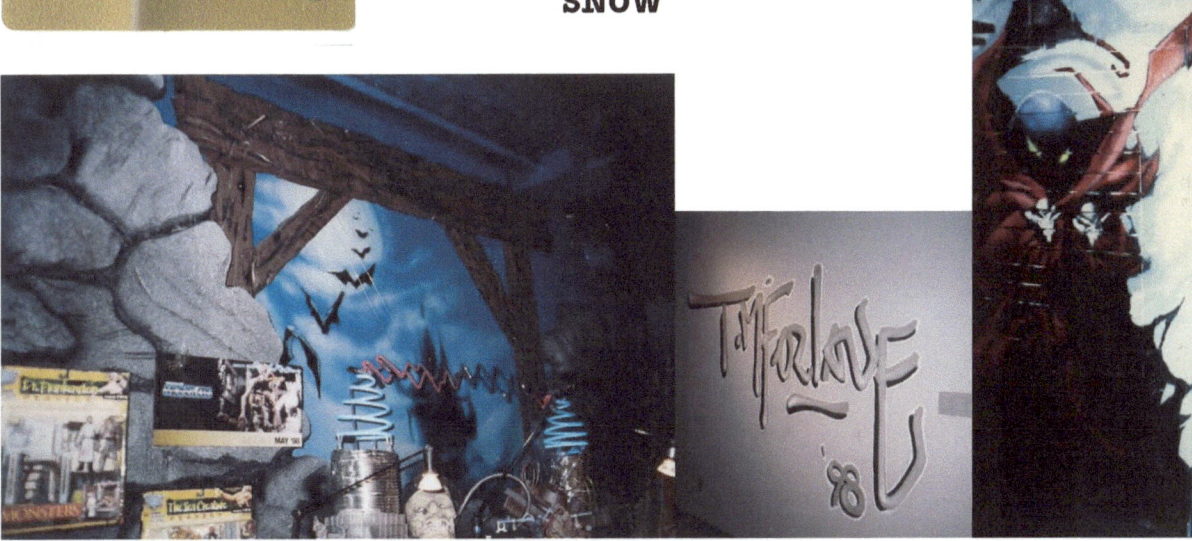

Subsequently, the next seven years working for McFarlane would prove invaluable for Snow. He would bounce between working at the showroom and painting prototypes at the McFarlane Design Studio in Bloomingdale, NJ. The combined experience of Tony Billetto and his cousin Ken Hoare would be an immense help in contributing to Snow's growth as an artist. Through their guidance and tutelage, Snow really began to excel. He was learning new and exciting techniques while exploring and experimenting with new mediums and materials.

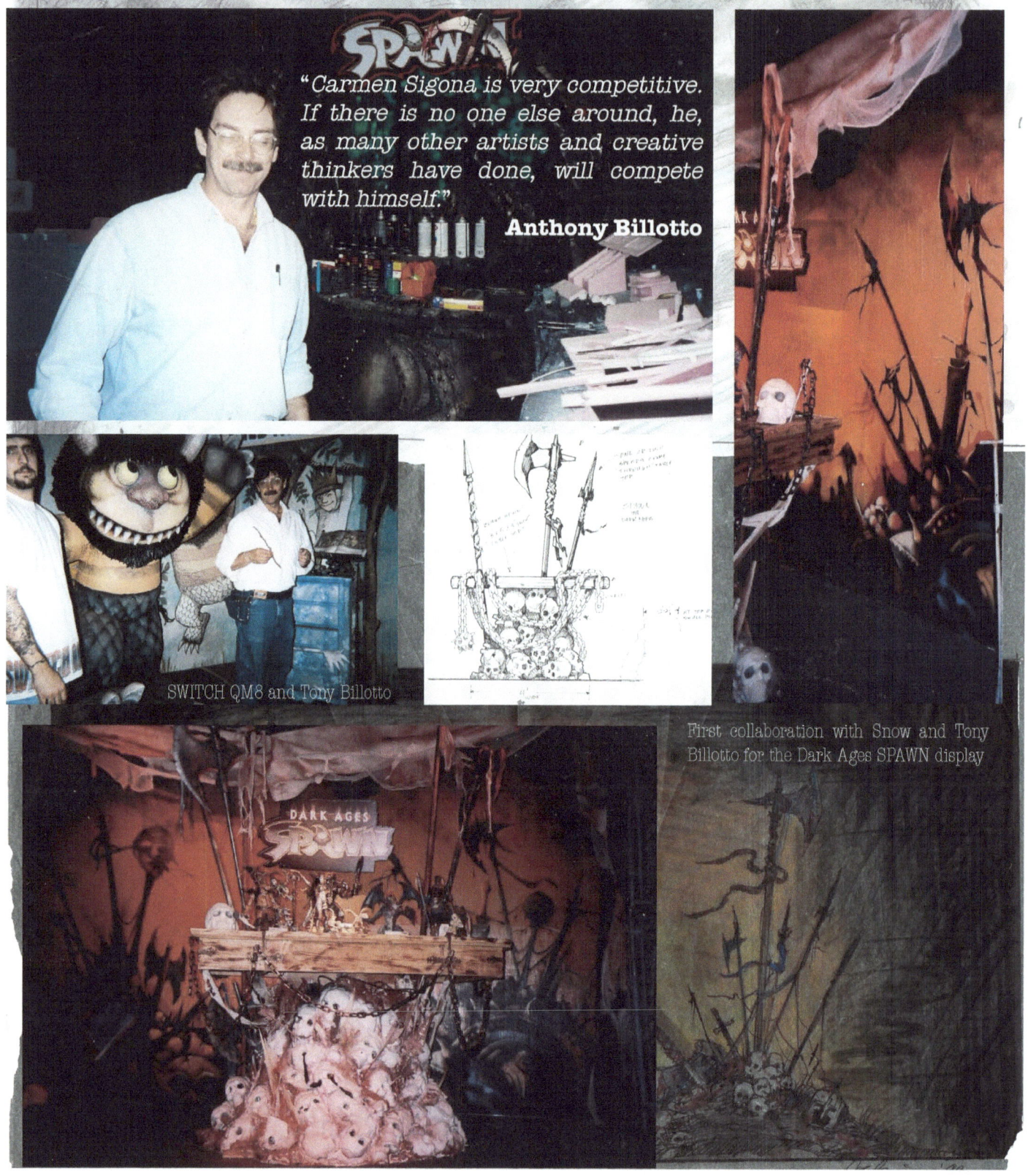

"Carmen Sigona is very competitive. If there is no one else around, he, as many other artists and creative thinkers have done, will compete with himself."

Anthony Billotto

SWITCH QM8 and Tony Billotto

First collaboration with Snow and Tony Billotto for the Dark Ages SPAWN display

The graffiti prodigy described their guidance as "getting 30 years worth of experience in just seven years". He basically received a "crash course" in showroom design and installation as well as prototype design and finishing. It was a very exciting time for Snow, and he enjoyed his newfound friendships. (Snow participated in the International Toy Fair from 1994 to 2001; sometimes working on two shows per year.)

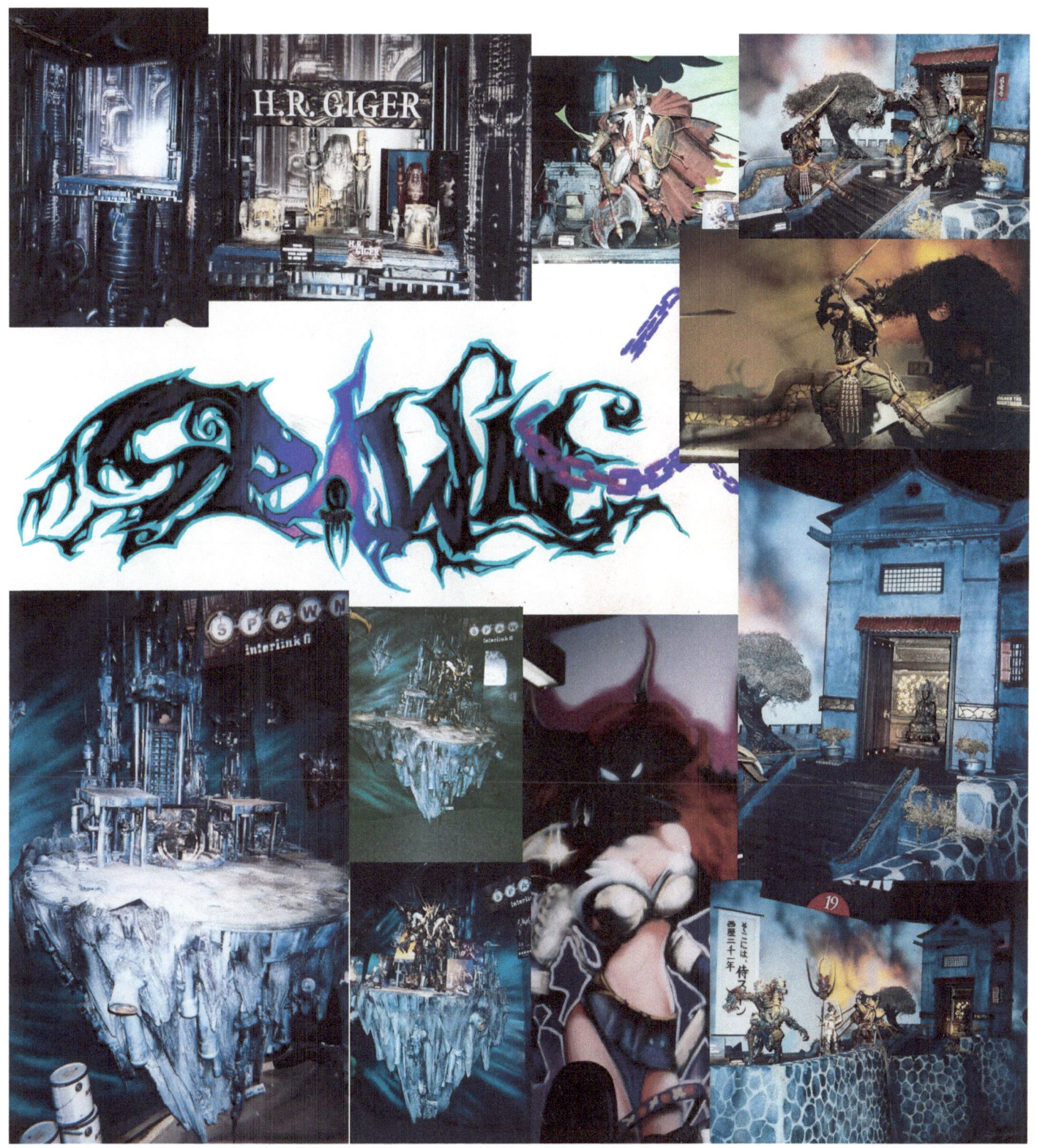

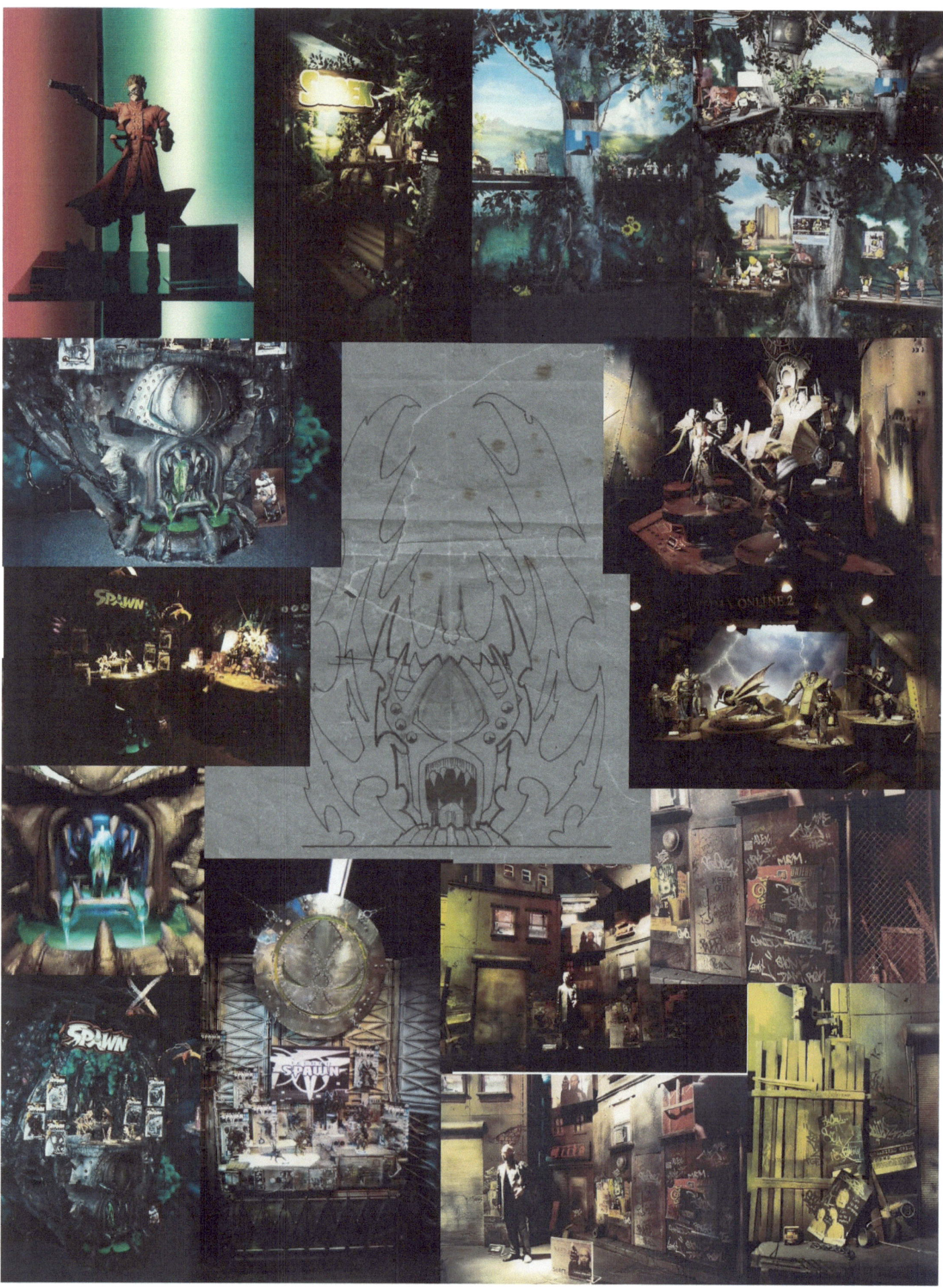

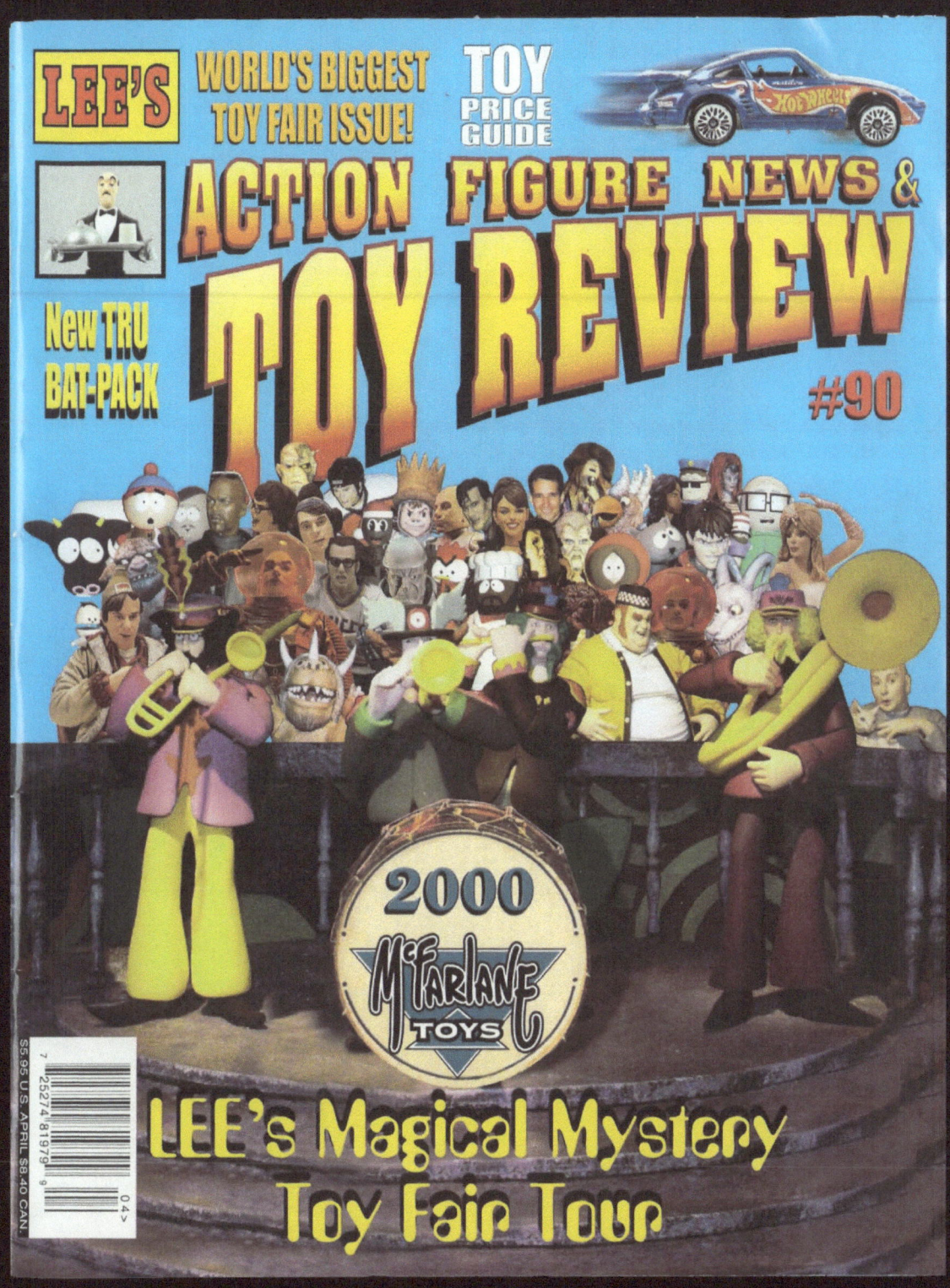

"Pound for pound, I know we were one of the hottest show rooms at Toy Fair every year. Funny thing is, we used to dumpster dive the big companies, like Habro, Mattel, etc., and reuse all of their discarded materials in our showroom. There was a lot of buzz in those days about the McFarlane showroom and how hot in looked every year. The inside joke amongst us was that we used the major companies' scraps to blow them out of the water."

SNOW

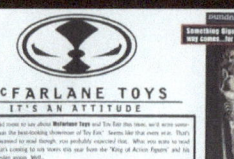

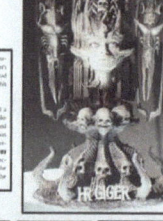

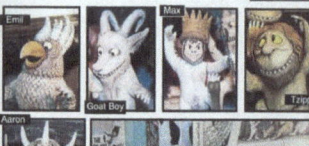

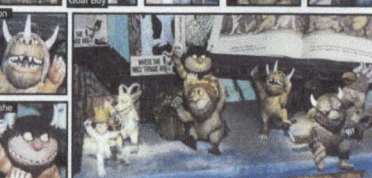

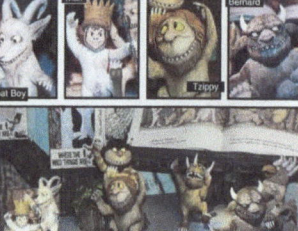

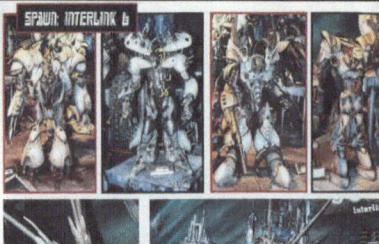

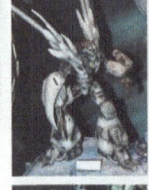

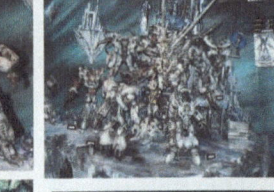

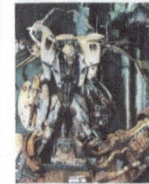

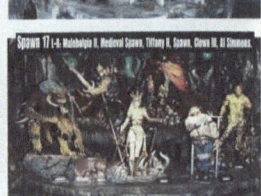

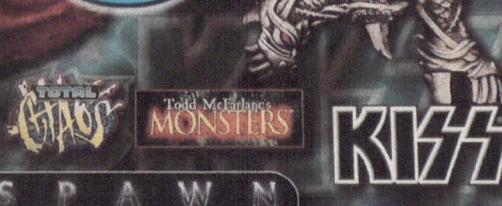

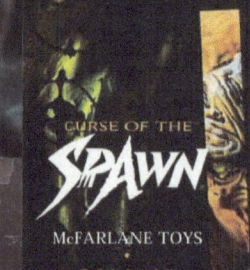

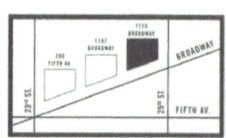

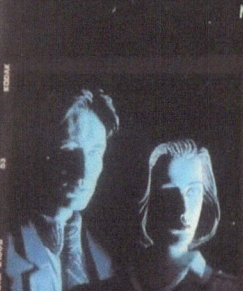

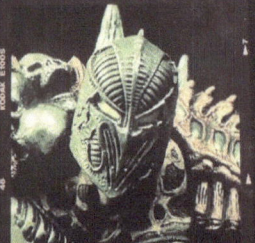

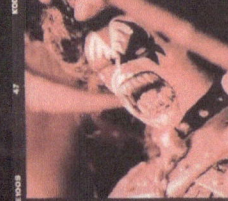

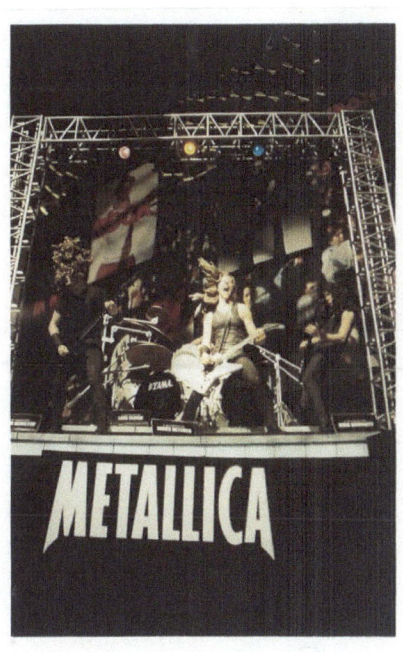

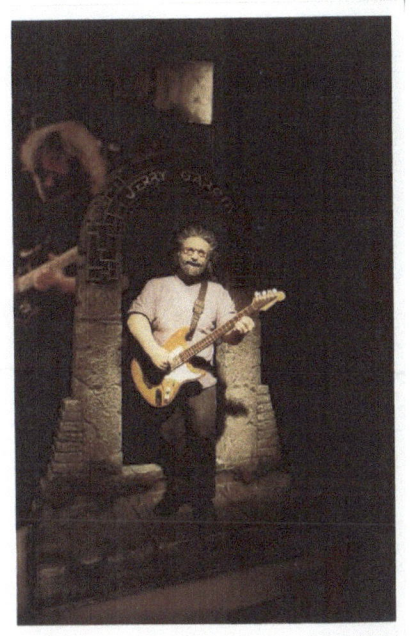

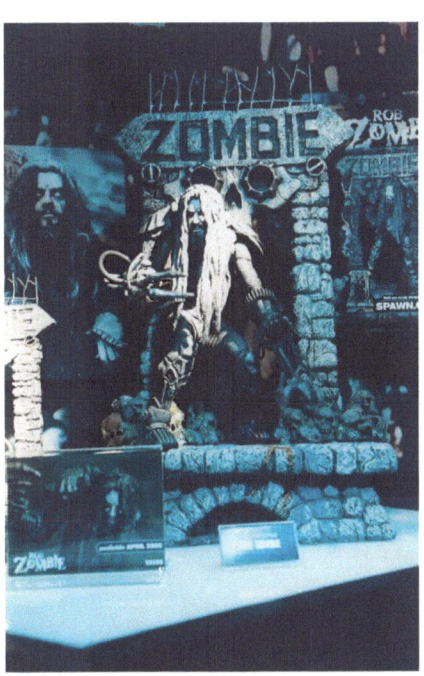

During his time at McFarlane Toys, Snow was privileged to work with many high profile sports and entertainment licenses and properties. Some of the people he was fortunate to actually meet included rock and roll icons Gene Simmons and Ozzy Osbourne, executives from Dreamworks (Shrek) and Fox (X-Files), Clive Barker, and comedian/actor Mike Myers (Austin Powers). Quick story....

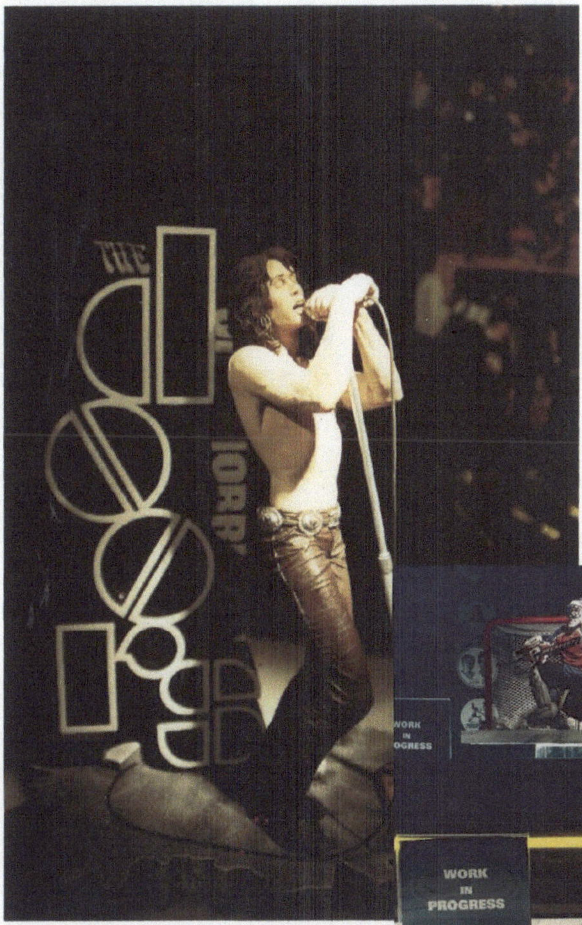

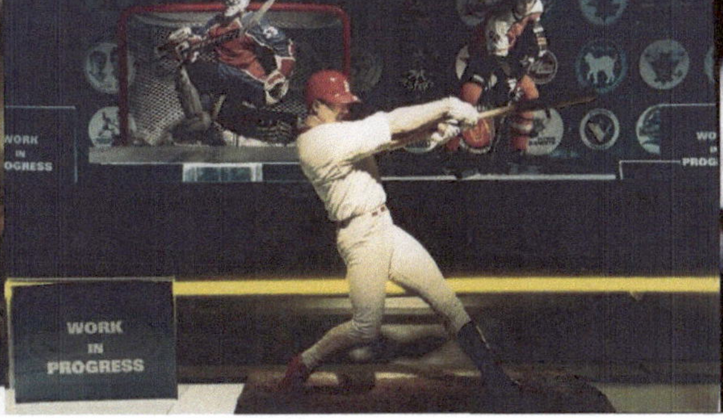

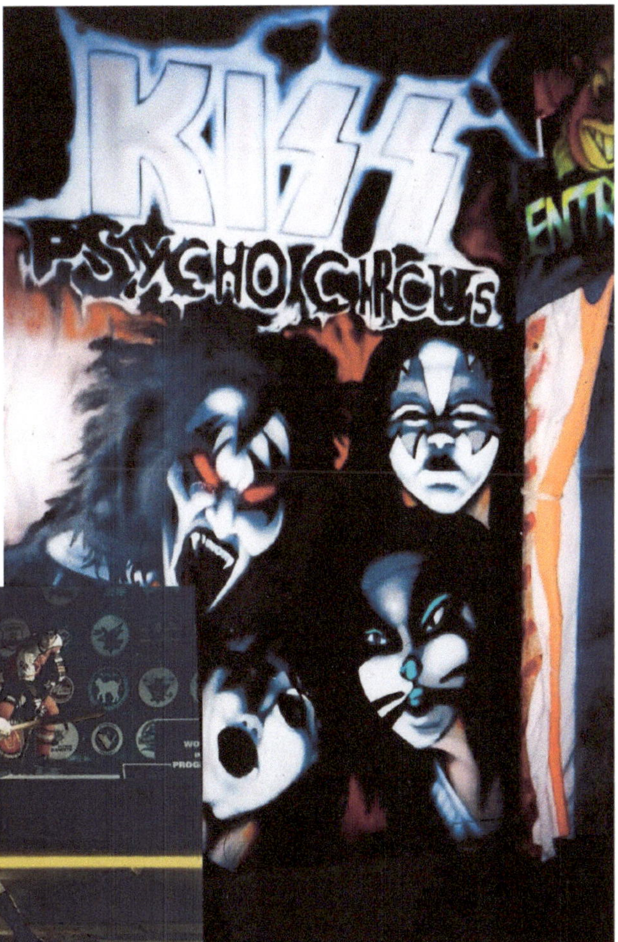

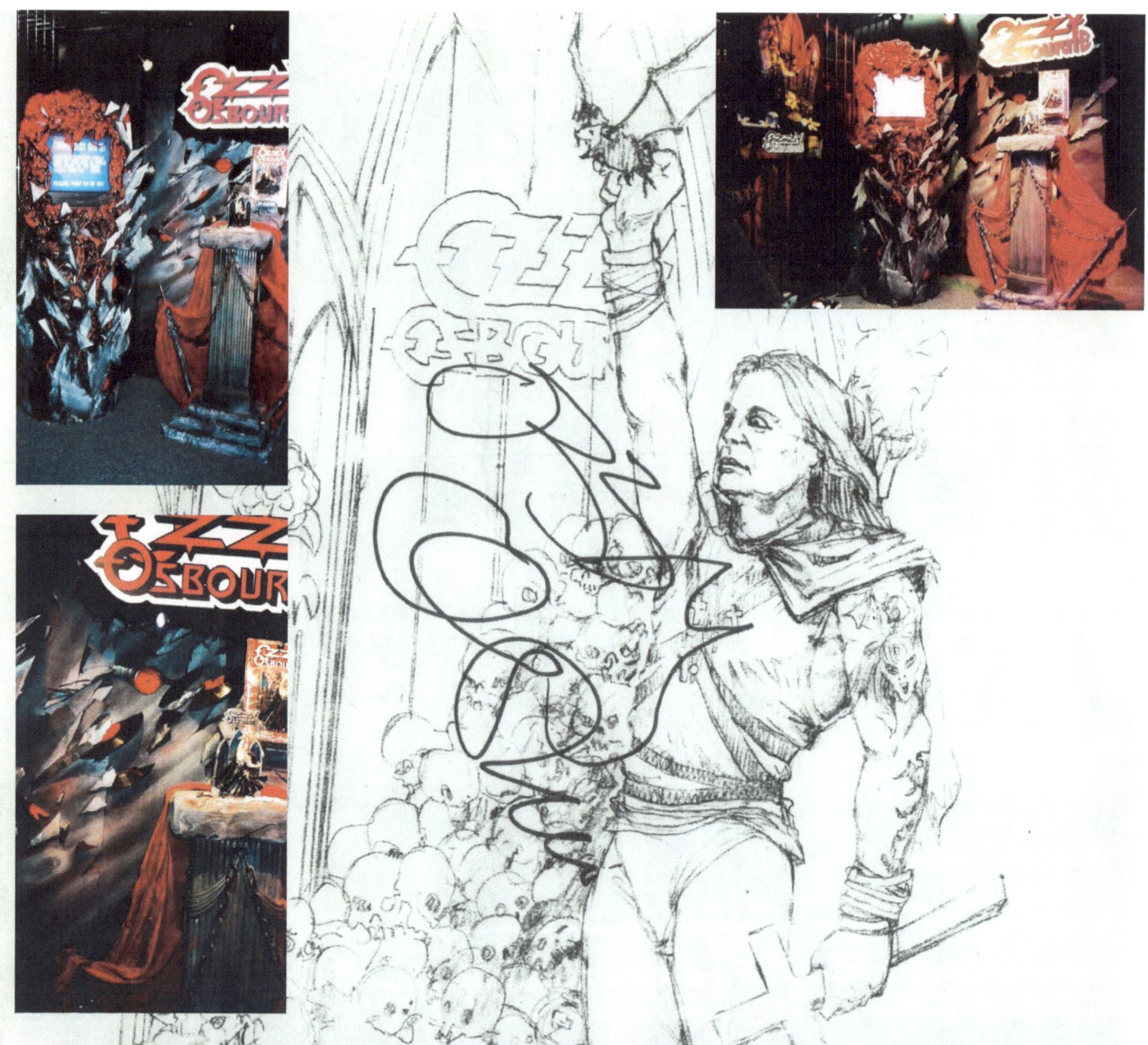

"Out of all the VIPs I got to meet while at McFarlane Toys, Ozzy Osbourne was by far the coolest! He was in town to promote the launch of his action figure and stopped by the showroom to hang out for a bit. He was amazed with the set and display that I had built for his action figure prototype. Ironically, it was the first display that I was given full and free creative license to design and build by myself! I had brought in a sketch and an illustration for him to sign. He was on his way out and finally remembered to sign them. Haha. He signs the sketch and hands it back to me. At this point he is holding the illustration up and while looking it over, he nods his head in approval and comments, 'Wow! This reminds me of the works of Frank Frazetta!' It was a huge compliment, as Frazetta is by far my favorite artist of all time! The only thing was, he misunderstood my request and walked away with my illustration! He said he was going to put it in his collection at his home. I only wanted him to sign it and didn't mean for him to keep it, but I didn't have the heart to ask him for its return. I guess it wasn't a loss, since I still had the signed sketch!"

SNOW on meeting Ozzie

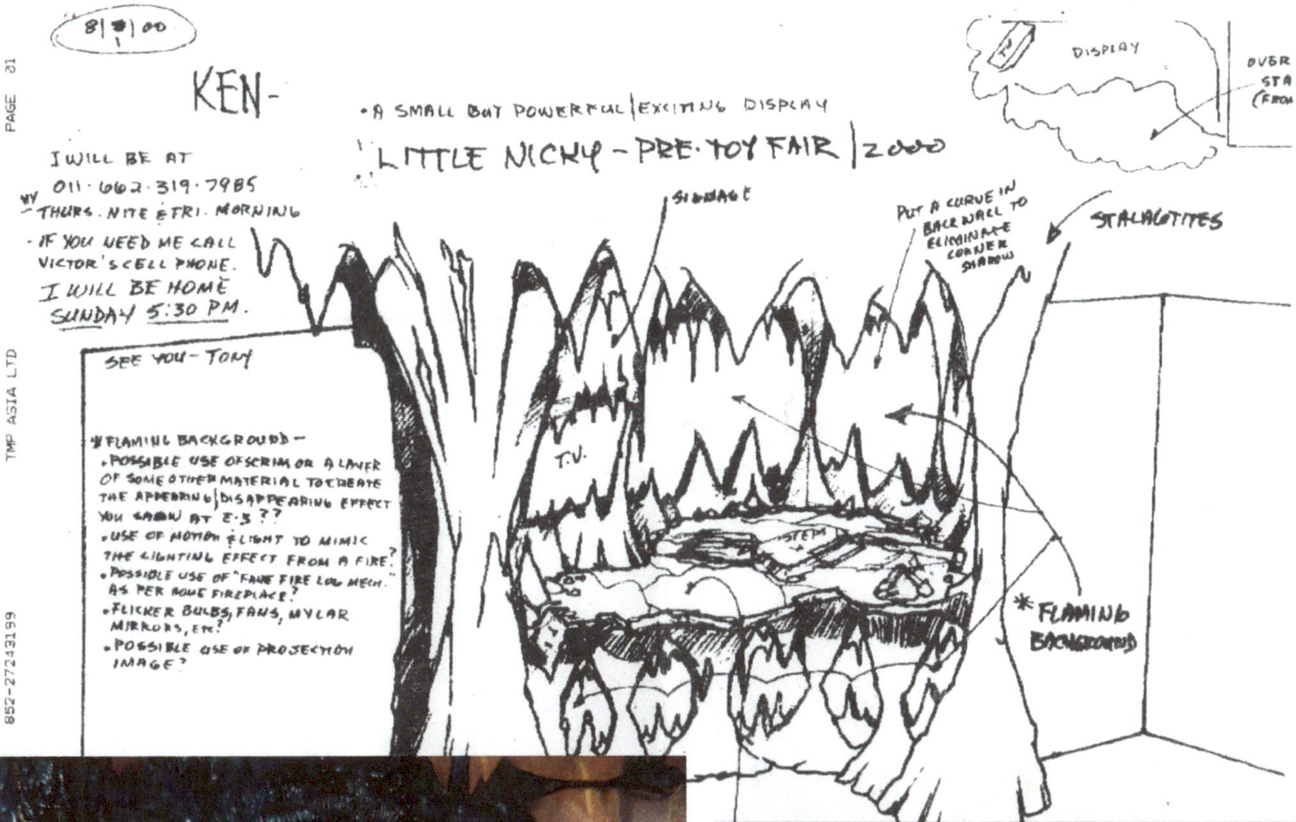

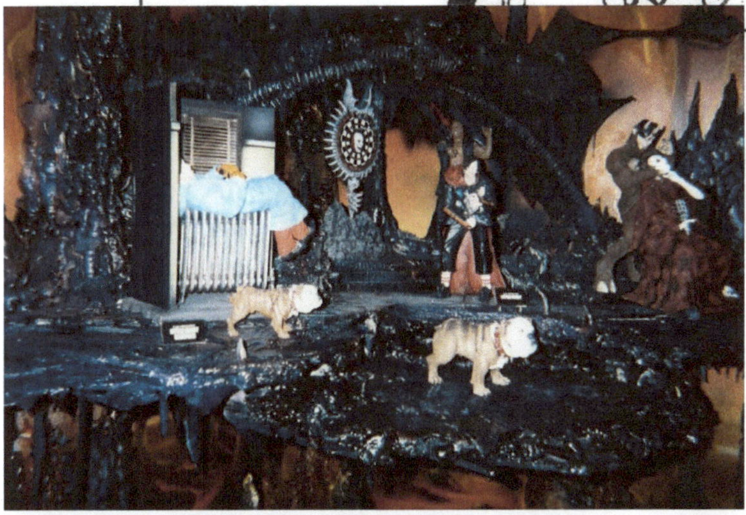

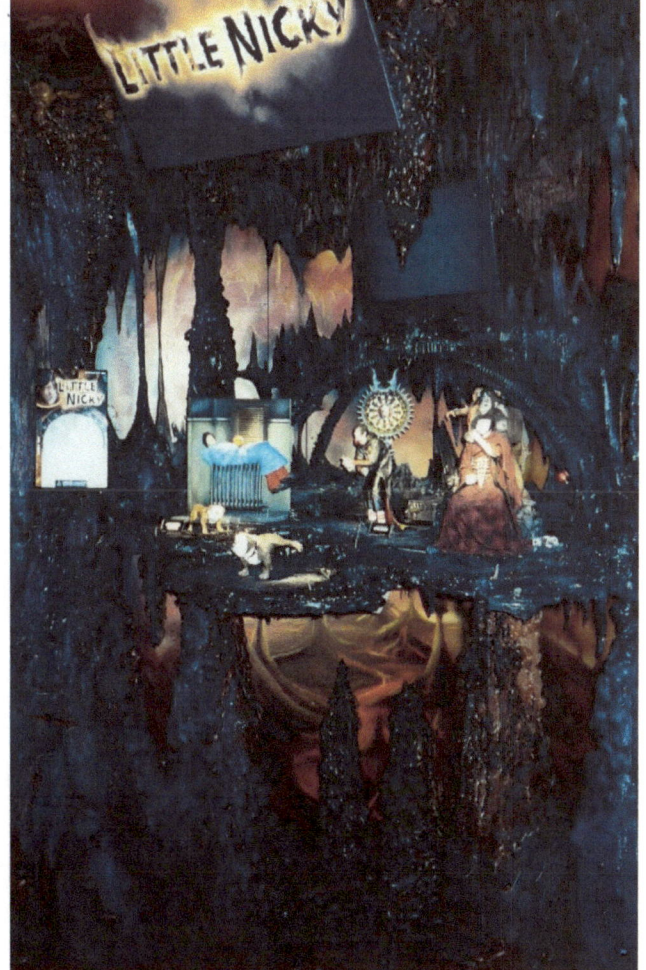

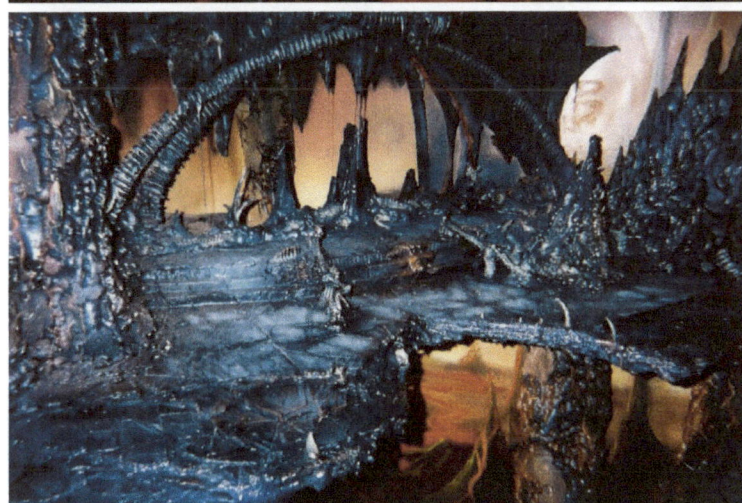

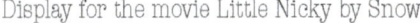
Display for the movie Little Nicky by Snow

McFARLANE DESIGN GROUP
15 HAMBURG TURNPIKE
BLOOMINGDALE, NJ 07403
TEL 201-838-7072
FAX 201-838-8202
MODEM 201-838-7469

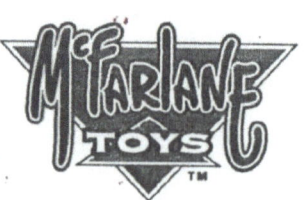

Carmelo Sigona
Snowstorm Grafx
254 Bloomfield Avenue
Apt 3L
Caldwell, NJ 07006

March 3, 1997

To whom it may concern,

One of the great surprises and successes we had at Toy fair '97 this past February was the outstanding mural work "Snowstorm Grafx" created for us in our New York City showroom. Carmelo Sigona and his partner did a fine job and we highly recommend "Snowstorm Grafx" to anyone in need of murals and / or custom art work..

Great job guys!

Sincerely,

Edward Frank
Anthony Billotto

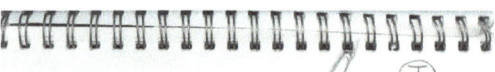

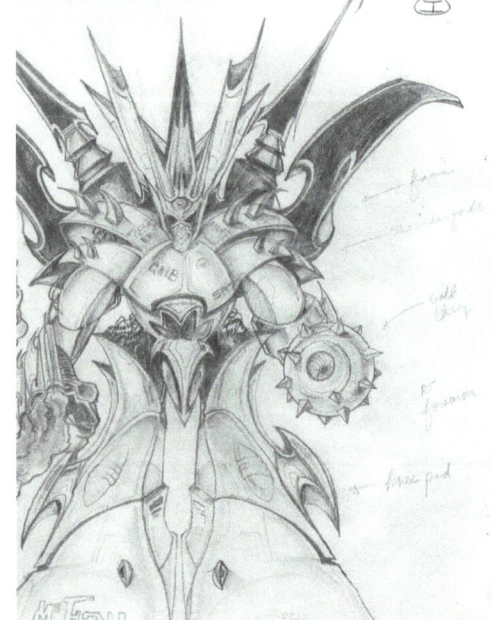

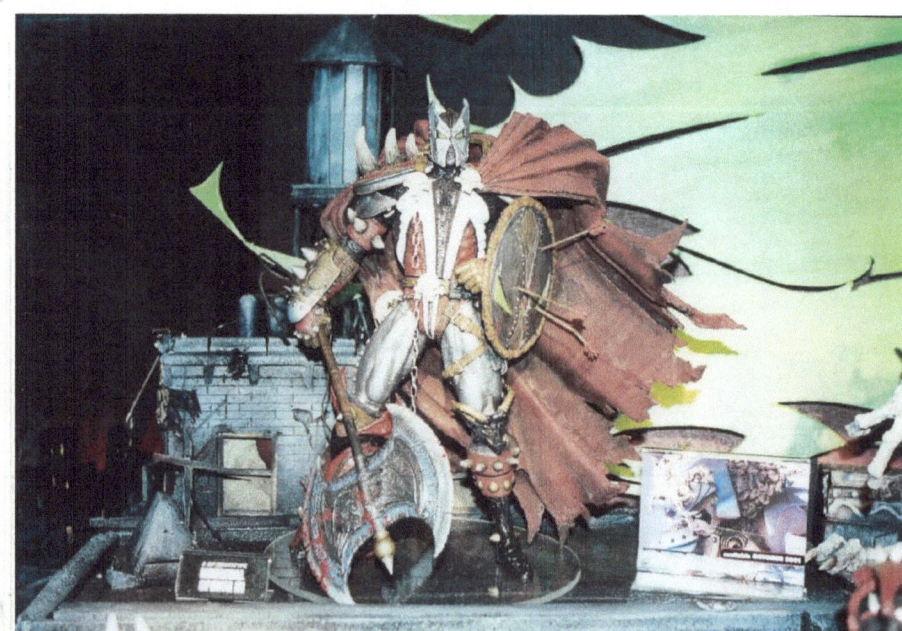

In typical Snow fashion, the showroom experience would not be a selfish one. The first chance he had, he shared this opportunity with his crewmates and close friends. Aside from recruiting the talents of Jamie HEF and CES FX, he secured employment for his late friend and own gifted protege, James CHILD Byrne Jr., SWITCH QM8, THEMO PFE, Dan "The Man" Marchese, and the masterful Masahiro Ito. "Masa" assisted in both the showroom and the design studio, where he worked as a sculptor and met toy sculpting legend David Cortes. (The two would later go on to work together under the INU ART banner.) Snow made many lasting friendships that he still treasures to this very day. Along with Jim Preziosi and the Four Horsemen design team, Oliver Brig was yet another talented model maker and dear friend of Snow's. Sculptor Ray Santoleri was hired later by Snow to sculpt the Jeru the Damaja action figure. The twins Rocco and Vinny Tartamella were also contracted much later by Snow to create toy prototypes for his own venture. Snow also worked briefly with Masa at The Source magazine. While there, Masa had introduced Snow to Jeru and then a bit later to GZA the Genius, Ghostface, Cappadonna, and Killah Priest, all of the Wu Tang Clan. Snow gave all these iconic MC's personal tours of the McFarlane Showroom. He described their reactions, "like kids in a candy store". This later led to many more opportunities that we will discuss a bit further in the second book, Volume Two.

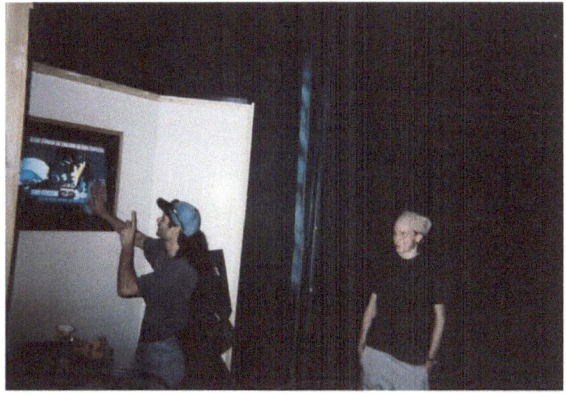

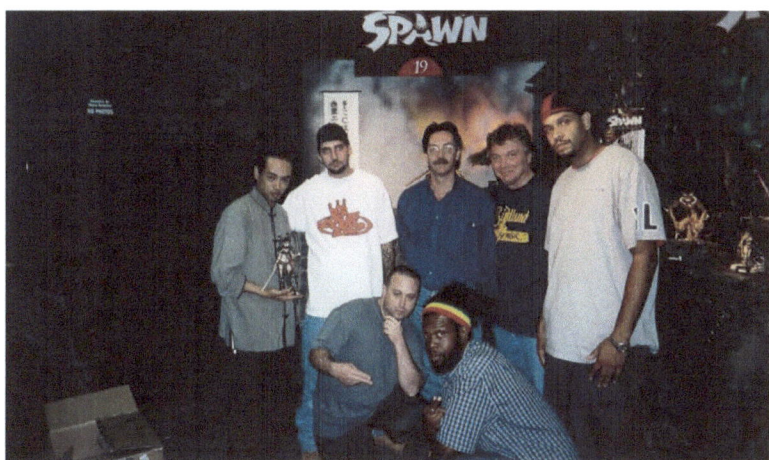

Standing: Masahiro Ito, SWITCH, Tony, Ken, DJ Tommy Hill
Bottom: SNOW, Jeru the Damaja

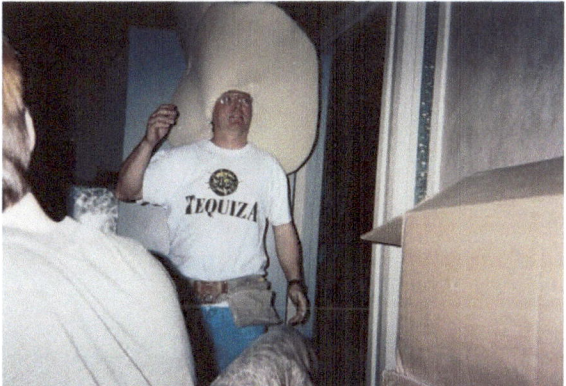

Our dear friend Ken Hoare (RIP) keeping the mood light

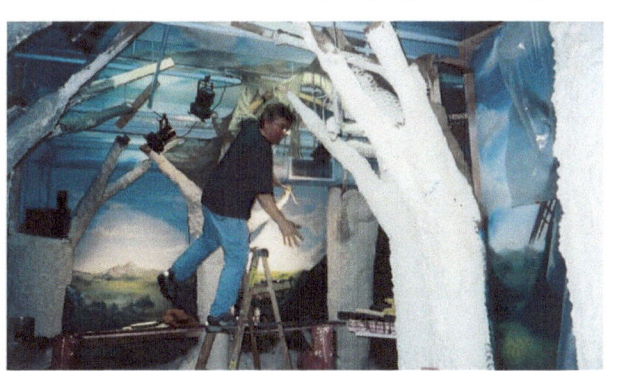

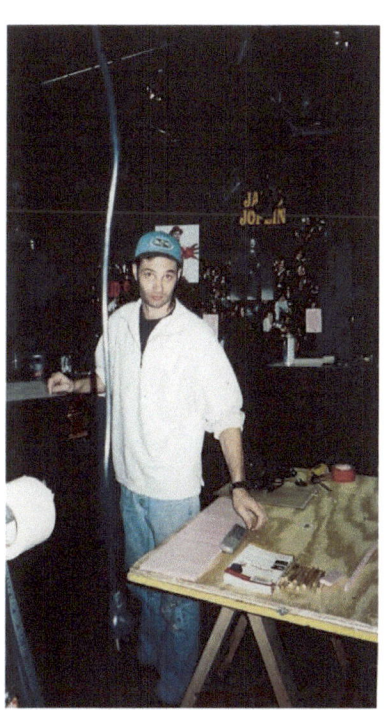

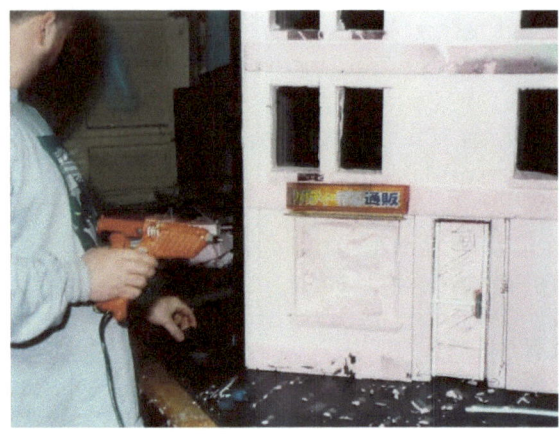

SNOW at work with his new medium

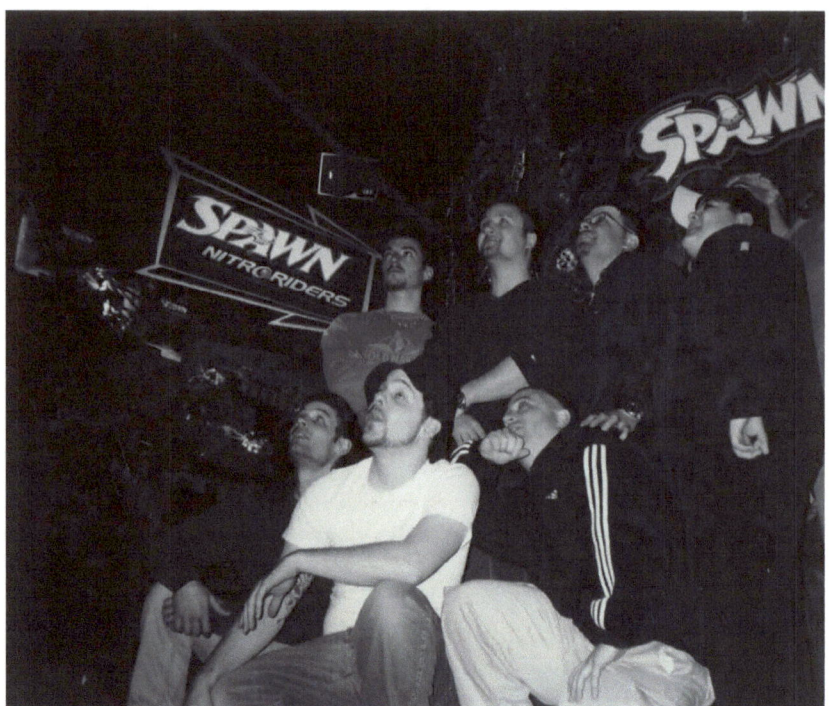

Top: Igor, Kaiz, ZAR, E-man, and Lil' ZAR
Front: Dan Marchese, JAE ONE, SNOW

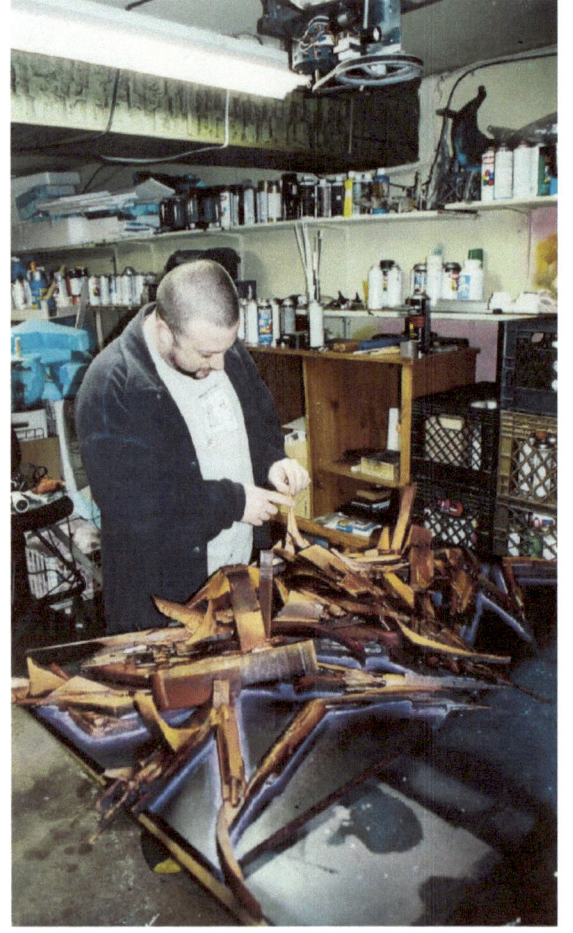

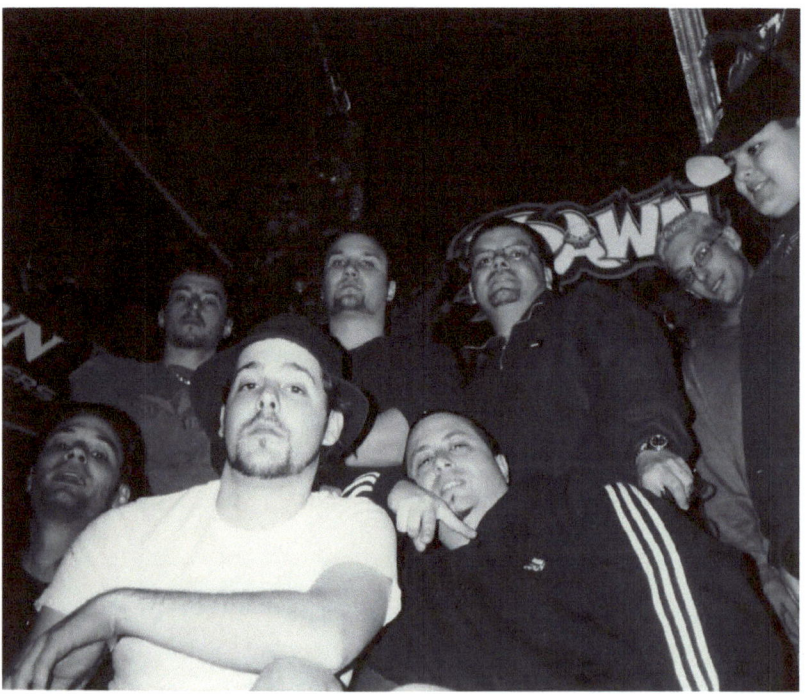

"It may surprising to hear the following, but many artists are not very creative. Many artists learn one of two techniques and rely on that narrow beam for the rest of their careers. Carmen is a true creative thinker and has the ability and drive to solve creative problems through any means available. His brain can bounce, twist, bob, and weave until a logical solution has been met."

Anthony Billotto

Snow's time at McFarlane Toys was not all steeped in the arts. He was part of Todd McFarlane's entourage on several occasions for various press conferences and tours. Snow traveled with Todd and the group to Toronto for Canada Day at Exhibition Stadium, former home of the Toronto Blue Jays. A baseball fan himself, Snow was thrilled to be on the field and in the dugout while Todd took batting practice with the team. He chatted it up with Jays pitcher, David "Boomer" Wells. Snow explained how he told Boomer that he was sorely missed at Yankee Stadium in the Bronx. I was not there, but I'm sure they discussed the no-hitter Wells threw while in Pinstripes.

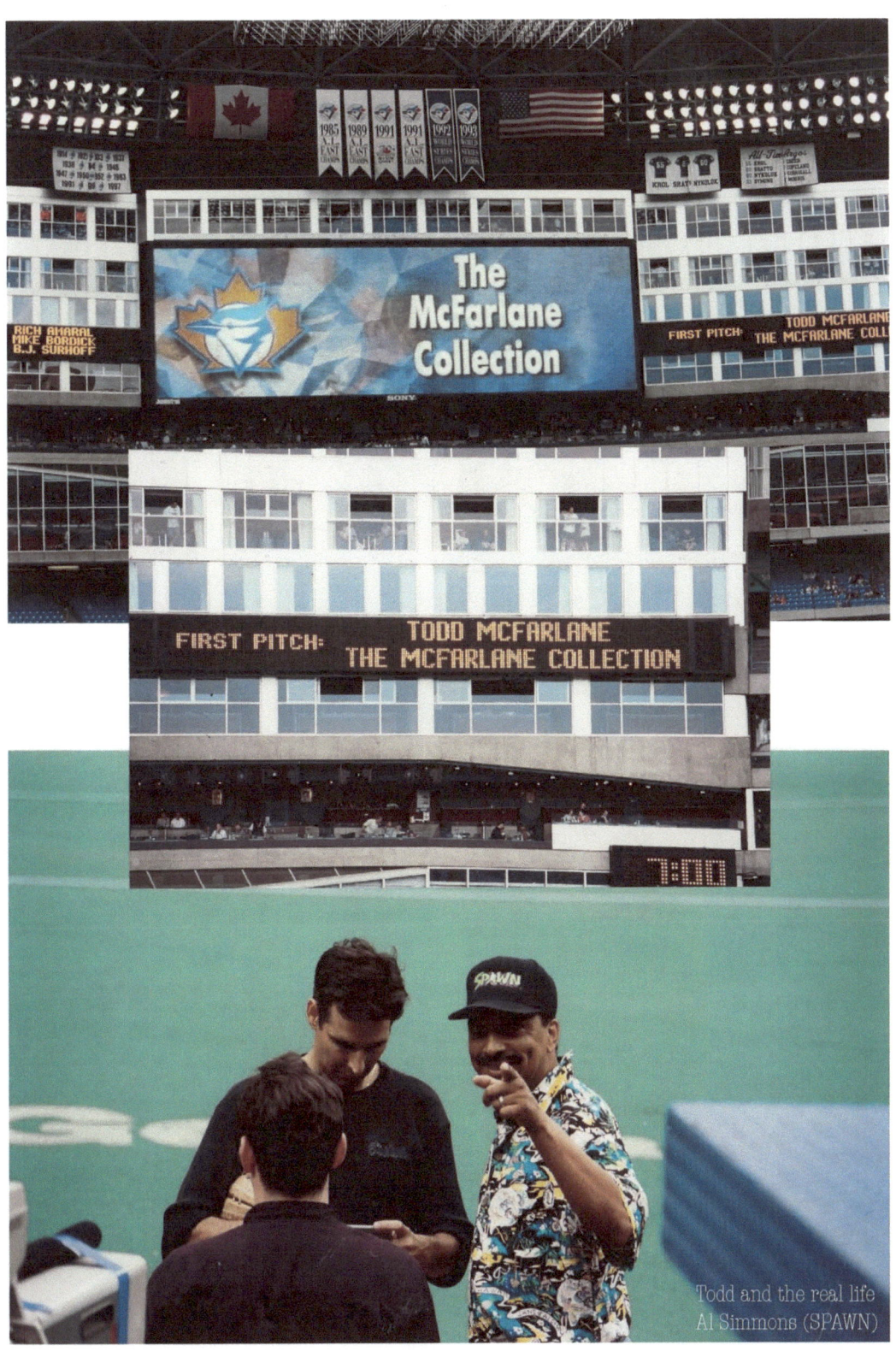

Todd and the real life
Al Simmons (SPAWN)

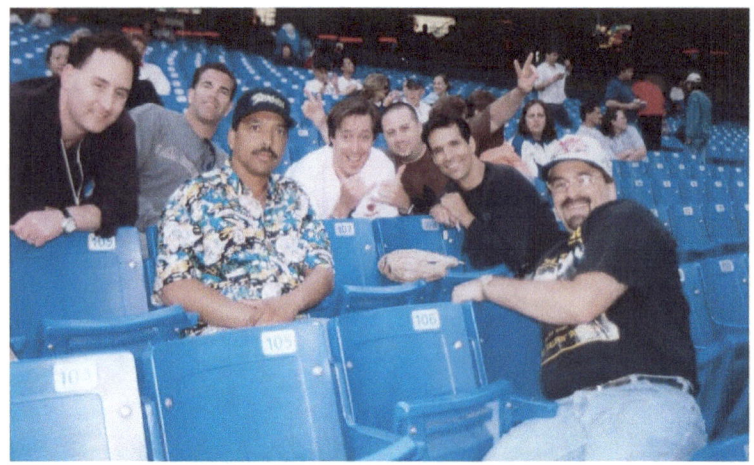

The McFarlane squad, including Al Simmons, Scotty Farrel, Snow, Todd himself, and Steve Hamady

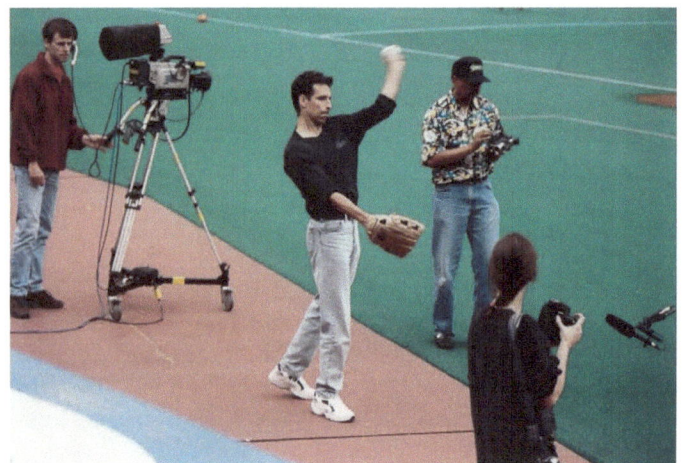

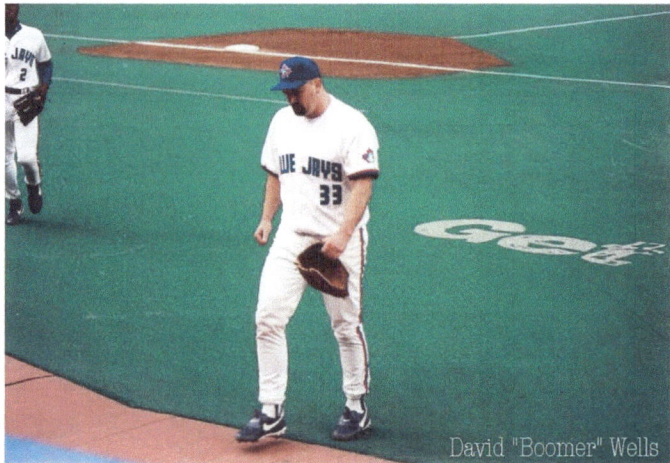

David "Boomer" Wells

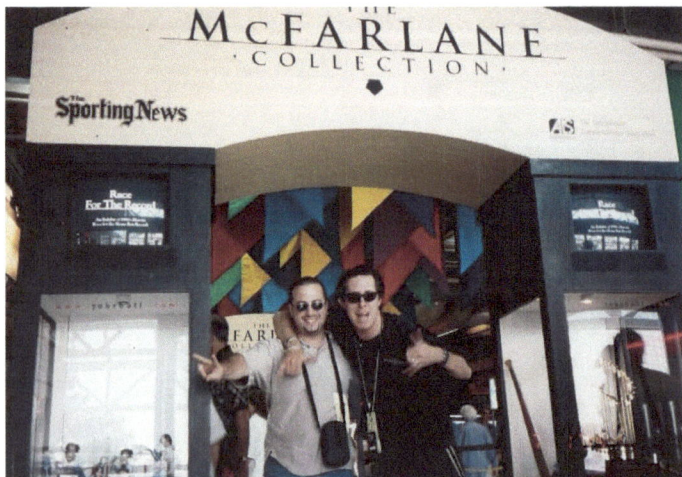

Snow with Scott Ferrall, sports talk radio announcer

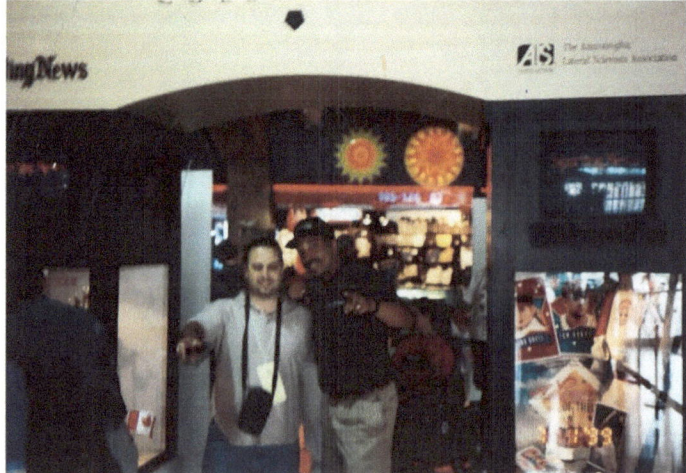

Snow and Al Simmons

Another exciting perk of the trip was having lunch with Todd and his entourage at Wayne Gretzky's own restaurant, with "The Great One" himself attending! There was a product launch party, and Snow was on hand to ensure that the paint applications on the prototypes were fresh and clean. It was a great time meeting "The Great One"!

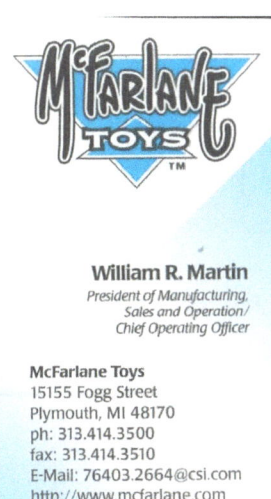

William R. Martin
*President of Manufacturing,
Sales and Operation/
Chief Operating Officer*

McFarlane Toys
15155 Fogg Street
Plymouth, MI 48170
ph: 313.414.3500
fax: 313.414.3510
E-Mail: 76403.2664@csi.com
http://www.mcfarlane.com

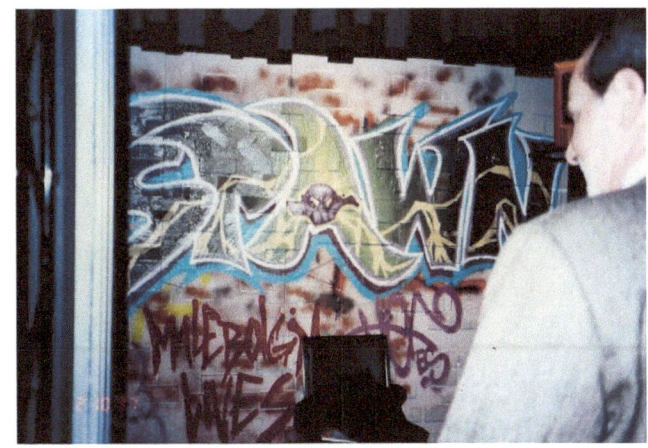

TMP executive Bill Martin checks out one of Snow's first pieces for the company.

"McFarlane Toys first used Carmen's (Snow's) talent in 1995, with Carmen painting a few great wall graphics depicting Spawn in our small toy space in Al Gilly's showroom in New York. We enlarged the wall art display to complete murals, when Gilly expanded our space in the showroom in 1996. The artwork drew so much attention from the buyers and supported the lines so well, we brought Carmen back in 1997 to create overall room themes, when we opened our own 5,000+ sq. foot McFarlane Toys showroom.

"In 1997, we created a showroom that featured individual presentation rooms for each of the McFarlane toy lines. Each room was unique in its appearance, as it related to the room's featured toy line. Carmen's graphics provided the continuity that kept all the individual themes intact as one cohesive environment, and depicted McFarlane Toys as the most creative company in the business.

"The foremost image I recall is when you entered the showroom. Carmen had created a reproduction of Spawn Alley from the movie by painting murals over constructed plaster walls. The lighting, props, and imagery made you believe you were on the movie set. Similar scenes and effects led you through the various presentation rooms, giving visitors a presentation that was part product exhibit, part carnival attraction. It was an experience that buyers, fans, and other toy executives wanted to be part of."

Paul Burke

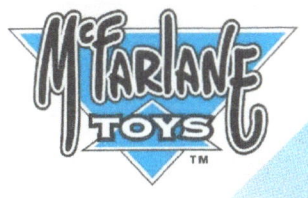

Paul Burke
*Vice Chairman/
Co-Chief Executive Officer*

McFarlane Toys
15155 Fogg Street
Plymouth, MI 48170
ph: 313.414.3500
fax: 313.414.3511
http://www.mcfarlane.com

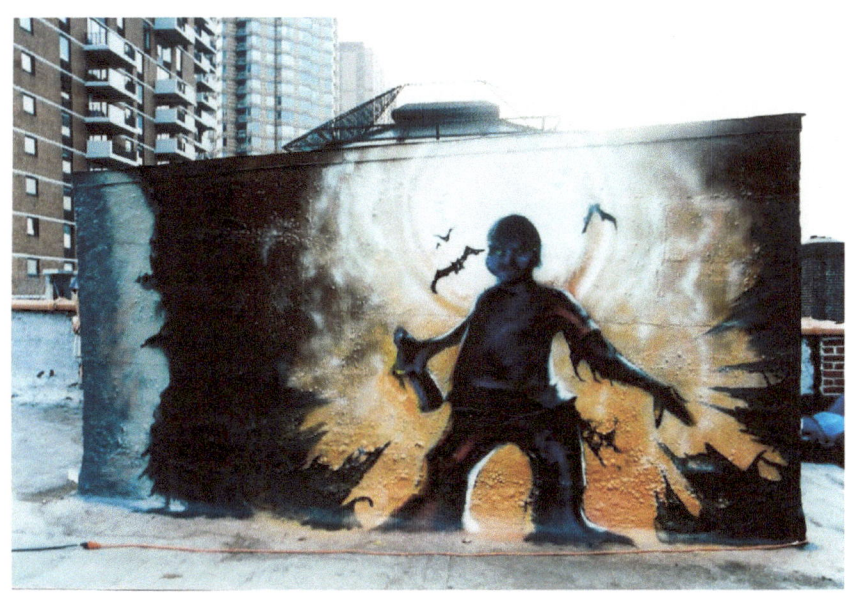

In 1999, Snow was also in attendance at The Plaza Hotel. The event was the unveiling of Todd McFarlane as the "mysterious crazy fan" who purchased the Mark McGwire 70th home run ball for $3 million. It was part of a public relations strategy (as well as it satisfied the collector in him) by Todd to purchase all the balls that Sosa and McGwire hit during that historical home run race.

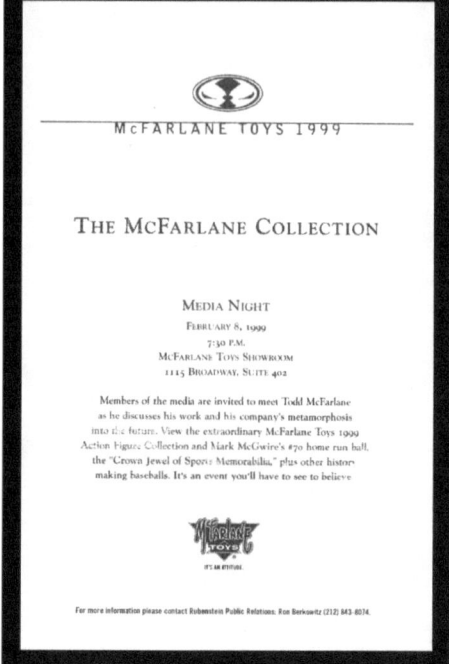

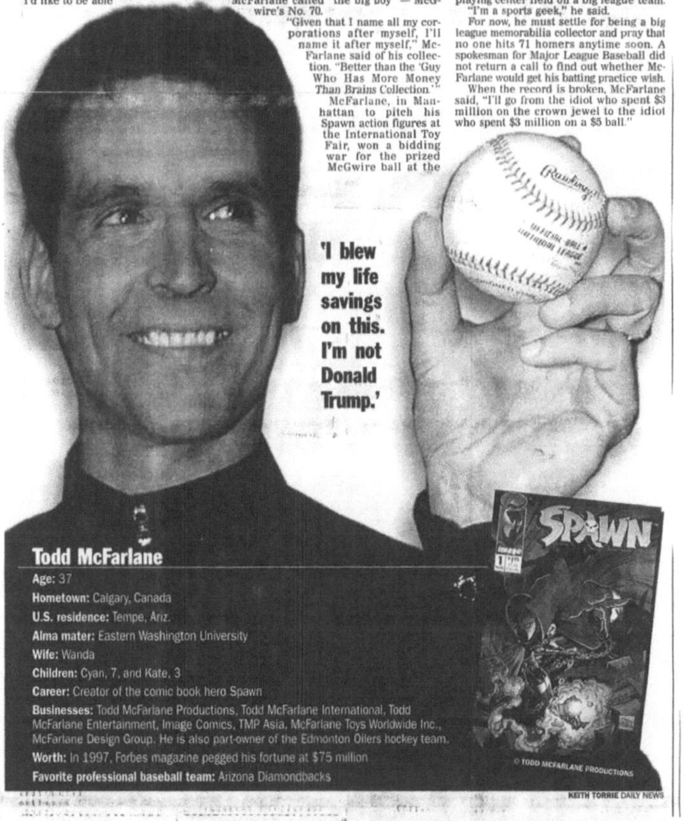

"It was definitely a cool experience, being a part of the press conference. All of the cameras and lights and microphones around us; it was definitely high energy."

SNOW

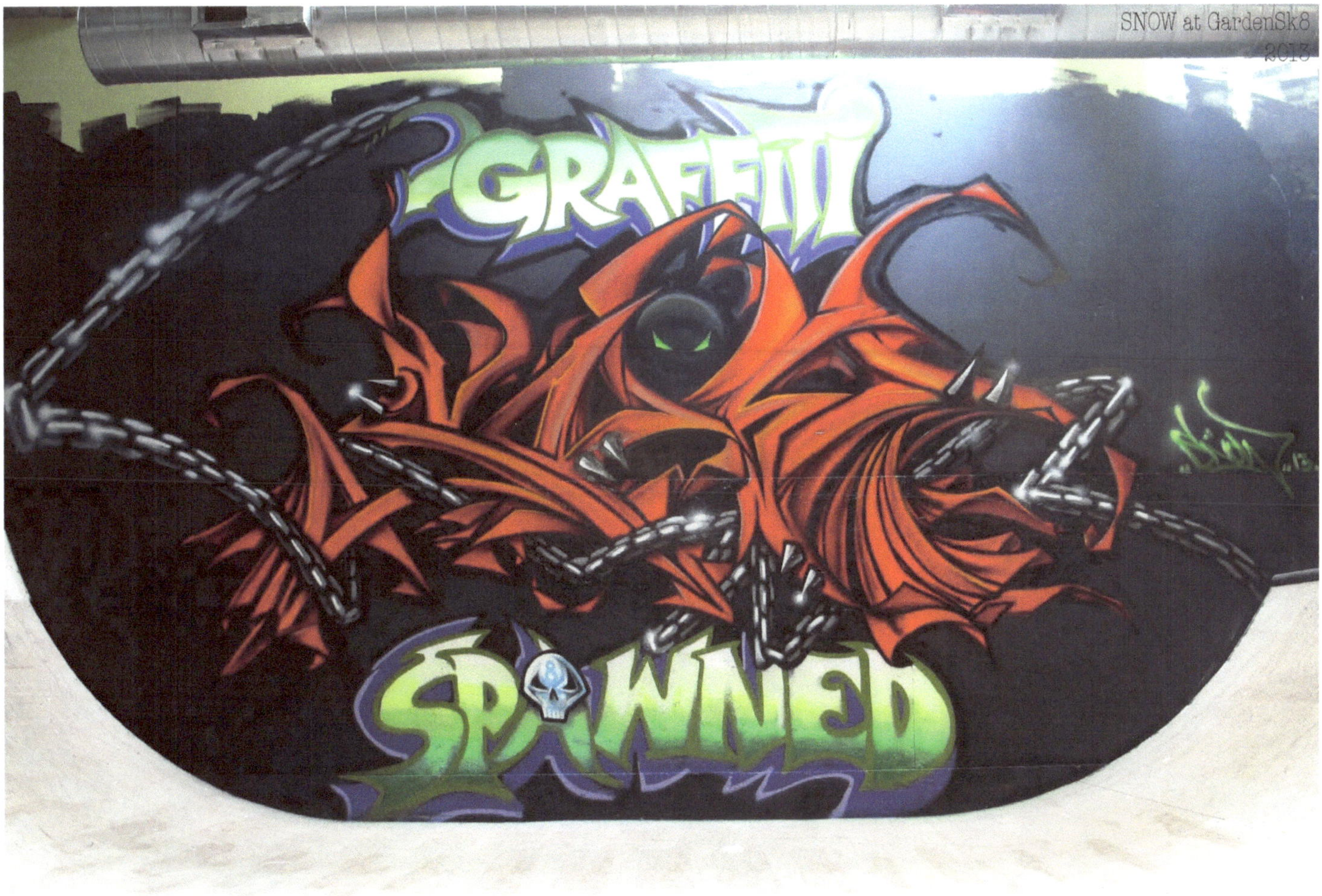

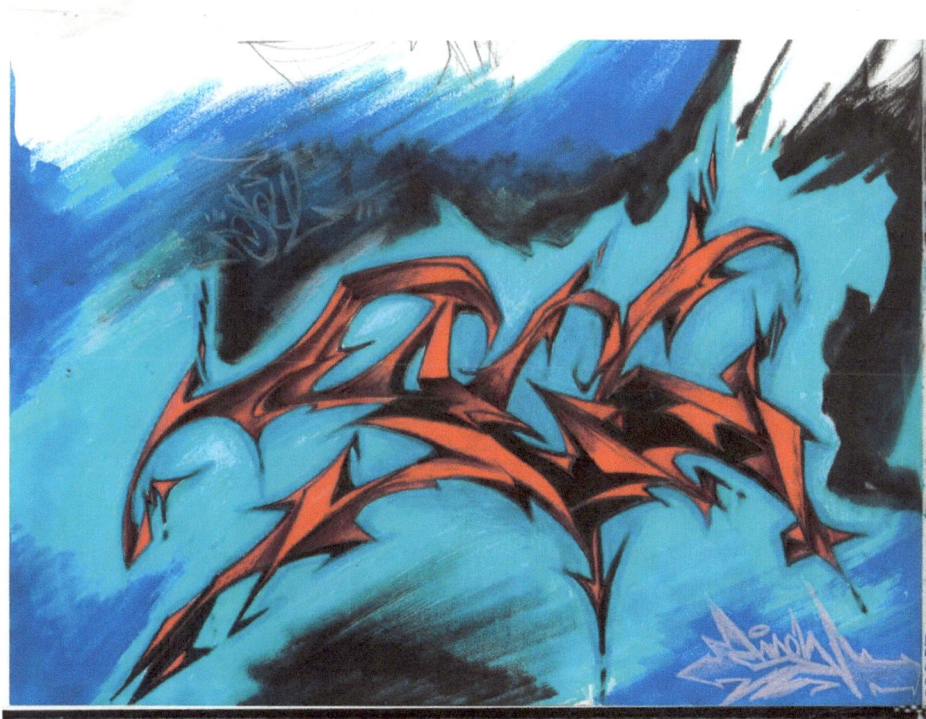

Old blackbook sketch that inspired this Spawn piece
1998

All and all, Snow's time at McFarlane Toys would prove invaluable and rewarding, and it certainly would be an enriching experience for the future graffiti legend. It was the experience Snow needed to evolve and become a serious force in the urban art world.

"I guess you could say I was graffiti spawned."
SNOW

Afterword

When we initially discussed this project, my intention was to plan the publishing of my original comic book series: Tales from the Mist ™. Instead, everyone felt that the time had come to tell my story and to showcase my works and accomplishments. While we gathered and prepared the content, we realized that there was so much material, it would be better to split the book into two volumes. The first volume gives you a glimpse of my early years, my foundation, and all of the adversity that I was determined to overcome. It closes with my continued development and the refinement of my methods and works.

The second volume will be more of an anthology of the latter half of my professional art career as it stands at the time of printing. Volume two promises to be delightful and will not disappoint!

Thank you for your continuing support and I wish each and every one of you peace and happiness!

Carmelo "Snow" Sigona

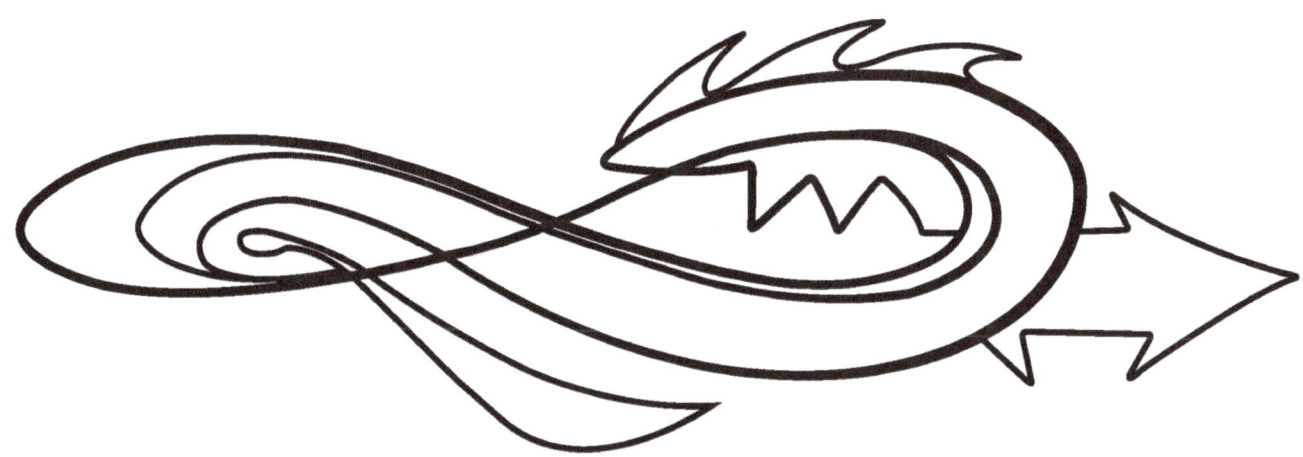

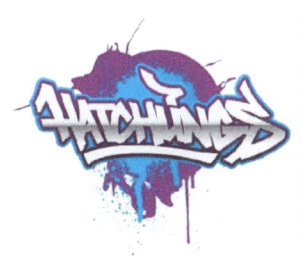 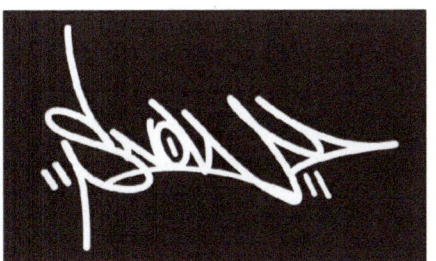 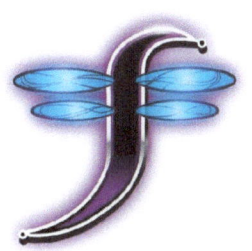 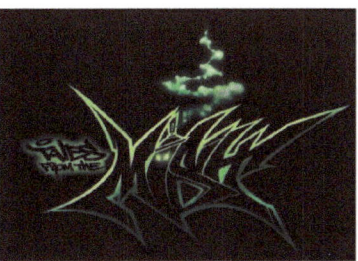

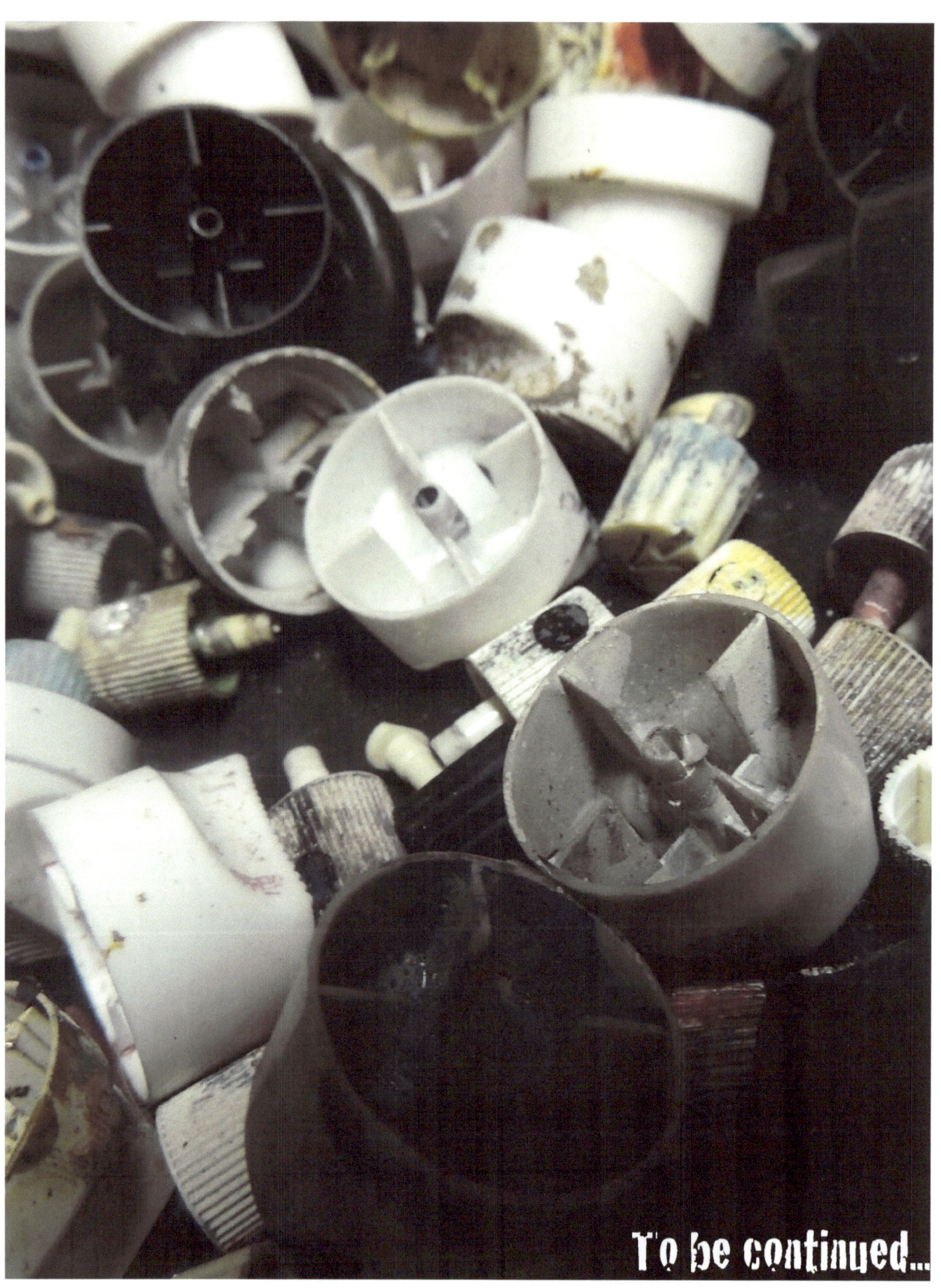

To be continued...